Colección Támesis
SERIE A: MONOGRAFÍAS, 325

THE REPRESENTATION OF THE POLITICAL IN SELECTED WRITINGS OF JULIO CORTÁZAR

Tamesis

Founding Editors
† J. E. Varey
† Alan Deyermond

General Editor
Stephen M. Hart

Series Editor of
Fuentes para la historia del teatro en España
Charles Davis

Advisory Board
Rolena Adorno
John Beverley
Efraín Kristal
Jo Labanyi
Alison Sinclair
Isabel Torres
Julian Weiss

CAROLINA ORLOFF

THE REPRESENTATION OF THE POLITICAL IN SELECTED WRITINGS OF JULIO CORTÁZAR

TAMESIS

© Carolina Orloff 2013

All Rights Reserved. Except as permitted under current legislation no part of this work may be photocopied, stored in a retrieval system, published, performed in public, adapted, broadcast, transmitted, recorded or reproduced in any form or by any means, without the prior permission of the copyright owner

The right of Carolina Orloff to be identified as
the author of this work has been asserted in accordance with
sections 77 and 78 of the Copyright, Designs and Patents Act 1988

First published 2013 by Tamesis, Woodbridge

ISBN 978 1 85566 262 9

Tamesis is an imprint of Boydell & Brewer Ltd
PO Box 9, Woodbridge, Suffolk IP12 3DF, UK
and of Boydell & Brewer Inc.
668 Mt Hope Avenue, Rochester, NY 14620–2731, USA
website: www.boydellandbrewer.com

A CIP catalogue record for this book is available
from the British Library

The publisher has no responsibility for the continued existence or accuracy of URLs for external or third-party internet websites referred to in this book, and does not guarantee that any content on such websites is, or will remain, accurate or appropriate

Papers used by Boydell & Brewer Ltd are natural, recyclable products
made from wood grown in sustainable forests

Printed and bound in Great Britain by
CPI Group (UK) Ltd, Croydon, CR0 4YY

To Sam, por darme alas...

Contents

Foreword	viii
Acknowledgements	x
Abbreviations	xi
Introduction	1
1. The Anti-Peronist Years	13
2. Action versus Inaction	69
3. Literature in the Revolution	111
4. Converging 'Lenin with Rimbaud'	156
Conclusion	196
Bibliography	201
Index	217

Foreword

This book analyses the evolution of the representation of distinct political elements through Julio Cortázar's writings, mainly with reference to the novels and the so-called collage books. I also allude to some short stories and refer to many of Cortázar's non-literary texts. Through this corpus, I trace a thematic thread showing that politics was present in Cortázar's fiction from his very first writings, and not – as the prevalent criticism and himself have tended to claim – only following his conversion to socialism after a life-changing trip to revolutionary Cuba. My analysis aims to show that in opposition to what many critics have argued, this crucial point in his life did not divide the writer into an irreconcilable before and after – the apolitical versus the political –, but rather, it simply shifted the emphasis of the representation of the political, which already existed in Cortázar's writings.

In order to trace this process, I carry out the analysis in chronological order, not of the publication of the works, but of the actual time when they were written. Therefore, in the first chapter, I look at some of the books written between 1948 and 1951, namely, *Divertimento* (1949), *El examen* (1950) and *Diario de Andrés Fava* (1951), focusing mainly on *El examen*; I then extend the analysis to *Los premios* (1960), written when Cortázar was already living in Paris. Chapter 2 focuses on *Rayuela* (1963) and the action/inaction dilemma as reflected in the novel's protagonist. The third chapter considers a period of conflict for Cortázar, as he tries to come up with a way in which to write literature for the political revolution of Latin America, without compromising his belief in artistic freedom. To elucidate this phase, I analyse *62/modelo para armar* (1968) on the one hand, and the collage books, *La vuelta al día en ochenta mundos* (1967) and *Último Round* (1969), on the other. The fourth and final chapter examines *Libro de Manuel* (1973), Cortázar's explicit attempt to converge literature, politics and history, and assesses the results of this effort to merge art and politics, allegedly without making aesthetic concessions.

Although there have been works analysing the political dimension of specific texts (particularly of his short stories), no study to date has analysed the evolution of the political element throughout Cortázar's writings, from the first unpublished novels to his later more experimental works. The originality of this book therefore lies in the tracing of this progression through an extensive analysis of these works. It also breaks new ground in that it refers to unpublished material (a selection of Cortázar's manuscripts from Princeton University Library), to the most recent posthumous publications (such as *Papeles inesperados* [2009]) and to a series of personal interviews with Argentinian writers associated with Cortázar. The research behind this book therefore hopes to bring unique insight that will further the overall understanding of this major and influential twentieth-century Latin American writer.

Acknowledgements

The original research upon which this book is based was made possible thanks to the generous support of the Miss Sym's Trust Award, the Roger and Sarah Bancroft Clark Charitable Trust Award and the John Orr Research Award from the University of Edinburgh. I am also grateful to the Society for Latin American Studies and the Abbey-Santander Group for facilitating the funds to carry out two research trips to Argentina. I would also like to thank Princeton University Library for giving me permission to quote material from the Julio Cortázar papers.

I would like to express my gratitude to the following writers and journalists who were kind enough to share with me their insights and thoughts on Julio Cortázar: Cristina Alonso, Roberto Fernández Retamar, Silvina Friera, Mario Goloboff, Liliana Heker, Ana María Ramb, Susana Reinoso, Saúl Sosnowski, Luisa Valenzuela and David Viñas.

I also wish to say thank you to every individual who, in some way or another, helped me along the way, be it intellectually, emotionally or logistically. My friends, my family, friends who are family, *del lado de acá y del lado de allá*: gracias.

I am eternally indebted to Dr Fiona Mackintosh and Dr Karl Posso for their discerning readings, inspiring criticism, constant support and admirable patience. Without them, this book would not be here today.

Abbreviations

It is customary for Cortázar to use noun phrases as character names in his novels. Throughout the book, I have chosen to keep these in their original with no added emphasis, so that the reader will find 'names', such as el insecto, el cronista or el que te dije, reproduced as seen here in the text.

To differentiate character names from the denominations that Cortázar gives to the groups of friends in the different books, I have chosen to mark the latter with inverted commas. This applies to, for example: 'Vive como puedas', 'la Joda' or 'Club de la Serpiente'.

Finally, certain words appear in their Spanish original and in italics. This practice has been used for words which can be understood by an English-speaking reader (for example, *pueblo*, *patria*, *porteño*, *hombre nuevo*) and also for terms that are particular to Cortázar's fiction and which English-speaking critics tend to leave in the original (for example, *microagitaciones*, *cronopio*).

After quotations from those of Cortázar's fictional works that are frequently used in the book, references are inserted in the text between brackets using the abbreviations listed below; this is followed by volume (when applicable) and page number. First editions are used, unless otherwise stated. All italics or bold in the quotations by Cortázar are the author's own emphasis, unless indicated otherwise.

D	*Divertimento* (Buenos Aires: Alfaguara, 1996)
DAF	*Diario de Andrés Fava* (Buenos Aires: Alfaguara, 1995)
EE	*El examen* (Buenos Aires: Sudamericana, 5th ed., 1992)
LM	*Libro de Manuel* (Buenos Aires: Sudamericana, 10th ed., 1993)
LP	*Los premios* (Madrid: Santillana, 1960)
LV	*La vuelta al día en ochenta mundos* (Mexico City: Siglo XXI, 31st ed., 2006)
PRO	*Prosa del observatorio* (Barcelona: Lumen, 1972)
R	*Rayuela* (Buenos Aires: Sudamericana, 1963)
62	*62/Modelo para armar* (Buenos Aires: Sudamericana, 1968)
UR	*Último Round* (Mexico City: Siglo XXI, 14th ed., 2004)

Debía encontrarme con una traductora polaca, especialista en Cortázar, que vino el año pasado a la Feria del Libro [en Buenos Aires]. No quería perderse ninguna de las mesas redondas de homenaje, y nos citamos a la salida de una de las más concurridas. Cuando me asomé a la sala, los panelistas, escritores también de la generación del '60, estaban entregados, con chistes e ironías, a la tarea de corregirse unos a otros sobre cuál era la gran parte de la obra de Cortázar que se debía despreciar y cuál la pequeñísima, en la que no se ponían de acuerdo, que se debería rescatar. Yo notaba que la traductora, en la primera fila, se ponía más y más nerviosa. Cuando llegó el turno de las preguntas quedaba tiempo sólo para una. Ella alzó la mano.

—Yo tenía entendido – empezó – que Cortázar era un gran escritor...

Su acento no dejaba saber si había desconcierto o ironía en su comentario. Uno de los panelistas, el más histriónico, retomó el micrófono:

—Era un gran escritor, sí, pero como dijo Ricardo Piglia: todo gran escritor tiene en la Argentina los días contados.

Risas, aplausos, y la gente empezó a salir de la sala.

Guillermo Martínez, 'Los días contados',
Crítica, 11 February 2009

Introduction

The motivation for this book arose from reading Julio Cortázar's *Libro de Manuel* and noticing a remarkable lack of criticism on that novel. It became clear that it was a book that critics remained reluctant to analyse in detail. In general, the novel is seen as exemplifying the 'politicised' Cortázar, the implication being that the politicisation process resulted in a deterioration of literary quality. This corresponds to the broader critical interpretative trend, whereby critics seem to accept unquestioningly Cortázar's own understanding that his first trip to revolutionary Cuba divided his personal life into a drastic before and after, into an apolitical Cortázar versus Cortázar the staunch socialist. Accordingly, the dominant critical tendency also sees that this event marked a watershed between the author's so-called 'apolitical' writings and those which express a given political conviction. In this sense, *Libro de Manuel* is categorised as Cortázar's 'political novel', emerging as the logical result of his conversion to socialism and the politicisation of his literature. This is a view that is prevalent to this day, with writers such as Enrique Guinsberg recently affirming that:

> Es muy conocido que, durante gran parte de su vida, Julio Cortázar nunca se interesó, y mucho menos escribió, sobre problemáticas sociales y políticas de su tiempo. Al contrario: siempre fue un escritor claramente afrancesado que se aleja definitivamente de Argentina para radicarse en París en 1951 […]. Recién es en la década de los '60 que comienza tanto su proceso de politización como un interés por América Latina que marcarían su camino futuro y lo seguirían hasta su muerte en 1984.[1]

On several occasions Cortázar himself claimed that it was not until his first journey to Cuba that he was confronted with history and, to an extent, with Latin American reality; as he put it: 'lo que me despertó a mí a la realidad latinoamericana fue Cuba'.[2] In turn, this sense of 'awakening', would lead him to maintain that his

---

[1] Enrique Guinsberg, '*El libro de Manuel:* Cortázar, literatura, política y quitinosidad', *El Sigma*, 16 March 2006 <http://www.elsigma.com/site/detalle.asp?IdContenido=9524> [accessed 24 March 2009].
[2] Julio Cortázar in Ernesto González Bermejo, *Revelaciones de un cronopio: conversaciones con Cortázar* (Buenos Aires: Edhasa, 1978), p. 135.

fictional work up until his final novel, *Libro de Manuel*, had been produced altogether 'outside history'. In 1973, comparing *Rayuela* with *Libro de Manuel*, Cortázar asserted that 'Entendí que *Libro de Manuel* era complementario de *Rayuela* [...] pero se da en una dimensión histórica, mientras que *Rayuela* se había dado en una dimensión exclusivamente individualista y fuera de la historia, porque yo también estaba fuera de la historia.'[3] An idea which he reiterates in his 'Corrección de pruebas' when, with regard to *Libro de Manuel*, Cortázar confesses that:

> comprendí que sólo escribiendo 'horizontalmente' podría transmitir sin demasiada pérdida los movimientos verticales de sentido, las interrogaciones de frontera. En los tiempos de *Rayuela* yo no tenía el menor apuro porque vivía al margen de lo histórico y sólo me interesaba una ontología, una búsqueda antropológica sin tiempo.[4]

Of course, being outside history is not possible; as the philosopher José Pablo Feinmann reminds us: 'la Historia nos elige, no podemos no-ser parte de ella, es esta pertenencia la que nos permite comprenderla'.[5] Yet, given the degree of involvement that becoming a socialist implied, in Cortázar's own rhetoric all writings up to and including *Rayuela* needed to have been written 'outside history'. This suggested that they contained neither social criticism nor any kind of political allusions that would indicate a degree of historical awareness. Iin forcefully and repeatedly affirming this, Cortázar reinforced the chronological political binary observed by critics. This process would be heightened, especially during the last two decades of his life, with statements such as that in 1977, where he claims: 'en mis primeros cuentos era el joven liberal [...] totalmente alejado del destino histórico de América Latina e incluso de mi propio pueblo'.[6] While it is certainly plausible to assert that Cortázar felt detached from the realities and the historical destiny of Latin America as a whole between his first fictional writings (in the late 1930s) and going to Cuba in the early 1960s, novels like *El examen* or *Los premios* show that this was not the case when it came to his 'propio pueblo', Argentina. In this sense his anti-Peronism was more active and considered than he later cared to admit.

Cortázar's biographer, Mario Goloboff, has antagonised many literary critics by affirming that there are not two distinct periods in Cortázar, but rather that:

---

[3] Norberto Colominas and Osvaldo Soriano, 'Julio Cortázar: lo fantástico incluye y necesita la realidad', *El País*, 25 March 1979, pp. 3–7 at p. 5.

[4] Julio Cortázar, 'Corrección de pruebas', in *Convergencias/divergencias/tncidencias*, ed. Julio Ortega (Barcelona: Tusquets, 1973), pp. 13–36 at p. 20).

[5] José Pablo Feinmann, *La sangre derramada: violencia política* (Buenos Aires: Ariel, 1999), p. 127.

[6] Julio Cortázar in Joaquín Soler Serrano, 'Grandes personajes a fondo: Julio Cortázar' (Madrid: TVE, 1977) <http://video.google.com/videoplay?docid= 87411303624586627­32> [accessed 20 February 2009].

En su camino de aprehensión de los contextos cotidianos, interpersonales, sociales, pueden haber sido distintos los abordajes. Ello no autoriza a sostener, como suele hacerse [...] que hubo en Cortázar dos períodos o actitudes textuales diferentes, casi opuestos, sino que, sobre la base de una unidad esencial en su preocupación, hay manifestaciones diversas, quizá de otro signo, pero no radicalmente distintas.[7]

Bearing in mind Goloboff's interpretation of Cortázar's 'essential unity', I embarked upon analysing his writings (including his letters and critical essays) in order to trace his continuous evolution from the anti-Peronist *petit bourgeois* to the committed socialist intellectual, demonstrating that, from the beginning, the political consistently plays an intrinsic part in Cortázar's writings. Through close textual analysis, this book thus substantiates and expands on that which Goloboff has claimed. In addition, it shows that the understanding of there being two Cortázars, and two distinct periods in his literary production, was not merely a critical appreciation, as the biographer has it, but that in effect it was a notion that Cortázar himself believed in and promoted, despite and including all the contradictions implied in that vision. This analysis therefore argues that Julio Cortázar did not emerge as a 'political writer' as a result of his first trip to Cuba; rather, this trip was the catalyst for Cortázar to modify the role and the emphasis that politics had in his fictional work. Politics, understood within its broadest sense as social awareness accompanied by a will to modify the structures of power, was always present in Cortázar's writings, and did not emerge – as Guinsberg's quotation implies – from the writer's conversion to the Cuban cause and from his subsequent 'discovery' of Latin American reality. If being 'apolitical' meant not writing about the 'problemáticas sociales y políticas de su tiempo', then this book clearly refutes Guinsberg's view, demonstrating that in terms of showing a concern for the social and political realities of his time, there is a political element that can be traced throughout Cortázar's writings, from the very first texts. Although anti-Peronism dominated Cortázar's political preoccupations while he was writing the first fictional pieces, and during his early days in Paris, from around the end of the 1950s onwards his political interests would veer towards a more socialist understanding of reality, an ideological position which was crystallized and consolidated by the events in revolutionary Cuba, and by the general ideological tendency of many Latin American writers of the time (later to be loosely grouped as the 'Boom'). Accordingly, therefore, I would argue that *Libro de Manuel* was not Cortázar's 'first' or indeed only political novel, but rather it was the logical conclusion of a political as well as aesthetic evolution, where history, political realities and social awareness were constantly and visibly present.

---

[7] Mario Goloboff, 'En Cortázar no hay dos épocas', *Clarín: Revista de Cultura*, 10 November 2007, 5–6 at p. 5; personal interview with Goloboff, Café El Cisne, Buenos Aires, 27 November 2007.

The book concentrates on a selected corpus of texts. These comprise all Cortázar's novels as well as his two 'collage' books (*La vuelta al día en ochenta mundos* and *Último Round*), which work as a fundamental complement to *62/modelo para armar*. Given the vast amount of material provided by these writings, and as no comparable evolution to the one carried out here has been traced within the short stories, the latter have been used only as a tangential reference to the main analysis. The writings prior to *Los premios*, analysed in the first chapter, were mostly published posthumously and have remained, to this date, altogether unexplored by critics and scholars. For this reason they have been given precedence over the already extensively researched short stories. Since this book traces an evolution, the corpus is presented in chronological order, taking into account the year when a work was written as opposed to its date of first publication. This is particularly important in the opening part of the first chapter, which deals with the novels written between 1949 and 1951, which were all published posthumously, that is, after 1984.

In the evolution that this book presents, the different stages are not merely marked by representations of the political through the fictional texts, but also by Cortázar's own changing ideological positions *vis-à-vis* certain crucial socio-political and historical moments. For this reason the analysis relies progressively on Cortázar's non-literary texts, so as to provide a context in which to place the political element of his fictional writings. Bearing in mind that Cortázar himself promoted the interpretation of his work as one defined by a division between the apolitical and the political, the biographical framework is also key to elucidating some of the contradictions between Cortázar's self-construction, which proved so persuasive for many biographers and subsequent literary critics, and what his texts actually express.

Additionally, the deliberate broadness and fluidity of the term 'political' as used throughout the analysis serves to underline and respond to the ambiguities and inconsistencies in Cortázar's own use of the word and understanding of the concept. Moreover, as will become evident, by analysing Cortázar's letters, manuscripts and critical essays alongside his fictional work, some rhetorical patterns emerge, permitting a more complete and insightful understanding of Cortázar's political and aesthetic evolution. The purpose of referring to his non-fictional texts is thus also to provide a clearer sense of Cortázar's understanding of the political within his own fiction. At points this proves problematic given the lack of coherence that he shows between his ambitions, his theories and his writings. Yet, this very lack of coherence forms an essential aspect of Cortázar's evolutive process.

This book consists of four chapters. The first, 'The Anti-Peronist Years', deals with the posthumously published early novels – *Diario de Andrés Fava*, *Divertimento* and *El examen* – as well as with *Los premios*. Although the latter was written almost a decade after the other three texts, it – like them – allegorises the Argentina of the first government of Perón, which Cortázar had left behind to go to Paris in 1951. These texts are therefore grouped together. A large part of the chapter focuses on a detailed analysis of *El examen*. On the one hand, this is in response to the critical vacuum regarding this novel. On the other, and more important, a comprehensive treatment of the political element in *El examen* defines and demonstrates the ideological roots of Cortázar's political thought. It is therefore a key text for understanding how the political evolves in his writings.

An analysis of the political in *Rayuela* follows. It cannot be said that this is an explicitly political text; nonetheless, certain aspects of the novel are undoubtedly political, and have been consistently, and interestingly, ignored by critics. Particular attention is paid to Horacio Oliveira's 'dialéctica de la acción', that is, his unresolved dilemma with regard to political (as well as social and emotional) engagement versus his all-embracing attitude of 'no te metás'. It is demonstrated that Oliveira's quandary reflects Cortázar's own at the time: 'action versus inaction'.

The third chapter covers the period subsequent to Cortázar's first trip to Cuba, and begins by looking at some of the concepts that Cortázar, by now an openly converted socialist, was attempting to formulate in his search to write literature for and within the revolution, without sacrificing his beliefs in artistic freedom, rooted in what for him was the very influential tradition of the Surrealists. He refers to this endeavour as an 'opération analogue', and within this 'operation', a bifurcation in Cortázar's evolution can be identified. On the one hand, he writes what is usually seen as his most hermetic novel, *62/modelo para armar*, and on the other, a year either side of *62*, he publishes his two 'collage books': *La vuelta al día en ochenta mundos* and *Último Round*, where text and image combine to put forward ideas on humour, eroticism, jazz, literature and politics. The chapter shows the series of difficulties that Cortázar encounters in this period of aesthetic exploration, whereby he tries to propose new ways in which to manifest political preoccupations without subjecting his way of writing to dogmatic forms of revolutionary literature.

The fourth chapter centres on *Libro de Manuel* as Cortázar's open attempt to meld, as one of his characters puts it, 'Lenin with Rimbaud'. The bifurcation between a kind of literature that does not explicitly manifest any political dimension, and one that combines experimental techniques with the aim of putting forward – among other elements – a given political ideology, merges in this novel. The aim, as Cortázar would have it, was to write literature that would have some kind of 'use' in the political revolution of Latin America, while at the same time attempting to maintain the aesthetic precepts that he so fervently defended. In addition to a textual analysis of the novel, this chapter deals with the reception of the text so as to show the effect (or lack of it) that the book had, especially in Argentina, since this is mainly where Cortázar had hoped that the novel would be 'useful' in the context of the political struggles taking place there.

Within the vast amount of critical work on Cortázar, there are only three works dedicated specifically to the political in his fictional writings. The most recent, by the Argentinian Pablo Montanaro, entitled *Cortázar: de la experiencia histórica a la revolución* (2001),[8] promises an analysis from 'Casa tomada' to *Libro de Manuel*, but effectively only deals with the period surrounding the publication of Cortázar's final novel. Despite being selected as part of the 'Plan de promoción a la edición de Literatura argentina de la Secretaría de Cultura y Medios de Comunicación de la Presidencia de la Nación', the book has several factual errors (such as claiming that *Bestiario* was published in 1957, rather than in 1951). It dwells on the anecdotal and fails to draw an insightful analysis. Compared to Montanaro's work, *Julio Cortázar: de literatura y revolución en América Latina* (2000) by the Mexican Francisco de la Guerra covers a wider range of texts, yet it does not carry out a literary textual analysis of the books; rather, it presents them in a descriptive manner, for the non-specialist readership.[9] This means that its extensive general historical and political contextualisation becomes as important as the analysis of the books themselves, taking away valuable room for in-depth analysis and for the tracing of a logical progression in Cortázar's political ideology. Finally there is Sylvia Sarmiento Lizárraga's discerning and original thesis, '*Los premios, Rayuela, Libro de Manuel*: evolución del pensamiento político en la ficción de Julio Cortázar'. Despite the apparent coincidence of topic, the findings presented in this book do not reiterate those of Lizárraga. This is principally due to the fact that Lizárraga's thesis was presented in 1979 so it cannot take into account any of Cortázar's early, posthumously published, novels. Moreover, at points its analysis does not substantiate aspects or connections presented as facts. This undermines the reliability of the political reading; an example is the political analysis of *Rayuela* which is based on unsubstantiated subjective associations, such as the one between the name Rocamadour and the Roca-Runciman treaty.[10]

Various books provide an overview of Cortázar's *oeuvre*, but sometimes with the political element referred to only tangentially. In 1968 Néstor García Canclini applied what he calls 'una antropología poética' to Cortázar's writings in search of 'la experiencia poética de lo humano' in the texts.[11] The study is comprehensive, yet it leaves politics out altogether apart from a brief study of the short story 'Reunión' and the move towards an idea of 'el prójimo'. Jaime Alazraki's

[8] Pablo Montanaro: *Cortázar: de la experiencia histórica a la revolución* (Buenos Aires: Homo Sapiens, 2001).
[9] Francisco E. de la Guerra, *Julio Cortázar: de literatura y revolución en América Latina* (Mexico City: UDUAL, 2000).
[10] Sylvia Sarmiento Lizárraga, '*Los premios, Rayuela, Libro de Manuel*: evolución del pensamiento político en la ficción de Julio Cortázar' (unpublished PhD dissertation, University of California, 1979), p. 73.
[11] Néstor García Canclini, *Cortázar, una antropología poética* (Buenos Aires: Nova, 1968), p. 19.

Hacia Cortázar: aproximaciones a su obra (1994) is perhaps one of the most valuable references for this study. It sets out to cover the key moments of Cortázar's writing career, from his 1941 article on Rimbaud, to the expressions of postmodernism in *Fantomas contra los vampiros multinacionales* (1975). Although it puts forward some pivotal ideas for the study and understanding of Cortázar, it is substantially made up of a collection of articles which Alazraki produced at different points in his career. This means that the book is not an analysis of an evolution, bur rather of discrete aspects. Politics is referred to only in his analysis of history in *Los premios*.[12] One of Cortázar's closest friends, Saúl Yurkievich, also produced a study of Cortázar's fictional works: *Julio Cortázar: mundos y modos* (2004). Yurkievich, unlike Alazraki, includes Cortázar's attempts at writing theatre and concentrates on the poems as well as the novels and short stories. Overall, the book reads more like a personal homage than a critical study. And the political is only alluded to fleetingly towards the end of the book, as an attempt to define 'revolución' through the Cortazarian lens: 'Revolución: tiempo abierto, tiempo esponja, edad porosa, proyecto utópico'.[13] The title of Graciela Maturo's analysis, *Julio Cortázar y el hombre nuevo,* promised to be a key reference for the study of the political in Cortázar. However, with only one chapter entitled 'Escritos políticos' (to cover the writings of the period 'desde 1970 hasta 1983'), and a two-page subsection, 'El compromiso político', Maturo inevitably oversimplifies and effectively becomes an exemplary exponent of the premise that this book aims to challenge.[14] In this sense, Maturo's book is comparable to two of the most significant English-languague studies on Cortázar's longer fiction, namely, Peter Standish's *Understanding Julio Cortázar* (2001) and Steven Boldy's *The Novels of Julio Cortázar* (1980). Although both books carry out extensive analyses of Cortázar's *oeuvre*, they reiterate the critical pattern of the apolitical versus the political writings without much questioning. Thus, even though there is a copious amount of material published on Julio Cortázar, most of it tends to repeat the seemingly accepted critical model without bringing to the fore the political dimension of Cortázar's early writings. None of the works to date charts systematically the complex evolution of the representation of the political in Cortázar's novels and his other fictional writings.

This book therefore hopes to bring a new insight to the understanding of Cortázar, not only through a particular approach and analysis, but also through the incorporation of the most recent critical readings and publications, including the latest collection of Cortázar's previously unpublished texts, edited

[12] In Jaime Alazraki, 'Imaginación e historia en Julio Cortázar', in *Hacia Cortázar: aproximaciones a su obra* (Barcelona: Antrhopos, 1994), pp. 299–322.

[13] Saúl Yurkievich, *Julio Cortázar: mundos y modos* (Barcelona: Edhasa, 2004), p. 329.

[14] Graciela Maturo, *Julio Cortázar y el hombre nuevo* (Buenos Aires: Sudamericana, 1968; 2nd extended edition, 2004), p. 151.

under the title *Papeles inesperados*, which came out in May 2009. Moreover, exclusive material obtained from personal interviews with writers who were in some way associated to Cortázar is included, and reference is made to some of Cortázar's manuscripts held at Princeton University Library. The renewed interest in Cortázar brought about by the latest publications, and also by the twenty-fifth anniversary of his death in 2009 and the fiftieth anniversary of the publication of *Rayuela* in 2013, shows that this study is indeed timely. Furthermore, and perhaps most important, given the general lack of appreciation of Cortázar, especially among Argentinian intellectuals and academics, so well captured in Martínez's anecdote, this book aims to prove that Cortázar's works remain relevant, and his days are 'far from being counted'.

On a more theoretical level, the definition of the term political within this study, deliberately fluctuates from the very broad to the very specific. Although this may at first appear problematic, it is crucial to bear in mind that even political scientists find it difficult to limit the term 'politics' to one rigid definition. In *Politics: The Basics*, for instance, Stephen Tansey reflects upon the problematics of the term, stating that 'If we try to define "politics" more formally and precisely, we run into the sort of problems which will recur again and again in this book.'[15] And Adrian Leftwich, in his *What is Politics?*, writes: 'What is politics? This apparently simple question is not as straightforward as it may first seem, and it raises further and more difficult questions.'[16] Therefore, for the purposes of this analysis, it has been entirely appropriate that the term should be fluid, mirroring Cortázar's own evolutive and contradictory process, while also encompassing a broader, generally assumed meaning of what we perceive as political in our day-to-day life as readers. In an attempt, however, to provide some basic conceptual framework of what I have understood to be the meaning of 'political', I will nevertheless outline here those notions which I considered to be pertinent.

It is primarily useful to take into account the etymology of politics (from the Greek word *polis*, meaning the state or community as a whole) and the very early significances given to this term by Plato and Aristotle. In *The Republic*, Plato describes the *polis* or ideal state, and the means of dealing with the diversity of human afflictions in order to achieve that utopian society. For Plato, therefore, the term 'political' is linked to the processes whereby an ideal state may be realised. It relates to measures put into practice in the hope of creating a better society, of improving a given state of affairs affecting the community. Although Aristotle disagrees with some of the measures that Plato developed, he is also concerned about finding the best form of political community, so that the citizen can realise his ideal life.[17] It is in his writings on politics that Aristotle famously argues that man is by nature a political animal. In other words, human beings should consider and perform their

---

[15] Stephen Tansey, *Politics: The Basics* (London: Routledge, 2004), p. 3.
[16] Adrian Leftwich, *What is Politics?* (Cambridge: Polity, 2004), p. 10.
[17] Aristotle, *Politics*, trans. Benjamin Jowett (New York: Dover Publications, 2000), p. 54.

role within the *polis*, for 'he who is unable to live in society, or who has no need because he is sufficient for himself, must be either a beast or a god: he is no part of the state'.[18] So according to Aristotle, politics is not an abstract concept, but rather an inherent feature of mankind. Despite their differences, both Plato and Aristotle wrote political philosophy because they saw imperfections in the societies in which they lived. Based on Plato and Aristotle, it can therefore be deduced that when describing something as political, in classical terms, we are referring both to the way in which society is organised and ruled, and to the attempt to change how individuals think and act as part of that societal community.

In this analysis, therefore, the political is understood as a concept that structures the very way we, as individuals, view and interact with our socio-historical, cultural context. For the French thinker Jacques Rancière, in this sense, the essence of politics resides 'in acts of subjectivization that separate society from itself by challenging the natural order of bodies in the name of equality'.[19] I also take on board the views of critics such as Frederic Jameson who in his seminal book *The Political Unconscious* engages with the idea that although some literary texts include self-consciously political elements, every text is ultimately the expression of a political unconscious. This is not to say that that every work of fiction is a political manifesto, but rather that a work of fiction can – and for Jameson, should – be positioned within society along a political ideology and within a historical moment. In Jameson's words: '[This book] conceives of the political perspective not as some supplementary method, nor as some optional auxiliary to other interpretive methods current today [...] but rather as the absolute horizon of all reading and interpretation.'[20] I believe, as Jameson argues, that nothing, neither a work of art nor its aesthetic evaluation, can be devoid of politics. This book elucidates how the different expressions of Cortázar's political impulses appear in his writings.

In this regard, it could be argued that the present study follows a contemporary Marxist line of aesthetic analysis, in that literature is not understood as a mere 'reflection' of reality, but rather that the relationship between reality and Cortázar's fiction is assumed to be mediated and influenced by ideology throughout. Paraphrasing Jack Sinnigen, by ideology I mean a set of ideas that 'explain' reality or that provide, following Jean Touchard's reading, 'una guía para la acción'.[21] In other words, I understand ideology to be con-

---

[18] Ibid., p. 29.
[19] Jacques Rancière, *The Politics of Aesthetics*, trans. Gabriel Rockhill (New York: Continuum, 2004), p. 42.
[20] Fredric Jameson, *The Political Unconscious: Narrative as a Socially Symbolic Act* (London: Metheun, 1981), p. 17.
[21] Jack Sinnigen, *Narrativa e ideología* (Madrid: Nuestra Cultura, 1982), p. 81; Jean Touchard, *Historia de las ideas políticas*, trans. Julián Pradera (Madrid: Tecnos, 2000; first published 1961), p. 587.

cerned with, as Terry Eagleton writes, 'the question of the real and imaginary relations between men and their social conditions'.[22]

Reflecting on the role of politics within the context of Argentinian fiction, Eduardo Belgrano Rawson argued that 'lo histórico y lo político se hacen presente en la narración, más allá de si se lo propongan o no los escritores [...] desde la escritura, lo histórico y lo político no son categorías separadas de lo real (entendiendo lo real como el mundo de experiencias y de percepciones del escritor a través de la escritura)'.[23] The present analysis also bears in mind Rawson's elucidation, in the sense that I have identified and examined those instances in the writings that have manifested a critical stance on the historical and political circumstances that while shaping it, were also demonstrating Cortázar's own political ideology. As will become evident, Cortázar's political ideology fluctuated through his life. As he developed as a writer and as an intellectual, so his political ideology shifted from that of an anti-Peronist *petit bourgeois* to that of a supporter of the socialist revolution.[24] This book traces how his works mutated to reflect this.

Although on a day-to-day basis, the term 'political' seems to pose no ambiguities, assuming a common understanding of what is meant by it in the public sphere and largely related to the classic sense of Plato and Aristotle, when it comes to analysing a fictional text the term is difficult to pin down without establishing rigid parameters that would restrict an interpretative analysis. What do we mean exactly when we argue that a novel is political, or that it contains political elements? Does it come down to the contents of the text *per se*, or to the effects that these contents have on the reader and on the reader's views of the world? In order to enquire about the political influence that fictional writings can have, Michael Hanne poses the question: 'Can a novel start a war, free serfs, break up a marriage, drive readers to suicide, close factories, bring about a law change, swing an election, or serve as a weapon in a national or international struggle?'[25] Questions of this kind could be seen as naïve, oversimplifying the complex ways in which fictional texts can be said to be at work in the world or have an effect on society. For the argument of this book, the political is understood as a concept that structures the very way we, as individuals, view and interact with our socio-historical and political context. As Adrian Leftwich as-

---

[22] Terry Eagleton, *Criticism and Ideology* (London: Verso, 1978), p. 181.

[23] Eduardo Belgrano Rawson, 'Sacarse de encima la historia', in Leónidas Lamborghini *et al.* (eds), *La historia y la política en la ficción argentina* (Buenos Aires: Centro de Publicaciones Universidad Nacional del Litoral, 1995), pp. 67–93 at p. 88.

[24] 'Yo pertenecí a un grupo, por razones de clase pequeño burguesa, antiperonista': González Bermejo, *Revelaciones de un cronopio*, p. 119; 'Todo el período del primer peronismo del año 43, hasta que yo me fui en el 51, yo fui antiperonista': Evelyn Picon Garfield, *Cortázar por Cortázar* (Xalapa: Universidad Veracruzana, 1978), p. 51.

[25] Michael Hanne, *The Power of the Story: Fiction and Political Change* (Oxford: Berghahn, 1994), p. 1.

serts, it is not likely that there will ever be universal agreement on the definition of politics or the political.[26] Yet, within the breadth of the notion, I have especially taken on board Tobin Siebers's understanding of the political. As I will show in chapter 2 in particular, Siebers presents the concept of politics as the demand to take a position within society, to accept and assume responsibility for that participation or the lack of it, in relation to a system of government or of ideals. Thus, for Siebers, 'Politics demands that we risk taking a position, that we stand somewhere, that we decide, and that we accept as part of the political process the possibility that our positions, stances, and positions may go horribly wrong, nowhere, or miraculously right.'[27]

In his evolution from anti-Peronist to socialist, Cortázar always believed that no one, let alone a political ideology or a government, should force the writer to create following imposed rigid formulas. In this sense, intellectual dictatorship was for him as intolerable as a political one. When his literature reflected this belief, emphasizing for instance the central need for humour and playfulness as part of a political revolution (seen mostly in the collage books), criticism from the Left would accuse him of not taking politics seriously enough or of not being sufficiently committed to the revolutionary cause. In effect, the more Cortázar got involved in actual political struggles outside his world of fiction, the more emphatic his fear would become regarding the 'quitinización' or increasing rigidity of revolutionary processes. Consequently, towards the end of his life, Cortázar felt that his understanding of politics and the role that this had in his writings, was certainly different and tore him away from many of the 'protagonists' of the political revolutionary struggles.[28] As Peter Standish would argue, it is true that Cortázar's literature tends to lend itself to very diverse and multiple interpretations, because it is not a kind of literature of 'verdades únicas y absolutas'.[29] For this reason, the political dimension of his writings also varies in manifestation and meaning. However, this is not only because Cortázar disagreed with aesthetic dogmas, but also because he understood politcal revolution to be constant and all-embracing: 'El aporte de una gran literatura es fundamental para que una revolución política pase de sus etapas previas y de su triunfo material, a la revolución total.'[30] Hence, for Cortázar, a revolutionary novel is

---

26 Leftwich, *What is Politics?*, p. 12.
27 Tobin Siebers, *Politics of Scepticism* (New York: Oxford University Press, 1993), p. 8.
28 For example, after having met many people who were complicit members of the left-wing guerrilla groups in Argentina, Cortázar claimed that 'Me di cuenta de que esa gente, con todos sus méritos, con todo su coraje y con toda la razón que tenían de llevar adelante su acción, si llegaban a cumplirla [...] la revolución que de ellos iba a salir no iba a ser *mi* Revolución': Omar Prego Gadea, *La fascinación de las palabras* (Buenos Aires: Aguilar, 1984), p. 138. My emphasis.
29 Peter Standish, 'Los compromisos de Julio Cortázar', *Hispania*, 80/3 (September 1997), 465–71 at p. 469.
30 Oscar Collazos, Julio Cortázar and Mario Vargas Llosa, *Literatura en la revolución y revolución en la literatura: polémica* (Mexico City: Siglo XXI, 1970), p. 68.

not one that necessarily has a 'revolutionary content', but rather one that 'procura revolucionar la novela misma'.[31] This kind of observation has led to the conclusion that almost everything written by Cortázar, insofar as he tried to question received aesthetic – and political – norms and categories, tried to be revolutionary and in this sense, generally speaking, also political.

[31] Ibid., p. 73.

1

The Anti-Peronist Years

The Manichean view of Cortázar's *oeuvre* regarding the division between his apolitical versus political texts is largely reflected in the critical writing on his early works. For example, Graciela Maturo, in her analysis, *Julio Cortázar y el hombre nuevo*, provides a detailed description of *Divertimento* and *El examen*, yet she makes no tangible connection between these novels and politics or, more specifically, Peronism.[1] Likewise, regarding the short stories in *Bestiario*, Mercedes Rein asserts that 'no se justifica demasiado una interpretación metafísica, menos aún [...] una interpretación ética o política de esos cuentos'.[2] Continuing in this vein, Alfred Mac Adam states, in the introduction to his own English translation of *El examen*, that throughout the 1940s and 1950s Cortázar remained 'apolitical', and that *El examen* is 'above all a novel about Buenos Aires'.[3] In other words, it is apparent that the critical studies of the works written in this period follow and repeat the assertion that the political element in Cortázar became noticeable only after his conversion to socialism. However, this chapter will show that even the first steps that Cortázar took into the fictional realm were, in several respects, unequivocally political.

El examen and the gradual disintegration of hope

In June 1943, in a *coup d'état* known as the 'Revolución del 43', the Argentinian military put an end to a fraudulent era of corruption and authoritarian leadership, known as the 'década infame' (1930–43). What followed was a series of *de facto* governments, during which the figure of the then Colonel Juan Domingo Perón became increasingly central. The last of those governments – before Perón came to power – was that of General Farrell. When Farrell, who had been War Minister and Vice-President during the 'Revolución del 43', was nominated president in February 1944, Perón took over the posts vacated.[4] The advance of Perón within

---

[1] Maturo, *Julio Cortázar y el hombre nuevo*, p. 60.
[2] Mercedes Rein, *Julio Cortázar: el escritor y sus máscaras* (Montevideo: Diaco, 1957), p. 77.
[3] Alfred Mac Adam, 'Translator's Note', in Julio Cortázar, *Final Exam*, trans. Alfred Mac Adam (New York: New Directions: 2000), p. viii.
[4] Luis Alberto Romero, *Historia argentina* (Buenos Aires: Fondo de Cultura Económica, 2001), p. 92.

the military government, and in particular his alliance with the trade-union sectors, began to generate very strong opposition within, and beyond, the armed forces. Distrustful of the 'workers' Colonel' and pressured by public opinion, on 8 October 1945 the Army coerced Perón into resigning from all his posts; furthermore, to mark a more emphatic distancing from the public scene, Farrell had Perón imprisoned and sent to the island of Martín García, in the River Plate delta.

At this point Cortázar was no longer living in Buenos Aires. He had left the capital city in 1937 to be a schoolteacher at the Colegio Nacional of Bolívar, moving on in 1939 to teach at the Escuela Normal of Chivilcoy (both Bolívar and Chivilcoy being small towns in the province of Buenos Aires). By October 1945 he had been holding a lectureship at the Universidad de Cuyo, in Mendoza, for over a year.[5] On 16 December 1945 Cortázar wrote to his friend and former colleague from Bolívar, Lucienne de Duprat, telling her proudly that in Mendoza he had been physically involved in the political battle against the Peronists:

> Fui de los que se encerraron en la Universidad [...] con cincuenta alumnos y cinco colegas, vivimos cinco días completamente sitiados, recibiendo las consabidas bombas de gases, amenazas, etc. Por fin nos allanaron, estuvimos presos, y una simple circunstancia afortunada – el brusco vuelco del 12 de octubre – hizo que las cosas no pasaran a mayores [...]. Desde entonces hasta hoy, hemos continuado luchando por el ideal que defendemos.[6]

The lucky circumstance that saved Cortázar from spending a longer time behind bars was Perón's sudden imprisonment on 12 October 1945. Perón would be set free five days later, a date which became popularly known as the day Peronism was born, or in Peronist terms, 'Día de la Lealtad', which, once the Colonel was in power, was declared a national holiday.[7] On 17 October a massive march was organised among the working-class sectors to demand the release of their leader, then head of the Labour Ministry. Once freed, Perón gave a speech from the iconic balcony of the Casa Rosada, which would define the peculiar profile of the Peronist masses as well as of Peronist doctrine. Perón proclaimed:

> Que sea esta hora histórica cara a la república y cree un vínculo de unión que haga indestructible la hermandad entre el Pueblo, el Ejército y la Policía. Que sea esta unión eterna e infinita para que este pueblo crezca en la unidad espiritual de las verdaderas y auténticas fuerzas de la nacionalidad y del orden.[8]

---

[5] Jaime Correas, *Cortázar, profesor universitario* (Buenos Aires: Aguilar, 2004), p. 27.

[6] Julio Cortázar to Lucienne de Duprat, 16 December 1945, in Julio Cortázar *Cartas/1 1937–1963*, ed. Aurora Bernárdez (Buenos Aires: Alfaguara, 2000), pp. 189–90.

[7] Mariano Ben Plotkin, *Mañana es San Perón: A Cultural History of Perón's Argentina*, trans. Keith Zahniser (Washington: SR Books, 2003), p. 65.

[8] For the full text see José Luis Romero, *Las ideas políticas en Argentina* (Buenos Aires: Fondo de Cultura Económica, 1956), p. 254.

This bizarre identification of the people, the army and the police would inevitably lead to, in the words of José Luis Romero, a 'dictadura de masas, controlada, apoyada y dirigida mediante el aparato del poder'.[9]

When Perón won the elections in February of 1946, he had the support of the masses, the army and the police, as well as the endorsement – at least initially – of the Catholic Church. This new state apparatus came to be known as the 'nuevo orden', which required two different pillars of support, namely, the severe frame of mind of a Prussian-style army, and the adulation of the masses in whom aggressive sentiments could be stirred. Such aggression was succinctly depicted by Jorge Luis Borges and Adolfo Bioy Casares (as the fictionalised author Bustos Domecq) in their story 'La Fiesta del monstruo' (dated 1947 and published in 1955). Tulio Halperín Donghi further explains that the 'components' of this kind of state apparatus were individually identified as 'factores de poder', which included the army and the Church as well as 'la élite empresarial y sindical'.[10] Halperín Donghi presents Peronism as 'la solución para [el] Ejército [...] para las clases populares que se recuerdan marginadas [...] y para un movimiento obrero que ve abrírsele el camino desde la más remota periferia al centro mismo del sistema de fuerzas sociopolíticas'.[11]

The temporary subversion of the existing social order, which saw public urban space in the hands of the working classes, is at the centre of Cortázar's *El examen*. The representation of the masses in the novel, and of the group of Europeanised protagonists *vis-à-vis* the proletariat collective, reflects the influence that the Peronist 'new order' (or 'la nueva Argentina' as Perón called it), was having on the physical and ideological spaces traditionally occupied by the *porteño* middle classes.[12] The Peronist masses produce a contradictory reaction in the novel's characters. On the one hand, there is fascination for that unknown other – the 'bárbaros' as Sarmiento would have it – coming from the interior provinces to 'invade' the urban landscape, and on the other, there is revulsion for the so-called 'cabecitas negras'. An analysis of the anti-Peronist allegory in *El examen* identifies several elements whereby Cortázar expresses his criticism of the government and its methods, showing that *El examen* contains a well-defined political dimension. These elements are the 'democratisation' of culture, equated with its deterioration, and the portrayal of the Peronist masses. The first category encompasses the portrayal of the changes in university education, the usurpation of national symbols, the Teatro Colón 'affair', folklore and the invasion of the 'barrenderos'. In the second, the portrayal of the Peronist masses,

---

9   Ibid.
10   Tulio Halperín Donghi, *La larga agonía de la Argentina peronista* (Buenos Aires: Ariel, 1994), p. 43.
11   Ibid., p. 18.
12   Perón's term 'la nueva Argentina' is explained in Pedro Santos Martínez, *La nueva Argentina 1946–1955 (Tomo 1 & 2)* (Buenos Aires: La Bastilla, 1980), I, p. 7.

the 'ritual del hueso', the Plaza de Mayo as a pivotal symbolic space, and Peronism as a form of political religion are significant.

Introductory lines, introductory note

El examen follows a group of five friends during one day and one night prior to a final university exam which two of them have to take. It is set against the surreal backdrop of a sinking Buenos Aires, invaded by a steadily thickening fog, bizarre flying mushrooms and choking fluff floating in the air. The gradual physical disintegration of the urban landscape is never explained in the plot; what is more, the characters do not find it particularly odd or threatening.

The novel begins with a phrase in French: 'Il y a terriblement d'années, je m'en allais chasser le gibier d'eau dans les marais de l'Ouest – et comme il n'y avait pas alors de chemins de fer dans le pays où il me fallait voyager, je prenais la diligence' (*EE*, 7).[13] The quotation, although we as readers are not told so, comes from *Le Rideau cramoisi*, a short story written by Jules Barbey d'Aurevilly, and published in 1874. When analysing the French text, Allan H. Pasco claims that in d'Aurevilly's text the role of allusion is so crucial that it gradually extends into one vast metaphor; in effect, according to Pasco, it is due to d'Aurevilly's masterful use of allusion and allegory that *Le Rideau cramoisi* continues to excite interest.[14] Using such a quotation as the opening lines to *El examen* thus brings the question of allusion, and therefore also of allegory, to the fore. For the analysis of the political element in the novel, this is undoubtedly an important factor. It is also worth recalling at this point that, as was the case with many Argentinian *literati*, Cortázar's main interests in literature at this early stage lay in European writers, especially French and British.[15]

Opening the novel with a quotation from another book, and in its original French, is also indicative of what Victoria Ocampo would recognise as the elitism of Cortázar's writings, which in turn plays a significant role in the author's anti-Peronist stance. Ironically, given that Ocampo was herself frequently accused of being 'afrancesada' and 'extranjerizante', she argues: 'Hecho insólito, el vulgo compra las obras de Cortázar [...] y se pasea con sus libros en Torino, o en subte o en colectivo. Sin embargo, Cortázar es netamente un autor para minorías, no para lectores a quienes ha de aburrir fabulosamente [...] porque no están prepara-

---

[13] In his English translation Mac Adam translates this fragment in a footnote: 'A terrible number of years ago, I set out to hunt wild fowl in the Western swamps – and since there were not railroads in the land in which I was to travel, I hired a carriage': *Final Exam*, p. 3.

[14] Allan H. Pasco, 'A Study of Allusion: Barbey's Stendhal in *Le Rideau cramoisi*', *PMLA*, 88/3 (May 1973), 461–71 at p. 461.

[15] To exemplify this, one only needs to take note of the modules that Cortázar proposed and actually taught at the University of Cuyo, namely, 'Poesía romántica a comienzos del siglo XIX' within the programme of European literature, and 'La poesía desde Rimbaud' as part of French Literature II: Correas, *Cortázar, profesor universitario*, p. 53.

dos para digerirlo y saborearlo.'¹⁶ Although Ocampo was referring to a phenomenon that related to a much later, established Cortázar, and *El examen* was written twenty years prior to this comment, the criticism still holds for the novel and also for the period in question. Quoting in French, Cortázar could certainly be seen as elitist, a self-image that he would have celebrated and encouraged at the time.¹⁷ For the reader who does not understand French, the quotation (read out loud in the novel by a 'Lector' as part of a French literature class: *EE*, 9) goes unnoticed, easily forgotten; for those who know the language, however, the phrase acquires a significant allegorical meaning. This is perhaps why Mac Adam, in his English rendition, deemed it necessary to provide English-speaking readers with a footnoted translation. In addition to the foregrounding of allegory implied, it is also important to relate these opening lines to Cortázar's own perception of the passing of time and of the changes of his own self-image within that. The distance in time that the narrator of the French text alludes to, through the nostalgic phrase 'Il y a terriblement d'années', reflects a certain feeling of loss that Cortázar perceived as a result of the Peronist political as well as cultural hegemony. The quotation is also imbued with a melancholia that Cortázar himself would relate to later on in his life, when he decided to write an introductory note to this early novel, although he would still choose to leave it unpublished.¹⁸

In the note, written more than thirty years after the novel had been completed, Cortázar mentions the supposed premonition, brought to his attention by friends, that the text manifests with regard to events that took place in Argentina during 1952 and 1953 (mainly, the death and public funeral of Evita Perón). Cortázar responds sceptically by asserting that, 'No me sentí feliz por haber acertado a esas quinielas necrológicas y edilicias. En el fondo era demasiado fácil: el futuro argentino se obstina de tal manera en calcarse sobre el presente que los ejercicios de anticipación carecen de todo mérito' (*EE*, 5). While *Le Rideau cramoisi* looks back to the past to recount a journey, *El examen*, told in the present, foreshadows a future that, according to Cortázar, is bound to be the repetition of that present. So much so that in the note he concludes that the novel remains pertinent (despite it being published over thirty years after it was written) because 'la pesadilla de donde nació sigue despierta' (*EE*, 5). Cortázar then stresses the need for *El examen* to be published given its 'libre lenguaje,

---

[16] Victoria Ocampo, 'Después de cuarenta años', *Sur* (July–August 1970), p. 325, as quoted in John King, 'Towards a Reading of the Argentine Magazine *Sur*', *Latin American Research Review*, 16/2 (1981), 57–78 at p. 71. With regard to the 'afrancesamiento' of Victoria Ocampo, Beatriz Sarlo argues that the writer was the 'epítome de[l] afrancesamiento' of the *porteño* elite: Edgardo Dobry, 'Entrevista con Beatriz Sarlo', *Cuadernos hispanoamericanos*, 618 (December 2001), 111–20 at p. 118.

[17] It is no coincidence, I think, that all twenty-four letters, dating between 1939 and 1945 and included in Mignón Domínguez's *Cartas desconocidas de Julio Cortázar, 1939–1945* (Buenos Aires: Sudamericana, 1992), have their heading and at least one entire paragraph written in English.

[18] Although written in 1950, *El examen* was not published until 1986.

su fábula sin moraleja, su melancolía porteña' (*EE*, 5). It is tempting to read this solemn statement as somewhat ironic, given that the novel suffered from indirect political censorship.[19] Moreover, the ending of the novel seems to be loaded with a moral: it is imperative to abandon, some way or another, Peronist Argentina. The freedom in the novel's diction, however, that Cortázar refers to can be traced – insofar as the ambiguity of the term permits it – in the very direct manner in which the characters express themselves within their situation. This is manifested particularly well through the character el cronista and his defensive attitude in the face of the invading other. Pursuing the allegorical dimension of the novel, and its political implications, and reminding ourselves that Cortázar did want this book to be published, but only posthumously, can *El examen* really be said to be a 'fábula sin moraleja', as Cortázar would have us believe?

Taking into account Cortázar's understanding of the role of collective memory under Perón, the novel's melancholia, particularly palpable in its ending, in the introductory note and in d'Aurevilly's quotation, can be understood politically. In a 1945 letter to another of his former teaching colleagues, recapping the events of that year, Cortázar remarks that 'he pasado por las más extraordinarias experiencias, suficientes para crearme una especie de nueva vida provisoria, artificial, dentro de la cual no tenían cabida mis recuerdos'.[20] In the analysis of this text, it is crucial to remember that *El examen* is written within Perón's Argentina, where, as the author implies, it is too painful to look back to other times. Indeed, this was one of the aims of the Peronist state which appropriated and reformulated many aspects of collective memory and of history as a whole.[21] If, for Cortázar, Argentina's present is a mere repetition of its past, the Peronist era becomes inescapably perpetuated – ironically, this is just as Perón himself liked to think of his political regime: as something eternal.[22] For an anti-Peronist, there are no railroads, as implied in the d'Aurevilly quotation; in other words, in Peronist Argentina there is no scope for progress, there is no room for remembering. Under the Peronist regime, it is pointless to hope for a better future, or a future at all, as the characters of *Divertimento* imply: 'Mañana. Qué imbéciles, todos' (*D*, 144).

---

[19] Regarding the rejection of *El examen*, Cortázar wrote : '[*El examen*] no se podrá publicar por razones de tema, pero me ha servido para escribir por fin como a mí me gusta, en plena libertad': Cortázar to Fredi Guthman, 3 January 1951, *Cartas/1 1937–1963*, p. 253. Officially, however, the book was rejected, by the then editor of Losada, allegedly because of the use of profanity and vulgar language in the text: Peter Standish, *Understanding Julio Cortázar* (Columbia: University of South Carolina Press, 2001), p. 207.

[20] Cortázar to Lucienne C. de Duprat, 16 December 1945, *Cartas/1 1937–1963*, p. 189.

[21] Plotkin, *Mañana es San Perón*, p. 51.

[22] At the Congreso Nacional de Filosofía, which took place in the Universidad de Cuyo in October 1949, Perón, who was there to inaugurate the event, finished his speech with a phrase that summarised the spirit of his political position: 'Sentimos, experimentamos que somos eternos': Correas, *Cortázar, profesor universitario*, p. 119.

Cultural democratisation/deterioration under Perón

University: 'La casa se viene abajo'

During the years of his first mandate (1946–51), Perón began to put into practice his long-term project for the popularisation/democratisation of culture. In general terms, this meant that the Peronist working class was allowed to enter those circles which up to then had belonged exclusively to the upper and middle classes. This involved not only actual centres of culture and education, but also, indirectly, certain streets and neighbourhoods. As part of this project, on 9 October 1947, the 'Ley Universitaria' (no. 13.031) was passed, its main tenet concerning the abolition of university fees. The law opened the doors of the universities to the more deprived sectors of society, yet it also detailed around fifteen different responsibilities with which students, lecturers and authorities had to comply.[23] Inevitably, the law had an immediate impact on the number of students attending university. According to Ángel Márquez the number of registered university students increased from 40,284 in 1945 to 138,871 in 1955.[24] At the University of Buenos Aires alone the numbers went from 17,742 in 1941 to 41,325 in 1951.[25] Although the law was not passed at a national level until 1947, before then there

---

[23] For the 'different responsibilities', see, for example, Art. 4: '(Funciones específicas). Las universidades no deberán desvirtuar en ningún caso y por ningún motivo sus funciones específicas. Los profesores y los alumnos no deben actuar directa, ni indirectamente en política, invocando su carácter de miembros de la corporación universitaria, ni formular declaraciones conjuntas que supongan militancia política o intervención en cuestiones ajenas a su función específica, siendo pasible quien incurra en transgresión de ello, de suspensión, cesantía, exoneración o expulsión según el caso. Esto no impide la actuación individual por la vía legítima de los partidos políticos, pero, en ese caso, actuarán como simples ciudadanos y no en función universitaria.' This Article and the full contents of the law can be found at the Comisión Nacional de Evaluación y Acreditación Universitaria (CONEAU) <http://www.coneau.gov.ar/archivos/543.pdf> [accessed 19 March 2008]. For the Radicales, this law would 'decapitar a las Universidades' and 'acentuar el régimen dictatorial': quotations from the Radical congressmen, Calcagno and Rojas respectively, taken from the debate regarding this law, Congress sessions of 23, 24 July 1947, reproduced in Santos Martínez, *La nueva Argentina*, I, p. 199. For Perón, this law was a way to pay homage to the historical heroes, for the good of the nation. Once it was passed, he declared that 'deseo anunciar que desde hoy quedan suprimidos los actuales aranceles universitarios en forma tal que la enseñanza sea absolutamente gratuita y al alcance de todos los jóvenes argentinos que anhelan instruirse para el bien del país. Para honrar a los héroes nada mejor que imitarlos', as reproduced in the decree's documentation at the Honorable Cámara de Diputados de la Provincia de Buenos Aires <http://www.hcdiputados–ba.gov.ar> [accessed 20 March 2008]. Perón's mention of heroes refers to Belgrano, intellectual, soldier and the creator of the Argentinian flag, who is known to have donated the money rewarded to him for his military victories in the fight for independence to the building of state-run schools in several cities of northern Argentina: Huberto Mandelli, *Las escuelas donadas por Belgrano y su reglamento* (Buenos Aires: Instituto Nacional Belgraniano, 1999), p. 50.

[24] Ángel Márquez, *Educación y Peronismo (1946–1955)* (Buenos Aires: Centro Editor de América Latina, 1984), p. 45.

[25] Argentina, Ministerio de Educación de la Nación, *Labor desarrollada durante la primera presidencia del General Juan Perón* (Buenos Aires: Ministerio de Educación, 1952).

had already been similar university reforms in different provinces. Cortázar experienced the beginning of this growth at first hand, having taught at the University of Cuyo – which Perón himself had taken to be 'modelo de *universidad justicialista*' – from July 1944 to June 1946.[26] It therefore comes as no surprise that in June 1946 Cortázar handed in his notice.[27]

In *El examen* the growth in student numbers is referred to sardonically. Staring at one of the university buildings and thinking about the reaction of her university teacher, Doctor Menta, Clara – one of the protagonists – reflects, 'No se pierden un aula, meten seis mil escuchas en tandas de a mil. Cuánto lamenta Menta no tener el Kavanagh' (*EE*, 14).[28] The democratisation of university education and the effects that this had on those who thus far had perceived tertiary education as a distinguishing element of their status, are behind some of the critical allegories in the novel. The fact that the narrative is centred around a university exam (which in the end fails to take place) is highly pertinent for understanding the text as an anti-Peronist allegory, since when looking at it in closer detail, there are several scenes that could be read as a criticism of the growth in university student numbers and, more specifically, of the deterioration of education as a result of Perón's policies. It is important to stress that the University as an institution is from the first page referred to by the characters as 'la Casa': 'La voz del Lector dejó de oírse; estupendo lo aislados que estaban los salones de la Casa' (*EE*, 9). Contrary to what could be expected, the term does not make the characters feel more at ease in the 'homely' environment of their university, quite the opposite. This unease alludes in turn to the sense of invasion from the point of view of the middle-class protagonists. The institution (like the city itself) has been 'taken over'; indeed, the university has become a 'Casa Tomada', to borrow the title of Cortázar's well-known short story, first published with the recommendation of Borges in 1946.

In this vastly expanded university, students – as they let themselves be passively indoctrinated by means of a newly imposed uncritical syllabus (*EE*, 9) – are regarded as 'parásitos'. Cortázar equates this phenomenon with Catholicism (a comparison that will recur at a later scene in the novel within the ritual of the Plaza de Mayo), as the narrator explains: 'Pero en la casa mandaba el doctor Menta, siervo de la cultura. Lea libros y se encontrará a sí mismo. Crea en la letra impresa, en la voz del Lector. *Acepte el pan del espíritu*' (*EE*, 11; my emphasis). Students accept unquestioningly, as they follow the education model of Dr Menta, sarcastically referred to as the 'siervo de la cultura'. This image, juxtaposing the 'casa' (or university, in this case) and God, possibly alludes to the government's involvement in the internal running of educational institutions. Perón in fact declared that he would not interfere with university issues, as long as universities did not

---

[26] Santos Martínez, *La nueva Argentina*, I, p. 204. Original emphasis.
[27] See 'Adiós Mendoza', in Correas, *Cortázar, profesor universitario*, pp. 107–13.
[28] Completed in 1935, the Kavanagh was the first skyscraper in Buenos Aires, and the highest building in Latin America for several decades; in other words, this was a vast space.

interfere with him; in his own words: 'Cada uno en su casa y Dios en la de todos'.[29] As a consequence, the narrator also explains that 'En un tiempo en que resultaba difícil dictar cursos interesantes o pronunciar conferencias originales, la Casa servía para mantener caliente el pan del espíritu' (*EE*, 12). Along with the impossibility of individual, critical thought, implied in the reference to the difficulty of carrying out 'interesting' or 'original' activities, the repetition of the phrase 'el pan del espíritu' makes explicit the degree of political indoctrination going on at university at the time. The students must accept Peronist doctrines unquestioningly, like the word of God, while the university, like the Church, fulfils its function of keeping that word alive.

The 'lema de la Casa' (*EE*, 16) ironically reads (notably in French): *'L'art de la lecture doit lasser l'imagination de l'auditeur, sinon tout à fait libre, du moins pouvant croire à sa liberté – Stendhal'* (*EE*, 16); yet, as Clara remarks, the very referencing of the motto is wrong, for 'nadie ignoraba que la frase era de Gide, y que se la habían vendido al doctor Menta como buena' (*EE*, 16). The university is no longer the cradle of knowledge, but rather it has become the very house of ignorance and ideological manipulation. The sense of falsity and deceit is here indirectly emphasised by the allusion to Gide and his emblematic *Les Faux-Monnayeurs* (1925) in which, as Jean-Joseph Goux argues, the author fictionalises 'the shift from a society founded on legitimisation by representation to a society dominated by the inconvertibility of signifiers, that refer to one another like tokens in infinite slippage, with no standard or treasury to offer the guarantee of a transcendental signifier or referent'.[30] Furthermore, and again given its lack of interesting or original courses, university has become the epitome of the country's new state of affairs, as Cortázar would have it: stagnant and hopeless.

Outside the boundaries of the 'casa', the various ways in which the city is disintegrating symbolise the many different techniques that Perón used to impose his doctrine as the hegemonic ideology. This phenomenon is also metaphorically depicted in *Diario de Andrés Fava* as the protagonist imagines the following scene:

> Martínez Estrada hace una lectura sobre Balzac [...] el lector está frente a su público, pero un sistema de parlantes proyecta su voz desde el fondo de la sala, de manera que nos llega por la nuca [...] una voz viniendo por separado, desde la dirección contraria, *sound track* que (sospecha gratuita pero alarmante) a lo mejor no es la voz del lector, sino un doblaje (*DAF*, 31).

Similar to the appropriation of national symbols, here the voice of the 'lector' is dubbed by another, while at the same time the actual reader, Martínez Estrada, is

---

[29] The speech was delivered on 28 July 1947: Juan Domingo Perón, *Perón en doctrina: ayer, hoy y siempre* (Buenos Aires: Megalibros, 1997), p. 443.

[30] Jean-Joseph Goux, *The Coiners of Language*, trans. Jennifer Curtiss (Norman, Ok.: University of Oklahoma Press, 1996).

also replaced physically, overlapped by a disfigured face projected on to a screen. While the voice coming from the speakers overwhelms the listeners, metaphorically hitting them on their nape, the audience remains eerily appeased, having become used to the deformation of truth, in the face of this 'monstruoso divorcio' (*DAF*, 31) from reality. The cultural and intellectual deformation is mirrored by the monstrous taking over of the city.

In *El examen*, the 'comunicados del gobierno' are part of what is taking over and destroying the city, as they are equated with the 'trimartinos eutrapelios', the flying fungi (*EE*, 214). They are ubiquitous, as Andrés fastidiously claims, 'las radios de aquí no pasan más que boletines' (*EE*, 185). The dampness, which allows these fungi to reproduce and expand so quickly, is also obliterating any possibility of intellectual progress or education, as books rot away inexorably: 'Vea ese libro, cómo se arquea, qué aspecto tiene [...] Nunca creí que un libro pudiera podrirse [*sic*] como un hombre – dijo [Andrés]' (*EE*, 168). In addition, in this setting of decomposition both for books and men, words turn into 'pelusas'. Fluffy and wiry (reminiscent of the rabbits in 'Carta a una señorita en París'), these 'pelusas' get stuck in the characters' mouths, so that no utterance is possible. They are so light that they are blown willy-nilly into the putrid air; they are effectively unavoidable. Maintaining the matter-of-fact tone that prevails throughout surreal occurrences such as this one, Stella says: 'El aire está lleno de pelusas [...] Me acabo de tragar una', to which Juan replies, 'Son las palabras que dice la gente y que la niebla preserva y pasea' (*EE*, 83). Allegorically, this is Peronist homogenisation in process: like the parasitic students at university, Stella, by swallowing the floating 'pelusas', has now internalised someone else's discourse.

As the narrative progresses, the parallel drawn by Cortázar between the effects of living under Peronism and the all-embracing process of decay becomes increasingly apparent. The oppression is not just physical and symbolic; given the quasi-religious indoctrination of the parasitic students and the words that force themselves into the characters' mouths, it is also intellectual, ideological. So much so, that Andrés declares ironically, yet straightforwardly: 'No hay como tener ideas en este país' (*EE*, 27).

In *El examen*, the 'casa' or the university is directly functional, since it is the location of the final exam and the setting for the novel's circular structure (it opens at the university and it draws to an end with the characters departing, frustrated, after going to the university to sit their exam). In *Divertimento*, however, the university is only referred to as a common denominator from the past shared among the main characters: 'La Facultad juega un papel raro en esto, es el eje de donde parten los radios yo-Dinar y yo-Vigil-Renato' (*D*, 59).[31] In this other early novel, the university also seems to have been the centre of the protagonists' political

---

[31] This is an interesting image for when we come to analyse Horacio Oliveira's political past in *Rayuela*, stemming from the university days that he shared with Traveler and Talita.

struggle against the military government of Perón's predecessor, General Farrell. The narrator in *Divertimento* recalls:

> A Laura la conocí como estudiante, a Renato como fugitivo de la justicia, refugiado en una vieja sala de mayordomía cuando los jaleos de 1945. Los Vigil estaban con él y eran de otra Facultad, pero la coincidencia en nuestro antifarrelismo nos puso a todos en la misma sala. Renato nos fue utilísimo, ahora puede decirse que era el autor de aquel inmenso cartel que enarbolamos en el techo de la Facultad. (*D*, 59)

As the passage continues, the reader is allowed a glimpse of what could be the explanation for Cortázar's own disillusion in the face of Argentina's political scene after the 'jaleos' of 1945. In the light of his 1945 letters, the excerpt is also reminiscent of Cortázar's own days at the Universidad de Cuyo, when he fought 'por el ideal que defend[ía]'. El Insecto, the narrator of *Divertimento* who, like Andrés Fava and like the Minotaur in *Los Reyes* (1949), is a poet 'signado por la desgracia' (*D*, 92), reveals that: 'nuestra derrota posterior y la servil decadencia que le siguió [a la lucha antifarrelista] nos mantuvo juntos pero entregados solamente a nosotros, otra manera de perder el tiempo' (*D*, 59).[32] The narrator elucidates the apparent self-indulgent nature of the meetings of the group 'Vive como puedas', which in turn anticipates the idiosyncratic nature of *Rayuela*'s 'Club de la Serpiente', of *62*'s ambiguous 'la zona', and *Libro de Manuel*'s 'la Joda'.

According to el Insecto, the members of 'Vive como puedas' felt the need to turn in on themselves as a result of their failed political struggle against the Peronist regime and its 'servil decadencia'. Yet, despite the apparent egocentricity and detachment of the characters, analogous to Cortázar's perception of himself and his writings prior to his post-Cuba 'conversion', the political element nonetheless plays a key role in the behaviour and feelings of these

---

[32] It is relevant to mention here Steven Boldy's reading of King Minos in *Los Reyes*. He draws a connection between Minos and Perón, emphasizing even more the anti-Peronist allegories to be found in many of Cortázar's writings of this period. Boldy writes that 'El rey Minos en *Los reyes* usa al Minotauro y los tributos exigidos a los atenienses para sembrar el terror en éstos y en los egipcios y perpetuar su propio dominio. No sería inverosímil, pues, distinguir la sombra de Juan Domingo Perón detrás de Minos; sin que esta lectura agote, ni mucho menos, la riqueza y la resonancia del poema dramático. Los comentarios de Cortázar en una carta a Sergio Sergi son esclarecedores: "[Es una obra] incluso con referencias actuales, a la condición humana de nuestro días. Teseo es el orden, la ley. ¿Por qué mataba Teseo a los monstruos […]? Porque el monstruo es aquél que escapa a la codificación, es lo libre, el individuo puro, sin especie. […] El Minotauro representará pues al individuo libre y anárquico, y en cierta medida al poeta (anarquista espiritual)"': 'Prólogo: Cortázar antes y después', in *Julio Cortázar: obras completas*, II: *Teatro; Novelas*, I, ed. Saúl Yurkievich (Barcelona: Galaxia Gutenberg/Círculo de Lectores, 2004), pp. 9–39 at p. 11. Fort the full text of Cortázar's letter see *Cartas/1 1937–1963*, p. 222.

protagonists. It even seems that the active political struggle inspires a certain degree of nostalgia in the narrator, as he comments: 'Renato continuaba con la mano puesta en mi hombro mirándome con un afecto que me devolvió por un segundo a la oscura piecita de la Facultad donde él y yo planeamos lo del cartel contra Farrell' (*D*, 130). The nostalgia attached to past political activity fits in with the new state of affairs, for although under Perón access to university was free, inside the institution there was no political freedom.[33] In effect, the activities evoked by el Insecto would have become completely forbidden once the 'Ley Universitaria' had been passed. Andrés Fava, likewise, looks back to his more politically active university days. While he recalls a certain image of Clara, walking with a book in her hands, he says: 'Vuelta de esa felicidad que entonces, cuando éramos camaradas de la Facultad – No, nada vuelve como era' (*DAF*, 15).[34]

In *El examen*, *Diario de Andrés Fava* and *Divertimento*, the past experience of university days appears to be associated with a nostalgia that refers to an idea of youth and also to a way of life which was suddenly and drastically changed. This abrupt change would have been caused in reality by Perón's victory in the elections of February 1946; a change which in *El examen*, for example, brings about an existentialist mood, as the characters admit that 'Aquello [la realidad] empezaba a parecerse demasiado a *Huis Clos*' (*D*, 57). Alluding to Sartre's play introduces a sense of entrapment that increases as the narrative progresses.[35] This allusion will also remain at the centre of *Los premios*, where the characters, trapped on board a cruise ship, will be left with no choice but to face the reality of their unknown fellow passengers, as well as their own individual truth.

It could be argued that in *El examen* the idea of the final examination works as a metonymy for the situation at the university, and also as an allegory of the general uncertainty felt by the 'educated' class during the Peronist years; as Andrés puts it, 'el desconcierto total que esta civilización sin cultura crea en tantos pobres seres' (*DAF*, 35). While reiterating the idea implied in d'Aurevilly's quotation (of the lack of railroads and thus lack of civilization), with his 'pobres seres' Andrés Fava is also being clearly patronizing to those new ignorant, parasitic students. Martin Stabb claims that during the early Peronist years, the emerging generation of writers felt desperate in the face of a reality with such

[33] See n. 23 above for a full discussion of Article 4 of the 'Ley Universitaria 13.031'. Perón's words are also succinctly revealing: 'Si quieren hacer política que vayan al comité y no a la Universidad': Santos Martínez, *La nueva Argentina*, I, p. 201.

[34] The use of the word 'camaradas' instead of the more frequently used 'compañeros', denotes a specific political partnership (given the terminology, presumably of Communist or Socialist leanings). In addition, Andrés Fava could be deliberately avoiding the term 'compañeros' as this is intrinsically linked to a Peronist discourse. See, for example, Alicia Poderti, 'Peronismo/antiperonismo y el diccionario de los argentinos (1945–1976)', *Rábida*, 25 (2005), 109–18.

[35] Through a French reference, Cortázar also registers his disillusion with the local cultural scene as if preparing for his self-imposed exile in France.

simultaneously uncertain and restrictive prospects.[36] At the root of their desperation were deep-seated feelings of guilt for not speaking out against a pro-fascist government and, arguably, for having brought it upon themselves.[37] In 1953, the writer Ismael Viñas expressed this in the first issue of *Contorno*:

> Rebeldía, rechazo, desconcierto. Eso es lo que sentimos. El mundo, este mundo inmediato, nuestro país, nuestra ciudad, nos aprietan como algo de que somos responsables [...]. El momento por que atravesamos, de confusión y remoción [...] agrava nuestro desconcierto y nuestra sensación de culpa. Sentimos que de algún modo somos responsables por lo que los representantes del intelecto, por lo que los hombres del espíritu no han hecho.[38]

In the face of such uncertainty, the significance in the novel of the final exam is crucial for it fills the characters with a defined sense of direction, it provides them with a firm objective, as Juan puts it: 'El examen se le daba como un término fijo, una boya hacia la cual avanzar. Buena cosa los términos fijos, los exámenes. Ante todo un término fijo es como una marquita de lápiz en la regla graduada: precisa lo que antecede, marca una distancia' (*EE*, 46–7). The exam is the only fixed target towards which the group of characters can move, and it exists thus in an extremely confusing setting, where the fog makes it impossible to see and the 'pelusas' make it hard to talk and even to breathe.

At the same time, the exam represents the absurdity of bureaucracy and despair in the face of an unfulfilled struggle, symbolised by it ultimately not being taken, for no apparent reason. As the dialogue between Andrés and Clara unfolds, the reader finds out more about how this desperate situation is affecting Juan's state of mind:

> – ¿Y Juan está tranquilo?
> – Dice que sí, pero mirálo cómo gesticula. [...] Está furioso con todo, *le duele Buenos Aires*, yo le duelo, anda mal comido, bostezando. [...] Anoche me dijo, medio dormido: 'La casa se viene abajo'. Después se quedó callado, pero yo sé que estaba despierto. (*EE*, 37; my emphasis)

At this point, Juan appears to be the only lucid member in the group of pro-

---

[36] Martin S. Staab, 'Argentine Letters and the Peronato: An Overview', *Journal of Interamerican Studies and World Affairs*, 13 (1971), 434–55 at p. 442.

[37] Looking back at what it was like to be an anti-Peronist intellectual between 1945 and 1955, Ernesto Sábato takes this sense of guilt to an extreme, asserting that 'cada nación tiene también el rostro que inmanentemente se merece, pues todos somos culpables de todo, y en cada argentino había un fragmento de Perón': *El otro rostro del peronismo: carta abierta a Mario Amadeo* (Buenos Aires: Imprenta López, 1956), p. 34.

[38] Ismael Viñas, 'La traición de los hombres honestos', *Contorno*, 1 (November 1953), 7–12 at p. 9.

tagonists. Unlike his peers, and perhaps as a consequence of his own sensitivity, Juan is aware and understandably afflicted by the plight of his city and the collapse of the university. Significantly, Juan feels physical pain at the disintegration of his reality. The image of Juan embodying the pain caused by political matters is one that will recur in Cortázar's novels.[39] Moreover, it is interesting to note that in Juan's statement, 'casa' is written with a lower-case 'c'. When 'Casa' refers to the university as an institution, the use of capital 'c' becomes an ironic marker of respect for the degraded educational institution under the Peronist regime. Here it is plausible that the use of 'casa' is referring to a more all-encompassing home, namely, the homeland. Accordingly, for Juan the deterioration of the university system implies the disintegration of the entire nation. Similarly, for Andrés, the effect of the popularisation of tertiary education is perceived in the corrosion of the quality of intellectuals, which is what worries this character most. In addition, that same corrosion is reflected in the gradual putrefaction of the city: 'Es la *calidad* de nuestro intelectualismo lo que me preocupa. Le huelo algo húmedo, como este aire del bajo [...] lo que estamos haciendo es tragar este aire sucio y fijarlo en el papel' (*EE*, 38–9; my emphasis).

After meandering aimlessly through the streets of Buenos Aires all night, when the group finally makes it to the university so that Clara and Juan can sit their final exam, they find that access to the classrooms is denied. As it turns out, no one in the building has the keys, so effectively no one can enter the respective 'salones de la Casa' to take their respective final exams. Metaphorically, university education has been shut down. As a result, and in the middle of a chaotic scene, degree diplomas are handed out willy-nilly, an act that alludes directly to the gradual degradation of the quality of university teaching as a result of the rise in student numbers. In the end, the group of characters leaves the university ethically empty-handed, and for this reason arousing the attention of the porter, who is 'verdaderamente asombrado de verlos irse así con las manos vacías' (*EE*, 211). Ironically, their very decency makes them look suspicious. A sense of disapproval is expressed through their empty-handed departure, and this does not go unnoticed, for significantly those who leave are being controlled by the 'vigilante de la entrada [que] era ahora el vigilante de la salida' (*EE*, 211). Foreshadowing what would be the end of *Los premios*, with the blacklisting of those who had rebelled on board the *Malcolm*, this act of scrutinizing those who leave underlines the sense of inescapability felt by Cortázar living under the Peronist system and emphasised in the allusion to *Huis Clos*. Now that the 'new order' of things has left the characters without their main focus, that is, the final exam, their moral correctness and their need to escape turns the protagonists of this novel into pariahs. Refusing to conform to the new state of affairs, Juan,

---

[39] The metaphor also has echoes of Pablo Neruda's *Canto general*. When alluding directly to Valparaíso he writes: 'Me duele en ti mi pueblo, / toda mi patria americana': (Mexico City: Talleres Gráficos, 1950), p. 262.

Andrés, Clara, Stella and el cronista, have now been displaced within their own settings, and have become the other in a reality of usurped values.

The usurpation of national symbols

In the same chaotic scene during which diplomas are being handed out indiscriminately, Andrés is perplexed when he notices something taking place in the background: 'Mirá – dijo Andrés [...] En el recodo adonde habían llegado, dos individuos descolgaban un retrato. [...] Ya habían bajado otros dos cuadros y los iban apilando en un rincón' (*EE*, 196). Those national figures who had once welcomed the students into the university are now being reduced to a pile of objects in the corner, in an act that is symbolic of the gradual marginalisation of those who will not submit to the Peronist ideological hegemony. Andrés compares the portraits to values (moral, national and ideological) and loses hope at the realisation that 'los valores, esos retratos si querés, están inermes en las manos de los tipos que los apilan en un rincón' (*EE*, 197). The sense of marginalisation is emphasised by Clara, as she says: 'Vos te sentís acorralado. [...] Yo solamente puedo decirte que me siento atrapada [...] sola y a oscuras' (*EE*, 197). The portraits are being taken down to be replaced by others, as Andrés explains to Clara: 'Mudanza – dijo Clara. [...] No, no se mudan [dijo Andrés]. Los cambian por otros' (*EE*, 196). Given a compulsory measure issued by the Peronist government, it is highly likely that the new portraits that are replacing the old ones are those of Perón and of his wife, Eva Duarte. In addition to Andrés's remark, the narrator also comments on this change, and supplies another important detail by saying that: 'Se veían muy bien los muebles, una perchera, un paragüero, el retrato de San Martín' (*EE*, 211). The reference to San Martín's portrait, now also hanging on the wall, emphasises the possibility that the other portraits being hung are those of Perón and Eva for, according to Law 1474, under the Peronist regime, not only had all three portraits to be hung in all public educational institutions, but they also had to be displayed 'en lugar[es] de preferencia'.[40]

It is important to note that Argentina's 'liberator' General San Martín is given a significant place in the novel. He features in two other scenes besides the one just discussed. In all cases, the political significance of this figure for

---

[40] The 'Ley 1474' (1948) establishes 'que en las Escuelas se coloquen retratos del General San Martín, Presidente General Perón y de la Jefa Espiritual de la Nación Señora Eva Perón. Art. 1°.– Todas las escuelas de la Provincia y las oficinas de los tres poderes del Estado provincial deberán exhibir en lugar de preferencia los retratos del Libertador General don José de San Martín, del excelentísimo señor presidente de la República, General Juan Domingo Perón y de la Jefa Espiritual de la Nación, señora Eva Perón. Art. 2°. – El Poder Ejecutivo proveerá de dichos retratos a cada una de las reparticiones y escuelas de la Provincia': <http://www.gov.ar/LEYES/leyesv/1474.htm> [accessed 30 March 2008]. Although the law refers to schools and governmental offices only, by implication its strictures can be applied to other state-run educational institutions, such as state-run universities.

Argentinian history, and for Peronism in particular, comes to the fore. One of the other instances occurs during a scene with Abel in the Central Post Office, in which stamps become a symbol for the 'patria de los héroes' (*EE*, 96), and where the 'patria', in turn, is described as 'plana' (*EE*, 97) and 'disponible' (*EE*, 97). The hero has been reduced to a mere stamp – a flat, tiny, lifeless image. As such, Abel sadistically describes San Martín's inevitable destiny: 'el acendrado culto de millones de lenguas lamiéndote el pescuezo y millones de sellos rompiéndote la cara [...] en poder del destinatario y el sobre a la basura, con su cara, su gloria inmarcesible, San Martín entre fideos y pedazos de budín de sémola' (*EE*, 98). It is interesting that out of the group of protagonists, it is Abel who comes into close contact with the figure of San Martín, since he is the only character in the text who is not 'alive'. It is implied that he is the immaterial presence of Clara's dead lover, although he also seems to operate as Andrés Fava's imaginary *alter ego*. The novel leaves it ambiguous, yet the fact that it is ghost-like Abel who reflects so bitterly upon this patriotic figure links the image of San Martín to a notion of ethereality and death, in other words, to the past. As in the previous example, where Andrés understands the removal of portraits as equivalent to the suppression of national values, Abel's comments imply distrust of historical accuracy under Peronism. Dumping San Martín in the rubbish and piling up in a corner portraits of figures key to Argentinian education, represents an objectification and belittling of national symbols about to be taken over by a new, imposed set of Peronist values.

The sense of the end of a 'reliable' history embodied in irreproachable *próceres* is explicitly associated with Perón's democratisation of culture, whereby values, symbols and patriotic heroes that were already part of Argentinian historical mythology, were appropriated and given a new, Peronist meaning with the aim of rewriting 'official history'.[41] The figure most emphasised by the regime as part of this process was none other than San Martín. This not only generated a great deal of activity in the Ministry of Education, as Mónica Esti Rein explains in her chapter 'The Peronisation of the Schools', but additionally, the comparison drawn between the 'Libertador' and Perón had to be reflected in all school textbooks.[42] These school texts 'presented a portrait of San Martín next to that of Perón, both figures in military uniform and the pictures captioned in the same way: "The Liberator, General San Martín", and "The Liberator, General Perón"'.[43] Andrés Fava thinks of San Martín in terms of an ever-present symbol, haunting him like a relentless ghost: 'San Martín, el misterioso [...] tal vez, si le ar-

---

[41] For further discussion on the rewriting of official history in Argentina in the Perón era, see Santos Martínez, *La nueva Argentina*, II, pp. 320–35.

[42] Mónica Esti Rein, *Politics and Education in Argentina, 1946–1962*, trans. Martha Grenzeback (New York/London: M. E. Sharpe, 1998), pp. 72–3.

[43] Ibid., p. 75.

rancáramos el poncho, ya no estuviera él adentro' (*DAF*, 29).[44] Rather than representing the *patria*, through Perón's manipulation of icons and values San Martín has now become a symbol for the unreal, for a deceptive notion of history. Peronism, like San Martín's *poncho*, is a façade. This is how Borges, and also Bustos Domecq, tended to portray their upper-middle-class understanding (and dislike) of Peronism.

In 'El simulacro', for example, after describing the simultaneous vigils that took place when Evita Perón died, Borges concludes that history is unbelievable, and that in it resides, 'la cifra perfecta de una época irreal', where 'tampoco Perón era Perón ni Eva era Eva sino desconocidos o anónimos [...] una crasa mitología'.[45] As argued by Rodolfo Borello, for Cortázar (as for his characters), the Peronist regime was immersed in a sense of falsity.[46] In turn, that falsity was so powerful and ubiquitous that for Cortázar, as for many other intellectuals, it became immoral to inhabit Peronist Argentina. One of the ways to escape from this state of dishonesty was to go into self-imposed exile. This was precisely what Cortázar did in 1951; in addition, and as reflected in the fictional writings, this is also what Lucio Medina does in 'La banda', it is what Irene and her brother do symbolically when they abandon their 'casa tomada', and effectively it is what Juan and Clara do at the end of *El examen*.[47]

Returning to San Martín, the third and final prominent mention in the novel occurs when the narrator describes Salaver pulling out of his wallet a 'calendario de celuloide que por fuera tenía a una *glamour girl* [...] y por dentro [...] un excelente encasillamiento de 1950. Año del Libertador General San Martín'

---

[44] This image is reminiscent of Sarmiento's *Facundo*, when he asserts that in the inversion of roles, with the *poncho* as an epitome of the *gaucho*, the soldier will fail: 'Los papeles están cambiados: el gaucho toma la casaca; el militar de la Independencia, el *poncho*; el primero triunfa; el segundo va a morir traspasado de una bala que le dispara de paso la *montonera*': Domingo Faustino Sarmiento, *Facundo: civilización y barbarie* (Buenos Aires: Sopena, 1945), p. 95. Original emphasis.

[45] Jorge Luis Borges, 'El simulacro', in *Obras completas 1923–1949* (Buenos Aires: Emecé, 1974), pp. 789–90 at p. 789. This was first published in *El hacedor* (Buenos Aires: Emecé, 1960).

[46] Rodolfo A. Borello, 'Los liberales: de Borges a Murena', in his *El peronismo (1943–1955) en la narrativa argentina* (Ottawa: Dovehouse Editions, 1991), pp. 147–82 at p. 154.

[47] It is interesting to note how the sense of inescapability comes through. While, at the end of 'La banda', Lucio Medina leaves, throughout the short story the 'virus' seems to be spreading into all spheres of life. When Lucio goes to the cinema to see a Litvak film, instead of the movie, a Peronist music band appears on stage. This creates in Lucio a feeling of estrangement that takes him over, indeed, like a virus: 'Salí a la calle, con el calor pegajoso [...] me olvidé por completo de la película de Litvak, la banda *me ocupaba* como si yo fuera el escenario del Ópera': Julio Cortázar, 'La banda', in *Cuentos completos/1* (Buenos Aires: Alfaguara, 1994), pp. 348–51 at p. 350; my emphasis. (This was first published in *Final del juego* in 1956). Also, in *Divertimento*, the characters' obsession with the Ouija board or 'el ritual de la taza', as they call it, is at the centre of their activities. This ritual, whereby the protagonists communicate with the parallel universe of the dead and more specifically with Facundo Quiroga's wife, could be understood as an allegory for the false reality implied by Peronism, and also as a method of escape (*D*, 67–9).

(*EE*, 72). This is no coincidence. The figure of the *prócer*, like that of Perón, became especially ubiquitous in 1950, when – to commemorate the centennial of San Martín's death – the Peronist government decided to denominate the entire year as 'Año del Libertador General San Martín'. As expression of this decree, alongside patriotic celebrations, all official documents, as well as any book published during that year, had to be preceded by the motto 'Año del Libertador General San Martín'. In the novel, following the narrator's ironic levelling of San Martín with a 'glamour girl', the reader is provided with a list of cultural events taking place during that same year, yet not in Argentina: '(y en esa fecha en París, Yehudi Menuhin tocaba las sonatas de Bach para violín solo, / y en Papua estaba Edwin Fischer / y Arletty representaba "Un tramway nommé Désir" en París)' (*EE*, 72). Instead of succumbing, like the parasitical students at the 'Casa', to the veneration of imposed political figures – that is, San Martín and by implication also Perón and Evita – the narrator chooses to look to foreign artists (reiterating the idea already discussed with regard to Sartre and d'Aurevilly). It is moreover significant that all the events mentioned are taking place outside Argentina. The idea of the Liberator, achieving political as well as cultural sovereignty for the nation, is contrasted with this determination to be more up-to-date with what is going on in Paris than in Buenos Aires. It is of course at the same time another way of escaping an imposed reality.

The idea of travelling to an alternative reality can be related to Cortázar's ambitions at the time. Although (notably) in the published letters there are none from 1950, in the letters from 1949 there are several allusions to the author's desire to leave Argentina. More specifically, in a letter to his friend, the poet Fredi Guthman, Cortázar says, 'Preparo mi viaje. Parece que el "año santo" me ayudará a ir barato a Europa.'[48] From various letters and later interviews, it seems evident that Cortázar's plans for departure are closely linked to the political situation in Argentina under Perón, and emphatically to the university changes that came as a consequence of the regime. In another letter to Guthman, written from Paris soon after arriving, Cortázar clarifies that although they have allocated him a room in the Argentinian Hall of the Cité Universitaire, he has arranged private accommodation elsewhere because in the 'pabellón argentino [...] las cosas son una exacta prolongación del clima universitario argentino'.[49]

---

[48] Cortázar to Fredi Guthman, n.d. 1949, *Cartas/1 1937–1963*, p. 246. Coincidentally, and beneficially for Perón, 'el Año del Libertador' concurred with the 'Año Santo', which most probably refers to the 'Año Santo Jacobeo', the name given to those years in which 25 July falls on a Sunday. During such a year Roman Catholics can hope for total redemption of their sins, provided that they follow 'certain conditions' imposed by the Catholic Church. 1950 was a Holy Year, which meant that there would have been more demand for travel to Santiago de Compostela or even to Rome: Vatican City, 'El himno pontífico' <http://www.vatican.va/news_services/press/documentazione/documents/spssscv/inno/_scv_testo_it.html#Breve%20presentazione%20in%20spagnolo> [accessed 1 April 2008].

[49] Cortázar to Fredi Guthman, 8 October 1951, *Cartas/1 1937–1963*, p. 262.

In the fictional texts that Cortázar was writing prior to his departure, the sense of entrapment and of hopelessness with regard to the future is felt especially strongly by the character Andrés Fava, for example as he says: 'Después nada – la interrumpió Andrés [a Stella] –. Olvidáte de esa palabra por un rato' (*EE*, 216). For Andrés the future is so bleak that it is futile even to use the word 'después'. In addition, when talking to his former lover Clara, Andrés sees 'el cráneo de Clara bajo su rostro y su pelo. […] El cráneo hablaba. La muerte futura vivía bajo este humo, este hedor de la ciudad' (*EE*, 197-8). In his analysis of the 'melancolía porteña' of *El examen*, Patrick O'Connor defines the metaphor of the skull as a metonymy for the novel's mood.[50] While anticipating the hopelessness of the characters' fate within the framework that they inhabit, it is apparent that this image, as well as summarising the novel's mood, emphasises Andrés's understanding of the city's physical decomposition as a sign of their lifeless, hopeless future.

In *Divertimento*, written eighteen months before *El examen*, concern for a non-existent future is one of the prevalent themes. Towards the end of the novel, ironically as he proposes a toast, el Insecto announces: 'Mañana, que es la gran palabra, la gran dispensadora del aplazamiento […]. Mañana – repitió Marta, imitando mecánicamente el brindis –. ¿Cómo pudo imaginarse siquiera la palabra? Demain, tomorrow, mañana, qué horror' (*D*, 139). If there is no tomorrow, and history has become, as the narrator in *El examen* says, 'un momento, una mísera palabra' (*EE*, 97), which, controlled by the Peronist regime, 'resuena altisonante y almafuerte' (*EE*, 97), the protagonists are faced with a single dilemma or, according to Clara, 'un *cachet* ontológico' (*EE*, 223), namely: '*Irse, quedarse / Juego del ser / Apenas es – después – el antes*' (*EE*, 224). Andrés's pessimistic outlook is emphasised by Juan's inescapable equation. Given the consequences of Peronism, the characters feel that to live immersed in such falsity is immoral, and that the only solution ('la salvación' as Andrés would have it: *EE*, 197) is to escape in some way or another. Thus, Juan and Clara leave physically on a boat that sails out into the Río de la Plata (*EE*, 241), while Andrés, who professes 'Yo también me voy' (*EE*, 241), kills himself and also takes the life of his immaterial double Abel, in a kind of atavistic duel (*EE*, 243). In turn, Stella (who, in any case, 'no existe', as Andrés Fava writes in the last page of his diary, *DAF*, 52) seems to escape intellectually into her own state of oblivion, prioritising trivia such as 'el agua del canario y [el] alpiste' (*EE*, 244) over the pressing circumstances. Finally, the fifth member of the group, el cronista, instead of reporting on the crumbling of Buenos Aires, he 'dormía a gusto' (*EE*, 244). Possibly commenting on the 'dormant' state of serious journalism during Perón, el cronista is thus left to his own world of parallel, dream-like reality as the novel concludes.

---

[50] Patrick O'Connor, 'Melancholia porteña and Survivor's Guilt: A Benjaminian Reading of Cortázar's *El examen*', *Latin American Literary Review*, 23/46 (1995), 5–32 at p. 11.

It is clear, therefore, that one consistent idea emerges from Cortázar's writings during the Peronist years, namely, that it had become impossible to stay in an Argentina, which, according to Cortázar himself, had been transformed into 'un pequeño infierno, sin la grandeza del que imaginó Dante; infierno a medias y por eso doblemente cruel y mezquino'.[51] In *El examen*, hence, 'Quedarse es Abel', says Andrés (*EE*, 233); and since Abel is an intangible figure from the past, it is inferred that to stay means to die, to disappear like the city itself, as Juan puts it: 'Yo creo que Abel es como la ciudad, algo que *a bel et bien disparu*' (*EE*, 236).[52] In his diary, Andrés Fava makes this point clear: 'Lo cierto es irse. Quedarse es ya la mentira, la construcción, las paredes que parcelan el espacio sin anularlo' (*DAF*, 37).

With the loss of 70% of lecturers and academic authorities from all the national universities at the end of 1946, and the persecution of students for ideological reasons, for Cortázar, as well as for most of his early characters, the effects of the Peronist government on education meant inexorable deterioration.[53] This, together with a constant sense of persecution, would result in the collapse of the democratic university system, and also in the intellectual disintegration of an entire society. For those who, like the protagonists of the early texts, were at some point part of the academic world, Argentina became, as Cortázar would have it, inhabitable.

Given Cortázar's subsequent swerve to the Left, it may seem contradictory that he should have felt an urge to leave the country just when tertiary education had been made available to all sectors. Yet, it should be borne in mind that it was the increasing political clashes within the institution that forced the author, then lecturer, to quit. He had gone to Mendoza 'después de haber abandonado Chivilcoy bajo vehementes sospechas de comunismo, anarquismo y trotskismo'; paradoxically, he would shortly be classified by the same institution as 'fascista, nazi, sepichista, rosista y falangista'.[54] During his period at the Universidad de Cuyo, Cortázar thoroughly enjoyed the task of teaching, and although he was involved in the highly-politicised 'toma' of the university, the political atmosphere would only reinforce his intentions to leave.[55] Consequently, Cortázar thinks of himself

---

[51] Cortázar to Lucienne C. de Duprat, 16 December 1945, *Cartas/1 1937–1963*, p. 190.

[52] Prefiguring Horacio Oliveira – whose brother, like his own *alter ego*, Traveler, has never left Buenos Aires – Abel is an early embodiment of Cortázar's own divided self, leaving yet at the same time wanting to stay.

[53] See Silvia Sigal, 'Intelectuales y peronismo', in *Nueva historia argentina*, VIII: *(años peronistas 1943–1955)* (Buenos Aires: Sudamericana, 2002), pp. 501–46 at p. 501.

[54] These accusations came after Cortázar's refusal to kiss the ring of Monsignor of Mercedes when he came to visit the school at which Cortázar was working. They also stem from the fact that his classes on the 'Revolución del 43' had been 'altamente frías, llenas de reticencias y reservas': Cortázar to "Los Firmantes de una nota del Centro de Estudiantes de la Facultad de Filosfia y Letras de la Universidad Nacional de Cuyo (Mendoza)", 29 July 1944, *Cartas/1 1937–1963*, p. 201.

[55] For Cortázar's positive personal experience of lecturing at the University of Cuyo, see Correas, *Cortázar, profesor universitario*, p. 70.

as a teacher who is dedicated to literature and not to politics. It is interesting to note that in later years, when recalling this episode, Cortázar would underline the fact that he had felt forced to leave Mendoza 'a raíz del fracaso del movimiento antiperonista en el que anduve metido', a nostalgic reminiscence comparable to that of el Insecto and his anti-Farrell struggle.[56] Yet, in a later interview he states: 'En los años 44-45 participé en la lucha política contra el peronismo, pero cuando Perón ganó las elecciones presidenciales, preferí renunciar a mis cátedras antes de verme obligado a "sacarme el saco" como les pasó a tantos colegas.'[57] The subtle change in Cortázar's perception of his own reasons for leaving Mendoza, and ultimately for leaving Argentina, indicate a step in Cortázar's political evolution, whereby the clear change in political ideology is mirrored in the somewhat mythologised construction of his self-image.

Although Cortázar manifests strong contempt for the university reforms brought about by the Peronist regime, both in his letters and in his fiction, it is not the opening up of the university to all sectors that really pushed him out of Peronist Argentina, but rather the fact made progressively more evident that Perón's goal was to obtain total control of the universities on a nation-wide scale. Indeed, the 'Ley Universitaria' was in 1954 modified into a different law (Law 14,297) whereby it was specified that the national state would regulate the internal administration of all universities as well as being in charge of appointing authorities and issuing directives regarding the content of all courses offered.[58] This new law went so far as to specify that the aim of the university was to reaffirm national consciousness, to which end, for example, students had to become versed in national doctrine and the fundamentals of the 1949 Constitution.[59] As Tulio Halperín Donghi remarks, for Perón the university was not a matter of ideology, but rather, it represented 'un problema político'.[60] For Cortázar, this was only the beginning of a long process of the degradation or, as seen in *El examen*, the progressive putrefaction of Argentina as a nation.

'La degradación de algo hermoso'
In November 1947, Perón called for a gathering of Argentinian intellectuals in order to expound to them the importance of, and need for, a 'cultural revolution' as part of his project for a 'new Argentina'.[61] Although there were many artists

---

[56] Cortázar to Graciela Maturo, 3 June 1967, in *Cartas/2 1964–1968*, ed. Aurora Bernárdez (Buenos Aires: Alfaguara, 2000), p. 1154.

[57] Luis Harss, *Los nuestros* (Buenos Aires: Sudamericana, 1977), p. 264.

[58] See Eduardo Sánchez Martínez, *La legislación sobre educación superior en Argentina* (Buenos Aires: IESALC, 2002), p. 10.

[59] For further details on the content of Law 14,297, see Plotkin, *Mañana es San Perón*, p. 102.

[60] Tulio Halperín Donghi, *Historia de la Universidad de Buenos Aires* (Buenos Aires: Eudeba, 1982), p. 184.

[61] The 'intellectuals' included writers, historians, journalists, artists and musicians. For a list of names see Santos Martínez, *La nueva Argentina*, I, pp. 210–22.

and thinkers who could not tolerate living under the Peronist regime, there were others who showed their political support, through involvement in government cultural events, which generally took place at the iconic opera house, Teatro Colón. With the aim of extending its political hegemony to the cultural sphere, the Peronist government enforced what Raymond Williams calls a 'selective tradition', whereby 'autochthonous' aesthetic practices were preferred to those that were foreign or deemed to be of bourgeois taste.[62] Therefore, *sainetes* replaced operas, *chamamés* were to be preferred over rock and roll, and José Hernández had to be read before any foreign author, however classic.[63] Recovering those cultural practices and meanings allowed the Peronist regime to justify the binaries on which its ideology was based, such as: *pueblo*/oligarchy, autochthonous/foreign, proletarian/bourgeois.[64] According to this, as Miguel Ronzitti explains, national theatre was used to 'educar [al pueblo] por medio del arte, pulir sus imperfecciones y hacer que pueda asimilar las obras superiores de los creadores de cultura'.[65]

Among the earlier measures carried out as part of the so-called 'democratisation of culture' was the free staging of plays aimed at the working classes. For Perón there could not have been a more appropriate place to launch this theatrical endeavour than the Colón itself, epitome of traditional elitist icons of Argentinian oligarchy.[66] As Mariano Plotkin argues, this strategy represented another form of 'taking-over' of upper-class symbols by the 'descamisados'.[67] If Perón thought that he could rewrite history through the usurpation and replacement of patriotic symbols, artistic culture could also be given a different significance within society through the appropriation and reformulation of values within cultural spaces and cultural acts. To clarify and promote his plan, after the performance at the Colón of *El conventillo de la paloma*, the best-known *sainete* by Alberto Vaccarezza (who was one of the intellectuals present at Perón's talk for the 'cultural revolution'), Perón addressed the audience directly:

> [un muchacho] me dijo que *El conventillo de la paloma* en el Colón era un acto extraordinario. Como este muchacho constituye una parte del pueblo a la que me gusta consultar a menudo en forma fehaciente y objetiva, le

---

[62] Raymond Williams, *Marxism and Literature* (Oxford: Oxford University Press, 1977), pp. 137–9.

[63] For a more detailed analysis, see, for example, Carlos de la Torre, 'The Ambiguous Meanings of Latin American Populisms', *Social Research*, 59/2 (1992), 385–414.

[64] Cristián Buchrucker, 'Interpretations of Peronism: Old Frameworks and New Perspectives', in *Peronism and Argentina*, ed. James P. Brennan (Wilmington: Scholarly Resources Inc., 1998), pp. 3–28 at p. 13.

[65] Miguel Ronzitti, 'Segundo Plan Quinquenal y Teatro', *Talía*, 1/1 (1953), 20–35 at p. 29.

[66] See Alberto Ciria, *Política y cultura popular: la Argentina peronista 1946–1955* (Buenos Aires: Ediciones de la Flor, 1983), p. 34; Horacio Sanguinetti, 'Breve historia política del Teatro Colón', *Todo es Historia*, 5/1 (1967), 66–77 at p. 68.

[67] Plotkin, *Mañana es San Perón*, p. 64.

pregunté qué pensaba sobre eso, y me dijo: 'Es indudable que los "pitucos" van a creer que es una profanación [...] pero los otros van a creer que es un agravio para *El conventillo de la paloma*'. Es indudable que ése podría ser el sentir de mucha gente, pero nuestra intención es distinta. [...] Trabajemos por ir elevando la cultura de nuestro pueblo que es la verdadera cultura.[68]

These words exemplify Perón's inversion of the dominant values, all the more pertinent when made within such a bastion of high culture. In his populist discourse, *el pueblo*, once considered barbaric and uncultured, is now elevated to become the 'authentic', superior class. As with the educational reforms, these cultural impositions affected and alienated those who had thus far dominated that sector of Argentinian – mainly *porteño* – life. In other words, the middle and upper classes, the 'pitucos', who were being pushed out of the now vastly expanded universities, were also being displaced from their comfortable cultural niches.

In *Divertimento* none of these cultural reforms is directly referred to, yet it becomes evident that the protagonists would certainly belong to that social stratum that considered the cultural changes under Perón to be a 'profanation'. This is shown, for instance, through the fact that all the characters have a 'sirvienta' (see pp. 61, 77, 95, 102), which was then, an exclusive luxury of the upper classes. In addition, linking to Perón's own paraphrasing of the 'muchacho' at the Colón, the narrator of *Divertimento* shows the physical displacement of the higher classes as he describes that, while walking through the streets of Buenos Aires one night, 'Me gané algunos gritos de una patota esquinera: "¡Mirá el pituco, le está jugando a la escondida!"' (*D*, 81). In *El examen*, the changes of socio-cultural parameters are brought to the fore in one of the novel's central scenes, namely, the visit to the Teatro Colón. To this effect, within the characters' apparently random roaming through the novel, deciding to go to the Colón is highly significant.

The scene in question begins with Clara, her father Funes, and Juan travelling in a taxi towards the Colón, where they have agreed to meet up with el cronista.[69] As they are about to arrive, the taxi drives past the back entrance of the theatre, where in the space previously occupied by a café patronized

---

[68] *La Prensa*, 22 December 1953. See Yanina Andrea Leonardi, 'Espectáculos y figuras populares en el circuito teatral oficial durante los años peronistas', <http://www.unsam.edu.ar/home/material/Leonardi.pdf> [accessed 31 January 2008], pp. 1–10 at p. 10. For reference to Alberto Vaccarezza as an 'official Peronist', see Santos Martínez, *La nueva Argentina*, I, p. 213.

[69] Cortázar's choice of name for Clara's father is significant. It is most probably a homage to Borges and to his short story 'Funes, el memorioso', written six years before *El examen*. The choice of name could also be working at a metaphorical level underlining the need to remember in a society where symbols have been appropriated and, as Cortázar put it, one might feel forced to believe that there is no room for memories. In other words, having someone called Funes in the novel is surely a call for readers not to forget.

mostly by the theatre's musicians, there is now a 'marquesina *pour faire pendant*' (*EE*, 128). Observing such an 'obscenity' of a change, as Juan calls it (*EE*, 129), Funes says, 'Cómo ha cambiado todo en tan poco tiempo' (*EE*, 128), which adds to the narrator's own comment, 'Buenos Aires ya no es lo que era antes' (*EE*, 128). Complementing these two remarks, the narrator quotes in Latin: 'Non sum qualis eram bonae sub regno Cynarae' (*EE*, 128). Whether Cortázar took this quotation from the homonymous poem by the Victorian Ernest Dowson, or from its original source in Horace's First Ode, is not clear; either way, the quotation implies a preoccupation with decline and with the insufficiency of the present compared with the past, and like the opening lines of the novel, the case of the native is inevitably 'extranjerizante'.[70] In other words, and within the context of *El examen*, just by observing the urban changes around the Colón, the characters as well as the narrator become aware of a process of deterioration, and feel the need to express their disapproval of those changes brought about by the Peronist present *vis-à-vis* their liberal (and in their view, more cultured) past.

As soon as they step into the foyer of the theatre, the narrator describes how Clara stops to observe the people standing there: 'las caras blancas, caras grises, caruchas, carotas, caretas, caronas' (*EE*, 129).[71] The use of the colour grey and the respective negative deformations of the word 'cara', show that the alliterative description of the faces does not lend itself to a positive impression (it is actually implied that among them there are no people of 'piel oscura', as Juan tends to refer to people from the lower classes: *EE*, 90). During the intermission, Juan and el cronista go to stretch their legs, and as they look at the other people in the foyer, the narrator observes that 'Los grupos [de gente] [...] tenían un aire más deliberado que otras veces; y no era del concierto que se hablaba' (*EE*, 133). It could be deduced from the talk about 'censura' (*EE*, 131) coming from the balconies, the narrator's mentioning of 'pánico' (*EE*, 130) and

---

[70] See, for example, the interpretation of Dowson's poem by Rowena Fowler, in 'Ernest Dowson and the Classics', *Yearbook of English Studies*, 3 (1973), 243–52 at p. 248. Interestingly, the full phrase also appears in one of Cortázar's letters from 1966. In that case he uses it in a form of *post scriptum* to close the correspondence with Francisco Porrúa, writing: 'Qué carta infecta. *Non sum qualis sub regnae Cynara?* Pero volveré, volveré': Cortázar to Francisco Porrúa, 18 November 1966, *Cartas/2 1964–1968*, 1087; my emphasis. The last words in this letter (the repetition of 'volveré') are also noteworthy. It is possible that Cortázar is ironically emulating Evita Perón's famous and most probably apocryphal phrase 'Volveré y seré millones', which she is believed to have said before dying in 1952. In addition, it is interesting that Cortázar recurrently resorts to repetition, not necessarily to emphasise an idea, but rather to convince himself: see chapter 3 below.

[71] Choosing grey as a colour to describe people's faces recalls Oliverio Girondo, who in his 'Apunte callejero' writes 'En la terraza de un café hay una familia gris': *Veinte poemas para leerse en el tranvía* (1922), in *Obra completa*, ed. Raúl Antelo (Barcelona: Galaxia Gutenberg, 1999), pp. 3–28 at p. 12. Girondo's metaphor will have further echoes later on in the chapter, when considering how some of the characters, unlike Girondo, cannot reconcile the idea of literature, of high-art, with travelling on the tram.

the fact that 'la calle está bastante rara' (*EE*, 136), that fear is defining the atmosphere at the Teatro Colón. The source of that unease could be related to having to 'share' this centre of high culture with the other, namely, Evita's 'descamisados', the working classes, which the upper sectors can no longer avoid. Juan sums this up as el cronista asks him: '¿A vos te parece que aquí hay pánico? – No – dijo Juan, mirando los grupos [...] Son los romanos viendo entrar a los bárbaros' (*EE*, 134).[72] Although no 'barbarian' actually enters at this point, it is implied that the possibility exists, and that thanks to the changes imposed by Peronism to the *porteño* cultural scene, fear and trepidation now possess the habitual, upper-class opera-goers.

There is a particular moment in this section which epitomises the relationship between the protagonists and the invading Peronist masses, and which brings the political dimension of the book strongly to the fore. This is the violent incident that takes place between Funes and 'el tipo del peine' (*EE*, 144). This episode is crucial for the overall meaning of the novel: Cortázar even alludes to it as a synecdoche for the entire text.[73] The theatre toilet is crowded with men who are, 'aliviándose, fumando y riéndose', while others, 'esperaban turno para usar el peinecito de nylon sujeto con una cadena cromada a la repisa del lavabo' (*EE*, 141). Funes is in the queue patiently waiting to comb his hair. While queuing, he comments to a gentleman 'de pelo crespo [...] y acento alemán' (*EE*, 141) that things in the Colón are not as they used to be; and it is not because of the youth, as the German suggests, but rather, according to Funes, it comes down to the 'mala educación' (*EE*, 142).[74] Right after that comment, and just when it is Funes's turn to use the comb, another man cunningly pulls the chain attached to the comb, and swiftly snatches it from Funes's hand. This starts off a circus-like fight in which all the men

---

[72] The characters' comments at the foyer are reminiscent of Cavafys's emblematic poem 'Expecting the Barbarians', in which the poetic voice manifests very succinctly a need for barbarians if those in power are to be able to exert their position of authority and superiority. Yet, at the same time, they feel threatened by that very need. See, for instance the verses: 'What are we waiting for, assembled in the public square? / The barbarians are to arrive today [...] Why this sudden unrest and confusion? / (How solemn their faces have become.) / Why are the streets and squares clearing quickly, / and all return to their homes, so deep in thought? / Because night is here but the barbarians have not come': Constantine P. Cavafys, *The Complete Poems*, trans. Rae Dalven, intro. W. H. Auden (London: Hogarth Press, 1948), pp. 18–20 at p. 18. In the later *Libro de Manuel*, Cavafys appears as a reference 'a consultar' (*LM*, 85), so it can definitely be asssumed that Cortázar was aware of the writings of this author.

[73] In a letter to Porrúa Cortázar writes: 'Lo del *El examen* lo podríamos dejar quieto por ahora. Yo no me veo en eso, aunque también me da pena que se pierda la pelea por el peine': 14 August 1961, *Cartas/1 1937–1963*, p. 449.

[74] Funes's concept of bad education could be defined in opposition to the manner in which *Divertimento* presents the 'bien educados', namely, 'Habíamos escuchado jazz, después un tiempo del cuarteto de Britten y en general nos estábamos conduciendo como gentes educadas' (*D*, 63). That is, 'mala educación' equates with lack of culture.

present get involved. There is no physical description of the aggressor, apart from 'el tipo del peine' (*EE*, 144). Some of the men are 'rubios' and some are 'bajitos', and there is one 'morocho pesado' (*EE*, 145), who tries to hold the comb up high in an attempt to prevent the mob from getting to it. The comb finally falls inside a cubicle, bringing an abrupt end to the scuffle. The ridiculous nature of this long scene, which eventually results in the intervention of the police, is all the more accentuated when, while 'neatening' up Funes right after the incident, Juan 'sacó un peine del bolsillo y se lo prestó [a Funes]' (*EE*, 146). The sudden violent outburst from Funes over a comb, when he could very easily have borrowed Juan's or when as a well-off 'caballero porteño' he most probably had his own, seems to imply that there must have been a stronger, yet unspoken, reason for the aggression. A reason that can possibly be linked to the fact that the comb in the refined opera house's toilet now needs to be attached to a chain. That is to say, Funes's extreme reaction against this expression of bad manners could be seen to be a manifestation of his discontent in the face of the changes enforced by Perón. Funes resents the 'deterioration' in the kind of people now attending the Colón. He feels displaced. In the usurpation of the comb itself lies the symbolic appropriation by the lower classes of this cultural niche once only and exclusively occupied by the upper classes. As the sumptuous Teatro Colón adapts to Peronist doctrines, its middle-class protagonists are cornered by their own discomfort. Similar to what the narrator says about the use of music in official *comunicados* when played 'desde los parlantes en serie', the transformation of the Teatro Colón under Peronism is nothing but 'la degradación de algo hermoso' (*EE*, 47).

As part of Perón's attempt to realise the 'national popular' in contrast to the 'oligarchic' project, the 'Ley del 50 por ciento' was passed in 1947. This specified that 50% of the music played on national radio had to be Argentinian.[75] Tango and folklore, such as the *chamamé, chacarera, zamba* and *gato*, were thus brought to the centre of the national music scene. That which is generally referred to as folkloric music in Argentina originates from the so-called 'interior', that is from the provinces and regions beyond Buenos Aires, whilst tango was born in the low *barrios* of the capital city. The link between folklore and the provinces establishes by implication a connection between folkloric music and, as Ricardo Gutiérrez Mouat puts it, the 'Peronist masses that streamed into Buenos Aires from the provinces'.[76] In *El examen*, it is therefore ideologically coherent for el cronista to react violently against folkloric songs, as an indirect reaction to Peronism and the Peronist masses:

---

[75] Santos Martínez, *La nueva Argentina*, I, p. 216.
[76] Ricardo Gutiérrez Mouat, 'The Modern Novel, the Media and Mass Culture in Latin America', in *Latin American Literature and the Mass Media*, ed. Debra Ann Castillo and Edmundo Paz-Soldán (London: Routledge, 2000), pp. 71–102 at p. 97.

Cámbieme un peso en monedas de veinte – dijo el cronista. Si ese negro de ojos sucios se lo ponía a tiro de Würlitzer, seguro que la iba de chamamés. Tres en la lista impresa, la mar de chacareras y gatos. 'Odio el folklore', se afirmó a sí mismo. 'Solamente me gusta el folklore ajeno, es decir, el libre y gratuito para mí, no lo que me impone la sangre'. En general, las imposiciones de la sangre eran vomitantes. (*EE*, 32–3)

In an episode that is comparable to Funes's fight for the comb at the Colón, the imaginary battle that el cronista fights with the 'negro de ojos sucios' over the jukebox is once again a reference to the social clash between the middle-class characters and the Peronist masses. El cronista sees his blood, his 'Argentian-ness' as a metonymy for the imposed nationalism of this new political hegemony, and he is utterly disgusted by it. It is telling that in this crucial scene Cortázar chooses to use el cronista, who with his intriguing namelessness is a faithful stereotype of the middle-class *porteños*: 'tipo tranquilo con su pisito en Alsina al cuatrocientos y sus hábitos porteños: "buen ejemplo del no te metás"' (*EE*, 33). He has, in addition, 'vuelto hace poco de Europa, y trae sabiduría en las palabras' (*EE*, 35).[77] Two important traits of el cronista, and of the average middle-class *porteño*, are thus defined: their indifference to socio-political issues (with the infamous 'no te metás' attitude),[78] and the adulation of all things European ('ella estaba con la Cruz del Sur y yo prefería la Flor de Lis', admits, for instance, el Insecto: *D*, 90). These aspects position the liberal, Europeanised middle-class *porteño*, as in the case of the characters in these early novels, as well as Cortázar himself, squarely in opposition to Perón and the Peronist masses.

The words used by el cronista to describe the other man also eager to use the jukebox are blatantly insulting, yet his attitude emphasises the middle-class ideology of these characters. Furthermore, it underlines their resentment of the imposed national aesthetic and of the 'invasion' of space (physical and cultural) implied by the music and by the presence of the poorer other. The fight for dominance over the jukebox becomes so meaningful for el cronista that he chooses not to move from its side in order to prevent folkloric music from being played; as the narrator illustrates, 'El cronista escuchaba *London Again* [...] el Würlitzer [...] amenazaba con sus zambas y sus machichas, por eso el cronista prefería sentarse al lado aunque le partiera los oídos, y darle al Würlitzer más y más monedas para que solamente *London Again*' (*EE*, 32). Just as Funes refused to give up the comb, el cronista refuses to surrender to the musical prefer-

---

[77] El cronista is indeed a quite faithful representation of Cortázar himself who, at the time of writing *El examen*, was living in a flat in Suipacha 'al 1200', only a few streets away from the imagined residence of el cronista: Eduardo Montes Bradley, *Cortázar sin barba* (Buenos Aires: Sudamericana, 2004), p. 34.
[78] This is analysed in detail, through the figure of Horacio Oliveira, in chapter 2 below.

ence of the 'cabecita negra'. This is due to the character's belief that in that song in English, in that 'foreign folklore', lies his freedom. In turn, Andrés Fava refers more directly to the 'contamination' of national musical culture, as he writes: 'Ya que de música se habló, lo que a ti o a mí nos guste del *folk* – no completo la palabra porque está apestada' (*DAF*, 35).

Not all the characters in *El examen* are as physically antagonistic in the face of this threatening other as Funes and el cronista; however, they all find an instance within the text to somehow express their revulsion. While Andrés, Juan, Clara and Stella are travelling on the tram, Andrés – observing that Juan is reading – says to himself, 'Macanudo, escribí para que después te lean en los tranvías. [...] Total, a estas alturas del *emputecimiento local* un tranvía es la justa sala de lectura' (*EE*, 29; my emphasis).[79] Whereas for Juan, being in a cramped tram allows him a blissful 'pequeño nirvana de un cuarto de hora' (*EE*, 26), Andrés cannot reconcile public transport, and particularly under such conditions ('El tranvía colgaba de sí mismo, mujer que anda a tumbos llena de paquetes', *EE*, 26), with the act of reading. Opening a book in such a space, immersed in a mass of people, is for Andrés a consequence of the local 'emputecimiento' and cultural vulgarisation, in other words, this is a result of the contemptible deterioration of the city and of its culture.

There is another incident in the same journey that provokes a criticism of the masses and, as in the previous example concerning el cronista and the 'negro de ojos sucios', evokes the clash between social classes and political ideologies. When a group of 'barrenderos' gets on the tram and begins trying to clean amongst, and despite, the crowd, a confrontation occurs between them and some of the passengers, including our protagonists. Halperín Donghi's remark on the undeniability of Peronism as a 'revolución social' is relevant here: 'bajo la égida del régimen peronista todas las relaciones entre los grupos sociales se vieron súbitamente redefinidas, y para advertirlo bastaba [...] *subirse a un tranvía*'.[80] When the 'barrenderos' reach Andrés's shoes, he looks at the other passengers as he lifts his feet up. He observes that 'la señora de anteojos ahumados vigilaba *temerosa* el movimiento del mando de la escoba, y se arrimaba más y más contra un asiento' (*EE*, 30; my emphasis). The use of the verb 'vigilar' here reinforces the woman's fear, as she tries to hide behind her dark glasses which also function as a divisive barrier between her and the 'barrenderos'. The woman's terror is further emphasised by the description of the 'barrenderos avanzando', like an invading army, posing a threat to 'los pasajeros [que] se apretujaban cada vez más' (*EE*, 30). While, in the earlier example, el cronista responds against the 'invading other' with a physical attack, in this case, as the passengers on the tram retreat in fear at the proximity of the other, Andrés

---

[79] It is plausible to suppose that Andrés's comment could be alluding to Girondo's *Veinte poemas para leerse en el tranvía*.
[80] Halperín Donghi, *La larga agonía de la Argentina peronista*, p. 26. My emphasis.

and Clara respond to the situation with aloof humour, as they mock the idiomatic mannerisms of the 'barrenderos': 'Niñas, *se bajamo* en la esquina. – *Se bajamo* – dijo Clara' (*EE*, 31; my emphasis). In what appears to be a defiant act, the protagonists adopt for their own amusement the grammatically incorrect expression commonly used by the lower classes. Their mockery of the other's speech invokes a certain degree of fascination, reminiscent of that felt by lawyer Marcelo for the 'cabecitas negras' in the story 'Las puertas del cielo'.[81] It is precisely this repulsion/attraction duality that impels the group of characters to go to the Plaza de Mayo in order to be part of the 'ritual del hueso' and experience for themselves the overwhelming power, the 'hechizo' as José Luis Romero described it, of the Peronist regime over the masses.[82]

The Plaza de Mayo and the 'Ritual del Hueso'

Preoccupation with the deterioration of culture is expressed unambiguously by, and remains central to, these early texts. The feeling of estrangement that the psychology of the Peronist masses inspires in the characters is most clearly revealed through the detailed scene of the bone ritual. This episode has become renowned among critics for 'anticipating' what would be one of the best-attended public events in Argentinian history: Evita Perón's state funeral in August 1952, witnessed by more than two million people.[83] Yet, beyond this curious coincidence 'carente de todo mérito', if we recall Cortázar's introductory note (*EE*, 5), 'el ritual del hueso' is crucial in the novel as part of its expression of the author's anti-Peronist sentiment and therefore the political content of the text, for it explores the behaviour and psychology of the Peronist masses from the protagonists' middle-class, *porteño* standpoint.

Although it is getting late and it is only a few hours until their final exam (*EE*, 49), the protagonists decide to attend this extremely popular event, whose main focus is to see a bare bone being displayed in a crystal box at the centre of the Plaza de Mayo (the reader is not told why the bone attracts the masses; it appears that the characters themselves have no idea). As the group approaches the ritual, the description of the Plaza and of the Casa Rosada foreshadows the aggressive atmosphere of the ritual itself (*EE*, 47). Indeed, the fact that the ritual takes place at the Plaza de Mayo and that the characters

---

[81] Cortázar, 'Las puertas del cielo', *Cuentos completos/1*, pp. 155–64. This was first published in *Bestiario* (Buenos Aires: Sudamericana, 1951).
[82] Romero describes how the masses and even the Army would fall under the 'spell' of Perón. He asserts that 'La voz viril del presidente y la voz gutural de Eva Perón producían sobre las masas sin experiencia política una influencia intensa, ajena por cierto a los conceptos que solían recubrir, y que llegaban a la zona de los instintos [...] esa influencia prestaba al "nuevo orden" un apoyo equivalente en fuerza al que ofrecía la palabra severa [...] con que Perón se dirigía a sus camaradas militares en los actos castrenses y oficiales': *Las ideas políticas en Argentina*, p. 255.
[83] See Félix Luna, *La comunidad organizada* (Buenos Aires: Sudamericana, 1985), p. 56.

sense a violent atmosphere should be underlined. For the Plaza de Mayo is not only the natural gathering place for Argentinians in times of protest and celebration, but, under Perón, it also became part of the urban space appropriated by the leader and the masses. Mónica Deleis describes the historical meaning of the Plaza de Mayo thus:

> La Plaza de Mayo representa el poder político en la Argentina, por lo menos desde la Revolución de 1810. Pero en la Argentina de la segunda mitad del siglo veinte ha sido, además, el símbolo de la política de masas: para el imaginario colectivo 'llenar la Plaza', será la máxima demostración de apoyo popular, y para gobernantes, políticos y sindicalistas, el 'sueño dorado' de sus aspiraciones. Ningún presidente quedará tan asociado a las concentraciones masivas en la Plaza como Perón.[84]

Indeed, the connection between the Plaza de Mayo and Perón is such that the revisionist politician Arturo Jáuretche uses the term 'placeros' to refer directly to the Peronists.[85] If, following Pierre Nora's definition, the Plaza de Mayo had been a 'lieu de mémoire par excellence' in the historical liberal tradition of Argentina (most commonly associated with the Revolución de Mayo of 1810), Perón was able to usurp it and transform it into a Peronist *lieu de mémoire*.[86] To understand the full political implications of the bone ritual in the novel it is therefore important to bear in mind the associations made between the Plaza de Mayo and Peronism in the Argentinian collective imagination.

At the centre of the plaza, the obelisk (known as the 'Pirámide de Mayo') seems to be the only patriotic symbol left standing in the novel's sinking Buenos Aires: 'La tierra estaba blanda desde que habían levantado las anchas veredas para despejar la plaza [...] había que andar con cuidado [...] lo único sólido parecía ser la Pirámide' (*EE*, 49). Its base not only provides a solid structure for the characters to walk upon confidently; the obelisk also holds in place the sanctuary built around the bone (*EE*, 48). The 'Pirámide' is thus structurally as well as symbolically central to the allegorical ritual. Being the first patriotic monument ever built in independent Argentina, and bearing the figure of liberty on top, it is a symbol of the country's past working in two antagonistic dimensions. For the working classes the 'Pirámide' represents freedom from the previous oligarchy, whereas for the intellectual sector, the symbol of freedom at the top of a monument celebrating nationhood is contradictorily attached to

---

[84] Diego L. Arguindeguy, Ricardo De Titto, and Mónica Deleis, *El libro de los presidentes argentinos del siglo XX: la historia de los que dirigieron el país* (Buenos Aires: Aguilar, 2000), p. 199.

[85] Arturo Jáuretche, *El medio pelo en la sociedad argentina* (Buenos Aires: Peña Lillo, 1984), p. 248.

[86] Pierre Nora defines the *lieu de mémoire* as a historically constructed space in which collective memory crystallises: 'Introduction' to *Les Lieux de mémoire*, I : *La République* (Paris, Gallimard, 1984), pp. 3–27 at p. 19.

the oppression implied by the military presence and the excessive power of the state. When Clara cries out, 'Me hundo en la tierra a cada paso, estoy muerta de sed' (*EE*, 53), el cronista sardonically remarks, '¡Muerta de sed al pie de la pirámide! Ecco la imagen misma de la Patria!' (*EE*, 53). In other words, from the point of view of those now 'oppressed' by Perón, Argentina has become indifferent to those who used to rule and now have to be sacrificed for the *pueblo*. Furthermore, the feeling of thirst seems to be a motif in this early Cortázar, for Clara's thirst echoes Susana's in *Divertimento* (*D*, 72), where thirst works as a symbol for hopelessness. A notion which, in turn, matches Cortázar's feelings about Peronist Argentina and concurs with el cronista's perception of the *patria*'s abandonment and indifference.

As the scene advances, the 'Pirámide de Mayo' remains at the centre of the bone ritual. At one point, the narrator describes it as the 'gloriosa inmarcesible jamás atada al jeep de ningún vencedor de la tierra, columna de los libres sitial de los valientes', where 'LOS MONTONEROS ATARON SUS CABALLOS' (*EE*, 55). The ritual could well be foreshadowing events that would take place two years later; yet, with the mention of the 'montoneros' tying up the horses to the pyramid (a reference to the federals Francisco 'Pancho' Ramírez and Estanislao López coming to Buenos Aires with their victorious troops after the battle of Cepeda, in 1820), Cortázar is only proving what he claims in the introductory note. Drawing an analogy between the chaos that invaded the city during 1 February 1820 and the events of 17 October 1945, Cortázar shows that Argentinian history indeed keeps repeating itself. If we look at the description of that same day by the historian Jorge Abelardo Ramos, written in 1959, the similarities between his writings and Cortázar's fictional account are uncanny:

> La noche había caído sobre la ciudad y seguían llegando grupos exaltados a la Plaza de Mayo. Jamás se había visto cosa igual excepto cuando los montoneros de López y Ramírez, de bombacha y cuchillo, ataron sus redomones en la Pirámide de Mayo, aquel día memorable del año 20. [...] ¿De qué abismo surgía esta bestia rugiente, sudorosa, brutal, realista y unánime que hacía temblar a la ciudad? [...] aquella noche inolvidable. [...] Miles de antorchas rodearon de una aureola ardiente, la mole espectral de la Casa de Gobierno.[87]

---

[87] Jorge A. Ramos, *Perón: historia de su triunfo y su derrota* (Buenos Aires: Ediciones Amerindia, 1959), p. 23. Accepting Ramos's description, *El examen*'s image of the Casa Rosada 'con luces en los balcones y en las puertas' also fits with the portrayal of the night of 17 October 1945. Compare also Plotkin's paraphrased description of 17 October 1945: 'In 1945 [...] partly as a protest against the opposition newspapers and partly as a means of obtaining light, the crowds had made improvised torches with these papers. In 1945, people on the balconies surrounding the Plaza de Mayo threw newspapers down to the participants so they could use them for torches': *Mañana es San Perón*, p. 65.

What made the day in 1945 so remarkable, apart from its political implications, is the fact that, according to popular history, the masses came to the Plaza de Mayo completely spontaneously, directly from their workplaces.[88] Andrés alludes to this when he states that 'Ninguna campaña publicitaria puede explicar ciertos furores y ciertos entusiasmos. Me han dicho que los rituales son espontáneos' (*EE*, 48). Given the importance that the events leading to 17 October have in the building of the Peronist mythology, and bearing in mind the Peronist understanding of *pueblo* and 'community' requiring 'organisation', it is perfectly comprehensible that el cronista – like many members of society at the time – should be sceptical about the alleged spontaneity of the masses and of the ritual itself.[89] He says, 'Un ritual no se inventa. [...] O se lo recuerda o se lo descubre' (*EE*, 48).[90] Whether spontaneous or state-organised, by fixing the place of the *pueblo* at the Plaza de Mayo and of himself on the balcony of the Casa Rosada, Perón turned the events of 17 October 1945 into a truly populist 'spectacle'.[91]

In the novel, Clara treats the ritual of the bone as a show, becoming increasingly captivated by it. Patronisingly (and consistent with her attitude when alighting from the tram), she admits, 'Me gustaría que me preguntaran sobre psicología de las multitudes, les contaría esto [el ritual] y asunto acabado' (*EE*, 49). Turning the masses into an object of sociological or anthropological study, and presuming that she understands the psychology of their behaviour, is a way of reducing and subordinating the other (similar to mocking the lower-class vernacular). When Clara finally manages to see into the 'círculo mágico' (*EE*, 49), the reader discovers that at the centre there is a woman in some kind of trance or 'histeria' (*EE*, 50). This woman is dressed in white ('alegoría de la

---

[88] See, for instance, Félix Luna's description of the phenomenon: 'comenzaron a llegar rotundos, desafiantes, caminando o en vehículos que habían tomado alegremente por asalto y cuyos costados repetían hasta el hartazgo el nombre de Perón [...] Venían de las zonas industriales aledañas a Buenos Aires. Nadie los conducía, todos eran capitanes': *El 45: crónica de un año decisivo* (Buenos Aires: Jorge Álvarez, 1969), p. 343.

[89] For many opposition newspapers (including *La Vanguardia* and *Orientación*) the events of 17 October 1945 had been organised by Perón from behind the scenes. According to them, the people who went to la Plaza de Mayo were not workers, but a strange combination of criminals and people of the lowest moral and social strata. For reproductions of the articles see Plotkin, *Mañana es San Perón*, p. 57.

[90] With el cronista's mention of the idea of 'discovering' a ritual, Cortázar could be making a passing allusion to Leopoldo Marechal, a writer he admired, who unlike himself became a fervent Peronist. According to his own account, Marechal became a Peronist after discovering 'la Argentina "invisible" [con] sus millones de caras concretas'. When seeing the masses approaching, Marechal says, 'Me vestí apresuradamente, bajé a la calle y me uní a la multitud que avanzaba rumbo a la Plaza de Mayo [...] Desde aquellas horas, me hice peronista': Alfredo Andrés, *Palabras con Leopoldo Marechal* (Buenos Aires: Carlos Pérez, 1968), p. 70.

[91] Emilio de Ípola, *Ideología y discurso populista* (Mexico City: Folios Ediciones, 1982), pp. 148–9.

patria nunca pisoteada por ningún tirano' [*EE*, 49], remarks the narrator ironically), and her hair is 'muy rubio desmelenado cayéndole hasta los senos' (*EE*, 49), significantly similar to Evita's hairstyle, as worn when outside official activities. The people surrounding the woman begin to chant: 'Ella es Buena [...] Ella es muy Buena [...] Ella viene de Lincoln, de Curuzú Cuatiá y de Presidente Roca' (*EE*, 50), and the narrator notes that 'todo el mundo peleaba por ver a la mujer que era buena, que venía de Chapadmalal' (*EE*, 51). The places that the crowd mentions are small provincial towns in Argentina, comparable, in size and idiosyncrasy, to Los Toldos, where Evita Perón supposedly came from.[92] It is interesting to note that Clara is truly horrified and scared not by the idea of a final exam, but by the realisation that she has joined the mass in their repetition of the idolatrising phrases; in her terror, there is also a sense of shame: 'Le entró miedo, y además el asco de darse cuenta que cómo había podido, cómo había podido y ya no hay marcha atrás [...] las cosas son IRREVERSIBLES' (*EE*, 50). Clara's reaction to her involvement with the 'hombres achinados' (*EE*, 50) becomes very fatalistic, as the character draws a direct analogy with ritual of the mass and Catholicism: having 'tragado la hostia, consentido' (*EE*, 51), Clara thinks to herself, 'Armagedón [...] Oh pálida llanura, oh acabamiento' (*EE*, 51). Involuntarily, Clara has followed Perón's 'new order', which brings together the masses and religion in their blind adoration of their patriotic leader. In a more indirect fashion, Juan later on also makes reference to this, when he says:

> Te criás en la estructura cristiana, reducida a no más que a un cascarón de tortuga donde te vas estirando y ubicando hasta llenarlo. Pero si sos conejo y no una tortuga, es evidente que estarás incómodo. Las tortugas, como el gran Dios Pan, han muerto, y la sociedad es una ciega nodriza que insiste en meter conejos en el corsé de las tortugas. (*EE*, 157)

Juan's mention of the Christian structure and the 'Dios Pan' (with the added oppressive simile of a 'ciega nodriza' enforcing an ideology on to those who simply think differently) establishes Peronism as a ritual-based political religion.[93]

By 1950 the regime held a definite monopoly over the public symbolic space. As Plotkin argues, Peronist doctrines themselves, along with the figures of Perón and Evita, became objects of public worship, concluding that, 'by

---

[92] The place of Eva Perón's birth is still disputed in the intricacies of Argentinian myth. Some historians maintain that she was born in the *campo* 'La Unión', 60 km south of the city of Junín, and twenty kilometres away from the town of Los Toldos. Others assert that she was born in Junín: Otelo Borroni and Roberto Vacca, *La vida de Eva Perón: testimonios para su historia,* I (Buenos Aires: Galerna, 1970), pp. 20–31.

[93] This paragraph also echoes the reference to university students accepting 'el pan del espíritu' at p.20 above.

1953, Peronism had become a true political religion'.[94] For Clara, no good can come of this blind submission to the 'good woman'; the fertile plains or green Pampas, a common metonymy for Argentina, have become colourless ('pálida llanura'), sterile and unpromising.[95] The Peronist masses have taken over the Plaza de Mayo, while allegorically Peronism spreads nationally like a 'virus tóxico', as the newspaper *Noticias Gráficas* described the party in 1956, uncensored, once Perón had been toppled.[96]

During the ritual, the characters express their estrangement in the face of Peronist reality through their class difference, which not only comes down to speech and manners, but also unsurprisingly to skin colour and facial features. El cronista ponders, '¿Cómo puede concebirse la unión de estas *negras cotudas* velando el santuario con esa jalea de manzanas von Supée...? ¿Qué hacemos aquí nosotros?' (*EE*, 53; my emphasis). In what Patrick O'Connor identifies as the 'second ritual' (the first being that of the entranced woman, the third the actual visiting of the bone), the cry of a boy leads the characters to what seems to be a ritual of child-sacrifice, carried out by 'un paisano de ojos rasgados y jeta brutal [que] estaba plantado a un metro del chico, con una aguja de colchonero, apuntándole a la cara' (*EE*, 52). The brutality of the 'paisanos' performing this act is contrasted immediately by Juan and el cronista having a conversation purely concerned with aesthetic style. Although, after witnessing the scene with the young boy, Andrés 'está blanco como una hoja' (*EE*, 52), he also joins in pedantically to declare that, 'El estilo ha muerto' (*EE*, 52). This once again shows the characters' attempt to resist the 'invasion' of the barbaric other through their frivolous conversations about all things cultural. It seems that in most cases of social confrontation taking place in the novel (at university, at the Colón, in the tram), the protagonists affirm themselves within their threatened position by clinging to matters that, in their own view, make them somewhat superior. It is interesting that *Rayuela*'s protagonist, Horacio Oliveira, will assume a similar attitude when observing images of torture.

---

[94] Plotkin, *Mañana es San Perón*, p. 45. According to Roberto Bosca, Peronism tried to replace the Catholic Church with its own 'political religion', with its own rituals and even a quasi-saint in Eva Perón: *La iglesia nacional peronista: factor religioso y poder político* (Buenos Aires: Sudamericana, 1997), pp. 78–90.

[95] This is an image that will recur in *Los premios*, especially through the voice of Persio. It is also possibly an allusion to (and in many respects an ideological alliance with) Borges's iconic use of the 'llanura' image, for instance in 'El fin' ('La llanura, bajo el último sol, era casi abstracta, como vista en un sueño' or 'un lugar en la llanura era igual a otro') and again in 'El sur' ('Ya se había hundido el sol, pero un esplendor final exaltaba [...] la silenciosa llanura'): *Obras completas 1923–149*, pp. 519–21 at pp. 519–20, and pp. 525–30 at p. 528, respectively.

[96] See Mariano Plotkin, 'The Changing Perceptions of Peronism', in *Peronism and Argentina*, ed. James P. Brennan (Wilmington: Scholarly Resources Inc., 1998), pp. 29–54 at p. 35. The notion of Peronism as a virus, as the 'muy argentino cianuro' as el Insecto says in *Divertimento* (*D*, 92), refers to an understanding of the Peronist phenomenon as something pathological.

In a 1944 speech Perón declared, 'No dividimos al pueblo en clases para lanzarlas en lucha, unas contra otras; tratamos de organizarlas para que colaboren en el engrandecimiento de la Patria.'[97] It is evident that the protagonists do not want to interact with the lower classes, let alone work with them; they are not interested, in other words, in collaborating in Perón's project. It is not simply a matter of will, but of physical revulsion. Juan – like Clara at the ritual – makes this plain when he claims that, 'No me importan ellos [esa gente de la Plaza de Mayo]. [...] Me importan mis roces con ellos [...] Esto es cosa de la piel y de la sangre. [...] Cada vez que veo un pelo negro lacio, unos ojos alargados, una piel oscura, una tonada provinciana, me da asco' (*EE*, 89–90).[98] Although curiosity about the unknown other seems to drive the characters close to the masses, it is irrational disgust that wins out and effectively repels them from accepting any form of social identification or contact with them. In the crude racism expressed by the characters, there is an inexorable sense of class awareness that is intrinsically linked with their irrevocable anti-Peronism; this, in turn, is a clear reflection of Cortázar's own standpoint at this period.

At one point Andrés is the only one in the group who seems to believe in the possibility of a unified collective (although not necessarily a *pueblo*), as he thinks that, 'en las pasiones, en el barro elemental somos iguales a cualquiera' (*EE*, 90). Yet this is later contradicted by his own intellectual (as opposed to Juan's brutally racial) differentiation, as he can only allow himself to build a rapport with the bookseller, that is, someone equally cultured, saying that, 'la fraternidad de los grupos, los equipos, las camadas [...]. Todo lo que podía decir, todo lo que valía, era la frase de Marlow al hablar de Lord Jim, *He was one of us*' (*EE*, 176–7).

Demarcation by class and race is unyielding. For the Peronist masses, thus, the protagonists are the 'Enemigos enemigos enemigos enemigos' (*EE*, 52), and as one of the orators at the ritual says to them: 'Ahora es el momento de comprender la salida' (*EE*, 56). Having eventually left the scene of the ritual, Juan, who has understood the orator's message, agrees with it as he comments: 'El orador estuvo bien' (*EE*, 58); but he also underlines one significant difference between him and 'them', namely that the orator 'encaja mucho mejor que nosotros [...] [porque] no dijo nada y lo vivaron' (*EE*, 58), whereas, 'Nosotros, los que deberíamos decir algo, aquí estamos como ves, hablándonos bajito por miedo a que nos muelan a palos' (*EE*, 58). Juan, adopting the position of the silenced thinkers, thus feels

---

[97] Perón's speech of 11 August 1944: Romero, *Las ideas políticas en Argentina*, p. 252.

[98] Juan's comment here is reminiscent of el cronista's disgust for the impositions of the 'sangre'. The imposition of national folklore generates in el cronista nothing but rejection. As a middle-class, anti-Peronist *porteño*, what runs through his blood has more to do with Europe than with a native Argentinian. Juan seems to share that, as he implies that his hatred for the 'cabecitas negras' stems from his blood. They are both estranged by that which, and those with whom, they are supposed to identify.

justified in his attitude towards the masses which is based on the intellectual oppression imposed by the system. The same intimidation that forced Cortázar out of the University of Cuyo – and, incidentally, removed Borges from his post as director of the city library to that of municipal poultry inspector – was also the reason why *El examen* failed to be published in 1951.[99] Perhaps this effective censorship is the most convincing confirmation that the manuscript was read as a political text; and, by extension, that its author was indeed politically critical and historically aware during the Peronist years.

Los premios and the journey towards ideological change

According to Graciela Montaldo, while Cortázar was trying to establish himself as a writer, Peronism became 'un elemento incómodo que sólo [servía] para poner de relieve la escasez de incentivos intelectuales en la Argentina a fines de los años cuarenta'.[100] During that decade, while Cortázar was earning a living teaching in the provinces, there were very few legitimate spaces where anti-Peronist intellectuals could find solace, and in this respect the *revistas culturales* played an important role. Among them, the most widely recognised was *Sur*, along with the literary supplements of the newspapers *La Nación* and *La Prensa*. During the turbulent transitional period after Perón's victory in the presidential elections of February 1946, Borges published Cortázar's 'Casa Tomada' in *Los Anales de Buenos Aires*, another important literary journal (December 1946), and had his sister Norah illustrate it. This story, which has now become emblematic of Cortázar's style, was also included in the second edition of *Antología de literatura fantástica* (1965), compiled by Borges in collaboration with Adolfo Bioy Casares and Silvina Ocampo. In this early text Cortázar's ideological and political dissatisfaction can already be perceived.[101] This is not only manifested in the story's allegory of the invasion of a monstrous other, but also through comments showing clear intellectual frustration, such as: 'Desde 1939 no llegaba nada valioso a la Argentina.'[102] Between 1948 and

---

[99] On Borges see further Plotkin, 'Changing Perceptions', p. 30.

[100] Graciela Montaldo, 'Contextos de producción', in Julio Cortázar, *Rayuela*, ed. Julio Ortega and Saúl Yurkievich (Madrid: Ediciones Unesco, 1991), pp. 583–96 at p. 586.

[101] One of the first critics to expose this interpretative trend was Juan José Sebreli who writes that '"Casa tomada" expresa fantásticamente esta angustiosa sensación de invasión que el cabecita negra provoca en la clase media': 'Clase media', in his *Buenos Aires, vida cotidiana y alienación* (Buenos Aires: Siglo XX, 1966), pp. 78–107 at p. 102. On a reading of Peronism in 'Casa tomada' and *Bestiario* see 'El peronismo toma la casa' and 'Tigres en la biblioteca', in Mario Goloboff, *Julio Cortázar: la biografía*, pp. 51–89. See also Carlos Gamerro, 'Julio Cortázar, inventor del peronismo', in *El peronismo clásico (1945–1955): descamisados, gorilas y contreras* Guillermo Korn ed. (Buenos Aires: Paradiso, 2007), pp. 44–57.

[102] Julio Cortázar, 'Casa tomada', *Cuentos completos/1*, pp. 107–12 at p. 107. This story was first published in *Anales de Buenos Aires* and then included in *Bestiario* (1951).

1953 Cortázar contributed eight pieces to *Sur*, in which alongside his discontent with the political situation in Argentina, his ideological differences with that particular journal (and with an entire sector of Argentinian intellectuals) had also begun to become visible.[103]

Cortázar's anti-Peronism would admittedly be the main factor behind his leaving the country for Paris in 1951, never to return to live in Argentina. Within a generalised alienation of the intellectuals from the Peronist regime, Cortázar's self-imposed exile could be said to be intrinsically linked to the deterioration of culture under Perón; or, in Cortázar's words, 'No me vine a París para santificar nada, sino porque me ahogaba dentro de un peronismo que era incapaz de comprender en 1951, cuando un altoparlante en la esquina de mi casa me impedía escuchar los cuartetos de Bela Bartok.'[104] However, the political circumstances that led to Cortázar's departure would later on prove paradoxical given his ideological commitments.[105] Hence, the hint of guilt identifiable in Cortázar's assertions of self-criticism is part of what obliged him to 'recant' his position within his own personal version of history. Furthermore, the fact that Cortázar never returned to live in Argentina would spark several debates, particularly during the 1960s, when Cortázar was criticised for allegedly refusing to renounce his bourgeois Parisian life and commit to the Latin American revolutionary struggle that he so defended.[106] Cortázar defended his life in Paris not as contradictory to his socialism or to the revolutionary struggles

---

[103] See King, 'Towards a Reading of The Argentine Literary Magazine *Sur*', p. 66.

[104] Julio Cortázar, 'Carta a Saúl Sosnowski (a propósito de una entrevista a David Viñas)', in *Obra crítica/3* (Buenos Aires: Suma de Letras, 2004), pp. 75–83 at p. 78. The letter was written on 20 September 1972 and it first appeared in *Hispamérica*, 1/2 (1972), 55–8. It was written as a response to an interview with David Viñas by Mario Szichman that also appeared in *Hispamérica*, in which Viñas cites Cortázar exemplifying the impossibility of political commitment from a self-imposed exile in France.

[105] This is why to an extent in 1972, the year of the quotation, Cortázar was trying somehow to justify ('incapaz de comprender') the anti-Peronism which by the 1970s was somewhat at odds with his socialism.

[106] Towards the late 1960s Cortázar debated with the Peruvian writer José María Arguedas about the necessary geographical position of the writer/intellectual. Arguedas was an 'indigenista' whereas Cortázar defended his 'European' standpoint. See, for example, Mauricio Ostria González, 'Sistemas literarios latinoamericanos: la polémica Arguedas/Cortázar treinta años después', in *Crisis, apocalipsis y utopías* ed. Rodrigo Cánovas and Roberto Hozven (Santiago de Chile: Prensa de la Universidad Católica de Chile, 2004), pp. 423–8. Cortázar also had a lengthy debate in various literary magazines with Liliana Heker regarding exile and the role of the intellectual during the years of the Argentinian dictatorship. The entire debate has been reproduced in *Cuadernos hispanoamericanos*, 517 (July–September 1993), 590–603, under the title 'La cultura argentina: de la dictadura a la democracia'. Information is also drawn from a personal interview with Liliana Heker, Buenos Aires, December 2008. In addition see José Luis de Diego, 'La transición democrática: intelectuales y escritores', in *La Argentina democrática: los años y los libros*, ed. Antonio Camou, María Cristina Tortti and Aníbal Viguera (Buenos Aires: Prometeo, 2009), pp. 49–82. See chapter 4 below for further analysis of this debate, particularly in relation to the politics of *Libro de Manuel*.

of Latin America, but rather as a different position from which to gain a better understanding of his country and continent. Montaldo elucidates the changing significance of Cortázar's self-imposed exile:

> El exilio es, ante todo, un lugar ventajoso que si en 1951 sustrae a Cortázar del asedio en que para él se había convertido el peronismo [...] posteriormente será el lugar que permite una 'mirada desde afuera', y por lo tanto más amplia, de la realidad latinoamericana con la que establece vínculos cada vez más estrechos. Alejarse permite, para Cortázar, ver en perspectiva y no necesariamente supone un 'irse'.[107]

With regard to his aesthetic production, Cortázar retrospectively saw his 'irse' as conveniently constructive, allowing him to relate differently to literature (and to his self-constructed image); as he put it in his now ubiquitously quoted phrase: 'De la Argentina se alejó un escritor para quien la realidad, como la imaginaba Mallarmé, debía culminar en un libro; en París nació un hombre para quien los libros deberán culminar en la realidad.'[108] This phrase summarises a transformation that was by no means immediate; *Los premios* (written during 1958 and published in 1960) is still rooted in the specific – past – reality of Argentina under Perón. So, although Cortázar might have intended it to be a book that 'culminates in reality', the reality with which the novel engages is no longer current, it belongs to a bygone historical period. Despite the fact that retrospectively Cortázar liked to imply that his one-way journey had an immediate effect on his development as a writer – and in turn on the impact that his writings would have on a particular reality – when his work from this early period is analysed it is clear that *Los premios* is still immersed in, and wrestling with, the Peronist reality that Cortázar had left behind. Even though by 1960 Perón was no longer in power, *Los premios* is nevertheless an allegorical political criticism of that regime. As with *El examen*, it is in that anti-Peronist allegory that the novel's most prominent political dimension lies.

The main allegorical element of the novel is found in the figure of the invisible monster and – as with 'Casa tomada' and *El examen* – in the inescapable sense of invasion that its presence provokes in the characters. There is also a more direct criticism through the nine interspersed philosophical soliloquies of

---

[107] Montaldo, 'Contextos de producción', p. 584. This is also reminiscent of Heideggers's comment on Hölderin's poem 'Return to the Homeland', in which he points out that it is necessary to distance oneself in order to embark upon the search for one's origins. To remain in one's homeland, suggests Heidegger, does not necessarily mean that one can be close to it: *Interpretaciones sobre la poesía de Hölderin* (Barcelona: Ariel, 1983), p. 45.

[108] Cortázar to Roberto Fernández Retamar, 10 May 1967, *Cartas/2 1964–1968*, p. 1136. The very spiritual connotations implied in the image of rebirth upon Cortázar's arrival to Paris, will be followed by the 'epiphany' later implied in Cortázar's first trip to revolutionary Cuba.

Persio who, like Andrés Fava before, is the expression of Cortázar's *alter ego*. In the words of Graciela Maturo: 'Apenas actor, solo en la proa, [Persio] es el lúcido testigo de lo que acontece en el barco. Pero también es transparentemente el autor [...] Persio-Cortázar deja fluir su pensar.'[109] Persio acts as the conscience at the core of the novel and his meditations on the 'Pampa del infierno' (*LP*, 263) – certainly comparable to Clara's previously quoted image of the 'pálida llanura' (*EE*, 51) – and the oppressed 'hombres de madera' (*LP*, 372), make him a sort of intermediary agent between the socio-political situation in Argentina and more fundamental philosophical questions (such as the meaning of man's freedom or his role in history) included in his meditations.[110]

Although *Los premios* is rarely referred to when elucidating the political element in Cortázar's writings, through the allegorical journey on board the *Malcolm*, the book represents a crucial phase in the development of Cortázar's political consciousness as expressed in his fiction. Opposing Cortázar's own implication that he was 'outside history' up until he wrote *Libro de Manuel*, this analysis provides further textual evidence to demonstrate that Cortázar was not only interested in political realities before the so-called turning-point brought about by his first trip to Cuba, but what is more this political interest formed a crucial part of his fictional writings from the very beginning of his writing career.

The novel, the monster

In 'Notas sobre la novela contemporánea' (1948) Cortázar elucidates his theoretical concepts of the novel, using certain striking metaphors: 'la novela es uno de esos monstruos que el hombre acepta, alienta, mantiene a su lado; mezcla de heterogeneidades, grifo convertido en animal doméstico'.[111] Cortázar maintains this imagery in another early article, 'Situación de la novela' (1950), where the novel, as distinct from poetry, is presented as 'la cosa impura, el monstruo de muchas patas y muchos ojos'.[112] Here, Cortázar further claims that man needs the novel

---

[109] Maturo, *Julio Cortázar y el hombre nuevo*, p. 87. When Maturo first wrote this in 1968 the novels discussed in the first part of this chapter had not yet been published. Therefore, although Persio remains one of the early manifestations of Cortázar's *alter ego*, he is not, as Maturo writes, the first one. It should be noted, however, that although Andrés Fava is clearly the first novelistic expression of Cortázar's *alter ego* (appearing in *El examen* and *Diario de Andrés Fava*, but subsequently also in *Libro de Manuel*), Persio remains a more defined and certainly more philosophical figure.

[110] For an analysis, for instance, of Persio's essentialism, and his understanding of rhythm at a profoundly ontological and metaphysical level, see Peter Dayan and Carolina Orloff, 'Finding rhythm in Cortázar's *Los premios*', *Paragraph*, 33/2 (2010), 215–29.

[111] This was first published in *Realidad*, 8 (1948) and reprinted in *Obra crítica/2*, ed. Jaime Alazraki (Buenos Aires: Alfaguara, 2004) pp. 191–204 at p. 193.

[112] Julio Cortázar, 'Situación de la novela', first published in 1950 and reprinted in *Obra crítica/2*, pp. 289–327 at p. 307.

'para conocerse y para conocer'.[113] He argues that since the beginning of the twentieth century the novel as genre has moved progressively towards a 'realidad inmediata', so that by 1950 what inspires novelists to write is the 'deseo visible de establecer contacto directo con la problemática actual del hombre en un plano de hechos históricos, de participación y vida inmediata'.[114] For Cortázar, the novel is therefore the literary genre that should allow man to know the world and, in particular, to know history and his own position in it. He affirms that the novel's basic aim should be 'llegar a comprender (en el doble valor del término) la totalidad del hombre persona', and that, in effect, novels are written either 'para escapar de la realidad o para oponerse a ella, mostrándola tal como es o debería ser'.[115]

It is apparent then that if he were following his own theoretical precepts, in writing an extensive novel (compared to his previous unpublished texts), Cortázar was at this point aiming to provide his readers with a universe that would allow them to think about themselves, whilst at the same time establishing a direct, immediate link – albeit perhaps a contestatory one – with a given historical reality. According to Cortázar's dichotomy, if we do not read *Los premios* as an escapist novel, we should analyse it evaluating to what extent it is a text that 'opposes' a given reality. In either case, Cortázar appears to bridge the two ideas when he concludes his essay by analysing the role of the characters; for him, within the context of modern reality, characters have an uneasy proximity to the readers. He asserts that:

> ya no hay *personajes* en la novela moderna; hay sólo cómplices. Cómplices nuestros, que son también testigos y suben a un estrado para declarar cosas que, casi siempre, nos condenan [...] ayud[ándonos] a comprender con más claridad la exacta naturaleza de la situación humana de nuestro tiempo.[116]

It is interesting to perceive the rhetoric of guilt emerging in this quotation. This is tangible in the idea of condemnation through an implied moral sentence, as well as to an extent through a sense of inescapable vigilance, with the characters bearing witness to something the individual should feel at fault with and responsible for. We should note, however, the use of 'casi', and the convenient gap in signification opened by it; this will prove important for understanding Cortázar's rhetoric of guilt post-Cuba, and his uneasy relationship with the role of the politically committed writer. Applying this notion to *Los premios*, the characters or 'accomplices' can be seen to be opposing and denouncing the reality of Argentina under Perón in a manner which is utterly unfruitful in the short term, but which in the future may lead to a more general and insightful understanding of an era.

---

[113] Ibid., p. 300.
[114] Ibid., pp. 315–16.
[115] Ibid., p. 315.
[116] Ibid., pp.. 302–3.

Despite his universalist rhetoric (implied in his 'situación humana de nuestro tiempo'), judging from the texts that Cortázar had written up to this point in time, his proposition regarding the role of characters seems to reflect not so much a general characteristic but rather one that is inflicted by his own circumstance. Cortázar explained this in a lecture he gave at Berkeley in 1980, in which, according to his notes 'en *Los premios* hay lo insólito, si no lo fantástico, pero el eje son los personajes, sus conductas y motivaciones. Sin saberlo realmente estoy descubriendo por primera vez a mi prójimo. Y con eso los problemas de su destino, su razón de ser'.[117] These theoretical concepts regarding the novel and the role of the characters, alongside a specific interest in the socio-political and historical context surrounding its plot and also the destiny of man in general, are brought into play in *Los premios*. Somewhat ignored by the critics, this, the first published novel by Cortázar, shows, in Maturo's words, 'su temprana preocupación por el destino de los suyos, su personal manera de sentir la realidad y su capacidad de organización estética'.[118] And although for some critics, like Mario Goloboff, the novel 'es una alegoría de la época del "desarrollismo", representado por el programa [...] de Arturo Frondizi', through textual analysis, *Los premios* can also be read as a political allegory, specifically linked to the first Peronist years rather than to the 'Revolución Libertadora' or to Frondizi's mandate.[119]

The novel tells the story of a random group of people from Buenos Aires whose common characteristic is that they are all winners of the state-sponsored lottery. This heterogeneous combination of people represents many different sectors of Argentinian society: from the *petit-bourgeois* couple, Lucio and Nora, to the very humble Presutti family. When they are all summoned to the 'London bar', however, instead of being presented with a cheque, they are told that their prize is a cruise on the *Malcolm* (not exactly a luxury liner, but rather a 'carguero', a 'barco mixto': *LP*, 65). The cruise will last 'tres o cuatro meses' (*LP*, 24) but the destination remains a mystery. Once on board, what is also kept

---

[117] Julio Cortázar Papers, Princeton University Library, Manuscripts Division, Series 1C, Box 2, Folder 43. It is important to note Cortázar's use of the present tense as opposed to the simple past ('sin saberlo [...] estoy descubriendo') to describe his personal evolutive process at the time of writing *Los premios*. Although it is evident that he is choosing that tense to talk about that process in a kind of narrative present, it also allows for an ambiguous reading, and even retrospective manipulation, of his own self. In addition, his admission of unconscious discovery excuses him for the uncomfortable politics of these early novels (those published, such as *Los premios*, and also those which were yet to be published).

[118] Maturo, *Julio Cortázar y el hombre nuevo*, p. 87.

[119] Goloboff, personal interview. Goloboff's interpretation is contradicted by direct allusions to Perón that appear in the text (such as 'el generalito en el poder', *LP*, 333) to refer to the government in question. In addition, the time frame seems to make it implausible for *Los premios* to be alluding to Frondizi's 'desarrollismo', since he governed between 1958 and 1962, and Cortázar claimed that he had finished the novel by 1958; in a letter of 30 May 1960, he wrote that *Los premios*, was 'la novelita náutica que escribí hace dos años': *Cartas/1 1937–1963*, p. 425.

undisclosed is why the passengers are not allowed access to the stern of the boat. This is where the novel's monstrous element tacitly resides. As the passengers insist on being told the reasons why they cannot breach the stern, the myth and fear of a monstrous presence increases. This brings about such a crisis that the journey eventually has to be truncated, and after only three days, the *Malcolm* is back in Buenos Aires, after a bizarre and intense journey to nowhere.

It should be underlined that it is the mere idea of there being a monster that affects the passengers, for the monster *per se* never actually shows itself, or acts in any way.[120] Their reactions and interactions are dictated by their fear of the unknown ('el miedo es padre de cosas muy raras', declares the novel's antihero, Medrano: *LP*, 91), but also by the threat that the unknown might take over – like in 'Casa tomada' – their enclosed space. The intrusion of the monstrous, like the gradual sinking of the city in *El examen*, introduces a fantastic element into the text, following Cortázar's notions that: 'lo fantástico es la indicación súbita de que al margen de las leyes aristotélicas y de nuestra mente razonante, existen mecanismos perfectamente válidos [...] que nuestro cerebro lógico no acepta'.[121] As readers, we know that it is illogical for there to be flying mushrooms and for no one to perceive that as abnormal; likewise, we deem it irrational for there to be an invisible monster on a boat, and for that to be ultimately the cause of someone's death (Medrano is killed as he tries to unveil what there is on the stern: *LP*, 396). Central to this fantastic dimension is the idea, in both *El examen* and *Los premios*, of an intangible yet ubiquitous presence that grows and takes over the space, be it physically or psychologically. Cortázar uses the fantastic within these novels in order to highlight, via allegory, specific aspects of the given logical reality from which the fantastic element emerges. In this reading, these aspects, emphasised through the use of allegory, are political, notwithstanding the inherent ambivalence of Cortázar's use of the fantastic. In turn, this is an ambivalence that will become more acute through Cortázar's aesthetic and political evolution.

In describing his own uncertainty regarding the creation of the monstrous element in *Los premios*, Cortázar places himself in the same position as his

---

[120] Taken into account here is Jacques Derrida's explanation of the monster, whereby it is not just a chimerical figure, but 'is always alive. [...] It is a species for which we do not yet have a name, which does not mean that the species is abnormal, namely, the composition or hybridisation of already known species. Simply, it *shows* itself [*elle se montre*] – that is what the word monster means – it shows itself in something that is not yet shown [....] it frightens precisely because no anticipation had prepared one to identify this figure': 'Passages – from Traumatism to Promise', in *Points... Interviews 1974–1994*, ed. Elisabeth Weber, trans. Peggy Kamuf (Stanford, CA: Stanford University Press, 1995), p. 386.

[121] Julio Cortázar in González Bermejo, *Revelaciones de un cronopio*, p. 78. Or, as Cortázar wrote in his lecture notes for Berkeley, 'lo fantástico es algo *que se presenta sin ser llamado*. Para mí ha sido siempre una 'irrupción' [...] ¿Qué es lo que irrumpe? Casi siempre una ruptura de la causalidad o la temporalidad, de las leyes físicas y psíquicas. "Todo iba bien, y justo entonces"': Cortázar Papers, Series 1C, Box 2, Folder 43.

characters: 'Me hallaba en la misma situación que López, Medrano o Raúl [...] tampoco yo sabía lo que había en la popa. Hasta hoy, no lo sé.'[122] Keeping the monstrous – that which is fantastic, but also allegorical – undefined, calls to mind several other instances when Cortázar, looking back on the inspiration for his own writings, chooses to retain the vagueness of central elements, apparently to avoid falling into categorical notions that would in turn restrict the artistic freedom that he deemed paramount. For example, he would deny any political intent in the writing of 'Casa tomada', as he did with regard to *El examen*.[123] Likewise, in the introductory note that he appended to *Los premios*, he clarifies: 'quisiera decirle [a usted, lector] [...] que *no* me movieron intenciones alegóricas y mucho menos éticas' (*LP*, 440; my emphasis). It is therefore to be noted how from very early on Cortázar would find it essential to include explanatory notes to his novels, expressing a seemingly imperative need to define his ideological position in relation to his fictions so as to leave no room for political (mis)understandings. It would appear that at this early stage Cortázar opts to hold the explicitly political at arm's length, in his understanding that if a novel is too political, it may lose aesthetic value. In other words, he is at this point of his evolution attempting to keep the explicitly political and the literary quite separate, even though his writings clearly contradict that. The vexed issue of politics versus aesthetics is thus one that appears from the beginning of Cortázar's writing career and is one that will preoccupy him right up to his final days, with *Libro de Manuel* being probably the most controversial, and in many respects damaging, of his creative outcomes.

In *Los premios* the political element is most prominently present in the form of the plot's central allegory of the invisible monstrous presence, invading the psyche of the characters. It can also be perceived, albeit more implicitly, in the development of a sense of solidarity with 'el prójimo' that some of the characters go through; or in a gradual belief in social unity, that comes as a consequence of the passengers' common fear of the unseen powerful enemy. For Jaime

---

[122] This is quoted in Harss, *Los nuestros*, p. 274, and also appears in Carlos Monsiváis, 'Bienvenidos al universo Cortázar', in *Julio Cortázar*, ed. Pedro Lastra (Madrid: Taurus, 1981), pp. 15–33 at p. 28. It was originally printed in *Revista de la Universidad de México*, 22/9 May 1968, pp. 1–10.

[123] In the case of 'Casa tomada', Cortázar explained to Omar Prego Gadea that the story 'simply' stems from a nightmare; in his words: 'Yo soñé "Casa tomada". La única diferencia entre lo soñado y el cuento es que en la pesadilla yo estaba solo. [...] Yo me defendía como podía, cerrando las puertas y yendo hacia atrás. Hasta que me desperté de puro espanto. [...] Era pleno verano, yo me desperté totalmente empapado por la pesadilla; era ya de mañana, me levanté (tenía la máquina de escribir en el dormitorio) y esa misma mañana escribí el cuento, de un tirón': *La fascinación de las palabras,* pp. 92–3. In his interview with Soler Serrano, confronted by the claim that 'Casa tomada' could be understood as an allegory of the invasiveness of the Peronist hegemony, Cortázar says: 'fue para mí una sorpresa, enterarme de que existía esa versión [...] mi interpretación de ese cuento es [...] el resultado de una pesadilla [...] el espanto total en estado puro. [...] La lectura política del cuento me parece válida, pero no es la mía': 'Grandes personajes a fondo: Julio Cortázar'.

Alazraki, the sense of solidarity palpable in *Los premios* is the basis for the political commitment that Cortázar assumed after the Cuban revolution, so that the 'responsabilidad humana' present in this early novel 'se convierte en responsabilidad política, en que el ahondamiento estético conlleva también un ahondamiento ético de la condición y situación del hombre en el mundo'.[124] Alazraki is right to introduce ethics into the question of politics in Cortázar's writings, for the ethical dimension of Cortázar's understanding of his active involvement in politics and of his 'duties' towards artistic creation is crucial in the evolution of his relationship with fiction and politics.

In *Los premios* the 'responsabilidad humana' is explored on several levels. Firstly, through the bonding of the passengers in the face of their common circumstances and in their reactions against the authority of the cruise. They are confronted by the impossibility of knowing, and thus controlling, the totality of their new temporary environment; consequently, some of them take action in order to find the hidden truth, and in so doing they take responsibility for each other. On a second, more metaphysical, level, there is Persio, who expresses his uncertainties about the human condition in general through autonomous, highly lyrical soliloquies, either in first person or through the omniscient voice of the narrator. Medrano, who emerges as the natural leader, determined to defy the authorities in defence of the rights of his fellow passengers, represents another aspect of collective responsibility.

Contrasting this exploration of solidarity, however, the novel simultaneously deals with the individual discoveries of certain characters in relation to their removal from their usual habits and social functions. Being on board the *Malcolm* is a departure from their known environment and routine, and also a temporary liberation from the oppressive socio-political situation that hinders their individual, critical development. Ironically, this oppression is 'praised' at the beginning of the novel by a policeman who says to the passengers: 'Ustedes saben lo que es el comunismo, vuelta a vuelta el personal se insubordina, pero por suerte estamos en un país donde hay orden y autoridad' (*LP*, 65). This sets the pattern for the division between the characters; that is, on one hand, those who support conservative views of authority (such as Restelli, who claims: 'El timón del Estado es cosa seria [...] y afortunadamente está en buenas manos [...] es necesario que haya una autoridad vigilante y con amplios poderes': *LP*, 115), and on the other, those who oppose it. This, nevertheless, does not simply translate into Peronists and anti-Peronists. It rather shows the complex – chaotic, as Persio claims – political situation that the novel condemns. It is apparent that the authorities and those with a conservative political ideology (like Restelli or Don Galo) strongly oppose communism, yet at the same time those with a more liberal tendency, and middle-class

---

[124] Alazraki, *Hacia Cortázar*, p. 311.

backgrounds, echoing their counterparts from *El examen*, cannot bring themselves to be comfortable with the working-class masses. Slightly more introspective than Juan in his comments in *El examen* after the 'ritual del hueso', Medrano talks about 'their' degree of responsibility for the level of ignorance of the lower classes, saying: 'Uno no puede ofenderse por la ignorancia o la grosería de *esa gente* cuando en el fondo ni usted ni yo hemos hecho nunca nada para ayudar a suprimirla. Preferimos organizarnos de manera de tener un trato mínimo con ellos' (*LP*, 126; my emphasis).

So while in *El examen* there was an irreconcilable division between the protagonists and the Peronist masses, it seems that in *Los premios*, at least for Medrano and his 'followers', there begins to be a possibility of overlooking political ideologies so as to live as equals. Therefore, if the novel as a genre is for Cortázar, at least at this point in his evolution, a way of knowing himself as well as others, and if he was – following his own theories – constructing his characters as witnesses of an era, it can be argued that the rejection of the monstrous presence in the novel, which could be read to represent the 'toxic virus' of authoritarianism in the hands of the Peronist regime, is bringing about an understanding of the other. Or at, the very least, that Cortázar seems to be showing in *Los premios* a willingness to begin to explore this through his fictional writings.

Los premios and history

Both *El examen* and *Los premios* express a political ideology that clearly opposes Peronism and translates into a deep-rooted unease in the face of a takeover by the working-class masses. Paradoxically, however, there is in these texts, although more palpably in *Los premios*, an emerging sense of the social collective and of political responsibilities towards 'el prójimo'. Furthermore, both texts put forward a visible concern for different aspects of Argentinian history, especially in relation to its vulnerability to political manipulation at the hands of Perón. In the case of *El examen* there was, for instance, to the appropriation of historical national symbols by the Peronist regime in order to extend its political hegemony to all spheres of society. In *Los premios* the characters allude to history as something negatively irrevocable or altogether non-existent. See, for example, this dialogue: 'No te rompás, Atilio –dijo Raúl–. La historia ya está escrita. –Ma qué historia– dijo el Pelusa' (*LP*, 428). For these characters, history has either already been predetermined by the political hegemony, as Raúl implies or, for sceptics like Pelusa – comparable to the figure of Abel in *El examen* – it has simply ceased to exist as a credible source of evidence by means of which to understand the present. Like politics, history is, and will remain, one of the main sources of reference in Cortázar's novels.

At the beginning of *Los premios* Medrano, in ironically critical mode, belittles the value of history by placing history and gossip on one same level, thus denying any possibility of credibility or significance being attached to it. He asserts: 'uno de mis defectos es la chismografía, aunque aduciré en mi descargo que sólo me interesan ciertas formas del chisme como por ejemplo, la historia' (*LP*, 33). The writing (and rewriting) of history under Perón was carefully controlled and manipulated. Perón's government also took control of the press and mass media in general, directly affecting the impartiality of the reporting of events, and hence, the day-to-day writing of history. In *Historia de la prensa*, Javier Rosado Álvarez explains for instance that:

> Durante los mandatos de Perón se producen situaciones difíciles para los medios de comunicación, ya que sufrieron la manipulación gubernamental, un terror constante y se produjeron numerosos asesinatos de periodistas, clausura de periódicos y una censura como nunca la había conocido el país, con listas negras de periodistas e intelectuales, prohibición de libros, filmes y revistas.[125]

If *Los premios* is understood as a fictional reflection of 1950s Argentina, it is no surprise that Medrano has lost his respect for history. Persio emphasises this by implying that history has become a mockery, a distorted version of the past, as he puts it: 'el pasado inútilmente desmentido y aderezado se abraza al ahora que lo parodia como los monos a los hombres de madera' (*LP*, 375). Persio, moreover, establishes an explicit connection between history and the authorities by stating that 'La historia del mundo brilla en cualquier botón de bronce del uniforme de cualquiera de los vigilantes que disuelven la aglomeración' (*LP*, 55). The metonymy of universal history shining in the button of a military uniform (and therefore being defined by it) stands in powerful contrast to Persio's use and repetition of 'cualquiera', which, through its inherent imprecision, belittles – as had Medrano – the credibility of history *per se*, and particularly, of the power of authorities. Yet this is only a semantic exercise, for in effect the power of authorities is affirmed in the novel, through the killing of Medrano, their suppression of the passengers' uprising and, indeed, their writing of the official version of events, or in other words, of history (*LP*, 437). Persio then alludes to the already prevalent threat that the military presence implied not just on board the *Malcolm*, but in Argentina as a whole: 'El vórtice que desde el botón amenaza observar al que lo mira, si osa algo más que mirarlo' (*LP*, 56). In sum, what transpires throughout the narrative is a tangible perception that most of the characters no longer take history seriously, since it has been reduced to a distorted portrayal of the national collective past to suit those in power.

To live in a nation under such a constraining political hegemony is to submit ourselves to a state of falsity, thus becoming something that we are not. Remi-

---

[125] Javier Rosado Álvarez, *Historia de la prensa,* dir. Alejando Pizarroso Quintero (Madrid: Centro de Estudios Ramón Aceres, 1994), p. 495.

niscent of Juan's words, of being forced to fit into the 'corsé de las tortugas' when being a rabbit (*EE*, 157), Persio claims:

> De cara a las estrellas, tirados en la llanura impermeable y estúpida, ¿operamos secretamente una renuncia al tiempo histórico, *nos metemos en ropas ajenas* y en discursos vacíos que enguantan las manos del saludo del caudillo? [...] ¿representamos en la tierra el lado espectral del devenir, su larva sardónica agazapada al borde de su ruta, el antitiempo del alma y el cuerpo, la facilidad barata, el no te metás si no es para avivarte? Destino de no querer un destino (*LP*, 334; my emphasis).

Persio's words come as a forceful reiteration of the ideas already expressed by Juan in *El examen*, lamenting the effects that the Peronist regime was having on the writing of history, with 'llanura' once again being the metonymy for a lost Argentina; this time it is not described as unfertile or hellish, but as idiotic and impenetrable. With the mention of 'el no te metás si no es para avivarte', Persio's reflection is also reminiscent of the el cronista's indifference, alluding incisively to a 'very Argentinian' attitude that will be embodied in *Rayuela*'s Horacio Oliveira. Unlike the socialist interpretation that Cortázar would later adopt, in *El examen* Juan feels that the history in which they are living, where they are forced to form part of a common 'barro' or 'río', is 'una historia sin historia o [una] historia [que] pertenece a otros' (*EE*, 41). Following on from Borges's notion of Peronism as 'una época irreal', and from Cortázar's own understanding of an era where, as quoted earlier, 'no tenían cabida mis recuerdos', the idea implied in these early novels is that Perón's Argentina is one which is suffering a process of progressive numbness or paralysis, where history is being re-written for instance through the forceful appropriation of national symbols and the inversion of cultural values. Therefore, whilst certain sectors of society, epitomised by the characters of *El examen*, *Divertimento* and the 'active' group of *Los premios*, wait for this 'virus' to pass, Argentina is 'un limbito, un entretiempo, un blando acaecer entre dos nadas' (*EE*, 103), or as Persio puts it, 'un ciego acaecer sin raíces' (*LP*, 264).

The notions of vulnerability implied in the word 'blando' recur both in *El examen* and in *Los premios*. If in *El examen* the insubstantiality of the sinking ground makes the characters feel helplessly paranoid (*EE*, 197), in *Los premios*, hope is completely lost, with Persio claiming: '[en Argentina] todo era un descenso' (*LP*, 347). Characterizing Peronism as a mere transitory phase ('un entretiempo') undermines the profound effect that the regime has on everyday reality and also on the future. Yet, the characters – and by implication, Cortázar, and anti-Peronist intellectuals – cannot anchor themselves in the past, because it is their own history which, remembering the thoughts expressed by Ernesto Sábato or Ismael Viñas, has caused this to happen, and which also prevents their destiny from being different. As Persio has it, they are destined not to want a destiny at all ('Destino de no querer un destino': *LP*, 334). This is also expressed by el cronista in *El examen* when he says,

> esto que flota en el aire actual, esta conciencia de que somos culpables de algo, de que estamos acusados. [...] No es [el pasado] quien nos acusa, sino nosotros mismos. Sólo que las piezas del proceso vienen del pasado. Lo que hicimos y lo que no hicimos, que es todavía peor. Este desajuste insalvable. (*EE*, 156)

This rhetoric of guilt and sense of historical responsibility is also expressed in *Divertimento*, when el Insecto, having shown nostalgia for the failed activist period at university, claims that 'Esta soledad, esta renuncia a la acción, recibirán sus merecidos (para ese día) epítetos. Cobardía de la generación del 40, etcétera. Tendremos nuestra buena lavada de cabeza en las historias de la literatura a cargo de un ecuánime dialéctico' (*D*, 104). Ironically, these words will be put to the test, when *Rayuela*'s protagonist, Horacio Oliveira, is seen trapped precisely in a dilemma between action and 'renuncia a la acción'.

The passengers as revolutionaries

In his essay 'Power and Strategies', Michel Foucault argues that, 'there are no relations of power without resistances. [...] Resistance to power does not have to come from elsewhere to be real, nor is it inexorably frustrated through being the compatriot of power'.[126] The predominance of one discourse always results from struggles over definition and authority. Foucault sees the defining examples of resistance at work in the transgression and contestation of societal norms, in the frustration of power and in the aesthetics of self-creation.[127] This concept of power and resistance can be applied to *Los premios* in an analysis of the passengers' actions and their implications from a political perspective. For although the passengers are not a solid group of friends sharing daily life in exile as in *Rayuela*, nor, as will be the case of *Libro de Manuel*, an already constituted politically motivated group rebelling against bourgeois society, some of them are, nevertheless, united in their defiance of authority and in their search for knowledge and truth. It is this search which in turn gives hope for an early manifestation of the *hombre nuevo*, as Ernesto Guevara would define it after the success of the Cuban Revolution.[128] In Persio's understanding: 'Qué es entonces de nosotros y de la satisfactoria existencia donde la inquietud no pasaba de una parva metafísi-

---

[126] Michel Foucault, 'Power and Strategies', in *Power/Knowledge*, ed. Colin Gordon (New York: Pantheon, 1980), pp. 134–45 at p. 142.

[127] Jessica Kulynych, 'Performing Politics: Foucault, Habermas and Postmodern Participation', *Polity*, 30/2 (1997), 315–46 at p. 328.

[128] See Ernesto Guevara, *El socialismo y el hombre en Cuba* (Havana: Cuadernos Erre, 1965). This is discussed further at pp. 63–66 below.

ca [...] sino la verdad que muestra la tercera mano, la verdad que espera el nacimiento del hombre para entrar en la alegría' (*LP*, 332). The passengers' resistance to the authorities on the boat – but by extension also in mainland Buenos Aires – combined with their will to self-knowledge (or in Foucault's terms, their endeavour for an aesthetics of existence) translates in the novel into a political shift which brings to the fore the hope for a new man. It also emphasises the more theoretical aims expressed by Cortázar regarding the possibilities of the novel as a genre, namely, to allow man to know himself and his position in history.

The passengers share the will to leave behind what is known to them so as to be able to redefine themselves. Yet, it is crucial to note that what they want to leave behind is actually already a void: 'había tanto que borrar (pero no había nada, lo que había que borrar era esa *nada* insensata)' (*LP*, 20; my emphasis). This nothingness can be linked to the idea of Peronist Argentina as a 'limbito'. That is why, ultimately, it does not even matter that the journey is frustrated or that it only lasts three days, because, 'entre irse por tres meses o por toda la vida, no había demasiada diferencia' (*LP*, 27). What seems to matter is the rupture brought about by departing, and the consequent insight that the characters gain into their own suppressed reality. Not even the discovery of what is (or is not) in the stern is of importance, as Medrano admits when he witnesses the emptiness of the forbidden stern before being killed: 'La popa estaba enteramente vacía pero [...] no tenía la más mínima importancia porque lo que importaba era otra cosa, algo inapresable que buscaba mostrarse y definirse en la sensación que lo exaltaba cada vez más' (*LP*, 396). This is the moment when Medrano realises the importance of the process which has led him to enter the stern and 'see' the non-existent monster for himself. What Medrano cannot put his finger on is the sheer importance of the search for truth. Being able to question, to challenge, to demand explanations, provides him with a sense of freedom, which is fulfilling and invigorating; a freedom that, given the current state of affairs in his Buenos Aires, he has not previously been able to exercise. Discovering this makes Medrano feel invincible, as the narrator adds, 'No sabía por qué, pero estar ahí, con la popa a la vista [...] le daba una seguridad, algo como un punto de partida' (*LP*, 396). Whereas in *El examen* the final exam was seen a something positive because it gave the characters a sense of direction, a concrete objective to aim for in the midst of unfathomable chaos (*EE*, 46), being nevertheless an end point, in *Los premios*, the process of self-discovery on board the *Malcolm* is a starting point, a point of departure. In *El examen,* when that target fails to materialise, the characters need to distance themselves somehow; in *Los premios*, the fact that the cruise goes nowhere is irrelevant because what matters is the characters' individual journey into self-discovery, an exploration that would lead them closer to an understanding of the reality that they had left behind.

In the search to find the truth, the passengers separate into a 'passive' and an 'active' group. The 'active' group, led by Medrano, defines itself through resistance. Their members, as Alfred Mac Adam puts it, develop into revolutionaries through their acts.[129] They become, following Jessica Kulynych's reasoning, citizens who are fully aware of their own position in society: 'Often only the act of resistance provides any meaningful sense of "citizenship". [...] Where the space for action is usurped, where action in the strict sense is no longer possible, resistance becomes the primary vehicle of spontaneity and subjectivity.'[130] However, although the 'rebellious' characters become aware of their power as a collective to confront the authorities, this soon fades away with the death of their leader, Medrano. What could have been a radical change in their exercise of citizenship, ends up being obliterated by the circular return to an unchanged Buenos Aires, where they all go off in their different directions to continue living their lives as before. The character Paula puts it well. Once back in the city, she thinks to herself, 'Raúl sería siempre Raúl. Nadie le compraría su libertad, nadie la haría cambiar mientras no lo decidiera por su cuenta' (*LP*, 416). The sense of political hopelessness depicted here will see a dramatic change in *Libro de Manuel* for although the leader of the group in that novel also dies, there is a unifying hope for the future embodied in baby Manuel.

The *Malcolm* is an alternative space where the possibility of transgression and transformation occurs, yet it is also a location of pessimistic entrapment. References to the cruise ship as a place of incarceration are ubiquitous in the novel, most explicitly expressed by López: 'Hay algo en esa idea de las puertas cerradas que me joroba. Es como si esto no fuera un viaje, realmente' (*LP*, 159). Dominic Moran compares Cortázar's use of images of imprisonment to describe the socio-political field with those of Foucault, and claims that for the former it is ultimately an 'apolitical' question of delivering man from external or self-imposed forces of repression.[131] It can be argued, however, that Cortázar's use of these images is indeed political, since it is imprisonment in the *Malcolm* that pushes the passengers to question their present, and ultimately to follow Medrano in taking action. It is the fact of being trapped and having no choice but to face the other as well as oneself (reminiscent again of Sartre's *Huis Clos*, alluded to in *El examen*) that makes the characters aware of that 'prójimo', and of themselves in relation to their fellow human beings. In addition, the passengers' entrapment allegorically refers to Cortázar's feelings under the Peronist regime, which led him to make the decision to leave the country.

The transformatory process that the characters undergo, and the significance of their journey is summarised in the words of the character López:

---

[129] Mac Adam argues that 'la realidad de los pasajeros/revolucionarios viene a ser la vida del microcosmos.Tratan de romper el misterio, reflejo del misterio del país afuera del microcosmos, luchando contra el enigma':'*Los premios*: una tentativa de clasificación formal', in *Homenaje a Julio Cortázar*, ed. Helmy F. Giacoman (Madrid: Las Américas, 1972), pp. 289–96 at p. 294.

[130] Kulynych, 'Performing politics', p. 336.

[131] Dominic Moran, *Questions of the Liminal in the Fiction of Julio Cortázar* (Oxford: Legenda, 2000), p. 202.

> Todo estaba preparado para hacer de este viaje algo como el intervalo entre la terminación de un libro y el momento en que cortamos las páginas de uno nuevo. Una tierra de nadie en que curamos las heridas. […] Pero me ha salido al revés, la tierra de nadie era el Buenos Aires de los últimos tiempos (*LP*, 317).

There is thus a strong criticism of the socio-political situation of the Buenos Aires of the time. On a more metaphysical level, this 'tierra de nadie', while being reminiscent of *El examen*'s Funes and his disappointment at how things have changed in the capital city, resembles Persio's experience of the 'borde': 'todo es borde y cesará de serlo en cualquier momento, al borde Persio, al borde barco, al borde presente, al borde borde' (*LP*, 238). The emphasis on demarcation establishes, on the one hand, a differentiation between Persio's experiences and those of the others, yet it also most importantly emphasises the notion of being on the brink, on the verge of collapse, of disaster, of an abyss of uncertainty. Similar to Persio's 'borde' and to the 'intervalo' that his journey represents for López, within Cortázar's own personal journey *Los premios* could be seen as the transitional intermission between the isolated, anti-Peronist writer 'trapped' in Argentinian socio-political parameters, and the self-proclaimed 'Latin American' author, aiming to discover a way in which to create freely while fighting in solidarity with 'el prójimo' against the social injustices of an entire continent.

The *hombre nuevo* on the *Malcolm*

Although the term *hombre nuevo* (or 'novus homo' as it was known by the Romans) was coined well before the Cuban revolution, it is the meaning that Ernesto Guevara gave it within the socialist reform that he envisaged for all of Latin America that was particularly significant in the rhetoric of the Latin American intellectual of the New Left in the 1960s. Whereas for Marx the 'new man' is the individual who belongs to the communist society, which will allow the full development of man as a producer, with a universal understanding that will allow him in turn to enjoy material and spiritual needs with his political, aesthetic and moral aptitudes highly developed, for Guevara the conception of the *hombre nuevo* also implies an individual human interest, the development of social conscience and a process of self-education in order to achieve multifaceted, creative growth.[132]

In the novel, Medrano is significantly seen reading Miguel Ángel Asturias's *Los hombres de maíz*.[133] Obviously this choice of reading material is not coincidental. Deemed to be Asturias's masterpiece, it depicts the rebellion of a remote indigenous tribe against the desecration of their land and their annihilation by the

---

[132] See Guevara, *El socialismo*, p. 10.

[133] For a perceptive in-depth study, see René Prieto, *Miguel Ángel Asturias's Archeology of Return* (Cambridge: Cambridge University Press, 1993), especially 'Becoming Ants After the Harvest: *Hombres de maíz*' at pp. 85–160.

army. Through his reading, Medrano begins to understand that by rebelling against imposed authority one can begin to hope for a different reality, for the birth of a new man. Medrano thinks to himself: 'con cosas así se enciende a veces el fuego, de tanta miseria crece el canto; cuando todos los muñecos muerdan el último puñado de ceniza, quizá nazca un hombre' (*LP*, 359). Although it would still be some years before Cortázar spoke and wrote openly about his hope for the *hombre nuevo*, as Ernesto Guevara understood it, there is an awareness – and perhaps even a will to believe in it – already prevalent in this first published novel.

Among the precepts that Guevara postulates as the defining notions of the *hombre nuevo*, there is one which can be particularly related to the development of the characters on board the *Malcolm*, as Guevara explains that the *hombre nuevo* has to undergo a period of transition in relation to his old self, acquiring an awareness of himself as a creator and a transformer of reality. In his words:

> junto al trabajo que está todos los días realizando la tarea de crear nuevas riquezas para distribuir por la sociedad, el hombre que trabaja con esa nueva actitud se está perfeccionando [...] pero aún no es el verdadero hombre nuevo [...]. Todavía le falta lograr la completa recreación espiritual ante su propia obra sin la presión directa del medio social, pero ligado a él por los nuevos hábitos.[134]

To create the *hombre nuevo* implies developing 'new habits' which, in the process of dissociation from the old ones, would make man aware of his new position in society and the general improvements that his change will generate – materially but also spiritually – in himself and his 'prójimo'. Placing this group of people in circumstances that almost force the passengers to look into themselves and acknowledge their neighbours, reflects some of the socio-political ideas that Cortázar had begun to contemplate approximately a decade after leaving behind Peronist Argentina.

The *hombre nuevo* could be thought to be an active being, who experiences politics as a space where freedom is conceived as an incessant ethical practice, which validates itself by means of creating its own conditions for existing. Unlike the classic Greek notion of the politics-ethics relationship, whereby a moral attitude towards freedom was to be expected only from the noble, privileged castes, in the longing for the *hombre nuevo* everyone is worthy and capable of this kind of political (and ethical) activity. Taking this idea a step further, Foucault, in *La hermenéutica del sujeto*, establishes that,

> La necesidad [ética] del cuidado de uno mismo, la necesidad de ocuparse de uno mismo, está ligada al ejercicio del poder [...] ocuparse de sí mismo

---

[134] Guevara, *El socialismo*, p. 24.

es algo que viene exigido y además se deduce de la voluntad de ejercer un poder político sobre los otros. No se puede gobernar a los demás si uno no se gobierna a sí mismo.[135]

Pertinent to the notion of the *hombre nuevo* is Cortázar's choice of epigraph for the novel, a quotation from Dostoyevsky's *The Idiot*:

> ¿Qué hace un autor con la gente vulgar [...]? Es imposible dejarla siempre fuera de la ficción, pues la gente vulgar es en todos los momentos la llave y el punto esencial en la cadena de asuntos humanos; si la suprimimos se pierde toda probabilidad de verdad (*LP*, 7).

There is certainly a contrast between the role and treatment given to the 'gente vulgar' (*LP*, 7) and the disgust and revulsion felt by the protagonists of *El examen* for the 'masa peronista'. Although there is still a prevalent class differentiation among the characters of *Los premios*, they are all 'la llave y el punto esencial' of history and of truth. This realisation is present in Persio's final monologues, when his search for an aesthetic outlook shifts towards Latin American reality, aiming to discover indeed the *hombre nuevo*. Unlike in *El examen*, the fight in *Los premios* is set against the generalised oppression imposed by the 'gobierno actual' (*LP*, 114), or the 'generalito en el poder' as Persio calls Perón (*LP*, 333), rather than against the Peronist masses.

If, as Persio understood it, Medrano was a potential *hombre nuevo*, then his death seems to imply that there is no room for such a figure, at least not in the Argentina of the time. Either because of ideological compliance, fearful submission or individualistic interests, the characters that survive the journey on the *Malcolm* do not want to be responsible for preserving Medrano's legacy. As Lucio expresses it: 'Vos fijáte, tal cómo están las cosas en Buenos Aires, un lío así [el que causó Medrano] nos puede perjudicar a todos' (*LP*, 431). It is too risky, and ultimately, once they are back in Buenos Aires, his legacy is in conflict with their habitual attitude of 'no te metás'.

So, in Guevara's terms, despite their transformation on board the *Malcolm*, the passengers seem unable to leave behind their old bourgeois habits in order to adopt new ones, and, in so doing, become that 'new man'. Yet, Medrano's character alone represents an attempt – and in that sense, a hope – to create a new reality. Andrés Fava's vision of a new future in *Libro de Manuel* appears therefore to be symbolised in Medrano's hope for a new man, for a radical change in habits, for an understanding and pursuit of collective action. Although the political dimension of the novel seems to be mainly concerned with the rav-

---

[135] Michel Foucault, *La hermenéutica del sujeto*, trans. Ulises Guinazú (Buenos Aires: Fondo de Cultura Económica, 2001), p. 338.

ages of Peronism, it also shows a gradual shift in Cortázar's political ideology; a gradual departure from the bourgeois staunch anti-Peronist stance, towards a more humanistic understanding of the collective. This understanding is blatantly different from the portrayal of the collective in *El examen*, where through the ritual at the Plaza de Mayo, the fight over the comb at the Teatro Colón and the reactions towards cleaners on the tram, it is clear that there is as yet no desire for a united collective. There is, recalling Andrés's words with regard to the bookseller, or Juan's disgust at the 'roces con *ellos*', an irrevocable divide between *them* (that is, the Peronist masses) and the Cortazarian, middle-class protagonists.

Steven Boldy argues convincingly that the concept of the *hombre nuevo*, emerging as a consequence of rebellion and destruction, occurs not only in the later Cortázar, but rather can be perceived throughout his entire work.[136] Moreover its first and most prominent manifestation can be seen in *Los premios*. With *Los premios* Cortázar not only, as Alazraki puts it, 'hace su primera zambullida a las aguas de la historia', but also indirectly affirms that history and politics are already central to his fictional writings, and will remain so.[137]

Sailing towards the discovery of a continent

> un escritor es siempre un pequeño Cristóbal Colón
> [...] es alguien que sale a descubrir con sus carabelitas
> de palabras [...] el gran escritor descubre América
> pero no todos son Colón.[138]

'En lo más gratuito que pueda yo escribir', asserted Cortázar, 'asomará siempre una voluntad de contacto con el presente histórico del hombre, una participación en su larga marcha hacia lo mejor de sí mismo como colectividad y humanidad.'[139] Cortázar wrote this when he had already adopted socialism as his political ideology and was attempting to define his role as a committed Latin American writer, without sacrificing his belief in art for art's sake. What appears as a promise stemming from the political 'commitment' subsequent to his first trip to Cuba is nevertheless visibly palpable in his earlier writings of the anti-Peronist years.

A detailed analysis of the allegorical political element in *El examen* and in *Los premios*, as well as more tangential references to *Divertimento* and *Diario*

---

[136] Steven Boldy, *The Novels of Julio Cortázar* (Cambridge: Cambridge University Press, 1980), p. 16.

[137] Alazraki, *Hacia Cortázar*, p. 309.

[138] Julio Cortázar, as quoted in Saúl Sosnowski, 'Julio Cortázar ante la literatura y la historia', in Julio Cortázar, *Obra crítica/3*, pp. 9–31 at p. 30.

[139] Cortázar to Fernández Retamar, 10 May 1967, *Cartas/2 1964–1968*, p. 1141.

de Andrés Fava, demonstrates how, notwithstanding his own later public conviction, Cortázar did have a clear political consciousness from his first steps into the realm of fiction; a consciousness that is certainly expressed in his fictional writings. This confirms the conclusions of Mario Goloboff who claims that:

> Cortázar, en distintas épocas, va jalonando esa conciencia de los intelectuales de las capas medias argentinas y reactualizándose (como ellas) de modo permanente, hasta llegar con la revolución cubana a representarla también en su mirada hacia Cuba, y sus enormes primeros desafíos y sus primeros grandes logros. Y aún después, en la época de las dictaduras en el Cono Sur y de su lucha por las libertades democráticas.[140]

The author's subsequent assessment of his own views and writings during these Peronist years is more concerned with a change in his political stance that took place later, and which made his anti-Peronism irreconcilable and inconsistent with his new socialist, committed self. This is possibly the reason why Cortázar, after Losada's rejection of *El examen* in 1950, and despite having considered it complete, chose not to publish this novel, nor *Diario de Andrés Fava* nor *Divertimento*, during his life-time. In turn, this decision contradicts the significance of the 'libre lenguaje' that Cortázar himself praised in *El examen* (*EE*, 5). Underlining the freedom of its language and ideas, while at the same time being unable to face the political consequences that its publication might have brought upon him, in particular with regard to the depiction of the lower classes, establishes a pattern of ambivalence that characterises Cortázar's political evolution. This ambivalence places Cortázar not only in a conflictive position within his aesthetic project, but also, as the Cuban poet Herberto Padilla would put it, it would lead him to a place of 'political solitude'.[141]

Cortázar's own response to a possible political reading of the work that he produced during the first Peronist mandate is ambivalent. Recalling this period in an interview with Ernesto González Bermejo in 1977, Cortázar goes so far as to claim that what he wrote then was escapist and reactionary; he asserts that 'nuestra condición de jóvenes burgueses que leíamos en varios idiomas, nos impidió entender ese fenómeno [el desborde popular]'.[142] It should be borne in mind that Cortázar's critical opinion of his political position during the Peronist years was retrospectively shaped by an adopted discourse inspired by his 'epiphanic' trip to Cuba. Yet, when revisiting the early writings it seems difficult to deny the political commitment of contemporaneous phrases such as 'Desde

---

[140] Goloboff, personal interview.
[141] Herberto Padilla, 'Imagen de Cortázar', *La Nación*, 28 April 1985, pp. 20–1 at p. 21. For a detailed analysis of Padilla's quotation and its context see chapter 4 below.
[142] González Bermejo, *Revelaciones de un cronopio*, p. 119.

entonces hasta hoy, hemos continuado luchando por el ideal que defendemos', which Cortázar proclaims so fervently in his fight against Perón.[143]

In the case of *Los premios*, although it was published when Cortázar was allegedly 'fuera de la historia', there are explicit, as well as implicit, elements through which his 'voluntad de contacto con el presente histórico del hombre' clearly emerges. The rhetorical discourse of Cortázar's paratext (including his letters and interviews) proves crucial to the attempt to achieve a holistic understanding of the moral imperatives attached to Cortázar's political viewpoints, as well as of his attitude towards aesthetic creation. Although *Los premios* and *El examen* tend to be excluded from the so-called 'political writings' in Cortázar's *oeuvre*, they are fundamentally political in their allegorical representation of the writer's anti-Peronist views.

Furthermore, it would seem that with *Los premios* Cortázar had stopped believing in a Rimbaud-like lifestyle, where he would live 'completamente aislado y solitario [...] leyendo y estudiando [...] millares de libros'.[144] Instead, he had begun to develop an interest in man's relationship with his fellow human beings, which translates in the novel as a realisation of the collective and of the possibility of the revolutionary *hombre nuevo*. Concern to express solidarity with 'el prójimo', or in Cortazarian terms, 'el descubrimiento de mi prójimo, de mis semejantes', marks a noticeable shift in Cortázar's political journey as seen through his fiction.

Los premios is generally considered an important stepping-stone in the narrative evolution of Cortázar, yet almost exclusively in aesthetic terms (in relation to characterisation, the notion of *figuras*, the role of the fantastic). However, as well as showing that the novel encompasses a rejection of Perón's oppressive regime, an attempt has been made here to elucidate that the inner journey of the passengers towards a revolutionary stance of resistance – through an expression of human solidarity and understanding – reflects a marked level of political preoccupation felt by Cortázar, prior to his much-vaunted 'despertar a la historia' brought about by revolutionary Cuba. What in *Los premios* takes place at the hands of the passengers will eventually lead – through the ethical action/inaction dilemmas of *Rayuela*'s Horacio Oliveira – to the activities of 'la Joda' in *Libro de Manuel*, dissolving habits and conventions through the characters' urban revolutionary plans and their *microagitaciones*.

---

[143] Cortázar to Lucienne C. de Duprat, 16 December 1945, *Cartas/1 1937–1963*, p. 190.
[144] For Cortázar's solitary Rimbaud-like lifestyle, see Harss, *Los nuestros*, p. 263.

2

Action versus Inaction

Whereas in the case of *El examen* and *Los premios*, ideological criticism of a specific political hegemony, namely, Peronism, is undertaken through an allegorical representation, in the case of *Rayuela*, the political element is present within a very broad sense of the meaning of politics, as opposed to the specificity of a given political ideology. This political element is primarily located in the ethical dilemmas of the novel's protagonist, Horacio Oliveira. As he reflects upon ethical, ideological and political concerns, and as he sinks into an attitude of passive acquiescence towards life, the reader – who thanks to Cortázar's constant jibes at the *lector hembra* via Morelli's theories and through the novel's structure has already been prodded into a less passive state than the reader of *El examen* or *Los premios* – is simultaneously confronted by the same questions. This is part of a process that could be seen as Cortázar's attempt to contribute towards a change within the ideological consciousness of his readership. Although other political elements manifest themselves explicitly in the text, Oliveira's action versus inaction quandary, with regard to his individual social commitment as well as political involvement in general, is the most prominent political consideration within the novel.

Tobin Siebers's understanding of politics, as elucidated in his study of scepticism, is relevant for this analysis, in particular his argument that 'politics demands that we risk taking a position, that we stand somewhere, that we decide, and that we accept as part of the political process the possibility that our decisions, stances and positions may go horribly wrong, nowhere, or miraculously right'.[1] In his sense, the fact that in *Rayuela* Oliveira seems incapable of taking any kind of ideological, ethical or even emotional position throughout the novel, has in many instances political implications, in the very broad sense of the term, such as how we understand the relationship between an individual and his *polis*, his society. What Cortázar identified early on in his fiction as the very *porteño* attitude of 'no te metás', widespread in the Argentina of Perón (and infamously radicalised during the country's last military dictatorship), is embodied and hyperbolised in Oliveira. Yet, crucially, whereas the reader could accept previous embodiments of this attitude

---

1 Siebers, *Politics of Scepticism*, p. 8.

without feeling personally implicated in conflicts of a political, ideological or ethical nature (for example the behaviour of el cronista in *El examen* or Restelli's praise of authority in *Los premios*), in the case of Oliveira, this seems to be different. For what the reader might 'observe' and 'live' vicariously through the character could generate, at key points, serious ethical discomfort and unease. It is in these moments that a certain political meaning is transmitted. Oliveira's attitude, combined with the inclusion of a number of 'real stories' within the fictional text, provides grounds for reflection upon a story being told that is parallel to the main narrative plot; a story that relates to issues outside the fictional world presented by *Rayuela*, and which requires insightful reflection on the part of the reader.

What Cortázar traditionally manifests in his short stories through an element in the narrative that shocks and dislodges the reader from the comfort of the fictional universe, is also present in *Rayuela* with an added implicit political signification. David Kelman explains this well when he claims that in Cortázar, and specifically after the Cuban revolution,

> the afterlife of storytelling [...] points to the possibility of a new political community that is not predicated on the full presence of the people, but rather on the transmission of a story. Politics can then be said to take place as the event of a transmission, and it is the function of the modern storyteller to tell the stories that are able to produce this kind of event.[2]

Setting aside what takes place during the reading experience, what has to be emphasised, confirming Kelman, is that the political in *Rayuela* relates to something which is not always explicitly spelled out in the narrative, but which rather gains meaning in the implicit 'transmission' of certain ideas. These are not (unlike in *Libro de Manuel*) politically biased, aiming to inculcate a particular political ideology; they are more fundamental notions concerned with a general choice between action and passivity in everyday life. It is worth remembering that *Rayuela* was written in times of radical ideological change throughout the world, and that Cortázar was part of much wider attempts to 'revolutionise' thought, intellectually, aesthetically and politically. As well as the Cuban revolution, and the consequent revolutionary politicisation of Latin America, at the time of the publication of *Rayuela*, there was also the decolonisation process in Africa, the Vietnam war, anti-racist rebellion in the US, all happening in an era when, as Claudia Gilman argues, politics was the yardstick by which every individual was measured.[3]

---

[2] David Kelman, 'The Afterlife of Storytelling: Julio Cortázar's Reading of Walter Benjamin and Edgar Allan Poe', *Comparative Literature*, 60/3 (2008), 244–60 at p. 245.

[3] Claudia Gilman, *Entre la pluma y el fusil: debates y dilemas del escritor revolucionario en América Latina* (Buenos Aires: Siglo XXI, 2003), p. 41.

At the time of writing *Rayuela* Cortázar had not yet openly adhered to a specific political ideology, though it is apparent that he was veering towards the Left. This begins to be articulated in *Los premios* with the characters' solidarity towards 'el prójimo' and the possibility of an *hombre nuevo* embodied in Medrano. This was not yet fully defined, however. While writing *Rayuela* Cortázar was, in many respects, searching for a political ideology: this search is at the core of the novel. As Carlos Fuentes put it, the very opening lines (if read as a *lector hembra*) give away 'la clave de [una] búsqueda inconclusa'.[4] And, as Néstor García Canclini points out, in that initial question lies 'la existencia entera del protagonista: interrogación permanente'.[5] It is this search, this permanent state of questioning which in turn made *Rayuela* one of the most important expressions of Latin American modernity, for in the novel, as Fuentes claimed, 'vemos mejor que nunca nuestras dudas, nuestras deudas, nuestras posibilidades'.[6] It is through that incessant questioning that Oliveira reveals his incapacity, and at times reluctance, to commit himself to any form of action. Cortázar does not aim to impose a reality upon the reader, but through Oliveira's unwillingness to risk a given position, he presents a crucial socio-political dilemma which was central to the political processes of the 1960s, and which remains equally significant for the reader to consider whatever the historical present. In many respects the kind of questioning prevalent in *Rayuela* would gradually acquire a more explicit tone over the course of Cortázar's evolution as a writer, as is clear from the recently published *Papeles inesperados*: 'problemas considerados como capitales en *Rayuela* pasaron a ser para mí algunos de los muchos componentes de la problemática del *hombre nuevo*; la prueba, creo, está en *Libro de Manuel*'.[7] However, in the vast amounts of criticism on *Rayuela*, there is virtually nothing that deals with its political dimension. While, at least superficially, the novel is more concerned with aesthetic experimentation and philosophical questions than with political issues, this does not mean that there is nothing political about it. It does however indicate a general disinclination to identify a political dimension in Cortázar's writings prior to his 'conversion', sustaining implicitly the critical trend that up until his visit to Cuba Cortázar's fiction was apolitical.

To elucidate the reading of the political in *Rayuela*, this chapter is divided into two main sections. The first offers an extensive analysis of the ideological dilemma faced by Oliveira throughout the novel, and how in turn this dilemma

---

[4] Carlos Fuentes, 'Cortázar: la caja de Pandora', in *La novela hispanoamericana*, (Mexico City: Joaquín Mortíz, 1969), pp. 67–77 at p. 70.

[5] García Canclini, *Cortázar, una antropología poética*, p. 45.

[6] Carlos Fuentes, 'Julio Cortázar, 1914–1984', first published in *Jaque*, Montevideo, 30 March 1984, reprinted in *Julio Cortázar a través de la prensa sudamericana*, ed. Perla Rosenstein (Buenos Aires: Instituto de Estudios de Literatura Latinoamericana, 1984), pp. 35–43 at p. 42.

[7] Julio Cortázar, 'Acerca de *Rayuela*', in *Papeles inesperados* (Buenos Aires: Alfaguara, 2009), pp. 173–5 at p. 173.

lays the groundwork for the political elements that emerge; how the political element is implicit in Oliveira's action versus inaction dilemma and what potential political 'afterlife' this might transmit to the reader through the story in *Rayuela*. Recalling Kelman, it is in the event of communication that the politics of a text can be located. The second section considers some of the more explicit, albeit isolated, political elements. These include several examples of the interpolation of 'real stories' into the fictional narrative which, together with the description of photographs of Chinese torture owned by the character Wong, serve to challenge the reader's position of comfort, aesthetically as well as ethically speaking.

The politics of 'No te metás'

In his article 'Apoliticidad o neutralidad política', the Argentinian sociologist Ezequiel Ander-Egg identifies and analyses the politics implied in choosing to remove oneself from anything apparently political. He claims that the alleged 'neutralidad política' that an individual adopts so as not to be stained by the 'dirty business' of politics, results in the formation of amorphous citizens, who become passive witnesses of their own destinies as the political hegemony makes choices on their behalf. These apoliticised individuals, like Siebers's sceptics, are epitomised by an attitude of 'no te metás', which is ironic since, as Ander-Egg argues, '[estas personas] no quieren meterse donde todos ya estamos metidos'.[8] In other words, thinking that we are outside politics just because we are not actively involved in it is a delusion for, according to Ander-Egg, even deciding to stay 'out' is in itself a political choice. Indeed, it is that apathy which, as well as having an impact on our fellow citizens within a given political community, directly benefits the political authorities in power:

> La neutralidad y la apoliticidad suelen tener una fachada que encubre y disfraza la cobardía y la complicidad que permite mantener un orden en el que está institucionalizada la injusticia y la dominación. La apoliticidad es, además, un artilugio de las clases dominantes, para que todos colaboren – no haciendo ni participando en la política – al mantenimiento del orden existente mediante el 'no te metás' y el descompromiso. Los despolitizados son un apoyo político al status quo: la apoliticidad es para la clase dominante una garantía que ayuda a perpetuar lo existente.[9]

Cortázar was always very aware of the attitude of political indifference attached to a particular ideology within Argentinian society. This is reflected in recurrent

---

[8] Ezequiel Ander-Egg, 'Apoliticidad o neutralidad política', in his *Formación para el trabajo social* (Buenos Aires: Humanitas, 1987), pp. 29–67 at p. 33.
[9] Ander-Egg, 'Apoliticidad o neutralidad política', p. 34.

allusions throughout his work. It appears in *El examen*, through the description of el cronista as a good *porteño*, who is '[un] buen ejemplo del no te metás' (*EE*, 33). It also appears implicitly in *Los premios*, through Lucio's disapproving attitude towards Medrano's rebellion against the authorities (*LP*, 431), and also in Persio's assertion (*LP,* 334). Cortázar even refers to this attitude as a metonymy for Argentina as a country, when in his 1950s poem 'La patria' he writes:

> Pero te quiero, país de barro, y otros te quieren, y algo
> saldrá de este sentir. Hoy es distancia, fuga,
> *no te metás*, qué vachaché, dale que va, paciencia.
> La tierra entre los dedos, la basura en los ojos,
> ser argentino es estar triste, ser argentino es estar lejos.[10]

Morevoer, in an interview that he gave to the magazine *Crisis* in 1973, Cortázar defines this attitude of apparent political neutrality when, reflecting upon the politics behind it, in particular with reference to the 1940s and 1950s, he claims: 'No puedo saber cuál es la situación actual en la mentalidad argentina, pero he conocido la de mi generación [...] ese famoso "no te metás" tan nuestro. Esa frasecita con la que alguien nos definió alguna vez, es decir la tendencia a delegar responsabilidades, a no asumirlas a fondo.'[11] Although *Rayuela* neither endorses nor proposes any particular political ideology, it is apparent that in Oliveira's inability to choose between being politically active or passive, there is an implicit portrayal of the 'no te metás' attitude. In addition, it is worth noting that although when he wrote *Rayuela* Cortázar might still have been searching for a political ideology that squared with his views, a work of fiction is never politically innocent, or as Guillermo Saccomanno would have it, when describing politics in the fiction of David Viñas and Jorge Luis Borges, 'no hay escritura desideologizada'.[12]

Perón's ghost

Following the 'Tablero de dirección', in which Cortázar sets out the two different ways in which *Rayuela* can be read, there are two epigraphs: one is a quotation from a Spanish translation of the Bible, dated 1797, and the second

---

[10] Julio Cortázar, 'La patria', in *Razones de la cólera*, a collection of poems written between 1950 and 1955, but printed for the first time in the first edition of *La vuelta al día en ochenta mundos* (Mexico City: Siglo XXI, 1967), pp. 43–9 at p. 44 (not reprinted in subsequent editions). My emphasis.
[11] 'Mi ametralladora es la literatura': interview by Alberto Carbono, *Crisis*, 3 (June 1973), 10–15 at p. 11.
[12] Guillermo Saccomanno,'Viñas de ira', *Página/12*, 9 July 2006 <http://www.pagina12.com.ar/diario/suplementos/radar/9–3106–2006–07–09.html> [accessed 10 September 2008].

is an extensive quotation from César Bruto's *Lo que me gustaría ser a mí si no fuera lo que soy*. César Bruto was the pseudonym adopted by the anti-Peronist writer Carlos Warnes, a key participant in the 1940s magazine *Cascabel*, known at the time for provoking a 'risa antiperonista' in its readers.[13] César Bruto was created especially for this publication, which eventually ceased production due to a shortage of paper, strategically commandeered by Perón. The aim of the work was to imitate the speech and behaviour of the proletariat, to mock the ignorance of the Peronist masses. Bruto's style is inevitably reminiscent of Roberto Arlt's urban anti-heroes. Like Arlt, Bruto also represents a given political ideology, especially through his use of satire. It was through humour that César Bruto marked the social as well as ideological differences between the witty middle-class (that is, his readers) and the 'brutos', or in other words, the Peronist masses.

Although quoting César Bruto is a subtle detail, it is one that certainly reinforces from the outset Cortázar's political stance, at least in relation to the Peronist Argentina that he had left behind. For certain critics, such as Peter Standish, the quotation from Bruto heralds the playfulness and artificiality of the novel, yet it can rather be argued that citing Bruto extensively is a politically-charged nod to the reader, and is also a homage to Warnes and his political humour.[14] It could even be said that the novel's protagonist, Horacio Oliveira, pays homage to Bruto throughout the novel, not only by using his apparently whimsical 'hache fatídica' (*R*, 397), but also through paraphrasing Bruto when describing Paris to Traveler: 'El tiempo [...] era muy variable, pero de cuando en cuando había días buenos. Otra cosa: Como muy bien dijo César Bruto, si a París vas en octubre, no dejes de ver el Louvre' (*R*, 233). In both instances, Warnes's humour is made evident and is to an extent emphasised by Oliveira's ironical tendencies. It is worth noting that when Oliveira travels back to Buenos Aires the figure of Perón becomes more prominent in the narrative, mainly through the protagonist's *doppelgänger*, Traveler. Oliveira, Traveler and Talita were childhood friends and shared political ideologies in their youth, as the narrator describes: 'de una juventud coincidentemente socialista [...] los tres amaban cada uno a su manera la lectura comentada [...] las posibilidades innegables de reírse como locos y sentirse por encima de la humanidad doliente so pretexto de ayudarla a salir de su mierdosa situación contemporánea' (*R*, 277). In the narrator's clarification of the three friends' shared ideals, there is a clear sense of nostalgia for a feeling of joy that is now only too distant (clearly reminiscent of similar instances in *El examen* and *Divertimento*). The narrator and the protagonist seem to overlap in this comment which is tinged

---

[13] This was explained by the cartoonist Carlos Trillo in an interview with Manuel Barrero for *Tebeosfera*, 10 July 2002 <http://www.tebeosfera.com/1/Documento/Entrevista/Trillo/1.htm>> [accessed 3 September 2008]. See also César Bruto, *Brutas biografías de bolsillo* (Buenos Aires: Ediciones Airene, 1972).

[14] Standish, *Understanding Julio Cortázar*, p. 98.

with arrogant sarcasm over the times when he used to believe in political change. Perhaps in view of their common politicised youth, Traveler deems it essential for his recently-arrived friend to be updated on contemporary Argentina. So, soon after Oliveira had disembarked from the boat that brought him from Paris, Traveler 'le contaba del circo, de K.O. Lausse y *hasta* de Juan Domingo Perón' (*R*, 235; my emphasis).[15] Bearing in mind that the preposition 'hasta' is generally used to indicate the addition of something or someone to a list with the supposition that what has been already listed was enough, its inclusion before Perón's name implies that the allusion to him was to be somewhat unexpected. Traveler mentions Perón along with boxing and work at the circus, that is, as an inevitable part of day-to-day life and interests. Whether the General is referred to as a figure of the past, or as a contemporary concern is ambiguous, yet given Lausse's peak of success and the brevity of Traveler's list of news items, it would be logical to presume that Perón might still be in power when Oliveira arrives in Buenos Aires.

Although somewhat reticent once back in Argentina, while in Paris Oliveira does refer to Perón. Significantly, in his allusions to the leader, the temporal ambiguity prevails:

> —Vos dijiste un día que el drama de la Argentina es que está manejada por viejos.
> —Ya cayó el telón sobre ese drama —dijo Oliveira—. Desde Perón es al revés, los que tallan son los jóvenes y es casi peor, qué le vas a hacer. (*R*, 155)

The use of the present tense by Oliveira in the sentence beginning 'Desde Perón', makes it once again difficult to determine whether or not Perón is still in power at the time when Oliveira is speaking. If he is, his mandate must be at least some years old for the change (for the worse, as Oliveira has it) to have taken place. On the other hand, if he isn't, it seems nevertheless that his influence on the youth is still having an effect on the country's general situation.

Sylvia Sarmiento Lizárraga, suggests that the central core of *Rayuela* is,

> la experiencia del personaje central *después* de la caída de Perón en la Argentina. [...] Toda esa confusión, esa oscuridad en la que se debate y que le llena de angustia se podría relacionar con la desilusión sufrida por los que se preocupaban verdaderamente por el destino de la Argentina y vieron la sucesivas traiciones a los intereses del país con la subida de Frondizi al poder.[16]

---

[15] In keeping with a very Cortazarian habit, boxing is made an important matter, in this instance through mentioning Eduardo Lausse, a middleweight boxer from Argentina who reached the peak of his career in the early 1950s, winning 14 fights, all of them by K.O. (hence the nickname): Horacio Pagani, 'El campeón sin corona', *Clarín*, 8 May 2005 <http://www.clarin.com/diario/2005/05/08/deportes/d-08901.htm> [accessed 20 June 2008].

[16] Sarmiento Lizárraga, *Los premios, Rayuela, Libro de Manuel*, p. 85. My emphasis.

It is feasible that the events in the novel are, as Sarmiento Lizárraga suggests, taking place after the 'Revolución Libertadora' had toppled Perón in 1955, but in the text this is left too ambiguous to be determined. Moreover, it is not clear whether Oliveira's torment and disillusion are exclusively linked to Frondizi's government, for although the protagonist is aware of the changes in the socio-political situation of Argentina, his preoccupation seems to go beyond the immediate government. Oliveira alludes to this when, in describing his typically Argentinian relatives to la Maga, he elucidates many of the characteristics that appear to have been central in the identity formation of his ancestors. He mentions traits which, as is seen in his sarcastic and scornful tone, Oliveira seems to deplore:

> mis dos honradísimos tíos son dos argentinos perfectos como se entendía en 1915, época cenital de sus vidas entre agropecuarias y oficinescas. Cuando se habla de esos 'criollos de otros tiempos', se habla de antisemitas, de xenófobos, de burgueses arraigados a una nostalgia de la estanzuela con chinitas cebando mate por diez pesos mensuales, con sentimientos patrios del más puro azul y blanco, gran respeto por todo lo militar y expedición al desierto, con camisas de plancha por docenas aunque no alcance el sueldo para pagarle a fin de mes a ese ser abyecto que toda la familia llama 'el ruso' y a quien se trata a gritos, amenazas, y en el mejor de los casos con frases de perdonavidas. (*R*, 529)

Oliveira was already disillusioned with his homeland before Frondizi, and thus also before Perón. In his 'tíos' Oliveira recognises the embodiment of a given society and, with wry sarcasm (emphasised by the use of the words 'perfecto', 'puro' and the derogative 'estanzuela'), the protagonist brings to the fore what he perceives to be some of the most shameful of his country's traits, namely racism, self-righteousness, hypocrisy and conformism. Oliveira moreover underlines this idea elsewhere in the novel, when he says: '[estaba] convencido de que a la Argentina había que agarrarla por el lado de la vergüenza, buscarle el rubor escondido por un siglo de usurpaciones de todo género' (*R*, 241).

The hopelessness that Oliveira feels for Argentina's past inevitably leads him to have no expectations for its present ('Claro que mi país es un puro refrito, hay que decirlo con todo cariño', *R*, 64), nor for its future ('[En la Argentina] se inventaba un futuro de frigoríficos y caña quemada', *R*, 272). And although the protagonist is inescapably defined by what seem to be irrevocably Argentinian categories ('[Oliveira] Era clase media, era porteño, era colegio nacional, y esas cosas no se arreglan así nomás', *R*, 29), his despondency and dissatisfaction are not exclusively associated with a post-Peronist Argentina. Rather, they are linked with general qualities that have defined the essence of Argentinian-ness, as a consequence of his own position in and outside that context.

Both the inclusion of an epigraph by César Bruto and the scattered allusions to the somewhat intangible yet influential presence of Perón, are important in the determination of the political dimension of *Rayuela*, in particular when it comes to understanding Oliveira's relationship with politics. Written after almost a decade of self-imposed exile largely prompted by Perón's regime, *Rayuela*, like *El examen* and *Los premios*, still shows the marks of fervent anti-Peronism, although to a much lesser extent. Nevertheless, the political dimension of the novel does not rest solely on its anti-Peronist 'residues'; rather, Cortázar's anti-Peronism sets a political framework within which to place the ideological attitudes of the novel's protagonist. If we think that the allegorical presence of Peronism, and in that sense of a political reality, pushed the characters of both *El examen* and *Los premios* to extreme situations (exile, suicide, sacrifice), in *Rayuela* the political framework that Oliveira has left behind, as it were 'del lado de allá', and which he revisits when he travels to Buenos Aires, does not inspire him to take any action, but on the contrary, it seems to have left him, politically and ontologically, in a state of constant suspicion, relentless questioning and paralysing doubt.

Horacio Oliveira's ideological dilemma

It is a commonly held view that Oliveira is experiencing the universality of human misery of 1950s Europe, where within the prevailing post-war existentialism, people are living in fear of a nuclear catastrophe.[17] Through his unfulfilled search, Oliveira embodies the anxieties of this period regarding the objectification and subordination of humanity which, as the character puts it, have become the 'gran costumbre' of Western man. In order to understand Oliveira's general attitude of 'no te metás' towards politics and life in general, and to see how he embodies a critical aspect of the political dimension of *Rayuela*, it is vital to refer to chapter 90, which centres on Oliveira's ruminations about, as he calls it, the 'dialéctica de la acción' (*R*, 420).

While Oliveira is pondering on the 'gran asunto' (*R*, 419), his friend Ronald approaches to invite him to come along to one of his regular political gatherings in support of the Algerian cause. From Oliveira's sceptical point of view, Ronald's active participation in the struggle for Algerian independence is merely 'unas confusas actividades políticas' (*R*, 419). Oliveira refuses to go with Ronald, yet for the rest of the day he cannot resolve the internal conflict that his friend's invitation has provoked in him: 'El mal gusto en la boca le había du-

---

[17] See, for instance, Kathleen Genover, *Claves de una novelística existencial en* Rayuela *de Cortázar* (Madrid: Plaza Mayor, 1975), and Noé Jitrik, 'Notas sobre la "Zona sagrada" y el mundo de los "otros" en *Bestiario* de Julio Cortázar', in *La vuelta a Cortázar en nueve ensayos,* Noé Jitrik et al. (Buenos Aires: Carlos Pérez, 1969), pp. 47–62. Cortázar would have been well aware of the anxiety in the nuclear era, having first-hand experience of working as a translator for the UN Commission for Atomic Energy in post-war Vienna in the late 1950's. See, for example, Cortázar to Jean Bernabé, 27 June 1959, *Cartas/1 1937–1963*, p. 394.

rado todo el día a Oliveira, porque había sido más fácil decirle que no a Ronald que a sí mismo' (R, 419). Through such phrases, repression and denial can be perceived in the protagonist. The omniscient narrator captures Oliveira's tortuous self-justifications for his actions or, rather, for his lack of action: 'Hacía mal en no luchar por la independencia argelina, o contra el antisemitismo, o el racismo. Hacía bien en negarse al fácil estupefaciente de la acción colectiva y quedarse otra vez solo frente al mate amargo, pensando en el gran asunto' (R, 420).[18] These opposing positions with, on the one hand, Ronald's moral, political conscience and, on the other, his own intellectual tendencies, leave Oliveira paralysed in a dilemma; his immediate 'solution' is to decline Ronald's invitation and with it the entirety of his political proposition. Oliveira can appreciate that there might be benefits in fighting for certain causes (hence, the moralistic 'hacía mal en...'), yet he also sees these political struggles as subordinate to his main ontological search, to his quest to unravel the 'gran asunto', which for him appears not to be political in any direct sense. However, that the character should be troubled by a dilemma implies that although Oliveira is cynical about the 'generosidad fácil' (R, 420) of collective political action, nonetheless, there is in him an apparent will to believe in some kind of political ideology, which would require, as Siebers would argue, the (political) risk of taking a stance.

Reflecting upon this, it becomes clear that the choices that the character considers viable are completely removed from any kind of direct political action, be it collective or individual. In Oliveira's own words, these choices would be:

> más allá de los compromisos personales y los dramas de los sentidos, más allá de la tortura ética de saberse ligado a una raza o por lo menos a un pueblo y una lengua. En la más completa libertad aparente, sin tener que rendir cuentas a nadie, abandonar la partida, salir de la encrucijada y meterse por cualquiera de los caminos de la circunstancia, proclamándolo el necesario o el único. La Maga era uno de esos caminos, la literatura era otro [...] la fiaca era otro, y la meditación al soberano cuete era otro. (R, 299)

Oliveira's attitude towards political engagement thus becomes evident in this list of 'options', which defines his ideology and way of living: he seems to

---

[18] The image of staying, alone or at home, in front of the 'mate amargo' when confronted by a dilemma, is one that recurs within the novel itself and also in other texts written by Cortázar. In the story 'El otro cielo' (first published in *Todos los fuegos el fuego* in 1966), for example, the narrator/protagonist, faced with another political quandary, finishes the story by stating: 'Y entre una cosa y otra me quedo en casa tomando mate, escuchando a Irma que espera para diciembre, y me pregunto sin demasiado entusiasmo si cuando lleguen las elecciones votaré por Perón o por Tamborini, si votaré en blanco o sencillamente me quedaré en casa tomando mate y mirando a Irma y a las plantas del patio': *Cuentos completos/1*, p. 606. Rather than using the mate-drinking process as a stimulus to reflection and action, both Oliveira and the narrator/protagonist of 'El otro cielo' seem to choose it as a passive form of escapism.

equate a 'libertad aparente' with what Ander-Egg would call 'apoliticidad cobarde'. It is important to note that the moral obligation of being aware of one's position as part of a given society is something unbearable for Oliveira; so much so that he sees it as a 'tortura ética'. The 'mal gusto en la boca' that he feels after talking to Ronald becomes here an ethical torture linked to a sense of 'patria', of societal belonging. Awareness of being rooted in a given race, of being forced to identify with the restrictions of a given nation arouses in Oliveira a sense of citizenship and thus a sense of responsibility that he unavoidably equates with lack of freedom. Something in him refuses to be associated with the Argentinian collective. Given the broad time frame of the novel, and the anti-Peronist allusions, it would not be erroneous to assume that for Oliveira this collective, recalling the Borgesian image of the 'irrealidad' of Peronist Argentina, forms a society immersed in a sense of 'falsity'. Oliveira openly rejects this society. He wants to break free from it so as not to succumb to the easy categories that it imposes upon its citizens: 'Si algo había elegido desde joven era no defenderse mediante la rápida y ansiosa acumulación de una "cultura", truco por excelencia de la clase media argentina para hurtar el cuerpo a la realidad nacional y a cualquier otra, y creerse a salvo del vacío que la rodeaba' (R, 28).

Whether or not confined within a sense of nationhood, Oliveira insists that being part of a political struggle, facing up to the responsibilities inherent in belonging to a collective, is merely bravado arising from certain social expectations. He prefers to be completely alone, and hence 'apparently' free, rather than submit to a life of social and political commitment. But his guilty conscience will not leave him alone, since the mere fact of being aware that he is at a crossroads effectively annuls the possibility of total disengagement (hence, his freedom can only ever be 'aparente'). Oliveira considers love, literature, futile meditation and even laziness as possible ways out; yet these are not solutions but mere temporary escapes or, as Ander-Egg would have it, they are simple disguises to cover the complicity that allows the political hegemony of dominance and injustice to prevail. In any case, what would be the point of living if we escape from these very decisions that ultimately define us as human beings, and, as Aristotle would argue, as political animals? Oliveira wonders:

> Parado delante de una pizzería de Corrientes al mil trescientos, Oliveira se hacía las grandes preguntas: 'Entonces, ¿hay que quedarse como el cubo de la rueda en mitad de la encrucijada? ¿De qué sirve saber o creer saber que cada camino es falso si no lo caminamos con un propósito que ya no sea el camino mismo? (R, 299)

The paradoxical double negative reflects, and even mocks, Oliveira's lingering confusion. Despite his seemingly dogmatic views on the hypocrisy or ineffectuality of collective political action, and his dogged refusal to be part of it,

Oliveira has not resolved his dilemma with regard to political involvement. His capacity to do so is in doubt, for the quandary paralyses him not only physically (as he stands still at the corner), but also intellectually. The character is trapped by his incapacity to resolve his own ideological dilemmas.

By way of an answer, Oliveira distracts himself and refers to the power of authority as a forceful barrier to his intellectual process (another lame excuse): 'No somos Buda, che, aquí no hay árboles donde sentarse en la postura del loto. Viene un cana y te hace la boleta' (*R*, 299). Oliveira's implication of not being able to reflect upon these matters is linked to the presence of an authoritative threat, which in itself could be understood as a political criticism, comparable to *El examen*'s 'no hay cómo tener ideas en este país' (*EE*, 27). Nevertheless, although Oliveira may wish so in bad faith, he is not censored by authority, but rather, by his own path of reiterative banal introspection, leading to detachment:

> cuantas veces había cumplido el mismo ciclo en montones de esquinas y cafés de tantas ciudades, cuantas veces había llegado a conclusiones parecidas, se había sentido mejor, había creído poder empezar a vivir de otra manera, por ejemplo una tarde en que se había metido a escuchar un concierto insensato, y después. […] Después había llovido tanto, para qué darle vueltas al asunto. […] ¿Seguiría tocando el piano Berthe Trépat? (*R*, 300)

The conclusions that the narrator refers to do not solve anything; for Oliveira, there are no conclusions, only temporary interruptions in a cycle that will sooner or later recommence. Instead of trying to opt for action or inaction, Oliveira puts an end to his questions – and to the corresponding chapter – by wondering tangentially about Berthe Trépat.

Ironically, the Berthe Trépat scene itself had also occurred as a consequence of the protagonist's walking away from another 'corner of paralysis'. The beginning of chapter 23 reads: 'Parado en una esquina […] Oliveira se había puesto a mirar lo que ocurría en torno y que cómo cualquier esquina de cualquier ciudad era la ilustración perfecta de lo que estaba pensando y casi le evitaba el trabajo' (*R*, 112). In addition to the reiteration of the image of Oliveira trying to answer big questions while standing on a street corner, what also comes through in this quotation is the idea of observation as a means of avoiding constructive introspection. In other words, what is being underlined is the state of 'fiaca' as an actual ideological choice. Choosing between action or inaction, ethical responsibility or 'lazy' freedom is, for Oliveira, ultimately a chore, a 'trabajo' which he wishes someone else would do for him.[19] Oliveira's dilemma crystal-

---

[19] This will prove interesting in relation to Cortázar's own crossroads, his 'bifurcación', which was linked to his internal conflict concerning political commitment versus artistic freedom. In several instances Cortázar will resort rhetorically to a third-person tacit agent (such as 'me están llevando [a hacer algo]') to justify his actions (or indeed, his inactions).

lises the different ideological representations of the group of people on board the *Malcolm* (in *Los premios*), and its fundamental division into an active group, which believed in the potential for political change through collective action, versus a passive group, which preferred not to defy authority in order not to jeopardise their own individual positions in society. We could also compare Oliveira's dilemma with the opposition between Medrano and Persio in *Los premios*: Medrano, the politically committed, active citizen who sacrifices himself for the benefit of the collective, and Persio, the intellectual, passive figure for whom it is as important to think of the aesthetic meaning of a guitar painted by Picasso as it is to think of man's socio-political and historical destiny. These two characters represent opposing positions with regard to political commitment, and in this step in Cortázar's political evolution *Rayuela*'s protagonist embodies them both.

Oliveira's refusal to become part of a 'numbing' social struggle effectively boils down to very individualistic, capricious and, to an extent, cowardly attitudes. Yet, they are nevertheless based (at least partly) on empirical knowledge. In the novel, the protagonist's scepticism appears to be a reaction against 'algunos comunistas de Buenos Aires y de París, capaces de las peores vilezas pero rescatados en su propia opinión por "la lucha", por tener que levantarse a mitad de la cena para correr a una reunión o completar una tarea' (*R*, 421). Emphasising his criticism of political commitment as a selfish act, one that is carried out only as a way of justifying oneself to the other, Oliveira considers that a commitment to action is only a negation of the self or a hypocritical assault on a sacrificed other. Cynically, expressing the thoughts of the protagonist, the narrator remarks:

> Felices los que vivían y dormían en la historia [...] felices los que amaban al prójimo como a sí mismos. En todos los casos, Oliveira rechazaba esa salida del yo, esa invasión magnánima del redil ajeno, bumerang [sic] ontológico destinado a enriquecer en última instancia al que lo soltaba a darle más humanidad, más santidad. Siempre se es santo a costa de otro, etc. No tenía nada que objetar a esa acción en sí, pero la apartaba desconfiado de su conducta personal. (*R*, 420)

In attributing inherently individualistic and selfish motives to collective action – presumably based on his direct experience with the communists – Oliveira paradoxically also sees in that form of action a negation of the individual self, a negation that he refuses to accept. Unlike Medrano, Oliveira sees it as pointless to give up his own ontological search for the benefit of his fellow men. From the narrator's tone, moreover, we may perceive that Oliveira also rejects the self-congratulatory nature of those who follow the 'dogma' of political commitment, and surrender to it quasi-religiously (the phrase 'los que amaban al prójimo como a sí mismo' is unambiguously reminiscent of the Commandment 'Thou shalt love thy neighbour as thyself' or in Spanish, 'Amarás a tu prójimo como a ti mismo'). Given Cortázar's understanding of himself as someone who was living 'fuera de la historia' prior to his first trip to Cuba, it is very significant that the narrator here should mention so precisely, and with such scorn, those who happily live within – rather than outside – history, alluding to those who are actively involved in any form of process of political change. When reading Cortázar's later assertions it seems that the author became, ironically, the very embodiment of those individuals whom Oliveira mistrusts: 'escribí *Rayuela* para mí [...] muy poco después, ese mismo individuo emergió de un mundo obstinadamente metafísico y estético, y sin renegar de él entró en una ruta de participación histórica, de apoyo a otras fuerzas que buscaban y buscan la liberación de América Latina'.[20] This attempt to reconcile the aesthetic world with an active participation in historical processes was to become Cortázar's central challenge in his evolution, one leading to ambivalence and contradictions within his aesthetic project, which would culminate in his final novel, *Libro de Manuel*.

After travelling to Cuba, and converting to socialism, Cortázar thus presents his own ideological quandary as easily left behind, yet this is a simplification when it comes to his position regarding artistic creation. For Oliveira, however, the dilemma remains openly unresolved. He will not engage in any form of political struggle, yet he is still pulled toward some kind of collective solidarity. With hindsight, for Cortázar it was this kind of sporadic reflection that contained the most explicit political meaning of the novel. He declares so to González Bermejo:

> Sin todo lo que traduce *Rayuela* yo no habría podido dar este paso que me llevó bruscamente a descubrir, a través de la Revolución Cubana, una América Latina [...] ¿No dicen ya Oliveira y Morelli en *Rayuela*: 'mi salvación [...] tiene que ser también la salvación de todos, hasta el último de los hombres?'[21]

For Carlos Monsiváis this is a key statement in the political interpretation of *Rayuela*, for it leads to the radical questioning of Western culture and society: '¿A qué salvación se refiere [la frase en *Rayuela* "Yo siento que mi salvación..."]? Si atiendo al contexto de *Rayuela*, a la salvación que viene del rechazo de la Gran Costumbre, de la solidaridad, de la cultura sin la K decapitadora, de la fantasía que es continuo reemplazo de personalidades.'[22] Yet, although concerned

---

[20] Julio Cortázar, 'Acerca de *Rayuela*', written in 1973: *Papeles inesperados*, pp. 173–5 at p. 173.
[21] González Bermejo, *Revelaciones de un cronopio*, p. 78; Cortázar, *Rayuela*, p. 447.
[22] Carlos Monsiváis,'"¿Encontraría a la Maga en la manifestación?" Julio Cortázar y la política', *Revista de la Universidad de México* (2004), 16–19 at p. 17.

for the collective, this assertion remains within the protagonist's fundamental unresolved dilemma. Beyond Cortázar's somewhat selective view of his own character, it is Oliveira's reluctance to commit himself, either to action or to inaction, that is key to the political dimension of the novel. For in that reluctance, recalling Siebers, there is a will to exist and remain outside politics.

Nevertheless, despite his ideological immobility, his 'ataraxia moderada' as the narrator calls it (*R*, 30), and his 'no te metás' attitude, Oliveira is not by any means an apolitical being. The unresolved action/inaction dilemma, and the intellectual as well as emotional paralysis that this provokes in him, allows Oliveira – indeed, it almost obliges him – to stand back and observe both sides of the question (as in the example of him standing in the corner, 'mira[ndo] lo que ocurría en torno': *R*, 112). And although he is politically passive, it is through that detachment that Oliveira feels that he can truly observe the world (and believe in bad faith that he is not part of it). This correlates to what Cortázar was feeling at the time in relation to his own position in the world, and in particular, when it came to justifying his 'being' Argentinian and feeling in touch with Argentinian and Latin American political issues while living in Paris. For Cortázar it was the 'alejarse' (but not the 'irse') that allowed him to see with more insight the realities that he had left behind. In turn, as the readers discover the attitudes that resulted from Oliveira's observations, it seems that the character's action/inaction dilemma 'transmits' something implicitly beyond the text, perhaps a will to rebel against that acquiescence. This is in tune with what was taking place at the time when the novel came out, as Montaldo puts it: 'Las marcas que caracterizan al momento que Cortázar publica *Rayuela* se definen por esa suerte de voluntad conjunta de modificar los presupuestos ideológicos y las prácticas de la vida social y estética a través de la necesidad de "estar al día" en la cultura [...] acercarse a la política a través de variadas formas.'[23] So although *Rayuela* does not explicitly contain a political message, it does convey a spirit of rupture, which extends beyond its unconventional aesthetics. Presenting us with a protagonist who chooses to remain disengaged from his socio-political context can in itself be read as a provocation within the ideological 'subversion' that *Rayuela* came to represent.[24]

---

[23] Graciela Montaldo, 'Destinos y recepción', in Cortázar, *Rayuela*, ed. Ortega and Yurkievich, pp. 597–612 at p. 601.

[24] Montaldo writes: '¿En qué punto se contactan las superficies de las expectativas del público y la producción textual? Creemos que en varias cuestiones específicas pero ante todo en la propuesta "subversiva" que hace la novela, en la apuesta a una ruptura con lo tradicional desde el punto de vista ideológico y con lo convencional desde el punto de vista literario': ibid., p. 598. Also, on the back cover of the first edition of *Rayuela*, Francisco Porrúa described the novel as 'la construcción de una contranovela en lo literario y de una denuncia en cuanto a lo ideológico [ ] exasperada denuncia de la inautenticidad de la vida humana y de la literatura estética y psicológica [ ] *Rayuela* es un texto que vuelve obligadamente cómplice al lector [ ] que busca una apertura': as quoted in Montaldo, ibid., p. 603.

The politics of observing

Despite the fact that Oliveira feels he cannot trust the political discourse of the Left, he is not blind to social inequalities. This is not only implied in his reflection about the salvation of all men, but also becomes apparent in a few specific scenes in the novel. Famously, the scene between Oliveira and the *clocharde* is supposed to show the protagonist's complex interest and sadistic attraction for the marginalised in society.[25] At another point in the narrative, in a bar prior to attending Berthe Trépat's concert, Oliveira observes and meditates on class divisions: on one side workmen and, significantly, on the other side students writing and pseudo-philosophising about the workmen. Observing this, the protagonist remarks, 'De una caja de cristal a otra, mirarse, aislarse, mirarse: eso era todo' (*R*, 112). The conclusion at which Oliveira arrives seems to suggest a social criticism, since in the phrase 'eso era todo' there is an implication that the character thinks that it is not enough simply to observe the other and detach oneself without attempting to bridge the gap that divides and differentiates the crystal boxes, the social classes. Yet, that is exactly what Oliveira does, except that he does not engage in the pretence of theorizing about it like the students. Although he may seem too self-involved to engage in political debates or in active struggles, Oliveira is committed (albeit briefly) not to inaction, but rather to the rejection of action. His reasoning behind that rejection is that 'La renuncia a la acción era la protesta misma y no su máscara' (*R*, 29). In other words, he refuses to act in order to show his dissatisfaction with 'la parvedad del presente' (*R*, 29); because, as Oliveira has it, 'Creer que la acción podía colmar [...] era una ilusión moralista' (*R*, 29). Considering political action a moralistic illusion links to Oliveira's understanding of it being self-congratulatory, ultimately only beneficial to the satisfaction of the individual ego and conscience. However, as we read on, we understand that the character's rejection is also associated with a fundamental fear of unfulfilment, as Oliveira himself puts it:

> todo hacer significaba salir de para llegar a, o entrar en esa casa en vez de no entrar, o entrar en la de al lado, es decir que en todo acto había la admisión de una carencia, de algo no hecho todavía y que era posible hacer, la protesta tácita frente a la continua evidencia de la falta, de la merma. [...] Valía más renunciar que actuar. (*R*, 28)

It is through this kind of reflection that the implicit political dimension of the novel becomes more palpable, in the sense that such dogmatically uttered as-

---

[25] See, for instance, the analysis by Margery Arent Safir, 'Erótica y liberación', in Cortázar, *Rayuela*, ed. Ortega and Yurkievich, pp. 827–38.

sertions – especially the final phrase – 'Valía más renunciar que actuar' – call for the 'active' reader to react. This reaction does not imply political action, but a sincere questioning, on the part of the reader, of Oliveira's ideological values, of his exasperatingly passive attitude.

Logically, it does not seem feasible to expect Oliveira to believe in any kind of political struggle when, by his own confession, he is a complete nihilist: 'Abrazado a la Maga, esa concreción de nebulosa, pienso que tanto sentido tiene hacer un muñequito con miga de pan como escribir la novela que nunca escribiré o defender con la vida las ideas que redimen a los pueblos' (R, 27). If, up to this point, love, literature, pointless reflection and idleness were equally Oliveira's possible paths away from the action/inaction dilemma, now, while clinging to love, Oliveira brings together literature and political commitment only to equate them with a figure made out of breadcrumbs. The simile suggests that for Oliveira literature and politics are both equally futile given their fragility and temporary nature; like making things out of breadcrumbs, they are easily manipulated, and ultimately futile and temporary. Yet, if Oliveira seems so sure of his own nihilism, should he still be affected, even hurt, by the world that surrounds him, as Gregorovius has it (R, 79)? Why, if political action is simply meaningless, if there is nothing to be done about social inequalities, or the situation in Algeria? Should Oliveira be paralysed by his own ideological dilemma?

Unable to submit fully to an 'apoliticised' self, to a life of 'no te metás', Oliveira compares himself to other epic doubters, who ironically just like him were immortalised in fiction: '¿Qué hacer? Con esta pregunta empecé a no dormir. Oblomov, *cosa facciamo*? Las grandes voces de la Historia instan a la acción: *Hamlet, revenge!* ¿Nos vengamos, Hamlet, o tranquilamente Chippendale y zapatillas y un buen fuego? [...] ¿Das la batalla, Arjuna? No podés negar los valores, rey indeciso' (R, 31). Although, through his colloquial use of Italian the protagonist seems to empathise with slothful Oblomov, incapable of making a decision, he also feels close to Hamlet and Arjuna, who resolved their dilemmas by choosing the road of action (the Shakespearean character by avenging his father, and the Hindu hero by agreeing to take part in battle and become a warrior, despite his initial reluctance). Yet, Oliveira remains paralysed throughout the novel: can this be his 'active' decision? The narrator seems to think so, as he alludes to this by saying: 'Quietismo laico [...] atenta desatención. Lo importante para Oliveira era asistir sin desmayo al espectáculo de esa parcelación Tupac-Amaru' (R, 30). The description of this attitude is made with reference to Argentina, and the egocentrism of the Argentinians' relentless 'pontificantes homilías histórico-políticas' (R, 30). Oliveira wants to be detached from his own culture and also from religion, which is easily manipulated (at least within his Argentinian experience) by political interests. With the words 'atenta desatención', the quotation also underlines the protagonist's rhetoric of paradox: even when he decides that it is pivotal to give his undivided attention to something morally disturbing, he does it inattentively. Significantly, what Oliveira seems to consider important, in the midst of so much confusion and contradiction, is to be an unaffected spectator, even if that which is to be observed is as abhorrent as the tortures that the Spanish carried out on the Inca emperor (who, symbolically, is minimised in the narrator's sentence by being relegated to the secondary semantic role of an adjective). Oliveira puts this to the test when he gets to see Wong's photographic collection of people being tortured. Even if this observing of extreme human behaviour does not help the character to resolve his dilemma, it will surely add to the reader's understanding of his acquiescent attitude.

It is important to remark that while Oliveira cannot sleep because of his action/inaction dilemma, he can, nevertheless, be a willing observer. It is his ability to stand back and observe that differentiates the protagonist from his fellow countrymen, epitomised in Oliveira's brother and to some extent in Traveler, who from Oliveira's point of view are 'blinded' by the collective. Since Oliveira has not succumbed to the 'numbing' effects of the collective like them, he can rejoice in his self-proclaimed 'intelligent doubting', as the narrator puts it: 'la especie [vela] en el individuo para no dejarlo avanzar demasiado por el camino de la tolerancia, la duda inteligente, el vaivén sentimental' (*R*, 31). Unlike the protagonist, people like his brother are numbed by having to adhere to one side or the other: 'o negro o blanco, radical o conservador, homosexual o heterosexual, figurativo o abstracto, San Lorenzo o Boca Juniors, carne o verdura, los negocios o la poesía' (*R*, 31). His rejection of the dualisms that define, in this case, his compatriots, differentiates Oliveira from them, yet it also categorises him as another type of individual holding to a different troubling dualism: action or inaction. However, unlike the other dichotomies that he lists, this one is in his view an intelligent dilemma, one that could lead – as in the case of Cortázar himself – to creativity, and at the very least it is a dilemma that encourages non-conformity.

The distancing that the protagonist feels in relation to the masses allows him to assume the role of, as he calls it, 'espectador activo', which in turn makes him believe that he can look beyond and through the blinding hypocrisy of collective political action. As Oliveira elucidates: 'ser actor significa renunciar a la platea, y él parecía nacido para ser espectador en fila uno. "Lo malo", se decía Oliveira, "es que además pretendo ser un espectador activo y ahí empieza la cosa". Hespectador hactivo. Había que hanalizar despacio el hasunto' (*R*, 421). Oliveira's phrase stands out because of its seemingly contradictory terminology, and also because of his exaggerated use of the letter 'h'.[26] The reader has learned by this point in the novel that whenever Oliveira finds himself at a philosophical crossroads, he resorts to writing 'las grandes palabras por las que iba resba-

---

[26] The cinematic metaphor that Oliveira chooses to describe his being an 'active observer' recurs in *Libro de Manuel* with Andrés Fava and his cinematic dream, a *leitmotif* in the novel and the basis for his political transformation: see pp. 183–84 below.

lando su rumia' (*R*, 419), with an added 'h' at the beginning of words that do not take one. As well as being a tacit typographical tribute to César Bruto, the narrator elucidates that Oliveira 'usaba las haches como otros la penicilina' (*R*, 419). This, in turn, emphasises the idea that although detached and aloof, sceptical and pathologically lazy, the protagonist is nevertheless physically affected by the things that he observes, with the image of penicillin implying that Oliveira actually feels pain, or suffers from an injury that needs curing.

If in *El examen* the political circumstances, reflected in the physical deterioration of the city, become so unbearable that 'a Juan, furioso con todo, *le duele* Buenos Aires' (*EE*, 37; my emphasis). In the case of Oliveira, pain is caused not by his city, but by the situation of the world at large. According to Gregorovius, '[a Oliveira] le revienta la circunstancia. Más brevemente, *le duele el mundo*' (*R*, 79; my emphasis). It is important to note that although frustration seems to manifest itself through pain in both characters, their attitude towards that pain is significantly different. Juan is furious, witnessing the collapse of his city at the hands of an authoritarian regime; its disintegration hurts him because there is a fundamental *a priori* concern for that which is crumbling. In the case of Oliveira, however, the use of the expression 'reventar' to elucidate the emotions behind that pain is indeed ambiguous, and this ambiguity translates, once again, into contradictory feelings in the protagonist. Oliveira is not simply angry at the world's state of affairs, he is also fed up with it; the problems of the world weigh him down and he, in turn, cannot be bothered with them. Yet, Oliveira does not seem troubled by the antagonistic nature of his relationship with the pain that the world causes him. To an extent, he sees it as inevitable given that, as he explains:

> todo dolor me ataca con arma doble: me hace sentir como nunca el divorcio entre mi yo y mi cuerpo, *me lo pone* como dolor. Lo siento más mío que el placer o la mera cenestesia. Es realmente un lazo. Si supiera dibujar mostraría alegóricamente el dolor ahuyentando al alma del cuerpo, pero a la vez daría la impresión de que todo es falso: meros modos de un complejo cuya unidad está en no tenerla. (*R*, 406–7; my emphasis)

The division that pain imposes on Oliveira is in itself contradictory and unresolved: pain scares the soul away from his body but at the same time is a unifying force (epitomised through the image of the 'lazo'). Whether false or real, for Oliveira the pain that the world inflicts upon him is not ultimately about altruistic concerns, as in the case of Juan and his crumbling Buenos Aires; rather, what interests him is himself and his reactions (or lack thereof) in the face of that pain. This is also evident in the use of the reflexive pronoun in the phrases '*me lo pone* como dolor' and in the third-person impersonal 'el mundo en que *se vive*'. It is apparent that life is an imposition on the protagonist and, consequently, he feels that he cannot be responsible for it. Thus, Oliveira justifies himself for being 'unable' to be ideologically and politically committed to the world, to life. It is this same rhetoric of self-justification in which Oliveira takes refuge that Cortázar himself will seek when faced with his own political/ aesthetic dilemmas.

Yet, why should Oliveira feel physical pain for the state of the world, when he constantly tries to divorce himself from humanity? How can Oliveira want to be an 'active spectator' when he does not believe in any form of committed action? In a recurrent attitude of protective complicity, the narrator tries to answer these questions for the protagonist, claiming that 'Oliveira era incapaz de precisar. Se sabía espectador al margen del espectáculo, como estar en un teatro con los ojos vendados' (*R*, 422), failing therefore to scrutinise Oliveira's idea of the active spectator. Earlier on in the novel, however, la Maga – showing less mercy than the narrator – attacks the protagonist on precisely this point:

> —Vos pensás demasiado antes de hacer nada.
> —Parto del principio de que la reflexión debe preceder a la acción, bobalina.
> —Partís del principio —dijo la Maga—. Qué complicado. Vos sos como un testigo, sos el que va al museo y mira los cuadros. Quiero decir que los cuadros están ahí y vos en el museo, cerca y lejos al mismo tiempo. Yo soy un cuadro, Rocamadour es un cuadro. Etienne es un cuadro, esta pieza es un cuadro. Vos creés que estás en esta pieza pero no estás. Vos estás mirando la pieza, no estás en la pieza. (*R*, 32)

In this exchange, la Maga succinctly points out that Oliveira is never going to achieve the action that he talks about, for he is perpetually anchored in the act of looking, which in itself alienates him, strips him of presence. La Maga also criticises Horacio for being a witness, yet not in any active sense – that is, in the sense that it may have an actual impact upon someone, something – but quite the contrary. Through her analogy, she depicts the protagonist as someone so detached and involved in the act of (on)looking, that he distances himself from the reality that surrounds him, a reality that has become completely objectified; herself, Rocamadour, his friends: to Oliveira they are all mere aesthetic objects, worthy of observation.[27] As la Maga perceptively underlines, his act of looking prevents him from being. By levelling 'cerca' and 'lejos', furthermore, la Maga also alludes to the author's own situation,

---

[27] The notion of 'on-looking' as opposed to 'witnessing' comes from Gregory Rabassa's English translation of *Rayuela*. Rabassa chooses to translate 'hespectador hactivo' as 'whactive whonlooker': Julio Cortázar, *Hopscotch*, trans. Gregory Rabassa (New York: Pantheon, 1966), p. 418. This is interesting given the subtle difference in the degree of involvement between being a spectator and being an onlooker. The latter implies total passivity, whereas the former may involve some kind of participation, whether emotional or intellectual, thus, a more active role in relation to the 'spectacle' being watched.

trapped in the middle of cultural dichotomies.[28] The dialogue continues with Oliveira's patronizing remark, issued in self-defence:

—Esta chica lo dejaría verde a Santo Tomás —dijo Oliveira.
—¿Por qué Santo Tomás? —dijo la Maga—. ¿Ese idiota que quería ver para creer?
—Sí, querida —dijo Oliveira, pensando que en el fondo la Maga había embocado el verdadero santo. Feliz de ella que podía creer sin ver. […] Feliz de ella que estaba dentro de la pieza. (*R*, 32)

Oliveira defends himself from his lover's comments by being condescending (in keeping with his usual way of treating her) and effectively, detaching himself from the remark. His irony seems to mock la Maga's apparently ignorant, albeit 'blissful', state of mind. Yet, if the other instances when Oliveira resorts to this phrase to belittle others are recalled (those who 'vivían en la historia', 'han elegido', 'aman al prójimo como a sí mismos'), we could begin to wonder whether Oliveira is not in fact jealous. He would like to choose between action or inaction rather than be paralysed in his own ideological 'ataraxia', he would like to be 'en la pieza', rather than 'al margen del espectáculo', marginalised by his own intellectual incapacity to commit, to make a choice. But he cannot, or at least that is what he says to himself and what he believes.

In the novel, Oliveira never resolves his dilemma of whether or not to get actively engaged, be it socially, emotionally or politically. And although his quandary is not always framed politically in the novel, observing the protagonist through his reflections and contradictions invites, on the part of the reader, an identification or rejection of the protagonist's attitude. If the closest he comes to any kind of action is through his observing, it would appear that Cortázar demands the same from his reader. *Rayuela* is written for a reader who not only is expected to be 'active' in leaping between chapters, but also in allowing for the possibility of a questioning process. In recent criticism the active role of *Rayuela*'s reader is also understood within a political frame, for instance when Fernández Cubillos argues that '*Rayuela* como novela, como estructura, constituiría el esqueleto de un libro donde se traban una enorme diversidad de temas: amor, sexo, arte, jazz, política, que apelan a un trabajo activo del lector para completar su forma.'[29] Cortázar, with hindsight, refers to this in his interview with González Bermejo, when he claims that: 'La idea de *Rayuela* es una especie de petición de autenticidad total del hombre; que deje caer, por un mecanismo de autocrítica y de revisión despiadada, todas las ideas recibidas, toda la

---

[28] For Montaldo's elucidation of the changing significance of Cortázar's self-imposed exile see pp. 49–51, 83 above.
[29] Héctor Fernández Cubillos, 'La crítica de Nietzsche contra Occidente en *Rayuela* de Julio Cortázar', *Veritas*, 3/8 (2008), 97–126 at p. 103.

herencia cultural, pero no para prescindir de ellas sino para criticarlas.'[30] Within the novel, this is also explicitly spelled out by Morelli who, when trying to define the protagonist for his own book, elucidates what is behind the nonconformism of his creation:

> la actitud de mi inconformista se traduce por su rechazo de todo lo que huele a idea recibida, a tradición, a estructura gregaria basada en el miedo y en las ventajas falsamente recíprocas [...]. No es misántropo, pero sólo acepta de hombres y mujeres la parte que no ha sido plastificada por la superestructura social; él mismo tiene medio cuerpo metido en el molde y lo sabe, pero *ese saber es activo* y no la resignación del que marca el paso. (*R*, 392; my emphasis)

In Morelli's schema it is the knowing – as opposed to Oliveira's observing – that has to be active, in order to change something in the ideological structure that society imposes upon us. It is there that the 'revisión despiadada' that Cortázar talks about takes place. A revision that admittedly is not exclusively political but which, nonetheless, necessarily engages with politics.

It is interesting to mention here the definition that Víctor Flores García gives to this 'saber activo' in relation to philosophy. He mentions that the 'saber activo' is intrinsically linked to philosophy 'como dirección del mundo y de la vida', whereby once the individual is able to assume full responsibility for it, the 'saber activo' becomes a 'saber de la acción'.[31] Therefore, when Morelli refers to the 'saber activo' (as opposed to resigning to a life of automatisation), he is also alluding to a life of action where the 'saber activo' can lead to a politicisation of the character and his actions.

Through Oliveira it becomes apparent that to be aware of one's position as an observer in and of society, yet refusing to act upon that which is observed even when it seems to be socially unjust, ethically wrong or morally reprehensible, is – irrespective of political ideology – a political decision. In the Aristotelian sense of politics every citizen, in their quest for an ideal life, has to assume their role and position in society, so that everything that we do, or choose not to do, has an inherent effect on our neighbour and on the *polis*; our actions or inactions are to this extent always political. Referring back to Ander-Egg, and to the 'no te metás' attitude, there is no such a thing as an apolitical citizen. If someone chooses to stay 'out' of politics as an assimilated political act, then that person is not apolitical, but 'apoliticised'.[32] Bearing in mind Oliveira's considerations about his action/inaction dilemma, and the political implications of observing from a detached position, or detaching himself through merely observing, four short chapters (14,

---

[30] González Bermejo, *Revelaciones de un cronopio*, p. 72.
[31] Víctor Flores García, *El lugar que da verdad: la filosofía de la realidad histórica de Ignacio Ellacuría* (Mexico City: Universidad Iberoamericana, 1997), p. 142.
[32] Ander-Egg, 'Apoliticidad o neutralidad política', p. 33.

114, 117 and 15) can be analysed usefully. These chapters are tangibly political, since, through the description of photographs of torture, the insertion of 'extra-textual' excerpts on capital punishment and the narration of la Maga's rape, they put Oliveira's ethical and ideological reflections to a political and ethical test.[33]

The politics of 'real stories'

When following the 'active' reading (as specified in the 'Tablero de dirección'), the sequence of chapters 14, 114, 117 and 15 forms a distinct nucleus linking the fictional narrative to 'extra-textual' events or historical realities. Read as a sequence, they make a strong political impact within the text, an impact that is heightened in the context of Oliveira's unresolved dilemma. Whereas thus far the reader has only had to try to understand the protagonist's dialectical quandary on an abstract level, these chapters provide concrete material to challenge Oliveira's attitude of disengagement or, to use Ander-Egg's terminology, his 'descompromiso'. The fact that these sections are placed sequentially, moreover, emphasises their political significance, for the reader is given no fictional narrative in between which may bring a sense of escape or detachment. Without the 'cushioning' effect of a fictional narrator to mediate the information included in these extra-textual fragments, they arrive at the reader directly, therefore producing a shocking effect. As Kelman argues with reference to 'real' information being transmitted through fictional narrative, 'Without the advantage of any kind of mediation, information simply arrives and forces itself upon the receiver. Although it is supposed to present facts, what it transmits are not facts but rather the effect of shock.'[34] As Walter Benjamin explains, the storyteller is there to submerge the 'real events' into the lives of the characters.[35] Yet, by removing the storyteller from this sequence, it is apparent that Cortázar wanted to create a particular extra-textual focus that provides the reader with a kind of 'jolt', dislodging her/him from the 'reality' of the fictional text and therefore producing a more direct impact. Additionally, the fact that these segments are brief and very concise, heightens their shocking effect. A detailed analysis of this sequence shows how the implicit political signification of Oliveira's action/inaction dilemma becomes a more explicit provocation in the political dimension of *Rayuela*, giving rise to fundamental moral, social and political questions.

---

[33] Gérard Genette offers an extensive analysis of his re-definition of the different types of relationships inside and outside the fictional text: *Palimpsests: Literature in the Second Degree*, trans. Chana Newman and Claude Dowinski (Lincoln: University of Nebraska Press, 1997). Although no specific category is provided for 'extra-textuality', when I use the term 'extra-textual' I refer to the 'transcendence that unites the [fictional] text to the extra-textual reality', that is, the reality outside the fictional realm of the text, which cannot be linked to any other fictional text: ibid, p. 432.

[34] Kelman, 'The Afterlife of Storytelling', p. 249.

[35] Walter Benjamin, 'The Storyteller: Reflections on the Works of Nikolai Leskov', in *Illuminations*, ed. Hannah Arendt, trans. Harry Zohn (Glasgow: Harper Collins, 1968), pp. 83–107 (p. 149).

Wong's Pekinese collection (chapter 14)

The opening of chapter 14 finds a drunken Oliveira sitting on the floor of la Maga's flat. From a position where 'no se ven más que zapatos y rodillas' (*R*, 66), he strikes up a conversation with Wong, about whom the reader knows little except that he is also a member of the 'Club de la Serpiente'. It can be deduced from his name, and from Perico's rather brutal remarks, that he is probably of Chinese descent.[36] Yet, significantly, as well as pointing out that Wong is in charge of making the coffee when the 'Club' gathers (*R*, 75, 77, 79), and that his immigration status in France is somewhat dubious (*R*, 413), the characters only mention Wong's name in instances when torture, or any torture-like experience, is mentioned.[37] The reason behind this association is that Wong is preparing a 'colección pekinesa' (*R*, 164) of photographs of torture carried out in China at the beginning of the twentieth century. The images, as he tells us, capture the different stages of the deterioration of the body as the person is being tortured. Although most members of the 'Club' seem incapable of dealing with Wong's 'research material' – they either trivialise it through racist remarks or associate the idea of torture exclusively with Wong so as to detach themselves from that reality (*R*, 130) – Oliveira has a peculiar interest in finding out more about Wong's collection. Chapter 14 deals with Oliveira's relentless curiosity with regard to the exact contents of Wong's book, in other words to images of torture. While the reader 'observes' the protagonist scrutinising such images, it becomes increasingly evident that Oliveira uses his 'apoliticised' attitude to free himself from any kind of socio-historical responsibility. In his book on torture, Peter Reddy writes that

> torture is the ultimate act of state power. In arrogating to itself the capacity to torture its citizens, the state has assumed absolute power over them. What is there to do about this when the collective power of armies, governments and security forces holds the ultimate capacity to control? It can be said that knowledge of torture is itself a political act, just as silence or ignorance of it have political consequences. Therefore to speak of the unspeakable is the beginning of action.[38]

---

[36] Racist remarks about Wong are recurrent in the novel, with Perico saying things such as: 'Ahí viene Wong [...] el chino está hecho una sopa de algas' (*R*, 50). It could be said that this racism represents not only a condescending attitude on the part of Western men towards those from the East, but it also reflects the comparable middle-class *porteño* attitude, as seen in *El examen*, towards the (different, and presumed inferior) other. There is another example in chapter 96 when the 'Club' is trying to enter Morelli's flat: 'Que entre primero Wong', says Ronald, 'para exorcizar a los demonios. Oh, de ninguna manera. Dale un empujón, Perico, total es chino' (*R*, 436).

[37] For example, at one point Oliveira says to Ronald, 'Acércate aquí [...] vas a estar mejor que en esa silla, tiene una especie de pico en el medio que se clava en el culo. Wong la incluiría en su colección pekinesa, estoy seguro' (*R*, 164).

[38] Peter Reddy, *Torture: What You Need to Know* (Charnwood: Ginninderra Press, 2005), p. 203.

Bearing in mind Reddy's understanding of the concept, there is an interesting link between lack of action (not daring to speak about the unspeakable) and the 'no te metás' attitude embodied in Oliveira and discussed earlier through Ander-Egg's formulations. However, the protagonist's 'no te metás' reflex will be compromised by the close scrutiny to which he subjects Wong's photos.

After commenting nonchalantly on how much it is raining outside, Oliveira asks Wong, '¿Es cierto que usted prepara un libro sobre la tortura?' (R, 66). Wong is evasive; at first he says, 'Oh, no es exactamente eso' (R, 66), an ambiguous non-definition that he never attempts to clarify. At Oliveira's insistence, Wong merely remarks that 'en China se tenía un concepto distinto del arte' (R, 66). This evasive reply exasperates Oliveira, who claims that he is aware of the Chinese understanding of art since, as he puts it, '*todos* hemos leído al chino Mirbeau' (R, 66; my emphasis). Octave Mirbeau was not Chinese, and it is highly improbable that everyone (in the room) would have read him, of course. Yet the mention of the French author is very significant for the political implications of this chapter, since alluding to Mirbeau creates a specific connection between literature and the experience of torture.

One of Mirbeau's key texts was the *fin-de-siècle* novel *Le Jardin des supplices* (1899). In it, crucially for the argument of this chapter, torture is portrayed aesthetically, mainly from the point of view of Clara, the sadistic female protagonist who takes sexual pleasure in viewing how people are tormented and tortured while she strolls through the beautifully tended garden – the 'jardin des supplices'. The idea of an aesthetic value in torture is also represented in Mirbeau's text by a Chinese torturer who, through his ideals and practice of torture as an art, establishes himself in the novel as the artist figure, mirroring the archetypal, decadent late nineteenth-century French artist.[39] By stating that, 'L'art [...] consiste à savoir tuer, selon les rites de beauté dont nous autres Chinois connaissons seuls le secret divin', the torturer manifests his understanding of himself as an artist, based on his mastery of 'the rites of beauty', an appreciation that Clara shares and approves.[40] Through marrying aesthetic values with what the 'civilised world' considered to be morally unacceptable, Mirbeau was calling for a re-evaluation of art and its traditional canons, while at the same time bringing into question the moral precepts of Western man.

Thus, the allusion to Mirbeau in *Rayuela* becomes very significant in that the use of transgressive images in his fiction was part of an ambition to question and deviate from the accepted aesthetic norms of the time, something that Cortázar is also attempting to do with *Rayuela*. More specifically, the intertextual allusion to Mirbeau's aestheticisation of torture gives an aesthetic dimension to the atrocities

---

[39] For a close study of Mirbeau and his aesthetic ideas, see Christina Ferrée Chabrier, 'Aesthetic Perversion: Octave Mirbeau's *Le Jardin des supplices*', *Nineteenth-Century French Studies*, 34, 3–4 (2006), 355–70.

[40] Octave Mirbeau, *Le Jardin des supplices*, ed. Michel Delon (Paris: Gallimard, 1988), p. 206.

that Oliveira witnesses (through photographs) and about which the reader learns through him. Given that Cortázar was highly influenced by the writings of Bataille, Sade and to an extent Artaud, it is not surprising that he displays an interest in the eroticism of pain and suffering. In fact, Cortázar recognised that quite often there was a sadistic dimension to the erotic episodes in his fiction, but defended himself by saying that there was plenty of evidence, thanks to Baudelaire and Freud in particular, that the erotic and the sadistic were always closely related to each other, whether on a conscious or unconscious level. Cortázar also drew attention to the need to find ways around the taboos that stifle the expression of the erotic in Spanish-language fictional narratives, a subject that he also dealt with at some length in *Último Round*.[41] Yet, what makes the aestheticisation of torture different, and indeed political, is that while on the one hand, Oliveira seems to be completely alone in his pleasure (and ultimately, he does not even feel that, for he seems to be emotionally numb), on the other hand at no point does Oliveira actually find beauty in what he sees. He describes the horror, in detail, yet not with aesthetic admiration. As no importance is assigned to the pain or torture of others, the scene becomes increasingly uncomfortable for the reader. Even if we are not looking directly, we are voyeuristically seeing. This seeing or thinking about torture disrupts the narrative continuity. Even if Oliveira is observing with curiosity, there is no assimilation of the other as a 'prójimo'; the man being tortured in the picture becomes completely objectified. And the line between the aestheticisation of pain and disregard for the other can easily become blurred.[42] The fact that this chapter should be followed by a description of Lou Vincent's death in the gas chamber (chapter 114), or by the description of la Maga's rape in the 'passive reading' (chapter 15), is indicative of Cortázar attempting to provoke some degree of thought about the politics of torture, and also about individual responsibility *vis-à-vis* violent acts carried out upon our 'prójimo'.

Returning to the conversation between Wong and Oliveira, after Wong's evasive reply regarding the Chinese concept of art, Oliveira defies Wong by interrogating him rhetorically: '¿Es cierto que usted tiene fotos de torturas, tomadas en Pekín en mil novecientos veinte o algo así?' (*R*, 66), to which Wong, smiling, replies: 'Oh no [...] están muy borrosas, no vale la pena mostrarlas' (*R*, 66). Faced with reticence, a contradictory smile and persistent incongruity (for Wong was asked whether or not he had the photos, and not what state they were in), Oliveira insists further:

---

[41] See Standish, *Understanding Julio Cortázar*, pp. 128–9, and Evelyn Picon Garfield, *Julio Cortázar* (New York: Frederick Ungar, 1975), pp. 69–70.

[42] Alejandra Pizarnik already points to this, to the necessity of control, when she describes at the end of her *La condesa sangrienta*: 'Como Sade en sus escritos [...] la condesa Báthory alcanzó, más allá de todo límite, el último fondo del desenfreno. Ella es una prueba más de que la libertad absoluta de la criatura humana, es horrible': 'La condesa sangrienta', in *Textos selectos*, ed. Cristina Piña (Buenos Aires: Corregidor, 1999), pp. 18–137 at p. 137.

—¿Es cierto que lleva la peor en la cartera?
—Oh, no —dijo Wong.
—¿Y que la ha mostrado a unas mujeres en un café?
—Insistían tanto —dijo Wong—. Lo peor es que no comprendieron nada.
—A ver —dijo Oliveira, estirando la mano. (R, 66)

From the kind of reply that Wong provides each time, more than one aspect stands out. The repetition of the phrase 'Oh, no' is perhaps the most visually obvious, suggesting uncomfortable negation on the part of the character faced with Oliveira's inquisitiveness. These interjections are not always logical, in fact they represent the absolute opposite, as if the 'Oh, no' expressed an affirmation that Wong would rather deny. Contrary to what Wong claims, he does have photographs of torture, taken in Peking around 1920, and he does carry the 'worst one' in his wallet.

When Oliveira extends his hand, in a gesture implying both absolute demand and, at the same time, humble begging (especially when recalling that he is sitting on the floor), Wong 'se puso a mirarle la mano, sonriendo' (R, 66). Implied in the use of 'se puso' is a measured pause; Wong takes the time to stare at Oliveira's hand, emerging from below. Oliveira's perspective, described at the beginning of the chapter as 'un amistoso contento' (R, 66), becomes unsustainable when being stared at by Wong, so much so that Oliveira 'Bebió más vodka y cambió de postura' (R, 67). The discomfort previously sensed in Wong's clumsy answers (comparable to the 'mal gusto' left in Oliveira's mouth after rejecting Ronald's invitation) is now perceived through Oliveira's vulnerability. As readers we note that this is clearly not a comfortable situation. Wong's grin is perplexing; he, like the torturer in Mirbeau's novel, understands himself as an artist figure, and thus can take pleasure in these images of horror, which he deems artistic. Furthermore, Wong also takes sadistic delight in observing Oliveira desiring the images and in deliberately delaying talking about them and producing them. At the precise instant of handing over the photographs, the smile is so emphatic that it becomes a metonymy for Wong, as Oliveira puts it: 'En lugar de Wong había una sonrisa de gato de Cheshire' (R, 67). It is apparent that Wong is taking pleasure in his position of power, controlling and possessing the object of Oliveira's desire. Wong has not only become the smile of a Cheshire cat, but also 'una especie de reverencia entre el humo' (R, 67). Completely depersonified, it is the smile that gives the images to Oliveira: 'le pusieron una hoja de papel doblada en cuatro en la mano' (R, 67). The use of the impersonal third person plural creates a distance between the reader and an unfathomable Wong, while also taking tangibility away from the subject, so that all the attention falls onto Oliveira's hand, and effectively, in a kind of cinematic close-up, onto the image itself. As in the short story 'Las babas del diablo', the change of narrative voices underlines the fact that at times, when telling a story, it is the story (or in this case, the image) that tells itself: 'Va a ser difícil [contarlo] porque nadie sabe bien quién es el que verdaderamente está contando, si soy yo o eso que ha ocurrido, o lo que estoy viendo.'[43]

Once the images are in Oliveira's hand, the narration shifts from Oliveira's drunken perception of a 'foggy' Wong to a very meticulous description of the scene of torture captured on a single sheet of paper. The interest that Oliveira has in seeing these images wakes him up and allows him to focus despite his drunken state. As the detailed description – told from Oliveira's point of view – of this torture session progresses, it creates a sense of shock and physical disgust, not only because of what is actually being described, but also because of the unexpectedness of these images within the narrative flow of the novel. It is the 'unrelatedness' of this narration within the overall text, in combination with the grotesque imagery of a person being cut into pieces while still alive (while others simply observe) that forcibly removes the reader from his/her comfortable position reading the story of Oliveira looking for la Maga. This is an effect maintained by the sequence of chapters here analysed, shocking the reader with descriptions and ideas that relate to torture or capital punishment and which allude to actual historical and political affairs; that is to say, they refer to 'real stories' that happened 'outside' the realm of the fictional text, and which at this point are interwoven in the overall fictionality of the novel.

The description of the images occupies most of chapter 14, and since Oliveira is the only observer, the narration is the portrayal of the protagonist's gaze, travelling over the page with his simultaneous cognitive process. The description of the image draws a direct connection to the analysis of 'Chinese Torture' which Bataille includes in his *The Tears of Eros*. Were it not for the fact that Bataille's book was published a year after *Rayuela*, it could most certainly have been argued that Cortázar, given the influence that Bataille had on him, would have been thinking of the same images described in detail by the French writer. Claiming to have first seen the images in the publications by Georges Dumas (*Traité de psychologie*, 1923) and by Louis Carpeaux (*Pékin qui s'en va*, 1913), Bataille admits that the images 'had a decisive role' in his life, given their depiction of 'pain, at once ecstatic and intolerable'.[44] When reading Bataille's own experience and obsession with this particular image, Oliveira's detachment becomes all the more shocking.

It is therefore worth noticing that as soon as the sheet is in the protagonist's hand, instead of remarking on the deplorable scene of a person being cut into pieces, Oliveira calculatingly determines the measurement of the pole that the victim is tied to, the number of images on the page and the order of the sequence of images: 'El poste debía medir unos dos metros, pero había ocho

---

[43] Julio Cortázar, 'Las babas del diablo', *Cuentos completos/1*, p. 220. This was first published in *Las armas secretas* in 1959.
[44] Georges Bataille, *The Tears of Eros*, trans. Peter Conor (Hong Kong: City Lights, 1989), pp. 205–6. This was first published in French in 1961.

postes solamente que era el mismo poste repetido ocho veces en cuatro series de dos fotos cada una, que se miraban de izquierda a derecha y de arriba abajo' (*R*, 67). The description gets even more mechanical when clarifying that 'el poste era exactamente el mismo a pesar de las ligeras diferencias de enfoque', and almost in passing:

> lo único que iba cambiando era el condenado sujeto al poste, las caras de los asistentes [...] y la posición del verdugo, siempre un poco a la izquierda por gentileza hacia el fotógrafo, algún etnólogo norteamericano o danés con buen pulso pero una Kodak año veinte, instantáneas bastante malas. (*R*, 67)

The omniscient narrator exposes the viewer's knowledge of photography as very precise. Not only does he seem to know the brand of camera with which the photos were taken, but also, remarkably, the year in which the camera was manufactured. This emphasises the degree of coldness and detachment that Oliveira has towards the images while also depicting how detailed his scrutiny is; he is paying very close attention to the images, technically and aesthetically speaking, yet hardly on a human-to-human, empathic level.

Although the technical photographic knowledge is not something that the reader immediately associates with Oliveira, the subtle irony with which he describes the position of the executioner is perhaps more easily related to the protagonist. The antithetical kindness of the torturer towards the presumably Western photographers is emphasised by the ironic tone used by Oliveira. This, in turn, underlines his emotional detachment from the image since, as Linda Hutcheon claims, 'irony engages the intellect rather than the emotions'.[45] This irony is also reflected in the patronizingly imprecise mention of an 'American or Danish' ethnologist 'probably' observing the scene of torture with mere anthropological interest. This could also be read as a political comment (comparable to that round Mirbeau) regarding the relationship between the haughtiness of the Western man, embodied in this case by Oliveira, and his suffering, distant other. It is significant that while in chapter 1 the presence of the other shifted from the 'masa peronista' (in *El examen*) to an invisible monstrous element (in *Los premios*), here it has been weakened and belittled into something outside Oliveira, and effectively outside the fictional thread of the novel. The awareness of that responsibility, of thinking about it, has been implicitly transferred to the 'active' reader, who may continue with day-to-day life unconcerned by Oliveira's relationship with la Maga, but might find it more conflictive to forget about events that are known to have been 'real'. This will be key for the political dimension of *Libro de Manuel*.

---

[45] Linda Hutcheon, *Irony's Edge: The Theory and Politics of Irony* (London: Routledge, 1995), p. 14.

The account moves on to describe the progression of the torture session through the differences in the sequence of images. Thus the reader learns that:

> aparte de la segunda foto, cuando la suerte de los cuchillos había decidido oreja derecha y el resto del cuerpo desnudo se veía perfectamente nítido, las otras fotos, entre la sangre que iba cubriendo el cuerpo y la mala calidad de la película o del revelado, eran bastante decepcionantes, sobre todo a partir de la cuarta, en que el condenado no era más que una masa negruzca de la que sobresalía la boca abierta y un brazo muy blando. (*R*, 67)

It is interesting to note the levelling that Oliveira carries out between the degradation of the torture victim's body, progressively more mutilated as the eyes follow the sequence, and the bad quality of the film or the developing process. The use of the adjective 'decepcionante' shows, furthermore, that Oliveira's priority is commenting on the quality of the photos rather than on the state of the tortured man who becomes completely objectified when described by the protagonist as a 'masa negruzca'. As the chapter comes to its close, the description focuses on the last frame: 'Y si Wong desdeñaba la octava foto debía tener razón porque el condenado ya no podía estar vivo, nadie deja caer en esa forma la cabeza de costado' (*R*, 68). The use of the verb 'desdeñar' to refer to the image in which the torture victim appears to have died, is similar to Oliveira's own use of the adjective 'decepcionante' to refer to the entire sequence. This implies that both Wong and Oliveira are looking at these images from an aesthetic perspective, whereby they find it equally disappointing if the image becomes blurred or if the torture has ceased due to the death of the victim. It is this aestheticisation of torture which permits Oliveira to put a safe distance between himself and the images; for him, the photos are mere 'art scenes' rather than documentations of reality.[46]

Given that at no point does the reader get a hint of sadistic enjoyment from Oliveira's perspective, it could be argued that the protagonist has to understand the images aesthetically because, based on his own undefined ideological, ethical and political stance, he cannot even commit to reacting to what he observes. As Roland Barthes asserts in *Camera Lucida*, 'the photograph whose meaning [...] is too impressive is quickly deflected; we consume it aesthetically, not politically'.[47] When a photograph is too explicit in its political meaning, it ultimately fails to shock us. It is when the image is subtle that it haunts the viewer, and for that reason it penetrates the subconscious and fulfils its political goal in a much less radical, yet more lasting manner. Susan Sontag argues, perhaps more convincingly, that photographs of atrocities give

---

[46] See Regina West, 'La representación fotográfica en la literatura: el caso de *Cien años de soledad* y *Rayuela*', *Lucero*, 2 (1991), 59–72 at p. 69.

[47] Roland Barthes, *Camera lucida: Reflections on Photography*, trans. Richard Howard (London: Flamingo, 1984), p. 36.

rise to opposing responses, namely: 'A call for peace. A cry for revenge'; and if they fail to cause that in the viewer, they nevertheless generate 'the bemused awareness, continually restocked by photographic information, that terrible things happen'.[48] What is disturbing about this scene in *Rayuela*, is that throughout the viewing Oliveira seems to have no emotional response whatsoever. Despite this being consistent with his behaviour, it makes the reader uncomfortable, so that the provocation comes not only through the description of the images themselves but also through the protagonist's lack of response. Although this is not overtly political, it raises fundamental questions about the reader's position in society – and in particular with regard to the suffering of others, and to the reader's relationship to 'el prójimo' – so that it is implicitly political in a classical ethical sense. Moreover, if this scene is carried into a political scenario that requires action or involvement (for instance, Ronald's attendance at meetings for Algerian independence), Oliveira's detachment in the face of state-imposed torture, is equivalent to his 'descompromiso' or 'no te metás' attitude in relation to political affairs. This places him in direct opposition to Andrés Fava in *Libro de Manuel*.

Although Oliveira has appeared impervious throughout, towards the end of the chapter it is apparent that the images might start to have an effect on him, similar to that 'mal gusto en la boca' that Oliveira felt when he declined Ronald's political invitation:

> como siempre todo convergía desde dimensiones inconciliables, un grotesco *collage* que había que ajustar con vodka y categorías kantianas, esos tranquilizantes contra cualquier coagulación demasiado brusca de la realidad. O como casi siempre, cerrar los ojos y volverse atrás, al mundo algodonoso de cualquier otra noche. (*R*, 68)

Now that the images have been taken away, Oliveira is left with the idea of the photographs, and the 'reality' depicted in them. He suddenly feels the need to anaesthetise this 'grotesque collage' with alcohol and Kantian categories. And although the very idea of Kantian categories implies a will to understand, to conceptualise the images, at the same time it means that once categorised they can simply be left in the past, they can be put away somewhere 'behind' the world itself. This is what allows Oliveira to remain inactive, as Hécor Cubillos Fernández explains: 'Esto que Oliveira ilustra con sus sospechas de que hay "un detrás" del mundo en que vive, algo que escapa a la razón y a las narraciones que sostiene el mundo [...] desemboca en su deseo de la nada, representada en la inactividad, en el escapar del devenir, el quedarse inmóvil.'[49] This 'inactividad',

---

[48] Susan Sontag, *Regarding the Pain of Others* (London: Penguin, 2003), p. 11.
[49] Cubillos, 'La crítica de Nietzsche', p. 100.

in turn, allows Oliveira to avoid taking action or risking a decision, so that he remains 'quietecito sin hacer nada' (*R*, 71).

The mention of 'collage', on the other hand, as with the allusion to Mirbeau, shows Oliveira drawing a parallel between torture and art, to avoid assimilating the images of torture from an ideological, humanitarian or political perspective. This relates back to the fact that throughout the chapter torture is related to literature and visual art (photography or collage), but not to politics. The fact that Oliveira, although apparently affected, ends up avoiding the shock of reality and returning to his safe world is, on one hand, an affirmation of his incapacity to act – even if only to deal with his own reactions – and, on the other, it is an indirect provocation for the reader who is comfortably reading this novel. Cortázar, however, delays our return to the 'mundo algodonoso', for after this chapter, we are immediately confronted with the typographical reproduction of a newspaper article describing the last minutes of a man being killed in the gas chamber (chapter 114), or if we are a 'lector hembra', we read la Maga's account of being raped. In other words, it is significant that Cortázar, at this particular point, does not give the reader any kind of emotional relief; within the narrative texture, we cannot – unlike Oliveira – close our eyes and fall back into our anaesthetised existence; we can only do so if we close the book.

The meticulous description of the images, in combination with Oliveira's acquiescence, appears to provoke the readers into drawing their own conclusions regarding the character and the images. This would bring Cortázar closer to a Brechtian idea of catharsis, rather than the classic Aristotelian.[50] However, the novel does not intend to promote a particular political or moral message based on this visual 'lesson'; rather, it aims to emphasise the function of literature to unite men and women with their other, as Morelli succinctly puts it:

> Tomar de la literatura eso que es puente vivo de hombre a hombre. [...] Una narrativa que no sea pretexto para la transmisión de un 'mensaje' (no hay mensaje, hay mensajeros y eso es el mensaje, así como el amor es el que ama); una narrativa que actúe como coagulante de vivencias. (*R*, 400)

Evidently, the description of these images does not make the novel political. Yet, by including this kind of real 'vivencia' the text certainly creates in the reader a sense of unease. This unease is not exclusively political, yet the fact that it is linked to the protagonist's unwillingness to act leads to a more fundamental effect which is implicitly political. For in inducing the reader to react against, or identify with, Oliveira, Cortázar is also provoking us to decide between a life of (conscious) inaction, perpetuating an attitude of 'no te metás', or a life

---

[50] See Angela Curran, 'Brecht's Criticism of Aristotle's Aesthetics of Tragedy', *Journal of Aesthetics and Art Criticism*, 59/2 (2001), 167–84.

of commitment.[51] This is what is behind Sergio Ramírez's understanding of the political implications of *Rayuela*, when he asserts:

> ¿Por qué un guerrillero habría de leer *Rayuela*? Porque [...] las categorías éticas de *Rayuela* iban más allá de la patafísica, y ya se ve que llegarían a tener consecuencias políticas [...] porque planteaba las maneras de *no ser*, frente a las descaradas maneras de ser que ofrecían sociedades como las de América Latina donde no bastaría abolir las injusticias, sino buscar nuevas formas de conducta personal.[52]

An extra-textual death in the gas chamber (chapter 114)

From chapter 14 the reader of the 'active reading' is told to skip to chapter 114. There, they are confronted with what typographically appears to be a newspaper article. At first glance, it can be seen that the font is smaller than the rest of the narrative and that the text begins with an intriguingly incomplete date: '4 de mayo de 195...' (*R*, 479). The deliberate temporal imprecision is striking given the absolute specificity required of a journalistic text. However, incidentally, this turns out to be typical of the whole novel, where not even the characters themselves seem to be sure of the year in which they are living.[53] What appears to be a 'detail', capriciously undefined by the seeming distractedness of the characters, preoccupied with existential concerns beyond the temporal restrictions of a given period, here becomes a deliberate act of editing. In turn, the three dots replacing and erasing the exact year of the decade arouse suspicion with regard to the verisimilitude of the text. It appears to be 'real', that is, describing non-fictional events outside the fictional realm of the novel, but this deliberate imprecision diminishes the importance of the exact date: it does not effectively matter exactly which year it is. Given the contents of the 'article', what matters is the fact that in the 1950s people are still being executed. To this extent, the article could be seen as a denunciation embracing an entire decade.

---

[51] The fact that the other members of the 'Club' do not say anything about Oliveira's attitude to these images is also pertinent. Again, a parallel can be drawn with the Countess Báthory, as recounted in Pizarnik's *La condesa sangrienta*, where she writes (p. 135): 'Cabe advertir que al volverse la suerte contra ella, los Báthory, si bien no la ayudaron [a la condesa], tampoco le reprocharon nada'. In the same way, the 'Club' does not intervene when Oliveira is scrutinising the images, yet nor do they condemn him for not expressing any emotions about them. They are all, to some degree, accomplices in their inaction.

[52] Sergio Ramírez, 'El Evangelio según Cortázar', *Revista de la Universidad de México* (2004), 25–9 at p. 28. My emphasis.

[53] On two occasions the characters refer directly to the year in which they are living, and both times they allude to it with imprecision: '¿por qué estamos tan tristes, hermanos de mil novecientos cincuenta y pico' (*R*, 401); 'estamos en mil novecientos cincuenta y pico. Ya lo sé, coño' (*R*, 444).

As we reach the end of the section, it appears that it is not just the date which is incomplete, the text itself ends abruptly in the middle of a key sentence: 'Los testigos, entre los que se contaban tres periodistas de...' (R, 479). Indeed, most sentences in this fragment end and/or begin with three full points or, as they are appropriately called in Spanish, 'puntos suspensivos'; it is rather inserted, wedged in, as it were, like a piece belonging to a different puzzle.

The article deals with the death of Lou Vincent, 'ejecutado esta mañana en la cámara de gas de la prisión de San Quintín, estado de California' (R, 479). As in chapter 14, the description of the slow death process is very detailed. In effect, there are other striking similarities between the chapters, such as the use of the word 'condenado' to describe the victim or the general scenario of observers witnessing the process of somebody being killed. While in Wong's photographs there are three people, including the photographer, in this case, there are reportedly 'cincuenta y tres testigos [que] observaban a través de las ventanillas' (R, 479). There is, however, one crucial difference between the two chapters, and that is that while chapter 14 follows the narrative plot of the novel, and its contents originate from the descriptions of an omniscient narrator, chapter 114 is an extra-textual fragment, simulating an insertion of 'reality' or a 'real story' from outside the sequentiality and 'reality' of the narrative. In other words, the text is not introduced as a consequence of the fictional plot, nor does it have a direct effect on it or on the novel's characters (at least, not explicitly and not at this point).

Within Cortázar's fictional evolution, this is the first time that he introduces texts which typographically emulate newspaper articles. This technique will be further explored in his two collage books, *La vuelta al día en ochenta mundos* and *Último Round*, and will reach its fullest expression in *Libro de Manuel*. In all these subsequent examples, inserting newspaper-like fragments is central for the representation of the political dimension through his fiction. And although in *Rayuela* (and particularly in this chapter), we can begin to appreciate this political function, the insertion of extra-textual fragments emulating or reproducing newspaper clippings, recurs elsewhere in the novel but with absurd, even pataphysical intent. Chapters 130 and 150, for example, recount random episodes (in effect, 'prescindibles'), such as the risks of zips in trousers and the state of the broken leg of an English duchess. In both cases, they include captions showing their apparent verisimilar source, namely, *The Observer* and *The Sunday Times* respectively.[54] While these absurd examples contribute to the humorous aspect of the novel, chapters 114 and 117 differ precisely because of the gravity of the topics

---

[54] Other examples of this kind of extra-textual insertion can be found in chapters 119 and 146. *Rayuela* is knowingly also made up of many other extra-textual fragments (quotations from books by Bataille, Artaud, Cambaceres, Paz and so forth), which are included as separate chapters, or which are reproduced by Morelli as part of his 'Morellianas'. Reference here will be restricted to those fragments appearing in the form of journalistic articles.

with which they are dealing. Crucially, they are different because they put forward events that provoke questions about justice, punishment and marginality; in sum, they are 'real stories' that call for a necessary ideological response.

In the case of this sequence of chapters, the underlying theme is the same in all four; namely, the infliction of pain (mostly state-sponsored) upon others, and the witnessing – directly or indirectly – of that suffering. Although this fact *per se* is not political, the ethical questions raised by the presentation of these themes have a political basis and implication. Through the insertion of newspaper articles that emulate a reality outside the realm of the narrative thread, Cortázar brings a 'portion' of reality into the fictional text. So, while the reader can easily detach his/herself from the world of the characters, when 'facts' are presented as such, it generates more ethical questions at the moment when the reader chooses to close the book, if s/he pretends that those issues only exist in the universe of *Rayuela*.

Leopold and Loeb (chapter 117)

Chapter 117 is a first-person narration, with a reference at the end reading 'Clarence Darrow, *Defensa de Leopold y Loeb*, 1924' (*R*, 483).[55] The contents, and in particular the inclusion of the reference, appear to show that the text is part of, or aims to evoke, the legendary twelve-hour summing-up that the defence attorney acting for Nathan Leopold and Richard Loeb delivered at their trial, after they – aged 18 and 19 – had kidnapped and murdered a 14-year old boy simply for 'the experience'.[56] For this crime alone these middle-class youngsters would have certainly received a sentence of death by hanging. However, due to Darrow's insightful and philosophical defence speech, one of the most eloquent ever delivered against the death penalty, Leopold and Loeb were spared the rope and were instead sentenced to life-imprisonment. The excerpt included in this chapter (printed in a smaller font, as in chapter 114) concentrates upon that part of Darrow's speech in which he emphasises the subjectivity inherent in the distinction between good and evil. In his psychological study of the case, contemporary with the trial, Maurice Urstein remarks that, 'The act which created a stir far beyond this country is so frightful, psychologically so incomprehensible, so singular in its unfoldment [*sic*] that if Poe or a writer […] wished to unnerve his readers, no better tale could be invented.'[57] Urstein's paralleling of

---

[55] For the complete summing-up see 'Closing Argument: The State of Illinois versus Nathan Leopold & Richard Loeb. Delivered by Clarence Darrow. Chicago, Illinois, August 22, 1924', <http://www.law.umkc.edu/faculty/projects/ftrials/leoploeb/LEO_SUMD.htm> [accessed 20 June 2008].

[56] For details of the case, see, for example, Paula S. Fass, 'Making and Remaking an Event: The Leopold and Loeb Case in American Culture', *Journal of American History*, 80/ 3 (1993), 919–51.

[57] Maurice Urstein, *Leopold and Loeb: A Psychiatric-Psychological Study* (New York: Lecouver Press Co.: 1924); cf. Fass, *Making and Remaking*, p. 919.

the Leopold and Loeb case and a gripping fictional tale is relevant in that, through inserting this kind of extra-textual fragment, Cortázar is surely aiming to 'unnerve' his readers in a way that moves them to think about their own opinions and ideologies. This provocation is underlined by the fact that this fragment interrupts the narrative flow of *Rayuela*. The direct allusion to, and inclusion of, 'real' history is, furthermore, an explicit example of Cortázar's bad faith in claiming that until he went to Cuba, and up until writing *Libro de Manuel*, he was 'fuera de la historia'. Despite the fact that the kind of history alluded to through these excerpts is not contemporaneous with the writing of *Rayuela* – as it will be in the case in *Libro de Manuel* – it nevertheless shows that history and political affairs were constant sources of reference for Cortázar.

Although chapter 117 does not typographically emulate a newspaper article, the thematic link is maintained from the previous chapter, and also with chapter 14. The three sections deal with torture and capital punishment in different forms: to some extent, the diversity of the forms intensifies their political significance. In other words, torture, or being sentenced to death, is not just something that happens to one unnamed individual detached from the present time of the novel. It happened in China. It happened in the Unites States, in 'mil novecientos cincuenta y pico' (*R*, 444) and in 1924. It also happened to la Maga, in Montevideo. If the reader cannot endure the description on chapter 14 about the 'condenado' being tied to the post while parts of his body are being severed, and s/he chooses to move on to the next chapter, s/he will find another version of slow death carried out by state authority, also being mercilessly observed by witnesses. In the first instance, the torture is presented through photographic images, described to the readers by Oliveira; in chapter 114, however, the slow death of the 'condenado' is depicted in the form of a descriptive newspaper article. If again, in further discomfort, rejecting the disruption of his/her 'mundo algodonoso' of fiction the reader decides to leap to the next section, s/he will find that chapter 117 does not deal directly with a scene of torture or death, yet nevertheless it puts forward a pivotal reflection on capital punishment, which although brief, includes provoking explicit details (*R*, 483). Moreover, and not as a coincidence, in the same chapter, la Maga describes how she used to be beaten up by her father and how she was sexually abused by her neighbour. The sequentiality of these chapters is deliberately unrelenting.

La Maga's torture (chapter 15)

Following the excerpt on Leopold and Loeb, the reader is instructed to go to chapter 15, which begins thus:

> Entonces era tan natural que se acordara de la noche en el canal Saint-Martin, la propuesta que le habían hecho (mil francos) para ver una película en la casa de un médico suizo. Nada, un operador del Eje que se las había arreglado

para filmar un ahorcamiento con todos los detalles. En total dos rollos, eso sí mudos. Pero una fotografía admirable, se lo garantizaban. (*R*, 69)

The 'entonces' at the beginning of the opening line is left deliberately ambiguous (just as in the case of the date or final sentence in the newspaper article). It could be referring to the previous moment in the chronological sequence in the narrative – that is, to the end of chapter 14 – where Oliveira ponders on the possibility of closing his eyes and returning to his comfortable reality after seeing Wong's images of torture (*R*, 68). Equally, time might have passed between the end of chapter 14 and this 'entonces', when suddenly Oliveira introspectively makes a natural connection from one indirect experience of torture to another. One way or another, the images of torture have led Oliveira to remember yet another instance related to state-imposed death which, as in the case of chapters 14 and 114, was also witnessed; in this case, it was filmed. The vernacular 'nada' that the narrator uses to elucidate the details of the film that Oliveira was invited to see, is comparable to the sense of negation that Wong put forward before showing the photographs to Oliveira (through the repetition of the interjection 'Oh, no', and phrases such as 'no vale la pena mostrarlas', *R*, 66). The negation that prefaces the horror that follows, somehow belittles it as if the image itself, that is the filming of a hanging, was commonplace and not at all shocking. The narrator is careful to remark that this film included 'todos los detalles' and that, unlike Wong's 'instantáneas bastante malas' (*R*, 67), the film had 'una fotografía admirable'. The implication of trying to tempt Oliveira to see these images – even offering to pay him to do so – presupposes that he has an aesthetic as well as a voyeuristic interest in the contents of the film. This relates back to him looking at Wong's photographs and to the allusion to Mirbeau.

The description of the film that Oliveira received must have been detailed as well, for he notes that 'En el minuto necesario para resolverse a decir que no [...] había tenido tiempo de imaginar la escena y situarse, cuándo no, del lado de la víctima' (*R*, 69). This 'cuando no' stands out with irony, for as in the case of Wong's images, Oliveira does not feel inclined to side with the victim; in fact, it would appear that in his emotional as well as ethical acquiescence, he does not feel much at all. Oliveira acknowledges this, and tries to justify his own attitude, saying that 'Lo peor era que había mirado fríamente las fotos de Wong, tan sólo porque el torturado no era su padre, aparte de que ya hacía cuarenta años de la operación pekinesa' (*R*, 69). Within Oliveira's lame excuse of the passing of time, implied in the word 'peor' is a moral judgement that the protagonist passes on himself, or that the narrator inserts to redeem the character from his ethically and ideologically unsympathetic position.

When Oliveira announces that he is leaving the gathering, he is retained by a feeling of curiosity for the 'interviú sentimental' (*R*, 70) that Gregorovius is having with la Maga. The dialogue that is taking place between the two characters turns out to be crucial for the novel, for it is thanks to Gregorovius's questions about la Maga's past, that she recounts how she was raped at the age of thirteen. It becomes apparent, perhaps as a consequence of the psychological trauma and its subsequent denial, that for la Maga there is no sense of history. She says to Gregorovius: '¿A qué le llama tiempos viejos, usted? A mí todo lo que me ha sucedido, me ha sucedido ayer, anoche a más tardar' (*R*, 72); and further on in her account she adds: 'En Montevideo no había tiempo [...] yo tenía *siempre* trece años' (*R*, 72; my emphasis). Her sense of timelessness perpetuates the horror of her rape. This closeness with her past, a past fixed at the age when she was raped, results in a very detailed account of la Maga's experience.

Prior to the description of the rape, la Maga recounts how her father used to beat her up. This one day, 'mientras [mi padre] me estaba pegando, vi que el negro espiaba por la puerta entreabierta. Al principio no me di bien cuenta, parecía que se estaba rascando la pierna, hacía algo con la mano' (*R*, 73). Her unwillingness to identify, or to spell out that Ireneo ('el negro') was masturbating while watching her being beaten, shows that la Maga is still trapped in her teenage naivety. To the reader, the idea of there being an observer while someone is being physically abused inevitably echoes the scenes presented in the three previous chapters, with the difference that in this case – and returning to Mirbeau's protagonist, Clara – Ireneo is obtaining explicit sexual pleasure from watching the physical torment perpetrated on la Maga. The contents and arrangement of the chapters leading to chapter 15 accentuate the impact of the description of la Maga's abuse, while simultaneously bringing the idea of torture closer to the horizon of the text and the characters. In addition, the fact that the reader now learns about a physical ordeal undergone by the female protagonist, rather than reading indirect descriptions of Wong's Pekinese collection, or extra-textual fragments referring to 'real stories', highlights the political aspect of the other instances, since they all relate to torture that happened in the 'real' world, to actual human beings as opposed to fictional characters.

When la Maga, lost in her own narration of events, notices that Oliveira is trying to listen in, she says to him: '¿Por qué me mirás con esa cara, Horacio? Le estoy contando cómo me violó el negro del conventillo. Gregorovius tiene ganas de saber cómo vivía yo en el Uruguay' (*R*, 73), to which Oliveira acrimoniously replies, 'Contáselo con todos los detalles' (*R*, 74). Oliveira's dismissive comment ironically reminds us of the gruesome details included in the three previous chapters of this sequence, and of Oliveira's own seemingly sadistic predilection for 'todos los detalles'. It is, moreover, completely ineffectual, for la Maga has already given out the details of her traumatic experience. In any case, neither Oliveira nor Gregorovius seem to be paying her the attention that her account and her pain deserve. Further on in the novel, when the figure of 'el negro' comes up again between la Maga and Gregorovius, she has to clarify who this person was, and not only because Gregorovius cannot remember, but also because he had not even believed her in the first place. He says, '¿Entonces la historia del negro era verdad?' (*R*, 138).

It is interesting to note that Oliveira tries to justify his own detachment from the retelling of la Maga's rape, by asserting that 'en realidad todo se reduce a aquello de que *ojos que no ven*' (*R*, 70; my emphasis). The protagonist says this in relation to the incongruity of people being able to be upset at the 'muerte del rusito de la esquina o de la sobrina de la del tercero' and yet not be affected when one talks to them 'del terremoto de Bab El Mandeb o de la ofensiva de Vardar Ingh, y pretende que la infeliz se compadezca en abstracto de la liquidación de tres clases del ejército iraní' (*R*, 70). Oliveira leaves unfinished the idiom, which complete would read 'Ojos que no ven, corazón que no siente'; implying thus that since he was not there to witness the rape of la Maga, he is justified in not feeling any pain for her. Oliveira appears to be driven by one maxim, namely, of being 'active' in his inaction, of actively maintaining a detached attitude and not getting involved; in sum, he wants to live a life of 'no te metás'. As Cortázar put it, egoism was Oliveira's only guide: 'el egoísmo de tanta introspección y tanta metafísica era la sola brújula [de Oliveira]'.[58] Yet, as in Oliveira's statement here, although it would be easier for him to be unaffected, his action/inaction dilemma remains unresolved: as he tries to convince himself that if he is not there to witness the atrocity, it is acceptable (within his own parameters) not to feel anything, and therefore not to act, he considers socio-political events (the attack of Vardar Ingh, losses in the Iranian army).

A key feature linking this sequence of chapters is the insertion of 'historical' facts into the fictional frame of the narrative. Whether they are unaltered representations of reality or 'simulated slides' of the 'real' world outside the fictional text, is unclear and, furthermore, irrelevant. What is important is the defamiliarising effect caused by that doubt. In the case of *Rayuela*, as with *La vuelta al día en ochenta mundos* and *Último Round* – the provocation is itself part of the political efficacy of Cortázar's narration, whereby the effect is transmitted not in the content, but through the form. This sequence of four chapters intrudes into the fictionalised world of the narrative, causing with their political signification an unsettling effect on the reader.

The novel as revolver?

> 'usar la novela como se usa un revólver para defender la paz, cambiando su signo'. (*R*, 400)

Whether following the active or passive reading of *Rayuela*, it is only a few chapters into the novel that Oliveira displays his unresolved dilemmas between aesthetics and ethics (*R*, 27), and action or inaction (*R*, 31). The novel's politi-

---

[58] Cortázar, 'Acerca de *Rayuela*', *Papeles inesperados*, p. 173.

cal dimension is expressed implicitly mainly through Oliveira's quandaries between commitment and detachment or, as Jaime Alazraki sees it, between 'la *soledad* y la *solidaridad*'.[59] As Oliveira shifts in his ideological dichotomy, the novel presents political elements that, although they do not transform *Rayuela* into a political novel *per se*, nevertheless give rise to uncomfortable ethical as well as political questions that the reader cannot avoid, and which could challenge his political ideology. The novel does not aim for catharsis; rather, it seeks to instil in the reader a degree of estrangement that allows him/her to carry out a renewed reading of their own principles and of those of the socio-political space that they inhabit. Thus, as Morelli would argue, the novel – in this case, *Rayuela* – is a dynamic bridge which does not carry a specific message or a political slogan, but rather aims to function as a 'coagulante' merging all the different factors that should trigger the reader to reflect upon his/her own ideology as well as his/her own society and their position in it.

For some critics, such as Alazraki, *Rayuela* presents some fundamental contradictions when it comes to its political meaning, for while the novel 'cuestiona la realidad humana', it does not provide 'la acción para transformarla'.[60] This becomes evident in Oliveira's dialectical existence. On the other hand, critics like Jean Franco have argued that after the Cuban revolution, 'novels like *Rayuela* [...] spoke directly to an iconoclastic youth for whom social change was a matter of urgency and for whom the violence of the past [...] was an evil that only immediate action could overcome'.[61] This, in turn, agrees with what Cortázar himself perceived about *Rayuela* and revolutionary action a decade after its publication:

> mientras yo me distancio poco a poco de *Rayuela*, infinidad de muchachos aparentemente llamados a estar lejos de ella se acercan a la tiza de sus casillas y lanzan el tejo en dirección al Cielo. A ese cielo, y eso es lo que nos une, ellos y yo le llamamos revolución.[62]

My understanding is that *Rayuela* calls for a revisiting of the readers' ideological and political views, based on their degree of differentiation from, or identification with, Oliveira's 'no te metás' attitude, as well as on the degree of provocation caused by the discussions of torture. It cannot, as Alazraki hoped,

---

[59] Jaime Alazraki says that 'Horacio Oliveira se siente solo, se sabe solo y ve en esa soledad la condición para alcanzar su otredad, para poseerse entero, para realizarse desde su yo no conformado': 'Imaginación e historia en Julio Cortázar', in *Los ochenta mundos de Cortázar: ensayos*, ed. Fernando Burgos (Madrid: EDI– 6, 1987), pp. 1–20 at p. 2.

[60] Ibid. p. 4.

[61] Jean Franco, 'South of Your Border', in *The 60s Without Apology*, ed. Sohnya Sayres *et al.* (Minneapolis: University of Minnesota Press, 1984), pp. 324–6 at p. 324.

[62] Cortázar, 'Acerca de *Rayuela*', *Papeles inesperados*, p. 174.

provide the actions to transform the reality it questions, because ultimately that will depend on the reader. Alternatively, as Sergio Ramírez suggests, *Rayuela* cannot provide the answers because 'en las respuestas se incuba ya el error'.[63] It is precisely in the lack of answers that, according to Ramírez, the political lessons of the novel lie, that is, in the systematic destruction of Western values without the provision of any concrete answers apart from 'el salto al vacío'; because, as he argues, 'para construir, ya se sabe, es necesario primero destruir, ir a fondo en el cuestionamiento'.[64]

To claim that *Rayuela* directly contributes to political action would be a mythologised reading of its political content. It certainly calls for action, but for action that is individual and introspective. Whether that action then results in political commitment or a thorough re-evaluation of ideologies, cannot realistically be ascertained.

The implicit political dimension of *Rayuela* lies in the capacity of the book to make the reader think not only about the revolution of aesthetic conventions and narrative traditions, but also about the implications of a renewed political consciousness. It is not in vain that, when it was published, *Rayuela* was understood among intellectuals of the Argentinian Left to be a model for ideological questioning. Graciela Montaldo, for example, recalls: 'Desde la revista *Pasado y Presente* editada [...] por jóvenes intelectuales de izquierda [...] Schmucler lee a *Rayuela* casi como un acto revolucionario, y no duda en darle una filiación política'.[65] In this sense, whereas in *El examen* and *Los premios* the political dimension remained within the confine of allegory, in *Rayuela* the political is implicit and to an extent utopian, in that it relates to a necessity of questioning thought and behaviour, responsibility and awareness, outside the realm of the fictional text. This explains in part the novel's excellent reception among the intellectuals of the Left since, as Omar Prego Gadea elucidates, *Rayuela* 'coincide con una época de gran cuestionamiento entre la juventud latinoamericana, en una etapa de grandes sacudimientos históricos'.[66]

In response to the reading of *Rayuela* as a 'revolutionary' novel, Cortázar claimed:

> La noción de *Rayuela* como novela revolucionaria [...] es la que tengo yo también. Y no sólo yo, sino la crítica más lúcida acerca de *Rayuela* [...] que ha hecho hincapié en que un libro que no dice ni una sola palabra de política [...] contiene al mismo tiempo una serie de elementos explosivos que hay que considerar como revolucionarios.[67]

---

[63] Ramírez, 'El Evangelio según Cortázar', p. 28.
[64] Ibid., p. 29.
[65] Montaldo, 'Destinos y recepción', p. 608.
[66] Prego Gadea, *La fascinación de las palabras*, p. 114.
[67] Ibid., p. 188.

Rayuela cannot be said to be a political novel, yet as a text it does show that even before his pivotal trip to Cuba, Cortázar was a writer who was very much interested in politics, and was allowing this interest to permeate his fiction. While in the novels discussed in the previous chapter this interest concentrated on Argentinian socio-political reality, in *Rayuela* it begins to shift into more universal political concerns. However, it is worth noting that, due to the changes in the evolution of his political ideology, Cortázar felt increasingly detached from this novel claiming, in his 1980 Berkeley lectures, that *Rayuela* altogether lacked a political and historical dimension:

> Lo negativo [de *Rayuela*]: el excesivo individualismo, la falta de una dimensión política e histórica contemporánea. Pero ese mismo individualismo exacerbado permitiría después el paso del Yo al Tú y al Nosotros. Después de *Rayuela* todo se fue dando para llegar al *Libro de Manuel*'.[68]

This chapter has demonstrated that this is not the case. Contrary to assertions by both Cortázar himself and his critics that his novel is completely lacking in political content, *Rayuela* certainly contains 'more than just one word' of politics.

---

[68] Julio Cortázar Papers, Series 1C, Box 2, Folder 43.

3

Literature in the Revolution

The publication of *Rayuela* gave Cortázar extraordinary prominence on the Latin American and also international cultural scene. This largely coincided with Cortázar's 'conversion' to socialism, catalysed by his first encounter with Castro's Cuba. Based largely on his political adherence, critics and fellow writers constructed the image of the 'politicised Cortázar', marking a turning point in the understanding of him as a public figure but also of his fictional writings. The analysis thus far has tried to show that the so-called politicisation of Cortázar, and seemingly also of his literature, has been somewhat mythologised, and not just by critics, but also by Cortázar himself. Even the wave of articles that appeared in the Argentinian and Spanish press during 2009, commemorating the twenty-fifth anniversary of Cortázar's death, still refers to his first trip to Cuba as a precise point that defines Cortázar's 'before and after' politics, generally claiming that his 'good' literature ended when he became committed to socialism and to the Cuban Revolution: the Mexican critic Emmanuel Carballo stated, for instance, that 'su paso por la política nos robó libros que pudieron ser importantes'.[1]

Although the first trip to Cuba was certainly crucial for Cortázar, it should be noted that despite the fact that so much of the criticism is based on the 'before and after' politics marked by this 'precise' point in the writer's history, it is actually remarkably difficult to date the trip accurately. Cortázar travelled to the island for the first time between 1961 and 1963, yet it is unclear exactly when. Critics and Cortázar himself place this political turning point in different years. For example, in a series of interviews carried out during 1983 by Omar Prego Gadea, Cortázar asserts: 'esa primera visita a Cuba me colocó frente a un hecho

---

[1] See Fabiola Palapa Quijas, 'Elogian la vitalidad de la obra de Cortázar a 25 años de su muerte', *La Jornada*, 2 March 2009 <http://www.jornada.unam.mx/2009/03/02/index.php?section=cultura&article=a11n1cul> [accessed 2 March 2009]. For other examples, see also Florencia Abbate, 'Al borde del vértigo', *Página/12*, 12 February 2009 <http://www.pagina12.com.ar/diario/suplementos/espectaculos/subnotas/12837-3851-2009-02-12.html> [accessed 13 February 2009]; Sergio Otero, 'Julio Cortázar: 25 años de su muerte', *El Correo Gallego* 15 February 2009 <http://www.elcorreogallego.es/popImprimir.php?idWeb=1&idNoticia=395492> [accessed 16 February 2009]; and Ricardo Solís, 'A 25 años de la partida física del erudito, elocuente y memorioso Julio Cortázar', *La Jornada Jalisco*, 14 February 2009 <http://www.lajornadajalisco.com.mx/2009/02/14/> [accessed 15 February 2009].

consumado. Yo fui muy poco tiempo después del triunfo de la revolución – la revolución triunfó en 1959 y yo fui en 1961'.² Evelyn Picon Garfield's *Julio Cortázar* (1975), however, which puts together a series of interviews carried out during 1973, specifies that Cortázar's first visit to Cuba took place in 1963.³ From Cortázar's published letters, it is clear that during 1961 Cortázar left Paris several times to go to Vienna and Copenhagen, for work purposes, and to Italy and Spain on holiday; yet at no point during this year does he mention a trip to Cuba. Furthermore, and politically speaking, despite the success of the anti-Batista revolution in Cuba in 1959, between 1960 and 1962 Cortázar seems to be more concerned with the situation in Algeria than with anything happening in Latin America.⁴ Trying to establish the actual date of Cortázar's crucial first trip to Cuba is an intriguingly challenging task; this very difficulty underscores the mythologised nature of the event in which the precision of relevant facts has been altogether sidelined.

On 5 January 1962 Cortázar wrote to Francisco Porrúa giving extensive editorial instructions on *Rayuela*. He ends the letter by saying: 'Si te puedo escribir desde Cuba, recibirás la carta vía París', implying that a trip to the island is about to take place.⁵ It is not until his final published letter of 1962 that Cuba reappears. Dated 16 December 1962, and addressed in very idiosyncratic English to Sara and Paul Blackburn, it shows Cortázar flippantly telling his friends that: 'my old pal Fidel Castro [...] is inviting me to join the jury for their annual contest [...] we shall fly to La Habana on the 10 or 12 January [1963]'.⁶ Significantly, he adds that 'the invitation was so unexpected that I have not fully realised yet what it is going to mean to me. All this years [*sic*] I have been longing to go to Cuba to have a direct experience of what is happening out there, and suddenly... there we go!'⁷ Clearly, Cortázar had not been to Cuba before January 1963.

Needless to say, being interested in the Cuban revolutionary process was not unusual for a Latin American writer with left-wing sympathies in the 1960s. Wanting to be part of, and to believe in, a political movement that promised to bring social justice and cultural independence from the imperialistic dominance of the United States was in fact for many Latin American intellectuals the 'obligatory' step to take during this period. As David Viñas put it, in relation to meeting Cortázar for the first time in Havana: '[esa época] era la edad de oro de la revolución cubana. Todo el mundo estaba de acuerdo.

---

² Prego Gadea, *La fascinación de las palabras*, p. 208.
³ Picon Garfield, *Julio Cortázar* p. x.
⁴ See, for example, Cortázar to Jean Bernabé, 30 May 1960, and Cortázar to Eduardo A. Jonquières, 20 March 1962, *Cartas/1 1937–1963*, pp. 424, 471 respectively.
⁵ Cortázar to Francisco Porrúa, 5 January 1962, ibid., p. 467.
⁶ Cortázar to Sara and Paul Blackburn, 16 December 1962, ibid., p. 526
⁷ Ibid.

Era la revolución'.[8] So, although Cortázar had thus far expressed more interest in the political situation in Algeria than in Cuba, for example, Castro's invitation and seeing revolutionary Cuba first-hand, would cause a radical shift of priorities in Cortázar's political concerns.

An interest in socialism, and in politics and history more generally, had concerned Cortázar from his earliest fiction. Consolidation of a proven interest and a particular ideology, while accentuating his inclination towards socialism, nevertheless failed to eliminate lingering contradictory feelings exemplified in Cortázar's early fictional representations of the Peronist masses. As Carlos Fuentes put it: '[Cortázar] nunca separó los términos de las dos revoluciones, la revolución de afuera y la revolución de adentro [...] Cortázar vivió [...] el conflicto entre el afuera y el adentro de todas las realidades, incluyendo la política'.[9] It is the expression of these internal conflicts, that is Cortázar's attempt to manifest them through literature, which will concern us here. This chapter will analyse a period in Cortázar's artistic production that seems to be driven by an ethical guilt arising from the political reality with which he identifies after his trip to Cuba, and which he finds difficult to reconcile with his belief in artistic freedom. The dichotomy (between political duty and artistic freedom) is embodied in a sense of bifurcation whereby Cortázar tries to defend his principle of artistic autonomy while at the same time supporting the revolution in some kind of analogous, aesthetic 'operation', as Cortázar was to call it.

After *Rayuela*, where the political element is mostly implicit in Oliveira's unresolved dilemma between action and inaction, the next stage to be considered in the political trajectory of Cortázar's texts is marked by *62/modelo para armar* on the one hand, and *La vuelta al día en ochenta mundos* and *Último Round*, on the other. The latter two books are not narratives in the vein of the novels, but they do represent a crucial part in the evolution and exploration of politics in Cortázar's writings. In this period, between *Rayuela* and *Libro de Manuel* (that is, between 1963 and 1973), Cortázar also wrote fragments for a collaborative project, *Buenos Aires, Buenos Aires* (1968), with photographs by Sara Facio and Alicia D'Amico, as well as a collection of short stories entitled *Todos los fuegos el fuego* (1966). Since the publication of *Rayuela* marked such an irrevocable change in Cortázar's public profile, and given the fact that critics have generally understood the polarisation of Cortázar's writings as dating precisely from 1963, it is important that all these texts are analysed chronologically in order to trace the evolution of the political in them, and to show once more that there was no sudden 'politicisation' in Cortázar, but rather a change in the form and emphasis of a pre-existent dimension.

---

[8] David Viñas, personal interview, Buenos Aires, 17 December 2008.
[9] Carlos Fuentes, 'Julio Cortázar, 1914-1984', *Jaque*, 30 March 1984, reprinted in *Julio Cortázar a través de la prensa sudamericana*, ed. Perla Rosenstein (Buenos Aires: Instituto de Estudios de Literatura Latinoamericana, 1984) pp. 35-43 at p. 39.

Duty versus art: bifurcating paths

> 'Hay diferentes maneras argentinas de ser "culpable de literatura", de imaginar excepciones, individuos fuera de la especie': Julio Cortázar.[10]

The possibility of fundamental social and political change signalled by the triumph of the Cuban revolution was accompanied by a shift in the conception of the role of the artist and intellectual in Latin American society.[11] As a prime example of this, the so-called 'boom' in Latin American literature, emerging during the 1960s, was said to have its main foundation in political changes on the continent. Cortázar was to this extent not exceptional in being inspired by the social utopia that the triumph of the revolution represented; at least temporarily, many of the best-known figures of Latin American literature showed their support for the Cuban cause. Gabriel García Márquez, Mario Vargas Llosa, Carlos Fuentes, Mario Benedetti would all at some point believe that they could inspire radical political change through their literature.[12] Yet, while they were all united in the same cause, it was apparent that what moved some of these writers closer to Cuba depended upon factors that little had to do with political ideology. This was not the case for Cortázar; as Mario Vargas Llosa admits:

> En su caso, a diferencia de tantos colegas nuestros que optaron por una militancia semejante pero por snobismo u oportunismo – un *modus vivendi* y una manera de escalar posiciones en el establecimiento intelectual [...] – su mudanza fue genuina [...] y de una coherencia total.[13]

So, while in the case of many of writers belief in revolutionary Cuba was part of a historical facet or some kind of temporary and opportunistic ideological affair, for Cortázar Cuba meant much more. It became, in his words, his 'camino de Damasco'.[14]

In one of the most recent critical studies on Cortázar, the Mexican writer Ignacio Solares picks up on this image and compares Cortázar's embracing of socialism to a religious conversion.[15] With hindsight, Cortázar also described

---

[10] Quoted in Vicente Battista, 'La corteza de Cortázar', *El escarabajo de oro*, 40 (October 1969), 14-15.

[11] For further analysis see Claudia Gilman, 'El intelectual como problema', in her *Entre la pluma y el fusil: debates y dilemas del escritor revolucionario en América Latina* (Buenos Aires: Siglo XXI, 2003), pp. 143-88.

[12] See David Viñas *et al.*, *Más allá del boom: literatura y mercado* (Mexico City: Marcha Editores, 1981).

[13] 'La trompeta de Deyá', prologue to Julio Cortázar, *Cuentos completos/1*, pp. 13-23 at p. 21.

[14] Cortázar to Jean Thiercelin, 2 February 1968, *Cartas/2 1964–1968*, p. 1225.

[15] Solares, *Imagen de Julio Cortázar*, p. 100.

his first visit to Cuba as a quasi-religious experience, a 'llamada a la puerta', as he put it: 'cuando los cubanos me invitaron a ir como jurado del Premio de la Casa de las Américas [...] tuve la sensación de que *golpeaban a mi puerta*, una especie de *llamada* [...] estaba viviendo una *experiencia extraordinaria*, y eso me comprometió para siempre'.[16] It is important to understand how Cortázar later interprets his encounter with Cuba and to underline, as Solares does, the multiple religious connotations of the imagery through which Cortázar chooses to describe his 'epiphany'. For the morality attached to such imagery, the inherent sense of guilt and fear of failure that comes with any commitment 'para siempre' plays a key part in the analysis of the political element in Cortázar's writings from the late 1960s. Given his parallel commitment to artistic freedom, this will also lead Cortázar down very contradictory paths.

Even prior to what within Cortázar's sense of 'autofiguración' was an 'epiphanic' trip to Cuba, it becomes apparent that Cortázar gradually begins to feel a strong sense of duty. In Sartrean terms, his 'moral imperative' takes precedence over his 'aesthetic imperative'.[17] As the idea of the collective gains importance for Cortázar, so does his guilt at not being enough of a committed intellectual for his fellow Latin Americans. This is crystallised in statements such as that made in a letter to Ana María Barrenechea, a year after the publication of *Rayuela*, when he claims:

> Llega el momento en que se descubre una verdad tan sencilla como maravillosa: la de que salvarse solo no es salvarse, o en todo caso no nos justifica como hombres [...] no podemos refugiarnos cómodamente en el gran escape de la liberación individual [...] por eso el sentimiento de *culpa* de no estar haciendo nunca lo que debería hacer.[18]

The sense of guilt, generated by accepting and taking on his role as a Latin American intellectual in favour of the socialist revolution, is a major contributing factor to Cortázar's decision, at this point, to write literature in distinct ways: one expressing his wish for artistic freedom (and embodied in *62* and in most of the short stories in *Todos los fuegos el fuego*), and the other showing an explicit attempt to deliver a political message through a combination of narrative and visual techniques (as seen in *La vuelta* and *Último Round*). The very act of differentiating them also shows that although Cortázar supported Castro's revolution, he was reluctant to compromise and thus – in his view – restrict his artistic freedom for a political cause. In his words:

---

[16] Goloboff, *Julio Cortázar: la biografía*, p. 128. My emphasis.

[17] For Sartre there seems to be no possible clear division between art, politics and morality: 'Although literature is one thing and morality is a completely different thing, at the bottom of the aesthetic imperative we discern the moral imperative': *What is literature?*, trans. Bernard Frechtman (London: Methuen, 1950), p. 111.

[18] Cortázar to Ana María Barrenechea, 9 April 1964, *Cartas/2 1964–1968*, p. 699. My emphasis.

> el papel del intelectual o artista en el plano de la participación política no supone de ninguna manera una derogación o una limitación de sus valores o sus funciones puramente creadoras, sino que su creación literaria o artística se da hoy dentro de un contexto que incluye la situación histórica y sus opciones políticas, que de manera directa o indirecta se reflejarán en las fibras más íntimas de sus obras.[19]

Cortázar's ambivalent rhetoric is key to understanding how he was trying to fit into the 'situación histórica', without shifting his aesthetic ideas regarding the role and purpose of literature.

For the Cuban socialist cause, it would not be enough to allegorise a political reality or express an implicit fundamental dilemma; the committed socialist writer had to produce something that was immediate and explicitly in favour of the revolution. This impelled Cortázar to try to find a way to write literature that would be politically engaged without becoming a dogmatic or propagandistic form of 'political writing', that could manifest a political dimension 'de manera directa o indirecta'. Therefore, after publishing of *Rayuela*, and travelling to Cuba, Cortázar's fictional writings, rather than beginning the synthesis of the explicitly political and the aesthetic which Cortázar claims is fully realised in *Libro de Manuel*, instead bifurcate into what Cortázar called 'literatura pura', epitomised in the exploration of form of *62*, and work that was overtly engaged with a given political ideology, yet also lyrical, playful and aesthetically experimental, as seen in *La vuelta* and *Último Round*.[20] It is clear from his 1980 Berkeley lecture notes that Cortázar was aware of this differentiation:

> Cuba, catalizador. [...] Me siento implicado, concernido [...] me siento por primera vez latinoamericano. Empiezo mi trabajo *paralelo* de escritor partícipe. [...] Mi camino de ficción no cambia. Escribo *62*, *Todos los fuegos el fuego*, llenos de fantástico; pero a la vez polemizo (*La vuelta*, *Último Round*), ayudo a la lucha contra las dictaduras, Tribunal Russell, etc. Y hacia el año 1970 intento una convergencia (sin intención de sistematizarla): *Libro de Manuel*.[21]

He lays it out clearly: his role as a committed writer is not only a 'job', but is one that at this point is 'parallel' to his fictional path. What is more, he seems determined to emphasise that despite his taking on board this new role, his

---

[19] 'El intelectual y la política en Hispanoamérica', *Obra crítica/3*, pp. 151–75 at p. 161. This was originally published in a translation by Margery A. Salir in Jaime Alazraki and Ivar Ivask (eds), *The Final Island: The Fiction of Julio Cortázar* (Norman: University of Oklahoma Press, 1978), pp. 522–32.
[20] The term 'ficciones puras' is from Cortázar, 'Corrección de pruebas', p. 35.
[21] Julio Cortázar Papers, Series 1C, Box 2, Folder 43. My emphasis.

'camino de ficción' is not affected. For this reason it can be argued that Cortázar's aesthetic evolution after *Rayuela* splits into two paths of creative production that will run in parallel for a decade.

Writing as an analogous operation

Cortázar's letters are an invaluable source for understanding his intentions and motivations and as a context for his literary works. There are two quotations in particular that show how difficult this period was for him, insofar as being able to define the role of his literature within a political revolution. They also manifest how pronounced the sense of bifurcation became for Cortázar during this time. The first comes from a letter to Roberto Fernández Retamar, dated 10 May 1967:

> Ahora me sentía situado en un punto donde convergían y se conciliaban mi convicción en un futuro socialista de la humanidad y mi regreso individual y sentimental a una Latinoamérica de la que me había marchado sin mirar hacia atrás muchos años antes. Cuando regresé a Francia luego de esos dos viajes [a Cuba], comprendí mejor dos cosas. Por una parte, mi hasta entonces vago compromiso personal e intelectual con la lucha por el socialismo entraría, como ha entrado, en un terreno de definiciones concretas de colaboración personal allí donde pudiera ser útil. Por otra parte, mi trabajo de escritor continuaría el rumbo que le marca mi manera de ser, y aunque en algún momento pudiera reflejar ese compromiso [...] lo haría por las mismas razones de libertad estética que ahora me están llevando a escribir una novela que ocurre prácticamente fuera del tiempo y del espacio histórico [*62*] [...] mi problema sigue siendo un problema metafísico, un desgarramiento continuo entre el monstruoso error de ser lo que somos como individuos y como pueblos en este siglo y la entrevisión de un futuro en el que la sociedad humana culminaría por fin en ese arquetipo del que el socialismo da una visión práctica y la poesía una visión espiritual.[22]

From the very first lines it is clear that Cortázar by now believes in socialism as the only viable political system, not only for Latin America, but for the entire world. In the sentimental mentioning of Latin America as an ignored territory that he now is willing to confront thanks to Cuba, lies a romanticisation which is somewhat self-delusional for, as a self-acknowledged member of the Buenos Aires middle class, Cortázar would have tended to identify more with any European than with a Bolivian, Mexican or indeed a Cuban. Unlike Ernesto Guevara, Cortázar as a young writer and teacher had never shown any interest in exploring the interior provinces of Argentina, or the rest of Latin America: indeed Cortázar was 'sent' to work to the interior provinces, he did not choose to be there.

---

[22] Cortázar to Roberto Fernández Retamar, 10 May 1967, *Cartas/2 1964–1968*, p. 1138.

After this idealised statement, the sense of bifurcation begins to become increasingly apparent, when Cortázar speaks about the two things that he understood better after Cuba. If this were simply a list, enumerative adverbs such as, 'primero' or 'en primer lugar' could have been used to indicate the two items. However, through the use of 'Por una parte' and 'por otra parte', Cortázar positions his two affirmations as separate from one another, in effect, like two parallel paths. The first of the two statements refers to an already-existing, albeit vague, commitment to the fight for socialism, becoming firm and concrete. This convenient vagueness (comparable to the imprecision surrounding the date of his first visit to Cuba) creates a space for mythologizing in order to accommodate the new role of the committed socialist intellectual. The repetition of the verb 'entrar' ('entraría, como ha entrado') to demarcate and clarify that the change has indeed taken place, emphasises the sense of self-justification that Cortázar deems necessary in the face of other writers and intellectuals. It is worth pointing out that Cortázar wrote this in response to Retamar's request for his thoughts on the situation of the Latin American intellectual; a letter that, in other words, Cortázar knew would be published.

Nevertheless, and particularly taking into account the public nature of the letter, it becomes evident that Cortázar's commitment is not free of conditions, limited as it is to 'allí donde pudiera ser útil'. The personal 'colaboración' and 'compromiso', which apparently were so clear-cut in the first instance, are contrasted by Cortázar's 'trabajo de escritor' and 'manera de ser'. In other words, Cortázar is willing to sign his contract with socialism on a personal level, yet not as a writer. The personal commitment could be reflected 'at some point' in his aesthetic creations, but Cortázar's use of the subjunctive 'pudiera' following the open-ended deferral implied in 'en algún momento', is imprecise and deliberately ambiguous. It is important also to note how Cortázar employs the third person ('me están llevando') to detach himself from responsibility for the aesthetic destiny that has chosen him, and not that he has chosen. Furthermore, Cortázar's notion of his 'aesthetic destiny' is radically at odds with his personal political identification with Cuba, as he shows in another letter to Fernández Retamar, on one of the occasions when he returned to Paris from the island: 'Uno se va de tu isla con una honda herida, con algo que sólo poco a poco se va restañando [...] creo haberme identificado un poco más con mi destino [...] ahora me siento extranjero y solitario en París.'[23] It could be argued, incidentally, that this feeling of being an outsider in a European city does not come about because Cortázar happens to be more of a foreign than before, but rather because the previous mode of being foreign, manifested in *Rayuela* for instance, has been rendered untenable by his own feeling of guilt at the irreconcilability of his aesthetic freedom and his socialist commitment.

---

[23] Cortázar to Fernández Retamar, 20 March 1966, ibid., p. 1101.

The sense of duality is repeated, although with different contents, at the end of the quotation, when Cortázar refers to his 'problema metafísico', a reflection that underlines how he sees his dilemmas as being beyond the rationality of politics and hegemonic rule. For Cortázar, coming to terms with creating freely as an individual artist within a socialist revolution needs to be – like the inspiration for art itself – metaphysical. The second dichotomy that Cortázar presents comprises, as he understands it, the reality of what we are presently, as individuals and as peoples, *vis-à-vis* the utopian vision of a future society in which socialism would lay the practical basis for living, and poetry – and by extension literature and art in general – would provide the spiritual one. In Cortázar's own vision, art and socialism follow, at least at this point, distinct parallel paths.

The second extensive quotation which shows how Cortázar understands the role of his art within the revolutionary process, comes from another of his letters, on this occasion to the surrealist poet and editor Jean Thiercelin. In this letter Cortázar elucidates and fervently defends his political position, yet once again manifests a degree of guilt for not doing that which is expected of him:

> Bien sur [*sic*], je ne suis pas Che Guevara, je ne te parle de monter ver les guérillas, mais d'une opération *analogue* tout en restant (es c'est cela le problème) dans la poésie, dans la littérature, dans les seules choses que je sais faire. Cuba a été comme un chemin de Damas sans choc visible – car je vois maintenant qu'il y a longtemps que je marchais à ma façon par ce chemin. Je voudrais faire profiter l'Amérique Latine de cet hasard insensé qui m'a fait devenir une espèce de *maître à sentir* (plus qu'à penser) des jeunes de mon pays et des autres pays latino-américains. Écrire, bien sûr mais de façon que cet amour qu'on a pour moi se traduise en force, en levure, en révolution. Et quand je dis révolution, j'entends aussi la lutte armée, les 'quatre ou cinq Vietnam' que demandait le Che. Or, comment concilier ceci avec mon refus total de faire une littérature "révolutionnaire" dans le sens où l'entendent une bonne partie des cubains? [...] comment donner le maximum de force à un œuvre qui aujourd'hui est attendu comme une espèce de pentecôte ? Car il y a quelque chose de terrible dans cette prise de conscience de moi-même que je viens d'avoir à La Havane : c'est de savoir que je ne peux pas refuser, que *je ne veux pas refuser*, que je voudrais vendre le plus cher possible la peau, c'est à dire aider de la façon la plus totale la cause de la révolution tel que l'entend Cuba.[24]

The fact that Cortázar is writing in French sets out *a priori* a different tone and perspective with regard to his own self-projected image. He becomes the expatriate Latin American intellectual writing in French. Although by 1968 Cortázar had been living in France for over fifteen years, French is not his mother tongue.

---

[24] Cortázar to Thiercelin, 2 February 1968, ibid., p. 1224.

This slight linguistic distancing – equivalent to the use of third-person in the previous example – allows Cortázar to describe his own position within literature and the revolution, without committing himself fully, either semantically or politically. This detachment is emphasised by his alluding to an 'hasard insensé' that led him to become some kind of '*maître à sentir* (plus qu'à penser) des jeunes de mon pays et des autres pays latino-américains'. This idea (where 'm'a fait devenir' is as conveniently impersonal as the previous 'me están llevando') rids Cortázar of any sense of responsibility, since it is 'fate', and not him, that has chosen this path.

What is striking about this excerpt is how palpable and Manichean Cortázar's sense of a split between his convictions about aesthetic freedom and his political commitment has become, and also how many images and metaphors he carries forward from one letter to the other, even though they were written a year apart and to different people. If to Fernández Retamar he spoke of his own 'manera de ser' marking the direction of his writings, in this letter Cortázar writes about his own way ('ma façon') of walking the road to Damascus which is the allegory that he uses recurrently to refer to his 'awakening' to Latin American reality after his Cuban 'epiphany'. It is worth underlining that on this occasion Cortázar refers to the road to Damascus not in terms of a sudden moment of realisation, but rather as a continuation of a path that he had already embarked upon. In the same self-mythologizing manner in which Cortázar claimed that up until Cuba he had been 'outside history', and therefore also outside politics, he now declares contradictorily that this socialist commitment is not new to him, echoing his words to Retamar: 'mi hasta entonces vago compromiso personal e intelectual con la lucha por el socialismo'. The repetition of imagery (his 'conscience de moi-même') at different times and in different contexts emphasises Cortázar's construction of, and reliance on, a mythologised self, which he can – and will – alter with hindsight. It also brings to the fore his attempt to justify his personal acts and his aesthetic choices *vis-à-vis* the political demands of the time.

How, then, can Cortázar retain his artistic freedom while at the same time fulfilling his 'duty' as a Latin American intellectual within the revolutionary process? In attempting to reconcile these two imperatives, Cortázar comes up with the concept of an 'opération analogue' that he sees as parallel to Ernesto Guevara's guerrilla warfare. The word 'opération' denotes several fields of action. Whether in mathematical, medical or militaristic terms, it implies a task that needs to be precise, rational and calculated. In the quotation, the idea of an operation is also linked to the linguistic exercise of translation ('cet amour qu'on a pour moi *se traduise* en force, en levure, en révolution'; my emphasis). It is apparent that Cortázar wants his literature to be effective in all the possible connotations of the word 'opération'. It is also important that it takes place alongside the revolutionary struggle, emphasising once again the idea of operations running parallel. The 'opération analogue' that Cortázar wants to achieve 'dans la poésie, dans la littérature' is problematic, however, because literature and politics have to be reconciled 'de manera directa o indirecta', yet without compromising artistic freedom.

It is, therefore, his unwillingness to bring his own literature within the confines of his political commitment that generates in Cortázar an internal division, and a correspondingly deep sense of guilt, which manifests itself through the abundance of religious imagery, not only in this quotation but also in many of his writings during this particular period. In the French quotation the religious allusion is present in 'un chemin de Damas', and crucially as part of Cortázar's fundamental question: 'comment donner le maximum de force à un œuvre qui aujourd'hui est attendu comme une espèce de *pentecôte*?' (my emphasis). Cortázar even understands his work to be comparable in influence to the Holy Spirit. His literature, through the 'opération analogue' will make readers speak in tongues, spreading the language of the revolution. Cortázar wants to make sure, somehow – and this is the crucial point – that the tongues are those of the revolution, the 'lenguaje' of political action. These messianic comparisons – to Che Guevara, to the Holy Spirit – bestow upon Cortázar a binding sense of responsibility, while positioning him in a place of self-sacrifice, of heroism, of martyrdom, of being effectively 'culpable de literatura', as he argues elsewhere. Yet, the idea of having to conform to a readership that expects a degree of commitment traps him. As Cortázar puts it, this 'prise de conscience de moi-même' implies something 'terrible' ('quelque chose de *terrible*'; my emphasis), comparable to the 'monstruoso' in the letter to Fernández Retamar.

The sense of radical split deepens as Cortázar's ideas unfold in this letter, particularly when he asks: 'comment concilier ceci [the political commitment] avec mon refus total de faire une littérature "révolutionnaire" dans le sens où l'entendent une bonne partie des cubains?' The uncertainty implied in the lack of a concrete answer is contrasted with the dogmatic inflexibility of his 'refus total' and in the subsequent uses of this very verb (refuser). Cortázar refuses to write 'revolutionary literature' in strictly socialist terms.[25] He claims: 'je ne peux pas refuser [...] *je ne veux pas refuser*'. In contrast to the pervasive use of the present tense, the following part of the clause appears in the conditional, as he writes that: 'je voudrais vendre le plus cher possible la peau'. As in the previous case, when Cortázar uses the conditional to say that 'je voudrais faire profiter l'Amérique Latine de cet hasard insensé', the use of this tense emphasises the hypothetical

---

[25] Reference to revolutionary literature in socialist terms takes into account, for example, Trotsky's idea that: 'During the period of revolution, only that literature which promotes the consolidation of the workers in their struggle against the exploiters is necessary and progressive. Revolutionary literature cannot but be imbued with a spirit of social hatred, which is a creative historic factor in an epoch of proletarian dictatorship': 'Revolutionary and Socialist Art', in *Literature and Revolution*, trans. Rose Strunsky (Ann Arbor: University of Michigan Press, 1971). pp. 228–54 at p. 228. This was first published in English in 1925.

meaning of such statements, a contrast to the definition and solidity of the ideas previously presented. This in turn makes even more significant what Cortázar presents as a possibility in case his 'opération analogue' fails, namely, that if he is going to sacrifice his literature (a sacrifice implied in the 'vendre le plus cher possible la peau'), then he would like that sacrifice to have maximum possible material benefit for the revolution ('aider de la façon la plus totale la cause de la révolution'). This will not be something that Cortázar comes back to during this period, yet it is what *Libro de Manuel* symbolises and embodies in many respects.

These two important quotations therefore provide a crucial insight into Cortázar's guilt-ridden internal conflict, between a sense of revolutionary duty, and a seemingly unshakeable belief in artistic freedom. It is in this context that Cortázar will set out to write literature during his post-*Rayuela* period, seeking for a manner that he can deem analogous to the revolution in Latin America, while also faithful to his own aesthetic beliefs. Cortázar does not specify, however, in what way this parallel aesthetic production can be of visible political benefit to the Cuban and Latin American revolutionary process. Nevertheless, it will become clearer that finding the way to reconcile these conflicting demands was for Cortázar, at this point, a challenge of paramount importance, one intrinsically connected to politics.

62/modelo para armar: 'insolemente literaria'

In 1969 David Viñas published an article that seemed to go against the dominant trends in literary criticism of that time.[26] One year on from the publication of *62*, Viñas issued a warning regarding what he called the 'dangers' of Cortázar's increasing influence upon new writers. Being fascinated by the labyrinths of formal experimentation embodied by *62* – Viñas claimed – would lead to nothing but the characteristics that he associated with the writer of *Rayuela*, namely, 'arrinconamiento creciente', 'abdicación de todo proyecto modificador', 'desinterés', 'enclaustramiento y encierro total'.[27] For Viñas, therefore, *62* was part of a process of de-politicisation that could only lead to arrogant isolation from socio-political realities and to political impotence (or some kind of ideological immobility or 'ataraxia moderada' as we saw embodied in Oliveira). Oscar Collazos, likewise, argued that novels like *62* were turning their back on the political concerns of Latin America in defence of their avant-garde aesthetic exploration.[28] In the face

---

[26] David Viñas, 'Después de Cortázar: historia y privatización', *Cuadernos hispanoamericanos*, 234 (June 1969), 734–9.

[27] Ibid., p. 738.

[28] Collazos, Cortázar and Vargas Llosa, *Literatura en la revolución y revolución en la literatura*, p. 29. See also Juan de Diego, 'De los setenta a los ochenta: la curva descendente en la valoración crítica de Cortázar', in *Actas del II Congreso Internacional CELEHIS de Literatura* (2004) <http://www.freewebs.com/celehis/actas2004/> [accessed 19 November 2008].

of such criticism, Cortázar felt moved to defend the literary experimentation of his novel, claiming that he *had to* write *62* as the 'experimento de la experimentación' in an attempt to 'seguir adelantándose' (*UR*1, 260), or in other words, in order to continue to explore uncharted aesthetic territories, irrespective of what political ideologies dictated. Being well aware of the reactions that *62* would spark, even before it was published, Cortázar wrote in a letter to Jean Bernabé:

> Es casi *divertido* decirle que [...] me dispongo a corregir [...] una novela que encolerizará a todos mis amigos "comprometidos" puesto que la encontrarán *insolentemente "literaria"*; yo sigo creyendo que por muchos caminos se va a la libertad del hombre e incluso al hombre nuevo que buscaba y quería el Che.[29]

Continuing with the religious imagery, Cortázar borrows from the phrase 'todos los caminos conducen a Roma' to attack once again the political dogmatism of what it meant to be a 'committed Latin American writer', while emphasising that there should not be just one way of expressing that commitment through literature. In turn, the mentioning of the *hombre nuevo* and Cortázar's awareness of Che Guevara's socio-political ambitions, are reflected in the short story 'Reunión', written in 1964 and included in *Todos los fuegos el fuego*.

'Reunión' could be said to be Cortázar's first visible fictional attempt to reconcile his adherence to the Cuban revolution and to socialism with his artistic principles.[30] The story depicts a realistic recreation of the Cuban guerrilla in the *sierra*. Its protagonist and narrator is clearly Che Guevara himself. Discussing the motives that pushed him to write this story, Cortázar claimed:

> Si ser castrista es tener fe en un futuro socialista [...] de los países latinoamericanos, entonces soy castrista. [...] Pero el cuento ['Reunión'] no fue escrito *por eso*. La verdad, como siempre, es múltiple. En el avión, de vuelta de La Habana, leí el texto del Che, y me fastidió su pobreza literaria. [...] Puesto que yo era un escritor, ¿por qué no potenciar esa historia hasta un terreno realmente literario, que quizá le diera más realidad, en un sentido último, que esa mezcla de historia y de literatura mediocre que advertía el texto?[31]

---

[29] Cortázar to Jean Bernabé, 30 January 1968, *Cartas/2 1964–1968*, p. 1222. My emphasis.
[30] Cortázar, 'Reunión', in *Cuentos completos/1*, pp. 537–47. First published in *Todos los fuegos el fuego* (1966).
[31] Cortázar to Jean L. Andreu, 3 October 1967, *Cartas/2 1964–1968*, pp. 1195-6. It was fascinating to learn, in conversation with Roberto Fernández Retamar that when, after talking to Che Guevara about 'Reunión', Retamar informed Cortázar that Guevara had not rated the story very highly, Cortázar was altogether quite disappointed (not to say vexed). 'No le hizo mucha gracia, la verdad', Retamar claimed with irony: personal interview, 26 May 2009, University of Manchester.

Through Cortázar's explanation we get an insight into his rhetoric of self-justification, on the one hand, and also of extravagant aloofness, on the other. That he sees his literary skills to be greater than those of Che could be reasonable, yet it is interesting to note that Cortázar believes that by giving the text a completely literary dimension – rather than it being partly testimonial and partly 'mediocre' fiction – it would become 'more real'. This relates directly to his conception of writing literature as an 'opération analogue', whereby within his role as a writer, Cortázar writes the revolution as fiction in order to incorporate it to the reality of his readers.

It is due to its 'insolent literariness' that *62/modelo para armar* could be said to represent one of the two paths in Cortázar's post-Cuba split. Indeed, given its hermeticism, *62* exemplifies the path of the debatable 'ficción pura'.[32] Due to its content and its formal complexity, *62* has largely been considered an ahistorical and explicitly non-political novel; for critics such as Jason Weiss, this was only natural, for Cortázar had always insisted that his artistic freedom was not to be compromised to serve any purpose other than its own.[33] For other critics and fellow Latin American writers *62* was simply unacceptable if Cortázar were to be taken 'seriously' as a committed socialist writer.[34] Yet it is clear from Cortázar's letter – as he writes that he finds it 'divertido' to predict the polemic he will spark among 'committed' writers – 'seriousness' was never at the centre of Cortázar's concerns, even less so when it came to politics. On the contrary, he will insist on the urgent need for humour within the somewhat rigid political revolution. In effect, this is reflected in *62*:

> Ninguno de nosotros era verdaderamente serio […] y lo que nos había reunido en la ciudad, en la zona, en la vida, era precisamente un alegre y obstinado pisoteo de decálogos. Cada uno a su manera, el pasado nos había enseñado la inutilidad profunda de ser serios, de apelar a la seriedad en los momentos de crisis, de agarrarse por las solapas y exigir conductas o decisiones o renuncias; nada podía ser más lógico que esa tácita complicidad que nos había reunido en torno de mi paredro para entender de otra manera la existencia y los sentimientos, caminar por rumbos que no eran los

---

[32] As Luisa Valenzuela put it, '*62* es la novela [de Cortázar] más pura, estéticamente hablando': personal interview, Buenos Aires, 19 December 2008. Or, in the words of Beatriz Sarlo, '[*62*] es la más difícil, la más discutida y la más perfecta': 'Una literatura de pasajes', in *Escritos sobre literatura argentina* (Buenos Aires: Siglo XXI, 2007), pp. 262–6 at p. 265.

[33] Jason Weiss, 'Interstitial spaces (Julio Cortázar)', in his *The Lights of Home: A Century of Latin American Writers in Paris* (London: Routledge, 2003), pp. 81–93 at p. 91.

[34] Among other descriptions, Oscar Collazos claimed that works like *62* with its 'enunciados del estructuralismo europeo' led to nothing but 'el distanciamiento cada vez más radical de la realidad y su canalización, el olvido de lo real circundante, el aplazamiento de las circunstancias objetivas que lo rodean': 'La encrucijada del lenguaje', in Collazos, Cortázar and Vargas Llosa, *Literatura en la revolución y revolución en la literatura*, pp. 7–37 at pp. 10–11.

aconsejables en cada circunstancia, dejándonos llevar, saltando a un tranvía como lo había hecho Juan en la ciudad, o quedándonos en una cama como yo seguía haciéndolo con Nicole, sospechando sin razones ni demasiado interés que todo eso tendía o distendía a su manera lo que en el plano de la razón sensata se hubiera traducido en explicaciones, cartas, mucho teléfono y quizá tentativas de suicidio o viajes repentinos a la acción política o a las islas del Pacífico. Mi paredro, me parece, había sostenido alguna vez que nos basábamos mucho más en un mínimo común múltiplo que en un máximo común divisor, aunque vaya a saber lo que había querido decir. (*62*, 83)

So, although the novel is not explicitly political, it is permeated with the ideas that Cortázar was dealing with at the time, which inevitably included politics, with the expectations of committed literature and indeed, with the degree of seriousness with which political issues should be tackled within literature. As well as ideas like the ones cited, it could be said that like the 'Club de la Serpiente' in *Rayuela*, in *62* there is also a 'revolutionary' group, yet this is a group based upon a seemingly utopian point of view, which relates to the more *avant-garde* aim of wanting to break with the tradition of a pre-established order. Unequivocally less active than 'la Joda' of *Libro de Manuel* and their *microagitaciones*, the groups in *Rayuela* as in *62* present themselves as bourgeois, aloof and decentred (typically *avant-garde* as Jean Franco would argue), yet there is certainly a presence of a group concept somewhat unified by one drive in *62*.[35]

This novel, like most of the others, also begins with an introductory note. Here, Cortázar explains that this particular text stems from chapter 62 of *Rayuela*, in which Morelli establishes that in his ideal novel,

Todo sería como una inquietud, un desasosiego, un desarraigo continuo, un territorio donde la causalidad psicológica cedería desconcertada, y esos fantoches [los personajes] se destrozarían o se amarían o se reconocerían sin sospechar demasiado que la vida trata de cambiar la clave en y a través y por ellos. (*R*, 369)

Following Morelli's principles, *62* is a novel that defies standard notions of fixity in the reading experience, while challenging conventional formulations of linearity, characterisation and narratology. Unlike 'El Aleph', where Borges writes, 'Arribo, ahora, al inefable centro de mi relato; empieza, aquí, mi desesperación

---

[35] Jean Franco, 'Julio Cortázar: Utopia and Everyday Life', *Inti*, 10–11 (1979–80), 108–18 at p. 115. See also María Cristina Pons, 'Compromiso político y ficción en "Segunda vez" y "Apocalipsis de Solentiname" de Julio Cortázar', *Revista Mexicana de Sociología*, 54/4 (October–December 1992), 183–203.

de escritor', *62* has no thematic centre.[36] Ultimately, the very a-centredness of *62* must be understood paradoxically as the novel's unifying theme. It could be argued that *62* is that Flaubertian 'novela de la nada', which, more than a decade earlier, even before Morelli, Andrés Fava aimed to write (*DAF*, 112).[37]

The novel is thus a Morellian text that, among the other intentions laid out in chapter 62 of *Rayuela*, attempts to realise the 'old' Cortazarian idea of the 'figuras' (searched for by Persio in *Los premios*, imagined by Morelli in *Rayuela*).[38] The text is made up of unconnected fragments which, given its subtitle, the reader will hope to assemble somehow. In the introductory note Cortázar mockingly warns his readers that the assemblage that the novel requires will not be intra-textual, as it was in *Rayuela*, but rather, arguably as part of the book's 'diversas transgresiones a la convención literaria' (*62*, 7), the montage will be extra-textual, that is, it will take place *a posteriori* and outside the text. Cortázar explains that the montage which the reader is meant to carry out should be 'como una decantación posterior a la lectura, en la que el lector debe escoger lo que cuenta y lo que finalmente puede dar un sentido a tanta insensatez parcial'.[39] Within *62*'s 'exploración de lo exploratorio', as Cortázar put it, this could be how he intended to carry out the 'opération analogue': through the *a posteriori* mental process carried out by the reader in response to the novel's 'irrupciones intersticiales' (*UR*1, 261). Furthermore, the search for rational sense within 'tanta insensatez parcial' need not be restricted to the aesthetic realm of the novel, but could effectively be extended to the day-to-day world of the reader. This in turn relates to the understanding that Cortázar had of literature as a means to opening oneself to different views of reality. In a lecture he gave in 1980, and

---

[36] Jorge Luis Borges, 'El Aleph', *Obras completas 1923-1949*, pp. 617–28 at p. 624.

[37] This comes from the well-known notion by Gustave Flaubert, wherein he establishes that he aims to write 'un livre sans attache extérieure, qui se tiendrait de lui-même par la force interne de son style, comme la terre sans être soutenue se tient en l'air, un livre qui n'aurait presque pas de sujet ou du moins où le sujet serait presque invisible': 'Lettre à Louise Colet', 16 January 1852, in *Correspondance II*, ed. J. Bruneau (Paris: Gallimard, 1980), p. 31.

[38] The notion of *figura* is central to Cortázar's writings. It is worth bearing in mind how he himself defined it in his interview with Luis Harss: 'La noción de figura va a servirme instrumentalmente porque representa un enfoque muy diferente del habitual en cualquier novela o narración donde se tiende a individualizar a los personajes y a darles una psicología y características propias. Quisiera escribir de manera tal que la narración estuviera llena de vida, en su sentido más profundo, llena de acción y de sentido, y que al mismo tiempo esa vida, esa acción y ese sentido no se refieran ya a la mera acción de los individuos, sino a una especie de superación de las figuras formadas por constelaciones de personajes. [...] Quisiera llegar a escribir un relato capaz de mostrar cómo esas figuras constituyen una ruptura y un desmentido de la realidad individual, muchas veces sin que los personajes tengan menor conciencia de ello': *Los nuestros*, pp. 288–9. Through this explanation, Cortázar puts forward the main features of *62*. Yet although the notion of *figura* is mainly linked to this novel, it appears in Morelli's notes and is at the centre of many of Persio's formulations.

[39] Cortázar to Graciela Maturo, 28 February 1969, *Cartas/3 1969–1983*, ed. Aurora Bernárdez (Buenos Aires: Alfaguara, 2000), p. 1333.

known under the title of 'Realidad y literatura en América Latina', Cortázar claimed that 'la literatura no nació para dar respuestas, tarea que constituye la finalidad específica de la ciencia y de la filosofía, sino más bien para hacer preguntas, para abrir la inteligencia y la sensibilidad a nuevas perspectivas de lo real'.[40] To an extent, the very circularity of *62*'s structure could be emphasising an idea of the endless questioning of reality, a constant non-acceptance of our circumstances.[41]

Admittedly, unlike the novels discussed so far, there is no representation – 'de manera directa o indirecta' – of the political in this text. Yet, the fact that Cortázar wrote *62* after his political 'conversion' to socialism not only undermines the image of the politicised Cortázar, whose writings were supposedly hampered by his political views, it also puts forward Cortázar's firm belief in artistic freedom as a political act. In other words, *62* escapes the confines of revolutionary literature, which Cortázar understood to be dogmatic and inflexible, and exposes ideas that have more to do with a kind of 'internal', subjective revolution and questioning than with a collective, political project.

It should be noted, however, that despite the general thematic abstractness of *62*, there are indeed references to certain concrete political events, such as the Tutsi massacre in the then recently independent African nation of Burundi:

> ¿Leíste lo que pasó esta semana en Burundi, Celia? Desde luego, no sabes ni siquiera que Burundi existe, que es una nación independiente y soberana. [...] En Burundi hubo una sublevación, querida; los rebeldes se apoderaron de todos los diputados y los senadores, en total unos noventa, y los fusilaron en masa. Casi a la misma hora el rey de Burundi [...] se entrevistaba aquí con de Gaulle, gran ceremonia en un salón con espejos, zalemas y probablemente ayuda técnica y esas cosas. ¿Cómo no comprender que Marrast y Tell que son sensibles a cosas así, y hasta Juan que es menos sensible porque vive un poco de ellas, decidan que lo único posible es hacerle la vida imposible a un director de museo, o que hay que enviarle inmediatamente una muñeca a la amiga solitaria de la rué de la Clef?
> –Dan ganas de bañarla –dijo Celia que se preocupaba muy poco por los parlamentarios de Burundi–, de darle de comer, de cambiarle los pañales. Pero es falso, apenas la miras bien te das cuenta de que no es un bebé, y entonces [...]. Dormir entonces, el olvido pequeño... (*62*, 143-4).

---

[40] Julio Cortázar, 'Realidad y literatura en América Latina', *Obra crítica/3*, pp. 303–21 at p. 309.

[41] The final words of the novel ('Bisbis bisbis': *62*, 269), uttered by Feuille Morte and meaning 'repetition' times four, refer the reader back to the text just read, so that the text repeats itself indefinitely, 'el final como principio' (*62*, 77). As Blanca Anderson puts it, 'no hay principio ni final; estos son los orígenes de la novela que busca sus orígenes': *Julio Cortázar: la imposibilidad de narrar* (Madrid: Pliegos, 1990), p. 119. *62* begins with the act of reading (Juan at the Polidor restaurant, reading the book that he has just bought, reading the images in the mirror, and so forth), and it ends by alluding to the act of reading.

The portrayal of Celia as someone who would not have learned about the events that took place in Burundi, and is actually assumed to be altogether ignorant about the mere existence of Burundi, emphasises the characteristics of the group as a whole, and certainly indicates a degree of scornful criticism from the narrator's point of view. The characters' obliviousness is part of their recourse to absurdist provocation, which in turn should be compared to 'la Joda's' *microagitaciones* in *Libro de Manuel*. And of course this is not the sole point of comparison. The fact that an external, actual historical fact is being woven into, and made part of, the narrative plot of *62*, is at the centre of the political significance of Cortázar's final novel. In *The Novels of Julio Cortázar*, Steven Boldy argues that whereas in *Rayuela* the *figura* was formed by the repetition, or at least the influence, of the acts of partly the same group of people elsewhere, in *62*, 'the *figuras* are based mainly on independent literary texts and myths', such as Parsifal, Diana and Acteon, Heliogabalus and the vampirism motif.[42] The novel is a reflection of an infinite chain of other texts, emphasising the argument of *62* as a *figura*, in the sense that the novel is also being other novels at the same time of being *62*. Cortázar, as the 'author within the constellation', elucidates how this process came about: 'Apenas empezada la escritura de *62*, mis lecturas paralelas, hechas siempre al azar y cediendo a los caprichos del momento, fueron mostrando segmentos, versos, imágenes que no solamente coincidían con lo que yo estaba tratando de fijar en la novela sino que eran esa tentativa misma.'[43] This is not a dissimilar process from the one reflected in *Libro de Manuel*, where all those 'lecturas paralelas' are not mere allusions, or indeed *figuras*, but are an inextricable – and, indeed, very politically meaningful – part of the text.

Nonetheless there is an argument for the more holistic political significance of *62* as a symbolic act of defiant aesthetic freedom. The critic Francisco de la Guerra claims that the specific, explicit allusions to actual political events constitute an unambiguous political dimension. In his analysis of political thought in Cortázar, de la Guerra asserts, for instance, that the novel contains references to the recent killing of Che Guevara and, in particular, to the effects that this had on the author, exposing Cortázar's sympathies for Che Guevara and his support for the Cuban cause. De la Guerra claims that when Hélène imagines the relatives of the deceased Juan look-alike 'llorando solitariamente en el fondo de un water, avergonzados y temblando y cigarrillo' (*62*, 168), Cortázar is actually alluding to his own feelings on hearing about the death of Guevara.[44] This seems unlikely given that when Cortázar found out about Guevara's death he wrote to Fernández Retamar:

---

[42] Boldy, *The Novels of Julio Cortázar*, p. 117.

[43] González Bermejo, *Revelaciones de un cronopio*, p. 89; 'Se necesitaba que el autor formara de algún modo parte de la constelación', p. 94.

[44] Francisco E. De La Guerra Castellanos, *Julio Cortázar: literatura y revolución* (Mexico City: UNAM, 2000), p. 118.

> No sé escribir cuando algo me duele tanto, no soy, no seré nunca un escritor profesional listo a producir lo que se espera de él, lo que le piden o lo que él mismo se pide desesperadamente. La verdad es que la escritura, hoy y frente a esto, me parece la más banal de las artes, una especie de refugio, de disimulo casi, de sustitución de lo insustituible.[45]

In many respects, the aesthetic exploration which *62* epitomises, as well as manifesting a belief in artistic freedom, also confirms Cortázar's refusal to succumb to what Goloboff calls 'la comodidad intelectual'.[46] Rather than frequenting the familiar, profitable paths opened up by the success of *Rayuela*, Cortázar instead chose to venture into what for him were uncharted aesthetic territories, arguably as a way of inviting the reader too to question reality through different means.

This is what Cortázar would also try to explore in books such as *Prosa del observatorio* (1972), where, as Evelyn Picon Garfield succinctly puts it,

> Cortázar appears to emulate the interplay of light and dark in the photographs by juxtaposing observations on the sultan's exploration of the heavens two centuries ago with observations on scientific studies in our century of eel migration in the seas. In so doing, Cortázar considers broader issues: how man confronts the unknown and acquires information about it, and how that knowledge effects a continued investigation of reality or a complacent, passive satisfaction with it. [...] Cortázar broaches the universal dilemma of mankind bent upon seeking answers to enigmas that stubbornly resist both reason and experience.[47]

As in the case of *62*, in *Prosa* Cortázar goes beyond mere factual reality to investigate visual appearances, emphasising interstices, exceptions and strange analogies, rather than absolute, 'serious' truths. In effect, and as Picon Garfield argues, this 'interstitial alley' embodied in *Prosa*, astride two realities, reflects the actions of many of his fictional characters who, like the eels in *Prosa*, partake in the two worlds 'flotando entre dos aguas' (*PRO*, 15): the protagonist of 'Axolotl', Alina Reyes in 'Lejana' and of course, Horacio Oliveira and his dilemmas.[48]

---

[45] Cortázar to Fernández Retamar, 29 October 1967, *Cartas/2 1964–1968*, p. 1200.

[46] Goloboff, *Julio Cortázar: la biografía*, p. 187.

[47] Evelyn Picon Garfield, 'Julio Cortázar's "Redheaded Night": Or Notes on Ordering the Universe in *Prosa del observatorio*', *Review on Contemporary Fiction*, 3/3 (1983), 71–7 at p. 71. Significantly, the photographs that constitute *Prosa del observatorio* were taken by Cortázar in 1968 (the year in which *62* was published), during his visit to Jai Singh's observatories in India: *Prosa del observatorio* (Barcelona: Lumen, 1972).

[48] Picon Garfield, '"Redheaded Night"', p. 72.

As will become clear, in particular with reference to Lonstein in *Libro de Manuel*, what Cortázar is trying to show at this stage is indeed an exploration of the many ways in which to express political rebellion, which does not have to be by any means dictated by given dogmas. Revolution, Cortázar seems to be saying, is not just about the liberation of the collective and its historical destiny, but also of the individual and his/her desires. Like *62, Prosa del observatorio* insists on a kind of 'compromiso cortazariano entre lo fantástico y una estética revolucionaria', as Marcy Schwartz puts it, bringing to the fore aesthetic freedom in a world of urban alienation and transnational post-colonialism.[49] And Jaime Alazraki goes as far as to assert that '*Prosa del observatorio* entrelaza poesía, ensayo y ficción para producir un manifiesto político.'[50]

Nonetheless, the question remains: how can this 'exploración de lo exploratorio' be used to fight for, or contribute to, the revolutionary cause? Within Cortázar's utter refusal to write a dogmatic kind of 'revolutionary literature', *62* is part of the attempt to create an 'opération *analogue* tout en restant [...] dans la poésie, dans la littérature'. Perhaps *62* was for Cortázar 'la façon la plus totale' to fight for the *hombre nuevo* and for Cuba: attempting to awaken a sense of freedom through hermetic, aesthetic exploration. Cortázar expresses this possibility in his letter to Thiercelin in January 1968, when he asserts:

> Me creo bastante a salvo de ilusiones, pero hay a mi espalda treinta años de vocación literaria y de dedicación a la escritura; quisiera aprovechar todavía todo eso y a la vez encontrar *la fórmula central*, la clave que lo potenciara hacia lo que hoy me parece la obligación insoslayable de eso que llaman un intelectual.[51]

The search for that 'fórmula central' – parallel (as the phrase 'a la vez' suggests) to his artistic 'vocación' – correlates to the attempt to achieve the 'opération analogue', namely, being a committed writer without sacrificing the artist's freedom to explore new aesthetic possibilities.

The extra-textual montage that Cortázar calls for at the beginning of the novel could then be translated as a demand for the 'active reader' to convert the very abstract, metaphysical concepts presented in *62* into some form of political action that would be somehow useful in the revolutionary process. That action could even be reflected upon the freedom embodied in the writing *per se* of *62* in times of revolutionary struggle. Yet, when *62* came out, it was apparent that readers did not understand the idea that Cortázar was trying to put across. This

---

[49] Marcy E. Schwartz, 'Del lado de acá/del lado de allá: la mirada fotográfica de Julio Cortázar, entre continentes', *Matérika* 9 (2005), 28–39 at p. 32.

[50] Jaime Alazraki, 'Tema y sistema de *Prosa del observatorio* de Julio Cortázar', *La Torre* 1.1 (1987), 92–110 at p. 104.

[51] Cortázar to Jean Thiercelin, 30 January 1968, *Cartas/2 1964–1968*, p. 1221. My emphasis.

becomes evident when, in a letter to Graciela Maturo, Cortázar admits that writing *62* was in fact a mistake:

> me equivoqué conmigo y con ellos [los lectores]; debí llevar la sequedad al límite. [...] Finalmente *62* es un libro híbrido por debilidad mía, y no me volverá a suceder; o escribiré para divertirme [...] o llevaré hasta sus últimas consecuencias lo que pretendí sin lograrlo del todo en *62*.[52]

This self-confessed 'error' could be linked not to some aesthetic aspiration, but rather to Cortázar's wish to write literature as an 'opération analogue'. *62* could be seen, in other words, as Cortázar's last attempt at carrying out this 'opération analogue' without sacrificing his views on literature by having to create a very explicitly political text. Since Cortázar understood *62* as a failure in terms of its reception, he had to rethink his position in the light of his own internal conflict. Many critics would argue that Cortázar's 'vendre le plus cher possible la peau' came five years later, with the publication of *Libro de Manuel*.

Imagining the city: *Buenos Aires, Buenos Aires*

In addition to *62*, in 1968 Cortázar also published *Buenos Aires, Buenos Aires*, in collaboration with the Argentinian photographers Sara Facio and Alicia D'Amico. The book displays the photographers' black-and-white images of Buenos Aires alongside texts written by Cortázar. These are remarkable for their lyricism, each paragraph being a poetic description of typical scenes of the capital city, perceptibly rose-tinted. In this portrayal of – to use Susan Sontag's expression – the 'marginal beauties' that the photographs depict, and despite Cortázar's conversion to socialism having been consolidated by this time, the reader can still perceive a latent tension in Cortázar's relationship with the Peronist masses, though now overlaid with cynical scorn for the upper classes and their habits.[53] For example, he writes:

> los domingos son del pobre, inútil que yates y petisos de polo, inútil que autos con chofer y que mandatarios y estancieras en peristilos o palacetes, el domingo porteño es ese camión donde los muchachos se instalan a mama y a

---

[52] Cortázar to Graciela Maturo, 28 February 1969, *Cartas/3 1969-1983*, p. 1333. It is interesting that Cortázar should choose the adjective 'híbrido' to describe his novel, when its major 'fault', according to those intellectuals who criticised it, was that it was too hermetic and abstract, that it was, almost exclusively concerned with aesthetic preoccupations and challenges. It could be argued that, following the definition from the Real Academia Española of 'híbrido' as 'un individuo cuyos padres son genéticamente distintos con respecto a un mismo carácter', or 'todo lo que es producto de elementos de distinta naturaleza', Cortázar is here understanding *62* as the product of both his political and his aesthetic interests, yet only giving prevalence to one.
[53] Susan Sontag, *On Photography* (Harmondsworth: Penguin, 1979), p. 88.

tía, ponen el cajoncito de cerveza y los chorizos para la parrillada, la sandía, la radio, entre discusiones y silbidos y Dios querido carpeteá esa nube, a ver si ahora yueve [sic] justo cuando estábamos fenómeno.[54]

The emulation of the working-class vernacular, and its orthographical mistakes, reminds us of the moment in *El examen* when the middle-class protagonists adopt this same colloquial speech as a form of patronising amusement. At the same time, it is clearly comparable to Cortázar's short story 'Torito', in which however the emulation of working-class slang is based on admiration.[55] The crucial difference is that whereas in *El examen* (and some early short stories such as 'La banda' or 'Las ménades') the working class is portrayed as a mass, and their speech mocked with disdain, in 'Torito' the focus of emulation, although from a lower class, is a successful individual, someone who has stepped out from the mass, the Peronist mass. In *Buenos Aires, Buenos Aires* we see another step in that transition from disgust for the anti-Peronist mass, through appreciation for the individual that stands out from that mass, to sympathy for the lifestyle and values of the lower classes. Yet, that sympathy is here somewhat ambivalent in that what appears to be rooted in appreciation could equally be read as stemming from belittling disdain.

Buenos Aires, Buenos Aires is above all an unchallenging book of photographs; in other words, there are no images in the book that could be said to confront the reader with uncomfortable, provocative depictions of poverty or violence. The Buenos Aires of the late 1960s is portrayed as a city of culture, tradition and sophistication, as even the scenes of poverty are presented in an aesthetically pleasing manner. It seems that Cortázar's accompanying words aim to bring those that are left out of the pictures into the foreground, yet interestingly his discourse is still tainted with atavistic anti-Peronist biases.[56] His narrative picture of the poor therefore comes through as apprehensive, detached and stereotypical, far from how one would expect of a 'politicised' left-wing committed intellectual. Cortázar's other mixed-media work and collaborations, which include photographs taken by the writer himself and were published, like

---

[54] Julio Cortázar, *Buenos Aires, Buenos Aires*, with photographs by Alicia D'Amico and Sara Facio (Buenos Aires: Sudamericana, 1968), p. 148.

[55] The first-person narrator speaks only using this jargon being the lyrical incarnation of Argentinian lightweight boxing champion, Justo 'Torito' Suárez. Born in the very marginal barrio of Mataderos (hence, his nickname), Suárez, who fought in the early 1930s, was the first popular Argentinian boxing icon, bringing a radical social change to the sport itself, which, until then, was exclusively linked to the higher classes of Buenos Aires. 'Torito' first appeared in *Final del juego* in 1956, and was reprinted in *Cuentos completos/1*, pp. 360-6.

[56] 'Atavistic' because the Peronist mass which Cortázar seems to be criticising is one that in the late 1960s can no longer be identified as the working class. After the coup against Perón in 1955, and until his return from exile in 1973, Peronism divided into many different, even ideologically opposed, strands.

book-ends, on either side of *Buenos Aires, Buenos Aires* and *62*, attempt, however, to show something less contradictory through what may be called 'the politics of collage': *La vuelta al día en ochenta mundos* and *Último Round*.

The politics of collage

Although *La vuelta* and its stylistic sequel, *Último Round*, are nowadays reprinted as two-volume sets, they were both single volumes in their original edition.[57] In the case of *Último Round*, the original edition had a 'piso de arriba' and a 'piso de abajo', so that the reader could play at combining the upper part of the page with the lower one; the book is therefore in itself physically many books. The artist Julio Silvia, close friend of Cortázar's and collaborator on the book, explains the format:

> *Último Round* fue construido cortando las páginas, de modo que se crearon dos pisos autónomos. Esto permitía un arte combinatoria. El texto se podía leer de varias maneras. En todo esto hay un ejercicio lúdico, donde el actor es el lector, que puede elegir su lectura, la posibilidad de intercambiar texto e imagen. La idea también era un poco la del tarot, mezclar las imágenes de arriba con las de abajo, como los textos, en general, eran muy cortos.[58]

Both *La vuelta* and *Último Round* escape 'conventional' narrative forms, offering through their collage a compilation of poems, speeches, literary analysis, photographs, engravings, personal anecdotes, short stories, quotations, drawings and, indeed, political provocation. According to Alberto Giordano these books display purposefully disconcerting attributes for which the author wants to be

---

[57] After more than thirty years, in February and March 2010, these two collage books were reprinted in their original formats: *La vuelta al día en ochenta mundos* and *Último Round* by RM (Barcelona: 2010).

[58] Marisol L. Chávez, 'Entrevista con Julio Silva: papeles, trazos y testimonios', *Revista de la Universidad de México*, 51 (May 2008), 49–56 at p. 55. The comparison between the collage book and the idea behind the 'tarot' reminds the reader of Italo Calvino's *Il castello dei destini incrociati* (Turin: Einaudi, 1973), where tarot works as the basis for constructing the narratives. Both Cortázar and Silva would have been well-acquainted with Calvino's work; indeed, Cortázar quotes him on the cover of *Último Round* (*UR*1, front cover). The reference also appears in the poem 'El gran juego' (*UR*2, 92–3) where the comparison between literature and tarot or, more precisely, a game of cards, is drawn again: 'pero no sé si la baraja / la mezclan el azar o el ángel / si estoy jugando o soy las cartas'. This takes us back to the quotations analysed at the beginning of the chapter where Cortázar refers to the 'hasard' and the third-person phrase 'me están llevando' to indicate that that which he does or can do is ultimately out of his control, and thus, not his responsibility. See also *La vuelta*, pp. 53–5. The image recurs in *62*, when Juan tells Hélène: 'tú y yo sabemos demasiado de algo que no es nosotros y juega estas barajas en las que somos espadas o corazones [...] juego vertiginoso del que sólo alcanzamos a conocer la suerte que se teje y se desteje a cada lance, la figura que nos antecede o que nos sigue [...] la batalla de azares excluyentes que decide las posturas y las renuncias': *62*, 38.

known, namely: 'la informalidad, el sentido de lo insólito y excepcional, la voluntad de transgresión'.[59] Hence, after *Rayuela*, Cortázar's creative path bifurcates not only in terms of political expression, but also as regards the demands and expectations that he has about his readers. If in *62*, through its implicit fragmentary abstract images, Cortázar calls for a montage that is internal, extratextual and takes place *a posteriori*, in *La vuelta* and *Último Round*, the demand for response is immediate. Images are explicit and the montage, as well as intertextual, is intra-textual and simultaneous (that is, it does not take place *a posteriori*). In that immediate provocation lies the most prominent political element in these two collage books, one which is crucial to understanding the progression to Cortázar's final novel, *Libro de Manuel*.

As well as being part of the content, form becomes a vital element in the political dimension of *Último Round* and *La vuelta*. Both texts bring to the reader an awareness of what literature is and what the writer is expected to deliver. They also make the reader re-evaluate his/her position in the world, and question how that position is affected by everything and everyone around them. This is an idea that Cortázar had begun exploring in his early days and one that he had already tried to develop in *Imagen de John Keats* (written between 1951 and 1952) in particular through the notion of 'permeabilidad'. It is this 'permeability' which, as Santiago Colás argues, is at the root of Cortázar's broader conception of quoting and quoting oneself ('citarse').[60] This is manifested in the opening section of *La vuelta* when Cortázar elucidates: 'Se habrá advertido que aquí las citas llueven, y esto no es nada al lado de lo que viene, o sea casi todo. En los ochenta mundos de mi vuelta al día hay puertos, hoteles y camas para los cronopios, y además *citar es citarse*' (*LV*1, 9; my emphasis). Thus, within the book as well as intertextually, each fragment permeates through to other segments. In a technique that foreshadows *Libro de Manuel*, each piece of the puzzle that both *La vuelta* and *Último Round* represent, like the newspaper clippings in the final novel, is a quotation about Cortázar's day-to-day artistic life, yet they also function as citations of his understanding of contemporaneous political realities.

If *62* stems from chapter 62 of *Rayuela*, it could be said that both *La vuelta* and *Último Round* also emerge from that novel, in particular, from Morelli's concept of the 'novela almanaque', inspired by 'su lado Bouvard et Pécuchet, su lado compilador' (*R*, 376).[61] *Rayuela*'s extra-diegetic narrator clarifies that Morelli in

---

[59] Alberto Giordano, 'Cortázar en los 60: ensayo y autofiguración', in his *Modos del ensayo: de Borges a Piglia* (Buenos Aires: Beatriz Viterbo, 2005), pp. 169-76 at p. 171.

[60] For further analysis on quoting and quotations in Cortázar, see Santiago Colás, 'Writing Life and Love: Julio Cortázar and Gilles Deleuze', *Angelaki*, 2/1 (1996), 199–207.

[61] The concept of 'almanac' features prominently in Dadaism, with the *Dada Almanach* being one of the periodicals that the Dadaists published in 1920. See *The Dada Almanac*, ed. Richard Huelsenbeck, trans. Barbara Wright and James Kirkup (London: Atlas Press, 1993). When thinking about the collage nature of *La vuelta* and *Último Round*, Cortázar, influenced by Dadaism and Surrealism, would have been aware of how the Dadaists employed this concept.

fact 'llama "Almanaque" a la suma de su obra' (*R*, 376). Both ideas can be applied to *La vuelta* and *Último Round*, for they make up a collection of pataphysical (that is, that they deal with 'the science of imaginary solutions') aleatory ideas, while containing recurrent intertextual references.[62] For instance, in *La vuelta* there are allusions to *Rayuela*, *Los premios*, *Historias de cronopios y de famas*, and in some of the excerpts in *Último Round*, Calac and Polanco from *62* are the narrators.

The concept of 'almanaque' also refers to the 'almanaque del mensajero', an annual booklet that used to circulate in Argentina during the first half of the twentieth century. Cortázar himself describes it as he reminisces in his 1977 television interview with Joaquín Soler Serrano:

> El 'almanaque del mensajero' [...] estaba destinado sobre todo a la gente del campo, porque contenía calendarios, recetas de cocina, horóscopos, medicina del hogar, pequeños cuentos, poemas, acertijos, destrabalenguas [sic], laberintos para los niños [...] había de todo para la familia. Y claro en esas familias o analfabetas o apenas alfabetas, ese almanaque del mensajero, les cubría todo un año. Era útil porque les daba los elementos necesarios: cómo hay que curar la enfermedad de una vaca que se enfermó, ese tipo de cosas, y al mismo tiempo tenían un contenido estético, inocente, pero muy bello.[63]

The pictorial insertions bring to the books another of Morelli's notions, that of 'dibujar ciertas ideas' (*R*, 376). In addition, as in the original 'almanaque del mensajero', they establish a link between the utility and effectiveness of the visual aesthetic elements. The images are an attempt to finally break away from the desperate ineffability that haunts many of Cortázar's protagonists – from Andrés Fava to Horacio Oliveira, to *62*'s Juan – in the sense that they display visually what the characters cannot name. This, as we saw, would also be the case in the later *Prosa del observatorio*, where Cortázar once again considers the combination of images and text in the attempt to expose, in his words, 'Todo eso que no tiene nombre [y que] se llama de tantas maneras' (*PRO*, 23). The placing of images and drawings in these collage books emphasises Cortázar's increasing interest in the 'observable', and in the direct and immediate provoca-

---

[62] Alfred Jarry, who coined the term 'pataphysics, proposed: '[Elle] décrira un univers que l'on peut voir et que peut-être l'on doit voir a la place du traditionnel, les lois que l'on a cru découvrir de l'univers traditionnel étant des corrélations d'exceptions aussi, quoique plus fréquentes, en tout cas de faits accidentels qui, se redisant a des exceptions peu exceptionnelles, n'ont même pas l'attrait de la singularité': *Gestes et opinions du docteur Faustroll*, in *Œuvres complètes* (Paris: Laussane, 1950), pp. 187–254 at p. 21). Regarding the pataphysical content of these two books, Sara Castro-Klarén asserts that 'These objects are not so much works as acts of "pataphysical endeavour"': 'Cortázar, Surrealism and Pataphysics', *Comparative Literature*, 27/3 (1975), 218–36 at p. 234.

[63] Soler Serrano, 'Grandes personajes a fondo: Julio Cortázar'.

tion that images can arouse in the reader. This will be crucial for the representation of the political in *Libro de Manuel*, and it is also at the centre of the political manifestation of both *La vuelta* and *Último Round*.

La vuelta al día en ochenta mundos

The innovative nature of *La vuelta* within Cortázar's *oeuvre* certainly caught the attention of Argentinian readers, then avid consumers of Cortázar's texts. According to Eduardo Anguita and Martín Caparrós, who researched the cultural scene of the time, by May 1968, a year after the book appeared: '*Cien años de soledad* seguía en las listas de los libros más vendidos, aunque ahora estaba segundo después de *La vuelta al día en ochenta mundos* de Julio Cortázar.'[64] Far away in Paris, Cortázar also followed and recorded the success of his book, writing enthusiastically to Julio Silva in April 1968 to tell him that he had received a letter from the publisher with news that 'en la Argentina se agotó nuestro hijito y ya piensan en la segunda edición'.[65] It is important to remark that while in New York flower-power reigned and in Paris the students' demonstrations of May '68 were about to happen, in Buenos Aires, and in Argentina in general, the political situation was radically different, making the success of *La vuelta* an interesting fact, above all in political terms.

After a military coup deposed the democratically elected President Frondizi, in 1962, a series of military juntas governed Argentina for over a year, until elections were called in July 1963. Arturo Illia, of the Unión Cívica Radical, would be in power between 1963 and 1966 in what was only the second post-Peronist constitutional government. In contrast to Frondizi, the new Radical government gave more importance to Congress and the democratic political scene.[66] The openly democratic characteristics of Illia's government, added to controversial resolutions such as the relaxation on the prohibition of Peronist political parties (which had been in force since 1955), soon resulted in another military coup since, despite this being a democratically elected presidency, the military had not ceased to be firmly present and influential. In June 1966 the armed forces deposed Arturo Illia, and General Onganía, who had been Head of the Army during Illia's government, took his place. As soon as this nationalistic and highly conservative revolution was in power, the regime forbade all kinds of political activity: the judges of the Supreme Court were dismissed, all political parties became illegal, activity in Congress was

---

[64] Eduardo Anguita and Martín Caparrós, *La voluntad: una historia de la militancia revolucionaria en la Argentina*, I: *1966-1973* (Buenos Aires: Norma, 1997), p. 193.

[65] Cortázar to Julio Silva, 27 April 1968, *Cartas/2 1964–68*, p. 1242.

[66] According to the historian Luis A. Romero, Illia's presidency was characterised by a respect for democratic procedures, a resolve not to abuse presidential powers and a desire not to aggravate conflicts, in the hope that they would be resolved in time: *Historia argentina*, p. 149.

brought to an end and all elected provincial governors were replaced by military authorities.

The 'Onganiato', as Onganía's regime was known, aimed to 'tidy up' the political scene, and to quash the 'immoral' habits of Argentinians at any cost. Consequently, for example, the Instituto di Tella, famous cradle of Argentinian *avant-garde* art, was considered to be a 'foco de inmoralidad y descaro' and was therefore forcefully shut down; women were banned from wearing short skirts or trousers and from wearing their hair down if they were in public, and the police were authorised to stop any man in the street in order to shave his beard and/or cut his hair.[67] Long hair was considered to be a manifestation of sexual ambiguity and political rebellion, neither of which were tolerated. Despite, and because of, the oppression, this was also the time when in Argentina many clandestine, radicalised groups began to emerge. Such was the 'Resistencia Peronista' and 'La línea dura', which were based on Peronist ideals and for whom armed struggle to achieve their aims became the only option.[68] For many of these groups, the most significant of their objectives was to bring Perón back from exile in Spain, so that he could rule Argentina again.

Such was the socio-political reality when *La vuelta* was published in Argentina. To the military regime, it seemed that this was not a book worth censoring; in other words, its playful content was definitely underplaying the manifestations – and the 'danger' – of its political ideas, such as its anti-imperialism, its specific views against the war in Vietnam, its criticism of the capitalist system and, poignantly, its clear position against military authorities. This understanding of the 'harmless' humorous politics of *La vuelta* was also shared by those left-wing intellectuals writing in Argentina at the time (David Viñas and Liliana Heker among them), who considered themselves 'seriously' – rather than humorously – committed to politics and political writing. This was only a part of what would become a recurrent source of debate and questioning for Cortázar and his role as an Argentinian, committed to Latin American politics while living in France. In a conversation that took place in his home in Paris with visiting Argentinian writers, Nicolás Casullo and Jorge Carnevale, around the time of the publication of *La vuelta* (April/May 1968), Cortázar exposes, with humour, the difference between him and those 'serious' intellectuals back in Argentina:

> – La Argentina sigue siendo un páramo, igual que cuando usted [Cortázar] se fue, aunque hayamos leído a Sartre y algunos escritores se pasen el día hablando de compromiso del intelectual. O quizás por eso.
> – Claro [dice Cortázar], una cosa es un escritor *comprometido* y otra muy

[67] See Pablo Ponza, 'Los intelectuales críticos y la transformación social en Argentina (1955–1973)' (unpublished PhD diss. University of Barcelona, 2007), p. 261.
[68] See Lucas Lanusse, *Montoneros: el mito de los doce* (Buenos Aires: Ediciones D., 2005), p. 53.

distinta un escritor *casado*. No hay nada peor que un escritor que escribe para la victoria de la causa, ¿no?[69]

It was apparent that for many Argentinian and Latin American intellectuals, Cortázar's humoristic approach to politics, or his levelling of political reflections with pataphysical texts, could never be the work of someone faithfully 'wedded' to a political cause. This does not mean, however, that the political dimension of *La vuelta* is not prominent; on the contrary.

For Cortázar, humour was not the antithesis of political commitment. In actual fact, he was convinced that Argentina was in serious need of irony. As Claudia Gilman points out, Cortázar went as far as to denounce 'la seriedad de los pelotudos ontológicos', embodied for example in writers such as Ernesto Sábato.[70] In 'Más sobre la seriedad y otros velorios' – a text in praise of the wit of Bioy Casares, one of the few Argentinian writers who, according to Cortázar, understood the role of humour in literature – Cortázar wonders: '¿Quién nos rescatará de la seriedad?' (*LV*1, 54). Later on this idea is emphasised in a quotation borrowed from Man Ray: 'Si pudiéramos desterrar la palabra "serio" de nuestro vocabulario, muchas cosas se arreglarían' (*LV*1, 55). As Pedro Lastra correctly points out, the humoristic vein in Cortázar is influenced by the views of Macedonio Fernández, who in his text 'Para una teoría de la humorística' put forward a criticism of the so-called 'humorística realista' based on real-life situations, and proposed to replace it with 'humor conceptual', detached and independent from the extra-textual reality.[71] The idea of humour in Cortázar can also be linked – as we saw – to the pataphysics of Alfred Jarry as Cortázar makes clear in his interview with Evelyn Picon Garfield: 'Jarry se dio perfecta cuenta de que las cosas más graves pueden ser exploradas mediante el humor. [...] Pienso que eso debió influir mucho en mi manera de ver el mundo, y siempre he creído que el humor es una de las cosas más serias que existen.'[72]

Humour in *La vuelta* (and also in *Último Round*), far from provoking alienation or displacement, seeks the readers' sympathy through an identification with certain values which are both transgressive and attractive.[73] In turn, Cortázar's humour is inseparable from 'lo lúdico', which is at the centre of

---

[69] Anguita and Caparrós, *La voluntad*, p. 194. My emphasis.

[70] Cortázar to Francisco Porrúa, 5 January 1962, *Cartas/1 1937–1963*, p. 467. For Gilman's comment, see Claudia Gilman, 'Dame más', *Página/12*, 13 March 2000 <http://www.pagina12.com.ar/2000/suple/libros/00-08/00-08-13/nota1.htm> [accessed 5 January 2009].

[71] Macedonio Fernández as quoted in Pedro Lastra, *Julio Cortázar* (Madrid: Taurus, 1981), p. 110.

[72] Evelyn Picon Garfield, *¿Es Julio Cortázar un surrealista?* (Madrid: Gredos, 1975), p. 187.

[73] Giordano says: 'El intelectual formado en la 'alta' cultura [...] juega a la desestabilización de su arte y su figura política pero cuidándose de conservar los fundamentos morales que le dan al juego y a la desestabilización un valor trascendente': 'Cortázar en los 60', p. 171.

all of his writings, and goes against the kind of literature traditionally associated with political revolutions, such as social realism. With regard to this, Cortázar claims:

> esas asociaciones aparentemente ilógicas que determinan las reacciones del humor y la eficacia del humor, llevan al juego [...], lo lúdico es una de las armas centrales por las cuales el ser humano se maneja o puede manejarse en la vida. Lo lúdico no entendido como un partido de truco sino como una visión en la que las cosas dejan de tener sus funciones establecidas para asumir muchas veces funciones muy diferentes, funciones inventadas. El hombre que habita un mundo lúdico es un hombre metido en un mundo combinatorio, de invención combinatoria, está creando continuamente formas nuevas.[74]

Humour, together with collage-style insertions, will also be central in the manifestation of the political element in *Libro de Manuel*, in a notion more closely linked to an understanding of the absurd, as Cortázar would explain in 'Corrección de pruebas': 'yo los dejo decir porque si alguna cosa sé es que nunca encenderemos los verdaderos hornos sin echarle al fuego el deslumbrante kerosene de la paradoja y del absurdo'.[75] This idea is further emphasised by the article's closing lines: 'Sé que el asalto al chalet de Verrières y la liberación del Vip son de un absurdo total; me gustaría que alguien me explicara mejor lo que sucedió en Munich esa noche, y cómo sucedió. Ahora se dice que hasta Moshe Dayán estaba entre los policías alemanes. Vamos, viejo.'[76]

In *La vuelta*, faced with a collage of heterogeneous fragments, the reader looks in vain for an authoritative linking thread. A French advert for 'Old Spice' cologne (*LV*1, 62) is given the same visual as well as formal importance as a quotation by Bertolt Brecht (*LV*2, 186), a photograph of the 1940s English serial killer John Christie (*LV*2, 94), or a critical reflection on Cortázar's political ideology (*LV*1, 35). For Sara Kastro-Clarén *La vuelta* is therefore an endeavour to multiply, and by doing so abolish, the idea of individual authorship as we have known it: 'The reader [...] will find himself reflecting on his own mind or his possible authorship. The text is thus a mirror.'[77]

Despite the effects of time upon matters that required urgent action in the late 1960s, the political content of *La vuelta* remains tangible, if uneven, given its collage nature. Although Cortázar presents his political views openly, he does not do so in isolation, but rather he combines them with a range of elements,

---

[74] Prego Gadea, *La fascinación de las palabras*, p. 68.
[75] Cortázar, 'Corrección de pruebas', p. 28.
[76] Ibid., p. 36. The events of Munich refer to the kidnapping and killing of members of the Israeli team by the Palestinian group, Black September, during the 1972 Munich Olympics.
[77] Castro-Klarén, 'Cortázar, Surrealism and 'Pataphysics', p. 234.

which relate broadly to forms of art and forms of creating art. Thus, the political contents of *La vuelta* shift from foreground to background, disappearing behind reproductions of paintings by Delvaux and drawings of the 'Rayuel-o-matic', to come to the fore in 'Vuelta al día en el tercer mundo'.

'Vuelta al día en el tercer mundo' (*LV2*, 114-19) is one of the most unambiguously political texts in the book. It comprises two sections, one dealing with war-torn Vietnam, entitled 'Informe de un norteamericano sobre el drama de la infancia en Vietnam del Sud', and the other, 'La desaparición de menores en Venezuela', which reproduces part of a report on the abduction of children to be sold on as 'lazarillos' for blind men in neighbouring Colombia. Radically detached from the playful or fantastic dimension of the previous segments (such as 'Estación de la mano' or 'Jack the Ripper blues') these are distressingly explicit manifestations of contemporary realities in the so-called developing world (the Vietnam war still being waged when *La vuelta* came out; the Venezuelan report had been written in 1966). As Dan Russek argues, in this section 'the authorial voice disappears, as if the main role of the author was to select and present to the reader the news of the moment'.[78] This, of course, will be brought to the fore in *Libro de Manuel*, where the 'news of the moment' will form part of the narrative itself, and not just textually, but also visually. It should be noted that within the segment's total length of five pages, two of them are dedicated to a black-and-white photograph in which the reader can see a young Vietnamese woman, carrying two children, escaping the ordeal of a burned-out village, visible in the background (*LV2*, 116-17).

According to William J.T. Mitchell's typology of images, a visual image is more persuasive than a perceptual one; in addition, it shows the qualities of precision and permanence that belong exclusively to graphic representation.[79] By inserting an image depicting such violence and desolation in the displacement of this woman and her two children, Cortázar is aiming to produce an immediate impact on his reader, which the visual testimony – as opposed to the written word – makes simply unavoidable. This combination of text and image, as Dan Russek would argue, is a way of constructing a meaning that provides a given 'truth'.[80] Accordingly, the photograph of this scene in Vietnam foreshadows the photographs of violence and poverty in Nicaragua that the narrator of 'Apocalipsis de Solentiname' projects onto the wall of his Paris apartment. The prominence that the photographic medium in its testimonial aspect adopts in *La vuelta*, and also in *Último Round*, is based on Cortázar's understanding of communicating urgent political realities. In this sense, returning to the notion of the 'opération analogue', at this point in his literary evolution, this combination of

---

[78] Dan Russek, 'Verbal/Visual Braids: The Photographic Medium in the Work of Julio Cortázar', *Mosaic: a Journal for the Interdisciplinary Study of Literature*, 37/4 (2004), 71–87 at p. 74.

[79] William J. T. Mitchell, *Iconology* (Chicago: University of Chicago Press, 1986), p. 10.

[80] Russek, 'Verbal/Visual Braids', p. 80.

fiction and testimony, art and journalism, humour and political commentary, present in the two collage books, shows Cortázar's more explicitly 'committed' attempt at writing a kind of literature within the revolution. So while 62 represents a strand in the 'bifurcation' of writing literature, an expression of artistic freedom without necessarily incorporating a visible political dimension, *La vuelta* and *Último Round* are Cortázar's attempt to explore a literary style and genre that can transmit a clear political message, without succumbing to rigid forms of revolutionary dogmatism or indeed of committed literature.

Another instance of explicit political commentary is the poem in praise of the 'piantados porteños' (*LV*2, 142-65), wherein Cortázar reproduces extracts of an epic poem on Argentinian history written by 'el Santo' during the 1940s. The last part of the poem reads:

> Edelmiro Farrell pasó a desempeñar el Poder Ejecutivo Nacional, el alejamiento del secretario de trabajo, Juan Perón, hizo promover / un movimiento popular que repuso al coronel el 17 de octubre de 1945; ganaron las elecciones / Juan Perón para presidente y Hortensio Quijano / vice, el 4 de junio se hicieron las consagraciones; / los recursos vitales, la Nación, los tiene en su mano. (*LV*2, 160)

After this quotation, Cortázar ironically adds: 'Muchos años esperé una puesta al día de **Los forjadores de la patria,** pero el Santo pareció entender que con Perón se le acababa el estro. A lo mejor pasó de la poesía a la importación de automóviles, eran cosas que se veían en esos tiempos' (*LV*2, 160). Cortázar personally identifies with the hypothesis that he invents to account for the truncation of el Santo's poem, a cynical allusion to the consequences of Peronism not only for poets, and by extension literature, but also for history as a whole. Although over a decade had gone by between the coup that deposed Perón in 1955 and the writing of *La vuelta*, it is remarkable how dominant the presence of Perón still is within Cortázar's interpretation of the present in Argentina. By the time *La vuelta* came out in Argentina, critical comments like this one would have created different ideological enemies from the ones that Cortázar would have made prior to his departure for Paris in 1951.

Peronism in 1968 did not have the same ideological implications and foundations as it had had almost two decades earlier, especially not for the youth, and in particular the middle-class militant youth, who in addition to clandestinely supporting and aiming to emulate the Cuban revolution, were becoming organised to fight for the return from exile of their ideological leader, General Perón. After 1955 Peronism became permeable to multiple discourses, those coming from Catholicism and nationalism, from historical revisionism and also from the radical Left.[81] Therefore, to criticise Perón in the late 1960s

---

[81] For a summary of the development of Peronism see, for example, Luis Alberto Romero, *Historia argentina*, pp. 38–52.

could even mean to be against the very same socialist ideals that Cortázar had recently embraced. Left-wing intellectuals were at this point also in favour of the 'Peronisation' of Argentinian intellectual spheres. As Oscar Terán describes: 'la política argentina había ingresado en una suerte de caldera del diablo donde se fundían las fuerzas más disímiles y enemigas'.[82] Thus, in the literary magazine *Crisis*, 'obligatory' reading for all intellectuals of the Río de la Plata in the 1970s, the articles presented a vision made up of the fragments that had been feeding the politically radicalised Argentinian imaginary during the 1960s. Lenin and Perón, José Hernández and Marx, Rosas and Mao, populism and Cuba, crossed and mixed with a coherence that could not have been possible a few decades earlier.[83]

The chameleon versus the coleopteran

From the beginning of *La vuelta*, with its overtones of self-victimisation, Cortázar clarifies his personal political position to the reader, underlining the importance that the author's political leanings have for the text. In 'Del sentimiento del no estar del todo', significantly a segment mostly dealing with aesthetic theories, Cortázar asserts:

> soy terriblemente feliz en mi infierno y escribo. Vivo y escribo amenazado por esa lateralidad, por ese **paralaje verdadero**, por ese estar siempre un poco más a la izquierda o más al fondo del lugar donde se debería estar para que todo cuajara satisfactoriamente en un día más de vida sin conflictos. Desde muy pequeño asumí [...] esa condición que me dividía de mis amigos y a la vez los atraía hacia lo raro, el diferente, el que metía el dedo en el ventilador. (*LV*1, 35)

Having a go at putting one's finger into a fan is not such an outrageously abnormal thing for a child to try, yet for Cortázar it seems to be indicative of how different he was. As with his identification with the isolated Minotaur in *Los reyes* – where he portrays the artist as the alienated figure – Cortázar still wants to cling to this Romantic notion of himself as the misunderstood, lone poet (a self-created mythologised conception that brings him closer to figures whom he admired, such as Rimbaud or Artaud).[84] What is worth noting in this quotation is that although Cortázar expresses his political stance straightforwardly, it is within that same discourse of somewhat self-pitying differentiation, reminis-

---

[82] Terán, *Historia de los ideas en Argentina*, p. 293.
[83] See María Sondereguer (ed.), *Revista Crisis: Antología 1973-1976* (Buenos Aires: Universidad Nacional de Quilmes, 2008).
[84] Moreover, in *La vuelta* Cortázar aligns himself with poets such as Shelley and Keats (*LV*1, 187-8).

cent of the idea invoked by the phrase 'vendre le plus cher possible la peau', that is, of 'having to' sacrifice his literature. He is not simply 'on the left', but rather, to his mind, he is inconveniently 'a bit further' to the left; further, that is, than 'donde se *debería* estar' (my emphasis). The coincidence is too striking and ideologically significant to be overlooked: Cortázar uses the same phrase in the story 'Reunión', where the narrator, a metaphorical embodiment of Che Guevara, reproduces the banal concerns of the revolutionaries while in the jungle: '"Si por lo menos nos pudiéramos sacar el barro", se quejaba el Teniente. "O fumar de verdad" (alguien, *más a la izquierda*, ya no sé quién, alguien que se perdió al alba)'.[85] Feeling the odd one out does not give Cortázar any freedom to defend the different position that he claims to be in; on the contrary, it burdens him with a sense of guilt, which seems to become increasingly more prominent the more actively involved he is in political causes.

Guilt is here communicated through the conditional use of the verb 'deber' and also of the word 'infierno', as well as in the ostentatious affirmation of Cortázar's oxymoronic 'terrible happiness'. Continuing with the self-punitory religious lexicon, in Cortázar's hyperbolic effort to explain and justify himself there is a serious degree of unease. He would like to write a kind of literature that is analogous to a political revolution, yet he does not seem to be entirely clear as to how he would go about doing this. He feels that he ought to, and thus feels at fault if he does not: a dilemma which invites a very Oliveira-like sense of immobility. The idea of the parallax, alluding to his ideological position but also to his Parisian perspective, is crucial to understanding Cortázar's struggle when attempting to reconcile politics and artistic creation. For, embedded in the notion of parallax is the idea of two points of view on the same project analogously coexisting, yet seeing it from different positions.

Cortázar does not want to conform to a fixed concept of the politically committed Latin American writer. His will to write literature as an 'opération analogue' to the political revolution not only forced a polarisation of his own writings into the exclusively fictional and abstract, and the experimental, playfully political, but in addition, when it came to what a committed Latin American writer should be producing, it set a difference between him and many of his contemporaries. The parallax here is thus threatening, for it isolates and generates incomprehension, yet that is the position in which Cortázar, unwilling to 'wed' his art to the artistic restrictions of the political cause he believed in, finds himself at this point in his evolution.

Cortázar explicitly confirms his political positioning again towards the end of *La vuelta*, when he claims that 'muchos no entenderán este paseo del camaleón por la alfombra abigarrada, y eso que mi color y mi rumbo preferidos se perciban apenas se mira bien: cualquiera sabe que habito a la izquierda, sobre

---

[85] Cortázar, 'Reunión', p. 538. My emphasis.

el rojo' (*LV*2, 193). As in the previous quotation, Cortázar seems to find it necessary to confirm and reiterate his political stance (as with his repetition of 'entraría, como ha entrado', in his letter to Fernández Retamar). The mention of the chameleon is not coincidental, for this quotation comes from 'Casilla del camaleón' (*LV*2, 185-93).

In this fragment Cortázar recalls having his 600-word manuscript of *Imagen de John Keats* inspected by someone 'con aire consternado' (*LV*2, 185) from the British Council in Buenos Aires at some point in the late 1940s. After recounting the anecdote to an imaginary interlocutor – a nondescript 'Señora' – Cortázar claims that: 'un escritor comprometido – usted me entiende – me señaló la necesidad de una ideología sin contradicciones [...] quizás comprenderá usted lo que sigue, la teoría de camaleones y gorriones de que se habla para incomodidad de buenas conciencias instaladas en verdades monocráticas' (*LV*2, 185-6). This comment, together with the anecdote, as Peter Standish argues, set the tone for what is to come in the rest of the segment, namely Cortázar's critique of ideological rigidity and systematisation, whereby the concept of the chameleon is opposed to that of the coleopteran (commonly known as a beetle, and appropriately illustrated on *LV*2, 187).[86] The former, comparable perhaps to a *cronopio*, is flexible, adaptable and open-minded, thus, at times also self-contradictory. It seems that Cortázar relies on this paradox as a way of being more honest with himself and with the outside world; and it is incidentally reminiscent of Oliveira and his ideological dilemmas. The coleopteran, on the other hand, has an exoskeleton and is rigid and inflexible. Cortázar therefore argues that those critics, journalists and intellectuals who have political agendas with regard to artistic creation are all coleopterans. They do not allow contradictory ideas. As he puts it, 'Pasa que el artista también tiene ideas pero es raro que las tenga sistemáticamente, que se haya coleopterizado al punto de eliminar la contradicción como lo hacen los coleópteros filósofos o políticos a cambio de perder o ignorar todo lo que nace más allá de sus alas quitinosas' (*LV*2, 186). To an extent, in his self-justificatory rhetoric, this is what 'allows' Cortázar to incorporate humour amidst his testimonial reproductions of the atrocities of Vietnam, and it is also what gives him the 'freedom' to get lost in aesthetic exploration and experimentation, as he does in *62*.

Omar Prego Gadea draws an analogy between the chameleon/coleopteran dichotomy and Cortázar's understanding of socialist politics in Latin America, such that a coleopteran becomes a symbol for 'ciertos procesos revolucionarios'.[87] Cortázar accepts Gadea's comparison and extends it, claiming that:

> En sus formas iniciales, esas revoluciones adoptaron formas dinámicas, formas lúdicas, formas en las que el paso adelante, el salto adelante, esa

---
[86] Standish, *Understanding Julio Cortázar*, p. 155.
[87] Prego Gadea, *La fascinación de las palabras*, p. 221.

inversión de todos los valores que implica una revolución, se operaban en un campo moviente, fluido y abierto a la imaginación, a la invención y a sus productos connaturales, la poesía, el teatro, el cine y la literatura. Pero con una frecuencia bastante abrumadora, después de esa primera etapa las revoluciones se institucionalizan, empiezan a llenarse de quitina, van pasando a la condición de coleópteros. Bueno, yo trato de luchar contra eso, ése es mi compromiso con las revoluciones, con la Revolución. Trato de luchar por todos los medios, y sobre todo con medios lúdicos, contra lo quitinoso.[88]

Cortázar's 'struggle' can certainly be understood and accepted within aesthetic terms, that is, not wanting to succumb to the rigidity of 'serious' literature; yet the question prevails: how is Cortázar's idea of commitment – fighting against creative inflexibility – contributing politically to a social revolution in Latin America? The answer, or rather the action, is not direct. In the case of *La vuelta*, the inclusion of photographs is part of Cortázar's attempt to provoke the readers, which might in turn (and only maybe) incite them to live their lives with a different understanding and awareness of reality. Although this is a more direct political provocation than that implied in Oliveira's action/inaction dilemma, Cortázar still does not provide, at least through his literature thus far, a practical 'revolutionary' answer which can be linked directly and explicitly to his 'opération analogue'.

Despite what could seem to be very specific concerns, Cortázar insists on the universality of *La vuelta*. Reminiscent of Persio's essentialism in *Los premios*, with a critical tone that resembles his reproach for the lack of humour in Argentinian literature, Cortázar writes that *La vuelta* will call for 'un sentimiento de substancialidad, a ese estar vivo que falta en tantos libros nuestros, a que escribir y respirar (en el sentido indio de la respiración como flujo y reflujo del ser universal) no sean dos ritmos diferentes' (*LV*1, 11). If, as Cortázar claims, this is a book about reviving and reshaping those fundamental qualities of man, of writing as a form of living, then along with pictorial art, music and literature, there should also be politics, the provocation of thinking politically. It is clear – and visible – that the text aims to affect, somehow, the general political conscience of the reader.

To end *La vuelta*, Cortázar remarks, with cynicism:

vivimos en un tiempo latinoamericano en el que a falta de verdadero Terror [*sic*] hay los pequeños miedos nocturnos que agitan el sueño del escritor, las pesadillas del escapismo, del no compromiso, del revisionismo, del libertinaje literario, de la gratuidad, del hedonismo, del arte por el arte, de la torre de marfil (*LV*2, 189).

---

[88] Ibid., pp. 221–2. Cortázar's words regarding the 'quitinización' of the revolution brings to mind Alejo Carpentier's *El siglo de las luces*, and the institutionalisation – and consequent disillusionment – of the revolutionary process. This causes Carpentier's pseudo-*alter ego* in the novel to claim: 'No valía la pena haber venido tan lejos [desde Francia/España a las Antillas] a ver la Revolución para no ver la Revolución': *El siglo de las luces* (Barcelona: Seix Barral, 1962), p. 89.

This enumeration clearly sums up the external as well as self-imposed accusations (political and moral) that affected Cortázar and forced him to justify himself incessantly. Even though both *La vuelta* and *Último Round* are attempts to demonstrate the ways in which 'hedonistic' or 'libertine' literature can at the same time be political, Cortázar's manifestations of guilt and self-justification are remarkably ubiquitous. So much so that in parts his literature appears to become political not because he has found a formula to write literature as an 'opération analogue' to the revolution, but rather because he is incessantly, and paradoxically, stating, even demanding, what is it that the committed or politicised writer should be creating. This is apparent in a fragment comparable to 'Casilla del Camaleón' in *Último Round* where, in a segment entitled 'El marfil de la torre', Cortázar writes: 'SIN EMBARGO / el escritor latinoamericano / debe escribir tan sólo / lo que su vocación le dicte / sin entrar en cuestiones / que son de la exclusiva competencia / de los políticos y economistas' (*UR*1, 148–9). Instead of challenging the inflexible exoskeleton, it seems that Cortázar has also become part of an aesthetic 'verdad monocrática' (*LV*2, 186), dictating the only acceptable manner in which he thinks things should be done, and literature should be written, for the benefit of the Revolution.

Último Round

In September 1968 Cortázar wrote to Francisco Porrúa elucidating the idea behind *Último Round*. He explained that he wanted it to be, 'un cuadernillo [...] que hiciera una segunda parte de *La vuelta al día en ochenta mundos* [...] de modo que habrá otro libro completo, que haré con Silva aunque dentro de un espíritu muy diferente del otro'.[89] Even if *La vuelta* and *Último Round* can be read as the first and second parts of the same literary project, there is, as Cortázar claims, a shift in 'spirit' that can be linked to changes within his aesthetic and political preoccupations. *La vuelta* explores a multiplicity of arts and media with the aim of highlighting playfulness, humour and the poetic character of artistic creation, combined with some political 'lessons' (see, for example, *LV*1, 7). *Último Round* also delves into poetry and imagination, but it includes more, and more poignant, political texts. It is apparent that the two years that separated the publication of these works had sharpened and hardened Cortázar's political resolve; perhaps there had even been a change in his position regarding what 'revolutionary literature' should be. Considering that those two years included no less momentous events than the death of Che Guevara, the May 1968 protests in Paris and an eye-opening personal trip to India, such an intensification of views seems entirely logical. In addition, it could be argued that it also related to the alleged 'failure' of *62*. By now Cortázar had to resign himself to the fact

[89] Cortázar to Porrúa, 23 September 1968, *Cartas/2 1964–1968*, p. 1273.

that his attempt at carrying out his 'opération analogue' had not succeeded in visible terms. He would have to try to demonstrate his political commitment in a different artistic manner, possibly in a less abstract (some critics would even say less ambitious) manifestation than the one epitomised by *62*. In other words, Cortázar would now have to 'vendre cher la peau', first by writing *Último Round*, and then, ultimately, through *Libro de Manuel*.

Certain critics, such as Solares, have argued that it was during the events in Paris in May 1968, that Cortázar's active political dedication came to the fore.[90] Mario Vargas Llosa recalls an anecdote that epitomises this moment, to an extent also 'epiphanic':

> Se le vio entonces, en esos días tumultuosos, en las barricadas de París, repartiendo hojas volanderas de su invención, y confundido con los estudiantes que querían llevar 'la imaginación al poder'. Tenía cincuenta y cuatro años. Los dieciséis que le faltaba vivir sería el escritor comprometido con el socialismo, el defensor de Cuba y Nicaragua, el firmante de manifiestos y el *habitué* de congresos revolucionarios que fue hasta su muerte.[91]

Undoubtedly this historical experience was crucial for the affirmation of Cortázar's political conscience, and indeed it appears prominently in *Último Round*. 'Noticias del mes de mayo' spreads over twenty pages, and includes texts by Cortázar as well as photographs of political posters and reprints of the graffiti covering the streets of Paris (*UR*1, 88–119). The revolts in Paris were also having a direct impact on Cortázar's political beliefs: not only was he out in the streets handing out leaflets, he also took part in the student occupation of the Casa Argentina, where, ironically, he had refused to live when he first arrived in Paris in 1951.[92] When it came to his fictional writings, his then most recent work had been *62*. In other words, although Vargas Llosa, for example, conforming to the critical pattern of the two Cortázars, pre- and post-Cuba, asserts that 'Este otro Julio Cortázar [el político] me parece menos personal y creador como escritor que el primigenio', Cortázar was at this moment perhaps being more innovative than ever before, in that he was attempting to follow two different creative paths: one, apparently exclusively concerned

---

[90] Solares, *Imagen de Julio Cortázar*, p. 114.

[91] Vargas Llosa, 'La trompeta de Deyá', p. 21. Evidently, Vargas Llosa's recollection is somewhat tinged by his own dose of mythologizing, especially when taking into account that he wrote this in 1992, following his own political shift from left to right and his disastrous candidacy for the presidency of Peru, as leader of the right-wing Frente Democrático.

[92] See pp. 30–31 above. The 'toma' of the Casa Argentina is also remembered in 'Noticias del mes de mayo', when Cortázar writes: 'A todo esto los muchachos argentinos me habían invitado a beber un vaso de tinto en su Casa de la Cité, y escuchábamos un disco de María Elena Walsh mientras Matta y Seguí empezaban a pintar en la pared a un general con cuatro patas cayéndose de un caballo con solamente tres' (*UR*1, 105).

with metaphysical and formal exploration, and the other, more explicitly – yet not exclusively – concerned with combining politics, humour, fiction and photography in the 'libros almanaque'.[93]

When it comes to the differences between *La vuelta* and *Último Round* it is important to analyse the notable change in the design of the covers. While the first edition of *La vuelta* uses an Escher-like drawing by Julio Silvia (in which two boys metamorphose into two giant frogs in Kafkaesque fashion), in *Último Round* the covers play as much of a textual role as the contents of the book. In the original edition, as well as in the two-volume pocket version, the covers emulate the typographical layout of a newspaper, with the words 'Último Round' seemingly appearing as its title. The tone of the material used in the covers is set by the multiplicity of messages and codes implied in the journalistic reproduction, and also by the subject matter of the fragments selected. For example, immediately underneath the main heading, there is a two-line quotation: 'Hay que soñar, pero a condición de creer seriamente en nuestro sueño, de examinar con atención la vida real, de confrontar nuestras observaciones con nuestro sueño, de realizar escrupulosamente nuestra fantasía' (*UR*2, front cover). No one other than Lenin is the referential source for these quasi-surrealist words. The quotation also relates to many of the slogans that appeared as graffiti during May '68 and which are reproduced in *Último Round*, such as the one that reads 'Sean realistas: pidan lo imposible (Facultad de Letras, París)' (*UR*1, 98). Yet, unlike most of the other fragments on the front cover, this quotation is not reprinted within the book nor does it allude to a specific text (as is the case with the 'Avisos Clasificados', for instance: '*JUGUETES*. ¿A la nena se le rompió la muñeca? Sin compromiso, consulte p. 248, tomo I': *UR*2, front cover). It could be argued that this highlights the importance of the quotation, emphasised also by its position. Paradoxically, though, the quotation is in such a small font that Lenin's phrase very easily goes unnoticed. This to an extent epitomises the aims of *Último Round*: to mock politics 'politically', while borrowing from *avant-garde* aesthetics; or, as Luis Justo puts it in his review of the book: '*La vuelta al día en ochenta mundos* es puramente eso, un libro-chiste. En *Último Round*, el marco de este género [...] Cortázar lo expande hasta lo irreconocible.'[94]

This can appropriately be applied to Cortázar's own ambition to create a kind of literature as an 'opération analogue' to the revolution. Lenin's quotation is ironically followed by another fragment, almost directly underneath, entitled: 'LA REVOLUCIÓN NO ES UN JUEGO' (*UR*2, front cover). This excerpt is addressed to a 'joven amigo', and it is a direct contraposition to Lenin's dictum, claiming: 'no se deje engañar por informaciones tergiversadas, no le haga caso a Lenin' (*UR*2, front cover). The fragment also offers a 'grave'

---

[93] The quotation from Vargas Llosa is from 'La trompeta de Deyá', p. 23.
[94] Luis Justo, 'Cortázar: ¿misticismo o arte-pop?', *Sur*, 325 (1970), 77–82 at p. 78.

warning to the reader: 'Cese de reir. NO SUEÑE. [...] Niéguese al delirio, a los ideales, a lo imposible [...] SEA SERIO. MATE LOS SUEÑOS. SEA SERIO. MATE LOS SUEÑOS. SEA SERIO. MATE LOS SUEÑOS' (*UR*2, front cover). Cortázar's repetition of these last two phrases in the short text highlights the ridiculous nature of such commands, emphasised by the visual authority suggested by the capitalisation. This, once again, makes reference to Cortázar's political views, and in addition to his understanding of literature in relation to politics. As in *La vuelta*, in *Último Round*, humour, irony and the absurd play a fundamental role in the representation of the political, and this is made clear from the very front cover.

The Cortazarian rules regarding the need for humour do not always apply when it comes to Cortázar laughing at himself. On the back cover, under the heading 'LAS GRANDES BIOGRAFÍAS DE NUESTRO TIEMPO', we read: '"el escritor Julio Cortázar, un pequeño-burgués con veleidades castristas". Ramiro de Casasbellas, PRIMERA PLANA, junio 1969 (Para más detalles, véase p. 265 ss., tomo 2)' (*UR*1, back cover). When the reader follows the clue, s/he finds that the text that Cortázar has linked to this description of himself is the emblematic 'Acerca de la situación del intelectual latinoamericano' (*UR*2, 265–80), where he writes to Fernández Retamar a sort of epistolary article (part of which is quoted at the beginning of this chapter) to be included in a number of the *Revista de la Casa de las Américas*. This is a text in which Cortázar tries to define what the role of the Latin American intellectual is and should be; yet above all, it is a space for Cortázar to justify his own position as an Argentinian who used to be 'casi enteramente volcado hacia Europa' (*UR*2, 269), but who can now have, thanks to his life in Europe, 'una visión desnacionalizada de la revolución cubana' (*UR*2, 268). In other words, while Cortázar preaches the need to take politics with more humour, when someone is being ironic about his politically paradoxical position, he needs to bring it to the attention of the reader by exposing the 'accusation' on the cover of this book, and by leading the reader to his own, very serious response.

Cortázar's wariness of politically dogmatic writing underpins fragments like 'Elecciones insólitas', where he takes a humorous approach to politics in general and to the lack of real free options within certain democracies, and the mistrust of those who choose 'differently' within a given system. The fragment reads: 'Como no está convencido, han empezado a pensar si no habría que tomar medidas para expulsarlo del país. Se lo han dado a entender, sin violencia, amablemente' (*UR*2, 210–11). The ironic tone of the text is further lightened by drawings by the Belgian artist Jean Michel Folon, depicting an expressionless man trapped in a cube the size of his body. Could this be a pictorial metaphor to show how politics is restricting Cortázar? According to his writings, rather than politics in general, what is restrictive and inflexible for Cortázar (or 'quitinoso' to follow the imagery from 'Casilla del Camaleón') is political commitment *per se*. This becomes clear in 'No te dejes', where Cortázar demands that the writer should not 'sell himself' to the 'formas públicas y espectaculares del "compromiso"' (*UR*2, 189). This is specifically addressed at socialism, as he states at the beginning of the fragment: 'Es obvio que tratarán de comprar a todo poeta o narrador de ideología socialista cuya literatura influya en el panorama de su tiempo' (*UR*2, 189).

Cortázar ends *Último Round* with an assertion loaded with sarcasm in which he notes that there is a 'justo, delicado equilibrio que permite seguir creando una obra con aire en las alas, sin convertirse en el monstruo sagrado [...] se vuelve el combate más duro que ha de librar el poeta o el narrador para que su compromiso se siga cumpliendo' (*UR*2, 189). The dichotomy between free artistic expression and committed literature is prevalent in *Último Round*, and through that repetition Cortázar emphasises his search for the 'delicado equilibrio' (comparable to the previously cited 'fórmula central' or indeed his 'opération analogue'), while at the same time justifying himself continuously for his decision not to 'sacrifice' his literature in the socialist cause. This refusal is not only apparent in the surreal, fantastic, humoristic and erotic contents of the book, but also, at the beginning of *El examen*, through Cortázar's use of foreign languages (French and English mainly). Thus, for example, in 'Que sepa abrir la puerta para ir a jugar' Cortázar reproduces fragments from Bataille in the original French and from Donleavy in English (*UR*2, 66–7), and in 'La muñeca rota' he quotes extensively from Nabokov, also in English (*UR*1, 257–9). In other words, if for Cortázar writing 'literature for the revolution' was not about simplifying or modifying aesthetic conventions or themes to fit an ideological aim, still less was it about the popularisation of language.

Último Round is not destined for the 'political indoctrination' of the masses; rather, its political 'usefulness' lies in its capacity to question and reconsider those values common to the influential middle class to which he belongs and which undeniably makes up the majority of his readers. It is worth noting that these were books that, given their editorial designs, were very expensive to produce, and hence unaffordable even to many middle-class readers especially in Latin America. As Liliana Heker recalls: 'Cuando *La vuelta al mundo* y *Último Round* salieron, eran libros carísimos. Como estudiantes universitarios, ¡no podíamos ni pensar en comprarlos! Para mí, eran una frivolidad [...] incluso la burguesía los usaba como libros simpáticos para regalar.'[95]

As well as the covers, another difference between *La vuelta* and *Último Round* is the prominence given to poetry. While in *La vuelta* there are only five poems by Cortázar, in *Último Round* poetry abounds. To an extent, this is an attempt to substantiate Cortázar's own romanticised perception of himself as a poet, yet it also emphasises the lyricism of the artistic dimension of the book. It is inter-

---

[95] Liliana Heker, personal interview, 19 December 2008, Buenos Aires.

esting that very few of the poems deal strictly with political issues. A crucial example is 'Álbum con fotos', where Cortázar comments on social reality through the contents of an imaginary album, containing photographs of children's faces; these are the 'verdadera cara de los ángeles / la cara de un negrito hambriento, / la cara de un cholito mendigando, / un vietnamita, un argentino, un español / la cara verde del hambre verdadera de los ángeles' (*UR*1, 157). The reference to photographs of children in dire poverty, and the discomfort caused to the middle-class eye, objectifying these scenes into 'holiday' snapshots, foreshadows the contents of the short story 'Apocalipsis de Solentiname' (published in 1976). Within *Último Round*, this poem also relates to the extensive 'Turismo aconsejable', where Cortázar intercalates his own views of Calcutta with stills from the Louis Malle film, *Calcutta* (1969).

Malle's documentary is essentially a visual tour of the city, focusing mostly on people living in slums or in the streets. Interspersed with the images is the narration, by Malle himself, which provides a framing for each image through cultural comment, statistics and historical information. Unlike Malle's more objectivised voice-over Cortázar's narration centres round his own description of what he has witnessed in the city. Unlike *Rayuela*, the atrocities that the text recounts are veiled in a wry sarcasm (with phrases such as, 'Algo verdaderamente pintoresco, inolvidable', *UR*1, 146), since the narration aims to emulate a form of tourist brochure for the European traveller (*UR*1, 129). In turn, this shows that the reader Cortázar had in mind when putting together this book was possibly someone who, like himself, would have been able to travel and to see other realities outside their own; the reference to the French director of course also assumes a certain level of education and socio-cultural status. It is apparent that if *Último Round* is to be politically useful it is through the re-contextualisation of these activities (travelling, going to the cinema, reading 'foreign' literature) into a framework of ethical and ideological questioning in the hope of awakening the reader's political awareness.

This is emphasised in 'Turismo aconsejable' where, contrasting the impersonal tone of the journalistic-like 'Vuelta al día en el tercer mundo' of *La vuelta*, Cortázar addresses the reader directly and repetitively through the use of 'Usted'. The illusion of a direct bridge – to bring in Morelli's metaphor – between Cortázar and his reader through the use of the formal second-person singular, is strategic, particularly at the end of the passage when Cortázar writes:

> el infierno es ese lugar donde las vociferaciones y los juegos y los llantos suceden como si no sucedieran [...] es una recurrencia infinita [...] cualquier día de cualquier mes de cualquier año en que usted tenga ganas de ir a verla [a Calcuta], es ahora mientras usted lee esto, *ahora y aquí*, esto que ocurre y que usted, es decir yo, hemos visto. [...] Vale la pena, le digo. (*UR*1, 146; my emphasis)

The extreme poverty that Cortázar saw in India affected him deeply, and sharpened yet more his social consciousness. As can be seen in his letter to Julio Silva from New Delhi in March 1968, he was no longer a mere 'aesthete': 'La India me muestra horriblemente lo que es el tercer mundo, y me siento muy mal y con una constante crispación de estómago; no soy, desde luego, el esteta que era en 1956, cuando me limitaba atentamente a ver lo bello de la India sin preocuparme demasiado por el resto, que es casi todo.'[96] When reading Cortázar's personal impressions, it could be said that the blending between the 'usted' (the reader, the European traveller, the 'aesthete of 1956') and the writer, is the coming together of Cortázar's divided selves (this is to an extent fictionalised through Andrés Fava and his 'internal revolution' in *Libro de Manuel*). Yet, while tacitly alluding to his old self, Cortázar is also turning the reader into a 'witness'. The 'recurrencia infinita' of poverty means that the scenes which Cortázar observed in India, the same ones that Malle captured in his film and which Cortázar reproduces in his text, will not have changed by the time that the reader encounters, imagines and to an extent witnesses, the reality that is presented before him/her.

The act of direct and indirect witnessing answers Cortázar's own demands, established in 'Acerca de la situación', namely that the writer should somehow bear witness to the realities of his own time. In 'Turismo aconsejable' that aim seems to be accomplished. The reader cannot avoid taking in, albeit briefly, the reality of poverty, of the marginalised, as photographs depicting this are interspersed between the textual fragments, and not in an aesthetically pleasing manner as in *Buenos Aires, Buenos Aires*. There will be moments of cathartic relief when skipping to sections such as 'Estado de las baterías' (*UR*1, 204-5) on the fantastic 'irrealidades' of *62*, or when delving into the pataphysics of 'En vista del éxito obtenido, o los piantados firmes como fierro' (*UR*1, 224-47). However, it will prove very difficult to ignore, let alone forget, the images that the reader has witnessed, especially when taking into account Mitchell's idea of the persuasiveness of the visual text. Cortázar has thus intercalated his political 'lessons' through images.

His difficulty in trying to reconcile politics and literature comes to the fore in 'Acerca de la situación', with statements such as: 'a mí me sucede estar empapado por el peso de toda una vida en la filosofía burguesa, y sin embargo me interno cada vez más por las vías del socialismo [...] no es fácil, *es un conflicto permanente* de un poeta con el mundo, de un escritor con su trabajo' (*UR*2, 273; my emphasis). This idea is reiterated at the end of the segment, when Cortázar elucidates his views on the role of the writer and claims:

> Insisto en que a ningún escritor le exijo que se haga tribuno de la lucha que en tantos frentes se está librando contra el imperialismo en todas sus formas,

---

[96] Cortázar to Silva, 9 March 1968, *Cartas/2 1964–1968*, p. 1237.

pero sí que sea testigo de su tiempo como lo querían Martínez Estrada y Camus, y que su obra o su vida [...] den ese testimonio en la forma que les sea propia' (*UR2*, 279).

Both *La vuelta* and *Último Round* represent Cortázar's singular way of being a witness politically to his own era. It could be said that this is in effect Cortázar's own 'façon', at this point in his aesthetic and political evolution, of walking the Damascus road.

A failed operation

I have tried to debunk a number of myths surrounding the figure of Cortázar and his commitment to the struggle for social justice in Latin America. Even his iconic first trip to Cuba, which is repeatedly taken as a landmark upon which to base the beginning of the 'politicised' Cortázar, is somewhat mythologised. Radical reassessment is called for. It should be clear at this point that although many critics still argue that there were two Cortázars, the apolitical *vis-à-vis* the committed socialist, and that this 'before and after' visibly determined the aesthetic quality of his works, politics was always present in Cortázar's writings, in the novels as well as in the more experimental books. Therefore the period between *Rayuela* and *Libro de Manuel*, when Cortázar travelled to Cuba and openly converted to socialism, does not symbolise a sudden politicisation, but rather, a shift in ideological beliefs, as well as an intensification of the role that politics played within his creative production. From the moment when Cortázar decides to adhere to the Cuban cause, he takes upon himself the task of proving how a kind of literature like the one that he creates (which is neither realistic, testimonial, nor populist) has a specific political function in relation to that particular ideological cause. Yet the dilemma is inexorable: how can he – the writer, the 'poet' – contribute to the revolution without giving up his artistic freedom and his will to explore the boundaries of literature?

It is in the period of aesthetic exploration that Cortázar tries to propose new ways in which to express political concerns without succumbing to dogmatic or propagandistic forms. He juxtaposes spheres that he knows are heterogeneous, without perhaps taking enough time to question or experience the difficulties of that very juxtaposition. In this sense, and as Alberto Giordano argues, Cortázar allows himself 'facilidades a las que por lo general renuncia cuando se ocupa de problemas estrictamente estéticos'.[97] This is exemplified in statements in which Cortázar asserts that the writer needed by the revolution is someone who encompasses 'una fusión total [...] de dos fuerzas, la del hombre

---

[97] Giordano, 'Cortázar en los 60', p. 175.

plenamente comprometido con su realidad nacional y mundial, y la del escritor lúcidamente seguro de su oficio'.[98] Through the books analysed in this chapter Cortázar's attempts to unite these two 'forces' have been elucidated. It is evident that although he might have been sure of his 'vocation', his determination to fuse art and politics without giving up the freedom to create spontaneously and freely was not an easy task.

Cortázar relied heavily on the self-construction, or as Giordano calls it, the 'autofiguración', of the image of the revolutionary writer which is based upon a version of commitment to literature as ingenious as it is inconsistent and deliberately ambivalent.[99] This is crucial when it comes to understanding the vagueness and ambiguity with which Cortázar deals with the function of the writer or of literature within the revolution, and indeed, when it comes to defining his own commitment as an artist. In sum, the bifurcation between Cortázar the playful writer and Cortázar the dutiful committed intellectual is one that, at this point, he himself cannot seem to resolve. During this period of production, his search for a literature through which he can unite both roles fills him with a persistent feeling of guilt from both sides of the dilemma: sometimes he feels that his literature is not committed enough to the political cause in which he believes; at others he is wary of veering too much towards a kind of dogmatism that would betray his own ideas of artistic freedom.

Through the literary production as well as the paratext, the years between *Rayuela* and *Libro de Manuel* represent a period of difficult transition for Cortázar. It is a time of profound, contradictory impulses on both a personal and a political level, emerging from an attempt to reconcile politics with poetics. Cortázar's rhetoric of guilt, duty and artistic inadequacy thus recurs in the works of these years. His bifurcation into two different ways of producing literature, in an attempt to contribute to the Latin American socialist revolution through an aesthetic 'opération analogue' seems to fail, by his own admission, at least as separate strands. It is therefore apparent that the more he struggles forcefully to incorporate a political dimension that can be seen analogous to the revolutionary process, the weaker Cortázar becomes as a writer of fiction. He will nevertheless move on to try new aesthetic forms in the attempt to unite both paths in his final novel, *Libro de Manuel*. Here the journalistic elements (photographs, newspaper clippings and official reports), present in both *La vuelta* and *Último Round*, are combined with a fictional (albeit less 'ambitious', when compared to *62*) narrative plot. This book, in its content the most explicitly political of the four novels that he published during his lifetime, represents the culminating stage in what Cortázar referred to as 'vendre la peau plus cher'. *Libro de Manuel* is a book that could be said to include, against

[98] Julio Cortázar 'Algunos aspectos del cuento', *Obra crítica/2*, pp. 505–34 at p. 528. This was first published in *Casa de las Américas*, 60 (July 1970), 24-35.
[99] Giordano, 'Cortázar en los 60', p. 175.

Morelli's own conceptions, an unambiguous political message. It is at the same time a fundamental part of the aesthetic corpus of a writer who did not want to abandon exploring aesthetic possibilities for the sake of artistic conformity, let alone for a given political ideology.

4

Converging 'Lenin with Rimbaud'

In 1970, during a series of debates between Oscar Collazos, Mario Vargas Llosa and Cortázar on the function of literature and the writer within the socialist revolution, Cortázar wrote: 'Uno de los más agudos problemas latinoamericanos es que estamos necesitando más que nunca los Che Guevara del lenguaje, los revolucionarios de la literatura, más que los literatos de la revolución.'[1] With hindsight, and through extensive study of Cortázar's letters and other paratexts, this assertion seems to have been more concerned with rejection of the so-called 'coleópteros' and their rigid, inflexible kind of literature, than with working towards a way of writing fiction that would somehow directly contribute to the socialist revolution. Yet, with characteristic ambivalence, Cortázar carefully avoids elucidating precisely what he meant, or how he might have intended to be that Che Guevara of language through his writings. His *Papeles inesperados* provides a partial explanation, since in one of his 'Entrevistas ante el espejo', he claims:

> hace unos meses dije [...] que necesitábamos muchos Che Guevara del lenguaje, es decir, de la literatura [...] lo que él [Che Guevara] hizo en el terreno de la acción *otros* deberán llevarlo a cabo en el de la palabra, que por ahora se está quedando atrás de los hechos revolucionarios en Latinoamérica. Una revolución que no abarque todas las estructuras de la personalidad humana, y la lingüística [...] es una revolución a medias, una revolución amenazada desde adentro mucho más que desde afuera.[2]

It is interesting to note how Cortázar delegates historical and political responsibility to an impersonal, third-person agent: 'otros'. This is comparable to his use of the impersonal third-person plural. It is 'otros' who are making Cortázar write a kind of literature that goes against his aesthetic ideals, but it is also 'otros' who should assume responsibility. Cortázar's idea with regard to his understanding of the revolutionary process is intrinsically linked to his views on the *hombre nuevo*, which is central to *Libro de Manuel* and is defined by Cortázar as 'el revolucion-

---

[1] These debates were published as Collazos, Vargas Llosa and Cortázar, *Literatura en la revolución y revolución en la literatura*. The quotation comes from p. 76.
[2] 'Arnaldo: aquí tenés el texto que necesitabas para preanunciar el libro': Cortázar, *Papeles inesperados*, pp. 441–5 at p. 444. My emphasis.

ario de fuera hacia adentro y de dentro hacia fuera'.[3] It is clear that his refusal to be a 'literato de la revolución' implied a desire to instigate, through his writings, that which he called the revolution from within, involving all the 'estructuras de la personalidad humana, y la lingüística'. Cortázar would therefore not only refuse to comply with the restrictions of, for instance, didactic social realism, but would also attempt to expose several issues that for him were still considered somewhat 'taboo' in Latin America (for instance, homosexuality, onanism or even the interweaving of politics with humour and eroticism). In his aim, therefore, to promote the revolution from within, in *Libro de Manuel* Cortázar brings to the fore erotic and humorous elements in an attempt to encourage, as he states in the novel's prologue, a socialist way of life 'con todo lo que supone de amor, de juego y alegría' (*LM*, 8), while at the same time attempting to merge 'Lenin and Rimbaud' (*LM*, 90). If his fears about the 'quitinosidad' of the revolutionary *literati* were already present a few years after his Cuban epiphany (as in the letters to Retamar and Thiercelin, and with the text 'Casilla del camaleón'), Cortázar would become all the more wary after the 'Caso Padilla'.

Herberto Padilla was a well-known Cuban poet who, although originally a supporter of the revolution, by the end of the 1960s had begun openly to criticise Castro's regime. After the publication of his internationally praised *Fuera del juego* (1968), the Cuban Union of Writers and Artists (UNEAC) pronounced his work to be counterrevolutionary, and Padilla was imprisoned.[4] Immediately after his sentence, more than eighty intellectuals from Latin America and Europe, who had enthusiastically backed the revolution, signed a letter expressing their disagreement and disillusion with the regime's methods, insisting that artistic freedom should not be curtailed, and demanding the release of the poet. Thanks to such international pressure, Padilla was released after a month. Nevertheless, on the day of his release, he confessed his own 'mistake' and performed an act of contrition and self-criticism in front of an audience.

Although Cortázar was among those who had signed the first letter, he refused to sign a second, more severe attack on Castro. Instead, in May 1971, Cortázar chose to send a personal letter to the then director of the Casa de las Américas, Haydée Santamaría, expressing his discontent, albeit with hyperbolic ambivalence. This letter was in fact his long poem, later published under the title *Policrítica en la hora de los chacales*.[5] Although Cortázar's 'criticism' am-

---

3   Julio Cortázar Papers, Series 1C, Box 2, Folder 43.

4   For a full account of the events see Luis M. Quesada, '"Fuera del juego": A Poet's Appraisal of the Cuban Revolution', *Latin American Literary Review*, 3/6 (1975), 89–98.

5   From the text it seems clear that Cortázar did not want to fall out with Castro or with Cuban readers. To that effect, he reduces the 'episode' to a 'crisis barata', ending the poem: 'Oye, compadre, olvida *tanta crisis barata*. Empecemos de nuevo […] / nunca estuve tan cerca / como ahora, de lejos, contra viento y marea. El día nace': Julio Cortázar, *Policrítica en la hora de los chacales* (Buenos Aires: Portocaliu, 1987), p. 28. My emphasis.

biguously contained judgement and praise, admiration and attack, the poem was made public through publication by the 'Casa'. However, from then on, Cortázar became a figure of suspicion for many Cubans, especially in the light of some of the articles that he wrote for the French press in defence of Padilla. In Padilla's own opinion, the suspicion that Cortázar now aroused in Cuba was the main reason why *Libro de Manuel* was never published or distributed on the island.[6] Padilla himself also recalls how the consequences of this episode indubitably tempered Cortázar's optimism for socialist Cuba:

> Las acusaciones e insultos que lanzó Fidel Castro contra los setenta y pico escritores y artistas que atacaron su política de 1971 [...] tuvieron una dolorosa repercusión en Cortázar. Y le sirvieron para conocer la verdadera naturaleza de su adhesión al proceso revolucionario cubano. Se descubrió súbitamente solo y vulnerable, atacado por la izquierda y la derecha, sin la inocencia con que lo justificaba la primera y sin el cinismo que siempre reclama la segunda.[7]

As Padilla suggests, Cortázar was aware of this sudden 'political solitude'. *Libro de Manuel* in many respects reflects this position, as well as Cortázar's consciousness of it, as he anticipates in the prologue that 'los propugnadores de la realidad en la literatura lo van a encontrar [al libro] más bien fantástico mientras que los encaramados en la literatura de ficción deplorarán su deliberado contubernio con la historia de nuestros días' (*LM*, 7).

In effect, once *Libro de Manuel* was published, Cortázar felt forced to defend himself and his work from the accusations of 'committed' writers and intellectuals, who saw in his notion of 'revolucionarios de la literatura' a concept that would not lead to any actual pro-revolutionary action. Some even believed that Cortázar did not take the political situation seriously enough. The militant Padre Carlos Mugica, for example, dismissed *Libro de Manuel,* asserting that 'la revolución no podía ser tratada como un juego'.[8]

After the 'conversion' brought about by his encounter with revolutionary Cuba, Cortázar claimed that from then on, everything he wrote would always

---

[6] Padella, 'Imagen de Cortázar', p. 21.
[7] Ibid.
[8] González Bermejo, *Revelaciones de un cronopio*, p. 125. Cortázar was not alone in his views; the Uruguayan Mario Benedetti also saw the need to defend a different territory for aesthetic creation within a certain political belief and struggle: 'el intelectual verdaderamente revolucionario nunca podrá convertirse en un simple amanuense del hombre de acción; y si se convierte, estará en realidad traicionando a la revolución, ya que su misión natural dentro de la misma es ser algo así como su conciencia vigilante, su imaginativo intérprete, su crítico proveedor': 'Sobre las relaciones entre el hombre de acción y el intelectual', in *Letras del continente mestizo* (Montevideo: Arca, 1972), pp. 20–57 at p. 30.

express a 'point of contact' with man's historical present.⁹ Although this came from the allegedly newly 'politicised' Cortázar, it is in fact a stance that is manifested from his very early writings.¹⁰ And although in his final novel, the political is more explicitly to the fore than previously, this did not imply that everything that Cortázar wrote after *Libro de Manuel* was wholly political, nor even as explicit in its politics. The accepted critical division between the apolitical and the politicised Cortázar, therefore, fails to give the full picture, either of the early work or of the writings subsequent to *Libro de Manuel*.

After a decade of trying to produce literature that would perform an 'opération analogue' to the political revolution, Cortázar arrived at *Libro de Manuel* where, as he understood it, politics and literature explicitly coexist and combine. As he puts it in the prologue: 'si durante años he escrito textos vinculados con problemas latinoamericanos, a la vez que novelas y relatos en que esos problemas estaban ausentes o sólo asomaban tangencialmente, hoy y aquí, las aguas se han juntado' (*LM*, 7). Yet, when *Libro de Manuel* was published in 1973 – despite or because of its explicit political contents – it was very poorly received, particularly in Argentina. It is apparent that, from then on, Cortázar's fictional writings would never again attract the same interest. The academic passing of judgement based on exclusively political criteria was noted by the Argentinian academic Roberto Ferro who wrote:

> Del mismo modo que *Rayuela* significó un trampolín que lanzó a Cortázar al centro de la escena, diez años después la aparición del *Libro de Manuel* parece liquidar su prestigio y el interés por su escritura futura. Curioso efecto el de estas dos novelas. *Rayuela* provocó la relectura de todos sus textos anteriores, que fueron leídos desde los modos de lecturas que imponían un texto generado a partir de una propuesta en la que algunos de sus componentes trastornaban la escritura desplegada hasta entonces. *Libro de Manuel*, en cambio, condicionó la lecturas de los siguientes libros de Cortázar.¹¹

With hindsight, it could be said that in many respects the poor reception of *Libro de Manuel* changed the relationship between Argentinian readers and Cortázar (both as a public figure and in his writings). For Cortázar himself, it put an end to his rhetoric of guilt and self-justification, in that it marked his last attempt to try to conform to what was expected of him as a 'committed' writer.

---

⁹ In the original: 'En lo más gratuito que pueda yo escribir asomará siempre una voluntad de contacto con el presente histórico del hombre, una participación en su larga marcha hacia lo mejor de sí mismo como colectividad y humanidad', 10 May 1967, *Cartas/2 1964–1968*, p. 1141.

¹⁰ Although in the case of *Los premios* this 'present' is rather a fossilised version of the present Cortázar left behind when departing to Paris in 1951.

¹¹ Roberto Ferro, 'Cortázar, la trasgresión permanente', *Las palabras y las cosas*, 10 March 1991, 10–15 at p. 14.

It took Cortázar four years to detach himself from the novel, and claim that: '[*Libro de Manuel*] fue escrito mal, es el peor de mis libros. [...] Lo hice como si me lo hubieran encargado'.[12] He also admitted to Liliana Heker that he wrote *Libro de Manuel* in a race against time because, given political and historical urgencies, he wanted the text to have an immediate impact.[13]

In the years after 1973, with the return of Perón to Argentina and the Peronists to power, the political panorama in Argentina would begin to change very quickly, becoming increasingly violent, with guerrilla groups playing a significant role. Cortázar's anxiety regarding the novel's publication can therefore be understood in relation to the political changes that were then taking place in Argentina.[14] In this sense Santiago Juan-Navarro is correct when he argues that, especially for Cortázar, had it come later, *Libro de Manuel* would not have had the same political effect.[15]

Before the disillusionment brought about by its critical reception, Cortázar believed that his text could have a 'useful' political influence: 'Pienso modestamente que este libro [*Libro de Manuel*] puede tener alguna *utilidad* para la causa de los presos políticos de toda América Latina, no solamente de Argentina. No me hago ilusiones sobre la eficacia de la literatura, pero tampoco creo que sea inútil.'[16] Although the revolutionary 'usefulness' of the novel is debatable, the book certainly served a material purpose, for Cortázar donated all its royalties to legal aid for political prisoners in Argentina. Also, when a year later the novel was awarded the Médicis Prize in France, he gave the prize money to Rafael Gumucio, representative of the Chilean civilian resistance against Pinochet's regime.[17] However, helpful these acts might have been, if *Libro de Manuel*'s contribution to the socialist revolution was to be limited to them, it would appear that Cortázar's ambition to merge literature with politics in a kind of operation that would be analogous to the revolutionary political process in Latin America, was somewhat demeaned by deeds of mere 'useful-

---

[12] Soler Serrano, 'Grandes personajes a fondo: Julio Cortázar'. Again, Cortázar's choice of words goes directly to the quotations analysed at pp. 117–18 above, when he opts for the impersonal third-person plural to justify his own actions, and avoids – at least superficially – taking full responsibility. See also pp. 80, 87, 95, 120, 156.

[13] '*Manuel* por razones obvias, fue una carrera contra el reloj (incluso salió cinco meses después de lo que yo hubiera querido)', Cortázar to Liliana Heker, 28 August 1973, *Cartas/3 1969–1983*, p. 1534.

[14] Outside the Argentinian context, the announcement of the withdrawal of US troops from Vietnam was also an important pressing political and historical event among others, which features prominently in *Libro de Manuel*.

[15] See Santiago Juan-Navarro, 'History and Self-Reflexivity in the Writings of Julio Cortázar', in his *Archival Reflections: Postmodern Fiction of the Americas (Self-Reflexivity, Historical Revisionism, Utopia)* (London: Associated University Presses, 2000), pp. 196–223 at p. 314.

[16] Cortázar in Carbono, 'Mi ametralladora es la literatura', 10–15 at p. 14. My emphasis.

[17] See Goloboff, *Julio Cortázar: la biografía*, p. 305.

ness'.[18] Was this what Cortázar had in mind when he aimed to write literature as a 'Che Guevara of language'?

Political structure

The politics of collage used by Cortázar in both *La vuelta* and *Último Round* is taken to extremes in *Libro de Manuel*, so that practically all the insertions (thirty-six out of a total of forty-two) deal exclusively with political issues, mainly centring on forms of political repression.[19] Although the novel's plot and themes also deal directly with political concerns (the urban 'revolution' of 'la Joda', Andrés Fava's quandary over action/inaction quandary, a kidnapping operation demanding the release of political prisoners), the collage format is a very effective manifestation of the novel's political dimension. This marks a crucial point in the evolution of the political element in Cortázar's writings, because although he had already shown an interest in inserting or alluding to extra-textual visual elements, this is the first time that he tried to combine that interest with the novel as a genre. This, however, does not originate in him suddenly becoming a politicised author, but rather it stems from the combination of wanting to subvert the dogmatic restrictions of 'revolutionary writing' while continuing to explore the aesthetic possibilities of fictional genres. Added to that is the concrete historical urgency of the time, and Cortázar's belief in using literature as his own 'weapon' in the socialist struggle, or as he put it: 'En este tiempo hay quien dice que lo único que cuenta es el lenguaje de las ametralladoras [...] cada uno tiene sus ametralladoras específicas. La mía, por el momento, es la literatura.'[20] Embedding typographical insertions, mainly containing news about human rights abuses, in the narrative layout of the novel, communicates (through their immediate visual impact) the urgency of the need to raise awareness about such violations as well as about the violent repression of left-wing guerrillas in Latin America. So how does this differ from Cortázar's understanding of *contenidismo*?[21] For it would seem that he is in effect putting

---

[18] This seems, moreover, to contradict the very Romantic idea of literature that Cortázar so fervently defended through his belief in artistic freedom. As Terry Eagleton wrote, 'Few words are more offensive to the literary ears than "use" [in the sense that "literature has a use"], evoking as it does paperclips and hairdryers': *Literary Theory: An Introduction* (Oxford: Blackwell, 1983), p. 208.

[19] For a detailed analysis of the inserted fragments see Emily D. Hicks, *Border Writing: The Multidimensional Text* (Minneapolis: University of Minnesota Press, 1991).

[20] Cortázar in Carbono, 'Mi ametralladora es la literatura', p. 11.

[21] In *Viaje alrededor de una mesa* Cortázar insistió on the need to distinguish between form and content, proposing the creation of a new kind of aesthetics with the power to counter the 'fossilisation' of language and literature. Once again, he showed his opposition to the typically revolutionary *contenidismo*. This was understood by Cortázar to mean 'la literatura al servicio de un contenido revolucionario', a literature that tended to present a narrow and simplistic vision of reality: González Bermejo, *Revelaciones de un cronopio*, p. 141.

his work at the service of a political aim. The answer would seem to be that the novel's other major preoccupations make it impossible to categorise it simply as a political or a 'contenidista' text.

Libro de Manuel describes the day-to-day reality of a group of friends, mostly Argentinian exiles, living in Paris. Parallel to the 'political' activities that most of them carry out within their group, 'la Joda', they all contribute to the writing of a book for baby Manuel, the son of two of the novel's protagonists, Susana and Patricio. The material that the characters put together for his scrapbook ranges from newspaper articles and advertisements to official government reports, and even to the typed minutes of a meeting between a journalist and Fidel Castro (*LM*, 273–9). The prologue to the book explains that these newspaper articles, which are reproduced in their original French, Spanish, Italian or English, were the actual articles that Cortázar read, cut out and kept as he was writing *Libro de Manuel*: 'No sorprenderá la frecuente incorporación de noticias de la prensa, leídas a medida que el libro se iba haciendo [...] las noticias del lunes o del jueves que entraban en los intereses momentáneos de los personajes fueron incorporadas en el curso de mi trabajo del lunes o del jueves' (*LM*, 7–8). As Cortázar further clarifies in his 'Corrección de pruebas', this had to be done in an attempt to '[contar] una historia que pretende reflejar también nuestra Historia de esta misma mañana', since in effect, 'la intención de inmediatez del libro [es la] única razón de su escritura'.[22]

Conforming to what by this point in Cortázar's evolution has become a pattern, the prologue (or introductory note) to the novel creates a space for Cortázar to explain himself and justify his book (despite him declaring that 'Los libros deben defenderse por su cuenta', *LM*, 8). Yet, the note would prove to be insufficient as, once the book was published, Cortázar time and again saw himself explaining to critics and fellow writers (and, indirectly, also to the readers) what it was that he had tried to do in and with *Libro de Manuel*. This to an extent showed that the book could not be 'useful' by itself as Cortázar had hoped. In a 1973 interview, for instance, he found it important to clarify that:

> [*Libro de Manuel*] es una tentativa de convergencia de dos cosas que yo había estado haciendo paralelamente. Por un lado estaba haciendo eso que llaman *literatura pura*, ficción, novelas y cuentos. Por otra parte, he tenido polémicas, he escrito cartas donde había referencias a mi militancia ideológica. [...] Esta vez me pareció que *tal vez* era el momento de intentar una cosa difícil de hacer, la de encontrar una convergencia en la que, sin perder el nivel literario, escribiera un libro que es una novela, que se puede leer como una novela, pero que contiene al mismo tiempo una visión más amplia, un contenido de tipo ideológico y político, actual y contemporáneo, y que no se queda en declaraciones líricas, sino que cita concretamente

[22] Cortázar, 'Corrección de pruebas', p. 27.

hechos. Por eso es que en el libro están los documentos. [...] Entonces me pareció que era necesario hacer esa especie de collage, donde existieran los documentos, las pruebas. El que quiera las verá, y el que no quiera verlas no las verá.[23]

Although once again Cortázar partially hides behind a rhetoric of ambivalence (with his use of 'tal vez' for example, or the third person of 'eso que llaman literatura pura'), it is obvious that when reading *Libro de Manuel* it is in fact impossible not to see the documents to which Cortázar refers. The act of not seeing would involve a deliberate decision to turn a blind eye to an evident reality; an attitude that, like Oliveira's 'no te metás', is in Cortázar's view politically and ethically to be condemned. The documents are inserted in the text to bring to the fore a reality for the reader to see and act upon. With time, the action implied in such 'witness' seems to be the prevention of historical amnesia. Cortázar alludes to this in his note with regard to the news of the killing of Israeli athletes in Munich and the total lack of journalistic coverage of the events happening at the same time in the Patagonian city of Trelew (*LM*, 9), where sixteen members of left-wing Peronist movements (ERP, Montoneros and FAR) were executed after they tried to escape from prison.[24] This view of the press as participating in a worldwide truth-selecting conspiracy is repeated in the novel through some of the comments that the characters make about the manipulation of information, as they read out the clippings.[25] The political meaning of the collage format of the novel, therefore, lies not only in the act of 'awakening' the reader to certain political facts that Cortázar considered important and wanted to put forward in their testimonial form, but also in the alienating effect that these insertions have precisely because of their testimonial nature.

The clippings, thus, represent the reality of the non-fictional world during the actual writing of the novel while they also constitute the frame of imaginary reality within which the characters exist. This double reality in the form of the novel becomes testimony to historical events but also of an aesthetic experiment. As Theo D'Haen points out:

> When the documentary materials become part of a work of literature, they are estranged from their natural sphere and instead of possessing the ephemerality of a newspaper article [...] they are embedded into a work of art which is supposedly eternal and which demands a different and increased

---

[23] Cortazár in Carbono, 'Mi ametralladora es la literatura', p. 12. My emphasis.

[24] An excellent account of these events was written by Francisco 'Paco' Urondo, later executed by the last military dictatorship: *La patria fusilada* (Buenos Aires: Tierra del Sur, 2007).

[25] For example, 'El informe señala que la tortura se aplica en general de manera científica (qué prostitución del idioma de los diarios, pensó petulante el que te dije, confunden cancha o técnica con ciencia)': *LM*, 243. See also *LM*, 32.

kind of attention from the reader. As a result, the horror of the events described is arrested and emphasised.[26]

Cortázar would have it that the 'rule of the game' is that these clippings represent, but also *are*, reality so that when combined with the absurd and humoristic elements of the novel, that 'reality' becomes more realistic: 'Lo "real": los recortes. Lo "absurdo": cosas como el pingüino para traer dólares falsos. La convergencia de eso vuelve más real la realidad.'[27] It could be said, though, that the insertions in fact underline the 'authenticity' of the fictional storyline with which they are linked (as in the case of André Breton's *Nadja* for example).[28] However, Cortázar's introductory note, telling us about the origins of the newspaper articles in the authoritative voice of Cortázar the author, provides a testimonial dimension to the insertions that the reader cannot then assume to be fictional. This quality is enhanced by the seemingly unaltered typographical reproduction of the insertions.

When a certain element such as a newspaper cutting, a governmental report, a diagram or a drawing visually interrupts the linearity of a conventional narrative layout, this has a direct and a somewhat destabilising impact on the reader. When turning the page of a book the eye is invariably caught by the unexpected. Once the unexpected has been incorporated into the visual field of that new page, the reader's eye involuntarily looks for a clue in the narrative which will explain, and thus justify, the presence of the unanticipated. In the novel, and for most of the insertions, the characters themselves explain the presence of an article or a report to the reader, as they choose to incorporate it in the book for baby Manuel. Moreover, they sometimes proceed to translate and comment upon it. This means that even though the reader might decide to skip visually the extra-textual insertion in his/her avidness to continue with the flow of the fictional plot, the contents of the fragments are nevertheless incorporated into the novel's narrative thread. Therefore, even if the reader chooses not to scrutinise the insertions, he/she will be 'forced' to read about them through the narrative. This emphasises the irony behind Cortázar's assertion that 'el que no quiera verlas [las pruebas] no las verá', for everything that is laid out typographically on what Parkinson Zamora calls the 'verbal surface of the narrative', is also explained within the narrative.[29] In other words, it is impossible for the reader not to see 'las pruebas'.

---

[26] Theo D'Haen, *Text to Reader: A Communicative Approach to Fowles, Barth, Cortázar and Boon* (Amsterdam: John Benjamins, 1983), p. 92.

[27] Julio Cortázar Papers, Series 1C, Box 2, Folder 43.

[28] In André Breton's novel documents (photographs, art reproductions, letters) are included to substantiate the authenticity of the underlying tragedy of the fictional story being told: *Nadja*, trans. Richard Howard (London: Penguin Books, 1999).

[29] Lois Parkinson Zamora, 'Movement and Stasis, Film and Photo: Temporal Structures in the Recent Fiction of Julio Cortázar', *Review of Contemporary Fiction*, 3/ 3 (1983), 51–65 at p. 60.

Whereas in *El examen* or *Los premios* the aim was to show political reality through allegory, in *Libro de Manuel*, with the intention of awakening the reader's political consciousness in a direct and more immediate manner, Cortázar wants to show political reality as 'it is', or at least, as he apprehends it through newspapers, official reports and so forth. Thus, it is apparent that Cortázar here has taken on board one of Bertolt Brecht's aesthetic precepts, namely that

> Realism is not a mere question of form. If we were to copy the style of [...] realists, we would no longer be realists. For time flows and methods become exhausted; stimuli no longer work. New problems appear and demand new methods. Reality changes; in order to represent it, modes of representation must also change.[30]

By playing with the reader's expectations regarding the visual representation of his novel, Cortázar emphasises the irrevocability of a given reality within the fictional narrative. In addition, through the visual effect of the insertions, he alienates the reader from his/her own place of comfort. Even if the reality presented is no longer 'real' as a present, it is real as history. This is what is so well achieved in short stories such as 'Apocalipsis de Solentiname' or 'Segunda vez'. Since the reader is aware of the 'reality' of the events depicted, the texts seem to be more categorical in the effects that they produce on the reader. In *Libro de Manuel* the aim is to destabilise the readers, yet what the novel also demands from them is that they fight against historical amnesia. As well as through the testimonial contents, this is put across allegorically in the final lines of the book, when Lonstein is at the morgue cleaning up a corpse, which we are meant to think is that of Marcos. The description of the body and its position draws a clear analogy between the novel's last scene and the well-known image of Che Guevara's corpse lying with his head slightly propped up, after being executed in the Bolivian jungle. Lonstein's aim is not simply to clean the dead body, but rather: 'convertirlo en un cuerpo que la esponja y el detergente lavarían hasta dejarlo blanco y puro, toda huella de la historia ya borrada' (*LM*, 386). In this sense, the insertions in *Libro de Manuel* want to leave those historical traces in the reader's mind, so that history and political truths are not altered, wiped out or forgotten.

The visual 'interruptions', in turn, have a similar effect to that which Walter Benjamin understood in relation to Brecht's theatre: '[by arresting] the action in its course [...] [the play] compels the listener [in this case, the reader] to adopt an attitude *vis-à-vis* the process, the actor *vis-à-vis* his role'.[31] *Libro de Manuel*

---

30 Bertolt Brecht, *Brecht On Theatre: The Development Of An Aesthetic*, trans. John Willett (London: Methuen, 1964), pp. 69–70.
31 Walter Benjamin, 'The Author as Producer', in *Reflections*, trans. Edmund Jephcott (New York: Schocken Books, 1978), pp. 220–38 at p. 235.

thus challenges the reader by combining revolutionary didacticism with *avant-garde* stylistic techniques, which is what prevents it from falling prey to *contenidismo*. These techniques are introduced with the ultimate aim of conveying political significance through the alienation produced by the 'authenticity' and contents of the articles enclosed. Although it may be argued that newspaper articles are familiar in a very mundane sense, when inserted within the fictional narrative they hinder the reader from fully surrendering to a fictional realm, and thereby have a disrupting, alienating effect on the reading experience.

Through the collage, Manuel's book is being created as the narrative progresses. The reader is hence effectively positioned where baby Manuel will be when he comes to read his book: 'Desorden lamentable de algunas páginas del libro de Manuel [...] sin embargo Gómez y Marcos e incluso el aludido terminan por reconocer que en esa recopilación al tuntún hay suficiente claridad si alguna vez Manuel es capaz de servirse comilfó de su aparato ocular' (*LM*, 307). The lack of explicit connection among the narrative sections emphasises the idea that, more than ever before in any of Cortázar's novels, the reader has to be an active participant in connecting and understanding the text as a unit. In this sense, the structure itself works as a medium to awaken the reader into the political reality that Cortázar presents through the inserted fragments. In Parkinson Zamora's filmic analogy of the novel, she argues that due to its fragmentary collage structure, 'the novel is a series of still shots to be contemplated and connected by the reader's efforts, rather than a moving camera which sweeps the reader along'.[32] This is also expressed almost literally in the text when, describing the death of Marcos, the narrator says: '[la] detención de la película que de un segundo a otro provocaría los silbidos de la platea' (*LM*, 362). Each inserted fragment represents in this sense a halt, not only in the visual flow of the narrative but also, crucially, in the continuity of the story. Consequently, through the political collage, the reader is expected to be emotionally drawn to the action of the plot, while at the same time alienated from it by the challenge implied in the novel's form and content. However, this inevitably ceases to surprise the reader as s/he works through the entire length of the novel; so that in the very repetition of the technique, the shocking effect that succeeds in the stories, in *Libro de Manuel* loses impact as the insertions gain predictability.

Cortázar was surely aware of the progressive loss of impact in the text, and perhaps for this reason opted to make some of the insertions physically impossible to read in full. In fact, some of them remain so unconnected that the reader must make an effort to decipher their meaning and narrative purpose. For instance, on page 213, a headline is reproduced in the middle of the page, without any introduction or commentary from the characters. The fragment reads: 'Amérique Latine. Argentine : querelles de généraux et luttes populaires' (*LM*,

---

[32] Parkinson Zamora, 'Movement and Stasis', p. 61.

213). Only a few pages on, another headline is introduced; this time it occupies the entire page, yet it is cropped, so that it cannot be read in its entirety (*LM*, 217; see Fig. 1). Examples like these not only alienate the reader in terms of interrupting the narrative flow, but also underline the effort and involvement expected from an 'active' reader who is expected not to fall into complacency.³³

Occasionally, Cortázar reproduces imaginary situations in which the reader might find him/herself while attempting to make sense of the

> erto M. Levings
> idente de la Rep
> litar. Asumirá el jueves 18
> Podría armarse en pie de
> Guerra a 150 hombres con
> las armas robadas en
> Uruguay. Preocupación

Figure 1

fragments inserted in the novel. In one instance, for example, we read how el que te dije tries to detach himself from the distractions of the domestic environment that he is immersed in, so as to take in the full significance of the newspaper article that he has in front of him. Thus:

> Aislándose del rumor, del chillido de Manuel en pro de los bombones, del gesto instintivo de Heredia [...] el que te dije alcanzó a hacer un hueco para leer por su cuenta las conclusiones del informe, la simple frase final que hubiera sido necesario repetir cada noche y día por todas las ondas, en todas las imprentas, desde todas las plumas [...] LA OPINIÓN PÚBLICA DE LOS PAÍSES CIVILIZADOS TIENE HOY UNA AUTÉNTICA POSIBILIDAD DE HACER CESAR POR MEDIO DE DENUNCIAS REITERADAS Y PRECISAS LAS PRÁCTICAS INHUMANAS DE QUE SON OBJETO TANTOS HOMBRES Y MUJERES EN BRASIL. (*LM*, 245)

This kind of 'lesson', shouted straight at the reader and at his/her passivity, makes Cortázar's own rejection of the inflexible didacticism in revolutionary literature (as implied in his view) somewhat hypocritical. For although, ostensibly, Cortázar is not promoting propagandistic dogmatic literature, at points in *Libro de Manuel* he does seem to simplify his own aesthetic tropes for the sake of one political message. It is this kind of 'concession' that constitutes a change in the representation of the political in Cortázar's writings, from *El examen* to this final novel.

In *La vuelta* and in *Último Round*, the collage technique was used to combine political excerpts with many that were completely unrelated to socio-political or historical concerns. The result was two works embodying the sum of the connections that the different fragments within them establish with each other. They include a political dimension, but not as unique unifying element, but rather as one more of the many fragments combined. In *Libro de Manuel* collage

---

[33] See also examples of this in *Libro de Manuel* at pp. 187, 196 and 332.

is used exclusively for political material; even those very few fragments which seem to bear no explicit relation to politics (such as the car advertisement [*LM*, 220], or a recipe for 'sándwiches fritos indicados para fines de semana' [*LM*, 347]), when combined with the others or with what the characters have to say about them, acquire a (direct or indirect) political meaning. Yet the collage is not the only representation of the political in the novel. In order to extend the meaning of revolutionary (both 'internal' and 'external') into other realms beyond the 'seriously' political, the collage structure is combined with other key elements, namely humour, eroticism and playfulness.

Eros and humour

Cortázar's views on humour were by no means put aside in *Libro de Manuel*. On the contrary, by the time that *Libro de Manuel* was published humour, together with eroticism and playfulness, had assumed a key role in Cortázar's conception of what 'revolutionary' literature should be about. Indeed, these elements became crucial in Cortázar's understanding of what the highest aim of the socialist way of life should be, as he elucidates in *Literatura en la revolución*:

> La sociedad tal como la concibe el socialismo no sólo no puede anular al individuo así entendido, sino que aspira a desarrollarlo en un grado tal que toda la negatividad, todo lo demoníaco que aprovecha la sociedad capitalista, sea superado por un nivel de su personalidad donde lo individual y lo colectivo cesen de enfrentarse y de frustrarse. La auténtica realidad es mucho más que el 'contexto socio-histórico', la realidad soy yo y setecientos millones de chinos [...] cada hombre y todos los hombres, el hombre agonista, el hombre en la espiral histórica, el *homo faber* y el *homo ludens*, el erotismo y la responsabilidad social [...] y por eso una literatura que merezca su nombre es aquella que *incide en el hombre desde todos lo ángulos* [...] que lo exalta, lo incita, lo cambia, lo justifica, *lo saca de sus casillas*.[34]

Cortázar's levelling of eroticism with social responsibility, or of humour with political action, would not readily be accepted by many left-wing intellectuals, who saw in Cortázar's tenets a superficial, even immature, attitude to politics, as opposed to political commitment. Figures like David Viñas thought Cortázar was not serious enough about politics, and therefore his attempts at writing 'political literature' could not be taken seriously. Yet for Cortázar the socialist revolution ought not to be based on dogmatic or inflexible views; that would inevitably lead to a dogmatic or inflexible system. 'La revolución', Cortázar claimed, 'no se hace con abejas u hormigas, se hace con hombres. Si los hombres

---

[34] Collazos, Vargas Llosa and Cortázar, '*Literatura en la revolución y revolución en la literatura*', pp. 64–5. My emphasis.

siguen defendiendo posiciones erradas o sectarias sobre lo que es bueno o malo, no son revolucionarios. Para mí, son contrarrevolucionarios.'[35] This showed his fundamental understanding of the meaning of the socialist revolution. Some critics, however, would, rather patronizingly, see his views as 'hermoso y pleno', but highly unrealistic.[36] Yet Cortázar did not, at least at this point, let himself be beaten by the inflexibility that he so despised, and therefore, in *Libro de Manuel* he deliberately interweaves humour, playfulness and eroticism with an unambiguous political dimension, in order to 'sacar de las casillas [al lector]'. Within the novel, this levelling also reads as a criticism of certain participants in the revolution: 'Gómez y Roland y Lucien Verneuil son de esos que repetirán la historia, te los ves venir de lejos, *se jugarán la piel* por la revolución, lo darán todo pero cuando llegue el después repetirán las mismas definiciones [...] y negarán la libertad más profunda, esa que yo llamo burguesmente individual y mea culpa' (*LM*, 76; my emphasis).

Cortázar's increasingly sharp sense of guilt at not doing what was expected of him as a 'committed' Latin American writer is modified in *Libro de Manuel*. It is apparent that he is no longer willing to 'vendre le plus cher la peau'. Rather, he appears willing to reconcile himself with the rhetoric of the 'pequeñoburgués' to emphasise once again the 'quitinosidad' of those who will 'jugarse la piel' in their attempt to take the revolution 'seriously'. So Cortázar contrasts those habits that are deemed bourgeois, with the dangers of political dogmatism; in the words of the protagonist, and *alter ego*, Andrés Fava:

> jamás habrá nada que me arranque esto que soy, al que escucha *free jazz* y va a acostarse con Francine en cumplimiento de ceremonias que no aprueban los jóvenes maoístas [...] [soy] pequeñoburgués contra los Gómez y los Lucien Verneuil que quieren hacer la revolución para salvar al proletariado y al campesinado y al colonizado y al alienado de eso que llaman con tanta razón imperialismo. (*LM*, 350)[37]

This is not to say, however, that Cortázar had stopped feeling guilty altogether. He was still, in many respects, standing in a position of 'political solitude' – to use Padilla's phrase – constantly receiving criticism from both the left and the right.

---

[35] Cortázar, *Policrítica*, p. 18.

[36] These are the words that the Chilean critic Volodia Teitelboim used to describe the quoted assertion: 'Epílogo', ibid., pp. 29–55 at p. 54.

[37] Andrés Fava's defensiveness of his right to listen to 'free jazz' (repeated also in *LM*, 147) is reminiscent of *El examen*'s el cronista and his fight over the jukebox. In that novel el cronista defends his right to listen to 'London again' over national folkloric tunes. An interesting parallelism seems to arise: Cortázar makes the link between the rigidity of the Peronist regime and the inflexibility of a socialist government.

When it came to generating the revolution from within something which he deemed fundamental for the development of the *hombre nuevo*, and which required humour and eroticism to be as central as concrete political ideals, although Cortázar would repeatedly defend his standpoint, he was not free of self-doubt. This is certainly identifiable in *Libro de Manuel*. In the words of el que te dije it is apparent that Cortázar's attempt to meld politics with literature sometimes made him wish he was altogether outside the realm of fiction, or that he could at least be a 'novelista puro':

> Cada vez me da la impresión de que estoy metiendo la pata y no el dedo [...] que en el fondo está mal lo que hago y que, por ejemplo, la libido no es tan importante para nuestro destino [...] vuelvo a escribir y me da asco [...] quisiera ser cualquier otra cosa [...] le tengo una envidia bárbara a los *novelistas puros* o a los teóricos marxistas [...] [tengo] miedo a estar equivocado, a que en realidad puede ser que la revolución se haga sin esa idea que yo tengo del hombre nuevo (*LM*, 233–4; my emphasis).

Almost a decade after writing *Libro de Manuel*, during the lectures that Cortázar gave at Berkeley, he would still defend ideas about the importance of a revolution 'from within'. With particular relation to *Libro de Manuel*, Cortázar wrote in his lecture notes that: 'Detrás de [*Libro de Manuel*] hay un deseo de ayudar a esa revolución de "dentro a afuera" que sigo creyendo imprescindible. El libro ataca diversos tabúes, empezando por el machismo, el puritanismo en materia erótica, los vocabularios obsoletos que usan muchos revolucionarios.'[38] This is indeed outlined in the novel's prologue:

> Más que nunca creo que la lucha en pro del socialismo debe enfrentar el horror cotidiano con la única actitud que un día le dará la victoria: cuidando preciosamente, celosamente, la capacidad de vivir tal como la queremos para ese futuro [...]. Lo que cuenta, lo que yo he tratado de afirmar, es el signo positivo ante la escalada del desprecio y del espanto, y esa afirmación tiene que ser lo más solar, lo más vital del hombre, su sed erótica y lúdica, su liberación de los tabúes. (*LM*, 8)

It is to this effect that throughout the novel characters are seen breaking many of the sexual taboos ingrained in Roman Catholic Latin America. This is not manifested simply through the presentation of Andrés Fava's sadistic pleasure in sodomizing his lover Francine (*LM,* 142, 150), but also for instance through the recurrent implied associations between sexual enjoyment and a revolutionary political utopia. A good example of this is the moment in the text when, as

[38] Julio Cortázar Papers, Series 1C, Box 2, Folder 43.

Ludmilla is climaxing with her lover Marcos, she thinks of 'la Joda's' revolutionary success: 'Perdida en el placer [...], hundiendo las manos en el pelo de Marcos lo llamó hacia lo alto, se abrió como un arco murmurando su nombre donde cualquier cosa empezaba desde otros límites [...] donde todo podía ser almanaques y barriletes [...] donde alguna vez la Joda podía tener todos esos nombres, todas esas estrellas' (*LM*, 263).

Already in *Último Round* Cortázar had referred to the 'underdevelopment' of Latin American literature in terms of expressions of eroticism. In 'Que sepa abrir la puerta para salir a jugar' Cortázar writes:

> entre nosotros el subdesarrollo de la expresión lingüística en lo que toca a la libido vuelve casi siempre pornografía toda materia erótica extrema [...] la colonización, la miseria y el gorilato también nos mutilan estéticamente: pretenderse dueño de un lenguaje erótico cuando ni siquiera se ha ganado la soberanía política es ilusión de adolescente que a la hora de la siesta hojea con la mano que le queda libre un número de *Playboy.* (*UR2*, 62)

For Cortázar, literary 'underdevelopment' with regard to eroticism was intrinsically linked to the socio-political underdevelopment of Latin America. When it came to his own literature, this kind of taboo acted as an aesthetic as well as a political challenge, and was as important as social transformation for a revolutionary. Nevertheless, in *Último Round* Cortázar confessed that he too had been a victim of the rigidity that reigned over Latin America with regard to the use of explicitly erotic language: 'El miedo sigue desviando la aguja de nuestros compases [...] en toda mi obra no he sido capaz de escribir ni una sola vez la palabra *concha*, que por lo menos en dos ocasiones me hizo más falta que los cigarrillos' (*UR2*, 83). In *Libro de Manuel*, Cortázar makes up for that 'wasted' time and has the characters confront and ridicule such taboos:

> ...carajo, puta, no encuentro las palabras.
> —Mezclás el argentino y el gallego en dosis iguales, polaquita.
> —Es que tengo la ventaja de no entender demasiado de qué se trata —dijo Ludmilla—. Al principio Andrés me hacía repetir cosas para reírse con Patricio y Susana, concha peluda y pija colorada, cosas así, a mí me suenan muy bonitas.
> —Son bonitas —dijo Marcos—, solamente que a veces la gente las usa mal, las echa a perder. (*LM*, 146)

Having Ludmilla utter these words, with the added encouragement of Marcos, removes the 'rigidity', the 'quitinosidad', imposed on these 'malas palabras' by Argentinian and Latin American society. The words ultimately are there to acquire the simple beauty (implied in the use of 'bonito') that the speaker wants to give to them.

Cortázar's attack on the 'lenguaje quitinizado' as he calls it, is part of his attempt to revolutionise literature from within, so that, in turn, man would know himself completely before moving on to fight for a revolution with a more 'highly developed' understanding of what makes us the people we are.[39] It was apparent that Cortázar was not just trying this in his fictional writings, but it was something that he perceived had to change in Cuba and in Nicaragua as well, as he tells Prego Gadea:

> En el *Libro de Manuel* yo di un paso adelante, incluso forzándome las manos a veces, porque estaba harto de haber discutido en Cuba acerca de problemas de tipo erótico, por ejemplo, y de tropezarme con la quitina. O el tema de la homosexualidad que ahora también es objeto de una discusión fraternal pero muy viva con los nicaragüenses [...] esa actitud machista de rechazo, despectiva y humillante hacia la sexualidad, no es en absoluto una actitud revolucionaria. Ese es otro de los aspectos que quise mostrar en *Libro de Manuel*.[40]

Homosexuality (touched upon in *Los premios* and in *62*) is brought to the fore in *Libro de Manuel*. We see, for instance, Patricio insisting that Susana should include in the book for Manuel a newspaper article dealing with homosexuals, assuring her that: 'Manuel te lo agradecerá algún día, ponele la firma' (*LM*, 319). In addition, Lonstein describes the homosexual adventures of his own youth. We are told in his erotic manifesto – entitled 'Lonstein on masturbation' (*LM*, 207) – that in his will to achieve a 'conocimiento total de los límites del placer, de sus variantes y sus bifurcaciones' (*LM*, 210), he had a homosexual relationship – significantly – with the 'cartero que me traía *Sur*' (*LM*, 207). However, it has to be said that homosexuality, especially in *Libro de Manuel*, although included in the narrative, remains somewhat tangential, if not altogether a token gesture. Hence, although he might have thought otherwise, Cortázar deals with it conservatively and not in ways that would break from any traditional views, let alone be revolutionary. The intention to change the 'actitud machista' with regard to homosexuality is clearly visible in *Libro de Manuel*. However, merely presenting homosexuality as a topic within the narrative is not enough to change an ingrained attitude.

Nevertheless, what remains clear is the fact that Cortázar is trying to criticise a certain level of hypocrisy within the socialist revolution insofar as homosexuality and machismo in general are concerned. This comes through in the novel both indirectly, and also with direct allegations such as that issued by Lonstein: 'Y después quieren hacer la revolución y echar abajo los ídolos del imperialismo o como carajo los llamen, incapaces de mirarse de veras en un espejo' (*LM*, 226).

---

[39] Prego Gadea, *La fascinación de las palabras*, p. 85.
[40] Ibid., p. 223.

As well as being the most outspoken critic of the acts of 'la Joda', Lonstein is the 'guru' of masturbation and erotic self-exploration. After going through his different experiences with both men and women, Lonstein confesses to el que te dije why now he simply prefers to be alone and resort to masturbation as a form of 'erotismo válido' (*LM*, 210). It is evident that el que te dije (who, as opposed to Lonstein, defends and reports on the acts of 'la Joda') is not comfortable with Lonstein's discourse, and almost involuntarily instils a sense of puritan shame in him as he asks: '¿no te resulta penoso hablar de todo eso?', to which Lonstein replies, 'Sí [...] por eso mismo creo que tengo que hablar' (*LM*, 210). Lonstein's response destabilises el que te dije, prompting him to question his own reaction and discomfort. In turn, the reiteration of Lonstein's 'expositions' throughout the novel, and the accompanying reactions similar to el que te dije's, manifest Cortázar's quasi-didactic ambition to break free from deep-rooted sexual taboos, so that through that process the readers can begin to analyse themselves, to get to know who they really are (or want to be), beyond imposed, inflexible categories. It is highly significant that Lonstein's erotic manifestoes tend to be linked to political reflections upon 'la Joda' and their revolutionary ambitions, for instance:

> Ahí los tenés a los muchachos, los estás viendo jugarse, y entonces qué; si llegan a salirse con la suya, y aquí vuelvo a extrapolar y me imagino la Grandísima Joda Definitiva, entonces pasará una vez más lo de siempre: endurecimiento ideológico, rigor mortis de la vida cotidiana, mojigatería, no diga malas palabras compañero, burocracia del sexo y sexualidad a horario de la burocracia, todo tan sabido viejo, todo tan inevitable. (*LM*, 227)

Lonstein's words are loaded with a kind of ideological resignation and political disillusion. It is even ironic to note that what he sees as the predictable consequences of political victory is comparable to the mood felt by the characters in *El examen* or *Divertimento*: the repetition of political systems that do not learn from previous mistakes; indeed, they are immersed in a generalised 'historical amnesia'. Yet, even though Lonstein anticipates and rejects what he sees as the inevitable 'quitinosidad' that will be born with the revolution, he nevertheless continues to help in the political operations of 'la Joda'. This certainly echoes Cortázar's own political position at the time of writing the novel.

Given his premise that 'Lo exótico abre todas las puertas' (*LM*, 105), Lonstein applauds the idea of transporting fake dollars from Argentina to Paris in order to support the kidnapping operation. The money will come hidden in the lining of thermal containers built especially for the absurd 'pingüino turquesa', which surreally will end up wandering on its own through the streets of the French capital (*LM*, 143-4). For Lonstein, the penguin is not absurd; it is one of the many elements that 'la Joda' needs to embrace – together with eroticism – so as to avoid a future which, although politically it might embody the socialist ideals for which they are fighting, in every other respect it might turn out to be rigid and dehumanised (as well as dehumanising). As he puts it:

> Cosas como la luna llena, el pingüino [...] mi hongo que crece [...] andá a explicarles a tipos como Gómez o Roland que también eso puede ser la Joda, te escupen en la oreja; por eso tengo miedo del mañana, che, cuando ya no estemos nosotros, cuando se queden solos. Todavía hay contacto, se puede hablar con ellos, pero lo malo es que son los mismos que un día te sacarán carpiendo. El mismo Marcos, ya verás. (*LM*, 106)

In such instances we see the epitome of the novel's purpose, that is, to try and take the meaning of revolutionary into other realms beyond the one considered to be 'seriously' political. The absurdist hilariousness embodied in the penguin and in Lonstein's 'hongo' as the phallic representation of his eroticism, are also to an extent part of 'la Joda' and their will to fight for a different political future. But Lonstein feels that he cannot be optimistic; in fact, the rigidity of the future is so imminent that he is already apprehensive. Even Marcos, the fervent 'seriously committed' leader of 'la Joda', will eventually stop listening to his own *compañeros*, as he – following Oliveira's views – becomes blinded by the collective.

If Andrés Fava is read as a committed version of *Rayuela*'s Oliveira, then Marcos could be said to be a radicalised version of Medrano from *Los premios*. His utopian socialist inclinations can be perceived through his political enthusiasm, his vitality and his language: 'su idioma corriente es como su vida, una alianza de iconoclasia y creación, reflejo de lo revolucionario entendido antes de todo sistema' (*LM*, 88). Although it seems that, ideologically, Marcos's group bears no relation to Lonstein's notions of 'un-rigid' revolution, he can nevertheless understand Lonstein and maintain, at least thus far in the novel, an open mind: 'Marcos sabía ver las cosas de más de un lado [...] lo había entendido desde un principio, desde la llegada de Lonstein a la Joda' (*LM*, 183). For Marcos, as for Lonstein, it is imperative to break free from taboos – sexual, moral, cultural and linguistic – with the difference that for Marcos the most important aspect of the fight against taboos is the social one. Like Medrano in *Los premios*, he aims to fight against oppression and towards the construction of the *hombre nuevo*.

How Marcos actually conceives of this *hombre nuevo* is left ambiguous in the text, yet it is clear that the hope for that new man, new future, is embodied in Manuel (see, for example, *LM*, 98, 150). In preparation for this new future, 'la Joda' not only prepares the book, the 'manual' of life, they also embark on an urban revolution through a series of *microagitaciones* around Paris. As part of their fight, and with the specific aim of demanding the liberation of political prisoners in several Latin American countries, 'la Joda' is also going to take part in the kidnapping of a person referred to as the Vip, the director of an Agency of International Espionage.

'La Joda's' ludic(rous) *microagitaciones*

'La Joda's' main kidnapping 'operation', like most of the newspaper articles, takes the reader directly to the Latin American context of political events surrounding the publication of *Libro de Manuel*. Within a specifically Argentinian context, the kidnapping of the Vip brings to mind the activities of guerrilla groups such as Montoneros, which had come to be known in the public domain, for instance, due to their kidnapping and execution of very prominent political figures such as former Argentinian president, General Aramburu, in 1970. Under the unifying aim of demanding Perón's return as well as fighting for radical political change in Argentina, Montoneros brought together people with very different ideological tendencies, from National Catholicism to radical Marxism. Perhaps it is not coincidental that the members of 'la Joda' also appear to defend slightly different, sometimes opposing, ideologies and values.

From the very beginning of the novel, the narrative voice underlines the differences among the group members as crucial in their revolutionary ambitions, 'puesto que se trata de individuos' (*LM*, 16). Their differences in fact also reflect the plurality and complexity of the ideological stance which keeps them together: 'Vos comprendés que traducir gauchistas por izquierdistas no te daría la idea precisa, porque en tu país y el mío eso significa una cosa más bien distinta […] Izquierdista o peronista o lo que venga no quiere decir nada muy claro desde hace unos años' (*LM*, 21). The conversation at this point goes no further, seemingly based on the characters' awareness of the potential hazards of dwelling too much on their own ideological nuances. Thus, Patricio ends the chapter thinking to himself: 'se hablará de cualquier cosa menos de la Joda' or, as the narrator clarifies, 'Le alcanzó otro mate *sin contenido ideológico*' (*LM*, 22; my emphasis).

When Marcos tries to give Ludmilla an explanation of the flaws and complexities of Peronism in relation to the revolution, the reader gets the most direct – though problematic – elucidation of 'la Joda's' ideological position. In a tone tinged with nostalgia for his homeland Argentina, Marcos tries to explain the difference between the 'peronistas de la vieja guardia' and the current Peronism as 'una fuerza o una esperanza' (*LM*, 261). When Ludmilla fails to understand, Marcos gives up trying to put simply something which is 'más complicado que la ley de alquileres' (*LM*, 262), and in his exasperation he finally exposes what could be said to be the political ideology of their group:

> Para nosotros, digamos para la Joda, todas las armas eficaces son válidas, porque sabemos que tenemos razón y que estamos acorralados *por dentro y por fuera*, por los gorilas y los yanquis e incluso por la pasividad de esos millones que esperan siempre que otros saquen las castañas del fuego, y además porque el sólo hecho de que los enemigos del peronismo sean quienes son nos parece un motivo más legítimo para defenderlo y valerse de él y un día […] salir de él y de tanta otra cosa. (*LM*, 262; my emphasis)

Considering the seriousness of the activities upon which they embark, Marcos's explanation seems dangerously imprecise, ambiguous and somewhat naïve. In fact 'la Joda' not only fails in its most important operation, but it also loses some of its key members: Marcos, Lucien Verneuil and el que te dije are all killed (*LM*, 361-3), while Oscar and Gladis are destined to meet their end at the hands of a member of the Agency (*LM*, 367). On the other hand, Marcos's imprecision is a reflection on many of the revolutionary armed groups that were emerging in Latin America which, given their ideological divergencies, had a short life (for instance, Uturuncos, FAP [Fuerzas Armadas Peronistas] or Masetti's 'guerrilla del Che').[41] In Marcos's assertion we see again Cortázar's determination to transmit the idea of the revolution 'por dentro y por fuera', and his condemnation of a life of passivity, of inaction, of 'no te metás'. However, this comes across as vague and, indeed, too ingenuous. The idea of 'acorralamiento', however, transmits a sense of frustration, which seems to justify the group's choice of methodology. This notion is present from the very beginning of the novel, when all the members of 'la Joda' are sitting down, facing a brick wall.

The brick wall image is reminiscent of one of Morelli's ideas in *Rayuela*, where the hole in the wall and the light that shines through it, work as a metaphor for the possibility of transgression and the 'infinitas posibilidades' of literature (*R*, 376). In *Libro de Manuel* the wall symbolises awareness of an absurd situation, because 'estar sentados en sus plateas delante de una pared de ladrillos [...] consiste para Susana, Patricio, Ludmilla, etc. en estar donde están' (*LM*, 17). In this sense, the absurdity of the scene is also reminiscent of *Los premios*, with a gathering of people on a journey, whose destination and duration remains unknown. For 'la Joda' the wall appears to symbolise that social and political 'acorralamiento' to which Marcos refers, and which they are out to topple. Although the enterprise may seem absurd, and many would rather carry on with their lives around that wall 'esperando como si la pared de ladrillos fuera un telón pintado que va a alzarse' (*LM*, 17), they are at least going to try; 'No se sabe bien cómo' but they know that 'ese absurdo de ir hacia lo absurdo es exactamente lo que hace caer las murallas' (*LM*, 17). Their rhetoric is very utopian indeed, sounding almost like the graffiti slogans on Parisian universities in May 1968 (reproduced in *Último Round*). With their different ideologies, personalities and nationalities, the characters are brought together by their will to reach that which lies behind the wall, even if they risk their lives in so doing:

> están mirando la pared porque sospechan lo que puede haber del otro lado: los poetas como Lonstein hablarán del reino milenario, Patricio se le reirá en la cara a Susana, Susana pensará vagamente en una felicidad que no haya

---

[41] See Julio Carreras, *La política armada: movimientos armados en Argentina* (Buenos Aires: Vergara Grupo Zeta, 2003), p. 4.

> que comprar con injusticia y lágrimas, Ludmilla recordará no sabe por qué un perrito blanco que le hubiera gustado tener a los diez años y que nunca le regalaron. En cuanto a Marcos sacará un cigarrillo (está prohibido) y lo fumará despacio, y yo juntaré tanta cosa para imaginar una posible salida del hombre a través de los ladrillos. (*LM*, 18)

So, while for Morelli the light shining through the hole in the wall represented literature, for el que te dije (the 'yo' narrating at this point) the space in the wall symbolises the possibilities of the *hombre nuevo* and of a better future (through the bricks). Although the ambitions of 'la Joda' may come across as noble and revolutionary, albeit naïve, the methods that they choose to carry out their ideals are not unrealistic but actually become so hilarious that they are in fact ludicrous (apart perhaps from their one failed grand operation).

In the novel, the 'attacks' that the group performs around Paris are called *microagitaciones*, and they are more akin to some kind of 'Dadaist provocation', as Steven Boldy rightly observes, than a violent subversion of bourgeois values for the good of a revolutionary end.[42] It could even be said that Cortázar's overall approach to revolutionary literature does not subvert the limitations of a Dadaist-like provocation. Within the novel, these provocations seem the natural approach for the group which, as Ludmilla puts it, does not see much difference between Lenin and Rimbaud:

> Cada vez me parece más complicado y más sencillo al mismo tiempo, como Marcos pero en un plano diferente aunque vaya a saber si es tan diferente, vaya a saber si entre Lenin y Rimbaud había tanta diferencia. Cuestión de especialidades, de vocabularios sobre todo, y de finalidades, pero en el fondo, en el fondo. (*LM*, 90)[43]

'La Joda's' *microagitaciones*, such as having all broadcasts on the radio translated into Romanian, or selling packets of cigarette containing nothing but cigarette ends, remind us, as Diana Sorensen argues, of some of the activities of the *cronopios* in *Historias de cronopios y de famas* (1962), rather than, as many critics who rejected the book in 1973 would claim, documenting the contemporary 'serious' activities of urban guerrillas operating in Latin America.[44] Yet, once again, precisely in the pataphysical element of their activities lies the

---

[42] Boldy, *The Novels of Julio Cortázar*, p. 167.
[43] Ludmilla's words recall, with a 'slight' political alteration, an idea expressed by André Breton, whereby he proposes a synthesis between Marx and Rimbaud. He writes: ' « Transformer le monde », a dit Marx, « changer la vie », a dit Rimbaud: ces deux mots d'ordre pour nous n'en font qu'un': *Position politique du surréalisme* (Paris: Editions du Sagittaire, 1935), p. 97.
[44] Diana Sorensen, 'From Diaspora to Agora: Cortázar's Reconfiguration of Exile', *Modern Language Notes*, 114/2 (1999), 357–88 at p. 386.

subversion and the humour. Cortázar is not trying to depict (nor defend) the methodologies of 'real' guerrilla groups. In that sense, as he has warned, reality is only present through the inserted clippings. Sorensen asserts that 'Cortázar's deliberate detachment from the practical aspects of the bourgeois order in favour of a surrealist cultivation of faculties centred on play and the unconscious, falls prey to the risk of futility'; yet if Cortázar had intended 'la Joda' to be a model to be followed, it would not be for its political revolutionary strategies, but rather, for its humoristic approach.[45] Nevertheless, even at the level of fiction the group suffers serious losses. After all, who would take seriously a group whose name, according to the 1973 *Diccionario de americanismos*, means: 'Broma o chiste que se hace a alguien con la intención de divertirse; Juerga, diversión informal, generalmente con baile, bebida y canto; Acontecimiento molesto o desagradable. Hacer a alguien objeto de bromas o burlas'?[46] In this sense, what seems futile and ironic is that critics should disregard the novel because they considered these 'revolucionarios' not to be credible.[47] However, this was – and continues to be – one of the main reasons why *Libro de Manuel* was rejected in Argentina.

The *microagitaciones* may not be effective in inspiring a socialist revolution, yet through their disruptions of everyday bourgeois assumptions at the most mundane of levels, 'la Joda' seems to be successful in provoking awareness of capitalist vulnerabilities within the *status quo*. Although, effectively, this does not lead to anything concrete in political or revolutionary terms, within the plot of the novel it is in contrast with the predictability of the inserted newspaper articles. It is as if Cortázar aimed at attacking the comfort of mundane middle-class existence on all possible flanks, so as to look beyond that 'mundo algodonoso' (to recall Oliveira's words).

Humour in 'la Joda's' acts leads to very serious consequences, and this cannot be ignored within the plot. Although the group does not appear to have a clear political aim that drives them to the *microagitaciones*, they do believe in risking their lives for a better future for Manuel (and all the 'Manueles' of the world). Their *microagitaciones* are intended to be contrasted to the 'seriousness' of 'real' revolutionary acts, yet not as their ridiculed versions, but rather their humorous, fictional counterparts, in a world imagined by Cortázar, where the 'real' element – as he put it – is the typographical insertions. Perhaps Cortázar's playful ambition was mistimed or, as Josefina Sartora suggests, maybe he was

---

[45] Ibid. p. 375.

[46] Alfredo N. Neves (ed.), *Diccionario de americanismos* (Buenos Aires: Sopena, 1973), p. 241.

[47] Héctor Manjarrez claimed, for example, that 'los revolucionarios que Cortázar describe en *Libro de Manuel* son lúdicos, chistosos, generosos, espontáneos; pero no son creíbles en absoluto [...] son increíbles, son inverosímiles; no existen': 'La revolución y el escritor según Cortázar', in his *El camino de los sentimientos* (Mexico City: Era, 1990), pp. 129–48 at p. 145.

being 'too' revolutionary in expecting humour to have a more transcendental role within political ideologies.[48] It seemed that although Cortázar brought the need for immediacy to the fore through the insertion and interweaving of testimonial text in the narrative, his notion of how humour and eroticism could also aid the revolution, failed to be grasped. It could even be argued that at the level of plot, humour does not achieve anything in political terms. There is one character, however, who as part of his political conversion, appears to embody the attempt to bring together humour, eroticism and freedom from taboos in general. This is Andrés Fava who – crucially – through the course of the narrative undergoes an inner transformation, which turn sceptical Oliveira-like passivity, into political action.

Andrés Fava and the internal revolution

In exploring the most prominent manifestations of the political dimension of *Libro de Manuel*, as well as the collage format, the role of humour, eroticism and the *microagitaciones*, it is also important to analyse the behaviour and thoughts of one of the protagonists, Andrés Fava. Through what might be called his 'internal revolution' he gradually moves from *homo ludens* to what Dellepiane calls a *homos politicus*.[49] It is surprising that none of the studies dealing with the politics of *Libro de Manuel* have discussed in depth the transformation of this character, and what it represents in political and biographical terms.

Andrés Fava was the sole character in the early *Diario de Andrés Fava* and was also one of the protagonists of *El examen*.[50] He was, in many ways, Cortázar's first *alter ego*. Although he commits suicide at the end of *El examen*, his namesake reappears in *Libro de Manuel* representing – like Oliveira in *Rayuela* – the *petit bourgeois* intellectual. Andrés lives in a world of constant ambivalences and contradictions, and in that sense he seems to be the prolongation of Oliveira; however, there is a crucial difference between the two characters, and that is that in *Libro de Manuel* Andrés Fava brings himself to make a decision, namely, to join 'la Joda' in their revolutionary actions. In Siebers's terms,

---

[48] 'Gran parte de la conmoción que produjo Cortázar se debió a la presencia permanente del juego y el humor, a lo que él ha llamado "la constante lúdica en su obra", que no es sólo un recurso narrativo, sino que cumple una función más trascendente. [...] Ya comprometido con las luchas políticas de Latinoamérica, propuso también que la revolución fuera *divertida* en *Libro de Manuel*, y nadie supo entenderlo: ¿tal vez fuera demasiado revolucionario?': Josefina Sartora, 'Jugarse la vida', *La Maga*, 5 (November 1994), p. 9. My emphasis.

[49] Ángela Dellepiane, 'Otra experiencia para lectores "salteados": *Libro de Manuel*', *Nueva narrativa hispanoamericana*, 5 (1975), 17–34 at p. 20.

[50] Cortázar, after declaring that they were not the same character, confessed: 'Mentí sin quererlo [...] Andrés es siempre el mismo Andrés, veinticinco años más tarde': Ana María Hernández, 'Cortázar: el libro de Andrés+Lonstein=Manuel', *Nueva narrativa hispanoamericana*, 5 (1975), 35–55 at p. 55.

in that risk of making a decision, he embraces his act as political. Therefore, in terms of Oliveira's quandaries, Andrés Fava rejects the 'no te metás' attitude and opts for a life of political action. This is significant not only with regard to the plot of the novel, but also insofar as its political content is concerned, for Andrés's choice proclaims a clear political ideology and a straight political message from Cortázar. Through Andrés Fava's dichotomies, Cortázar effectively shows his readers the conflictive processes that have led him to assume the active political role that he has chosen. The political meaning of Andrés's doubts is thus central to the representation of the political in the novel. By carrying out an analysis of the main aspects of his evolution through the text, it is possible to appreciate the complexity and implications of this character's decisions, but also, indirectly, of Cortázar's.

Andres's dilemma centres on the fact that he longs to change his vision of the world, but he is as dubious of his own longing as he is about the new alternative before him. He knows that he is trapped in a dichotomy, paralysed like Oliveira on a street corner, or, as el que te dije sees him, 'encaramado en un techo a dos aguas' (*LM*, 166). Andrés admits that his ideas might originate 'del esclavo de su bautismo occidental y pequeñoburgués' (*LM*, 167), which, when applied to reality, prevent him from being content and harm the relationships that he tries to establish with other people. This leaves Andrés with a perpetual sense of 'náusea y frustración, los reproches siempre dentro de líneas ortodoxas, los remordimientos y el mal gusto en la boca' (*LM*, 166). Yet, unlike Oliveira, who was also left with a bad taste in his mouth after being confronted with ideological matters, Andres's *petit bourgeois* bad conscience will ultimately win over, making him act upon that 'sensación de que había algo por hacer y que no había sido hecho' (*LM*, 167). However, he wonders whether the change that he desires concerns the benefit of 'el prójimo', or is rather a product of his own individualism: 'todo estaría en saber si realmente busco, si salgo a buscar de veras o si no hago más que preferir mi herencia cultural, mi occidente burgués, mi pequeño individuo despreciable y maravilloso' (*LM*, 170). On the other hand, the new alternative that socialism brings, at least at this point, makes Andrés suspicious about the total lack of individualism, and the elimination of personal liberty. Aware of this contradiction, Andrés thinks to himself:

> Cuando ves cómo una revolución no tarda en poner en marcha una máquina de represiones psicológicas o eróticas o estéticas que coincide casi simétricamente con la máquina supuestamente destruida en el plano político y práctico, te quedás pensando si no habrá que mirar de más cerca la mayoría de nuestras elecciones. (*LM*, 168)

Andrés's words seem to speak directly from Cortázar's own sense of disillusionment at the Cuban revolution. The bitter taste in the mouth left by episodes such as the 'Caso Padilla', and the reality of being caught between two positions, is epitomised in the novel by Andrés Fava. His ideological conflict could be said to be further mirrored in the two women in his life: Ludmilla and Francine. They could also be seen as the representations of politics and literature, with Andrés Fava's actions being a metonymy for Cortázar's different attempts at merging together these two forces in his life.

Andrés wants to be with both his lovers, he is not writing to compromise and lose either of them. He wants to join the two lifestyles that they lead in order, as he thinks, to give birth to something new and complete. In his words, his bigamy would allow him to 'liquidar la línea recta como la menor distancia entre dos puntos, cualquier geometría no euclidiana se me antojaba más aplicable a mi sentimiento de la vida, y del mundo' (*LM*, 167). Andrés Fava aims to unite 'el mundo Ludmilla y el mundo Francine [...] hasta tocar alguna vez con la mano del más extremo deseo un mundo Ludmilla–Francine' (*LM*, 167).

In Andrés's view, each woman represents quite contrasting ways of viewing the world. Ludmilla signifies enthusiasm, joy, the vitality of the new possibilities imposing themselves on history; she belongs to the 'tribe' of South Americans, and thus she is also a fighter against Western imperialism. Nevertheless, as Andrés understands it, Ludmilla's life also encompasses spontaneity and chaos, which at this moment in the novel Andrés presents as something negative: 'Ludmilla desde el desorden de una cocina donde pedazos de puerros habían quedado colgados en todas partes, el transistor vomitando Radio Montecarlo, un repasador asqueroso' (*LM*, 137). Francine, on the other hand, being French, embodies the old authority and traditional order; she represents respect for social conventions and cultural values, all that which 'civilization' is supposed to be about (according to the protagonist). Although Andrés is deeply infatuated by this figure, he understands that this order has had its day and now has to make way for a new one. Through a description of Francine's home and surroundings, he sees moreover that this way of life guarantees him no individual freedom: 'el departamento [de Francine] ordenado y preciso [...] biblioteca con la colección de la Pléiade y el Littré [...] los vasos tallados [...] Francine en su jaula precisa' (*LM*, 137). Although the triangular love affair seems to be a relational pattern in many of Cortázar's characters, in this novel Andrés Fava breaks away from it. Significantly in that breaking away he finds political meaning.

Andrés's initial rejection of 'la Joda' is linked to what he understands to be their very immature methods. Andrés cannot see how their *microagitaciones* are helping the revolution; he expresses this to Marcos, when he says: 'Cuando te enterás que [...] hay doscientos cincuenta mil presos políticos en este pañuelito de mierda, entonces tus fósforos usados no son precisamente entusiasmantes' (*LM*, 119). Later on, it transpires that what stops Andrés from getting involved with the group is his fear that if a revolution were to be successful, the new political hegemony could be in hands of individuals who might not understand, let alone take on board, the things that need changing beyond the political system itself. Thus, Andrés is scared that the new order might end up being rigid and stagnant, led by 'ideólogos de izquierda emperrados en un ideal poco menos que monástico de vida privada y pública' (*LM*, 27). Overall, Andrés's lack of political commitment derives, in a self-justifying manner, from his middle-class historical position. He can appreciate the possibility of a project for a revolutionary movement which might bring the freedom – individual and collective – that he desires. However, he is unable to pass his propositions to the active members of 'la Joda', because they see his ideas as the individualistic fantasies of a *petit bourgeois*. For the members of the group, Andrés's views are counter-revolutionary (echoing once again the Caso Padilla). Gómez, Verneuil and el que te dije all see in him an elitist: 'para un Patricio o un Marcos hay toneladas como Andrés, anclados en el París o el Tango de su tiempo, en sus amores y sus estéticas y sus caquitas privadas, cultivando todavía una literatura llena de decoro y premios nacionales o municipales y becas Guggenheim (*LM*, 77). And, as for Cortázar, what others see as 'elitism' is for Andrés part of his individual cultural freedom that he refuses to give up:

—El señor quiere cosas pero no renuncia a nada.
—No, no renuncio a nada, viejo [says Andrés].
—¿Ni siquiera un poquito, digamos, un autor exquisito, un poeta que sólo él conoce?
—No, ni siquiera.
—¿Su Xenakis, su música aleatoria, su free jazz, su Joni Mitchell, sus fotografías abstractas?
—No, mi hermano. Nada. Todo me lo llevo conmigo a donde sea. (*LM*, 147)

But the night comes when Andrés begins to change. It is the night when he performs an act of sodomy on an unwilling Francine; so, while he liberates himself from the taboos, Andrés begins his political transformation. Francine, as the embodiment of the old order, of the Western world, is now to an extent victim of Andrés's 'internal revolution': the oppressor is now the oppressed. During this night, they both begin to see Paris in a different light. Paris ceases to be one of the most beautiful cities created by civilization, and becomes a symbol for the decadence of capitalist society. All the aspects of Paris described by the narrator during that night seem to have corroded: 'la noche en su rutina de neón, papas fritas, putas en cada portal y cada café, tiempo de los alienados en la ciudad [...] más anclada en sí misma del mundo' (*LM*, 268). The air of deterioration and alienation (reminiscent of the desintegrating Buenos Aires in *El examen*) becomes deadly when Andrés and Francine enter the strip-tease club: 'un primer piso sobre el bulevar sucio de gente, neones cazamoscas de provincia [...] olor de encierro colectivo, guardarropa con vieja desdentada y números grasientos sobados' (*LM*, 269). Andrés wants Francine to see that all this human degradation is a result of the capitalist system which, in many ways, she in effect embodies. The epitome of all this poverty and misery is an old woman, who picks up cigarette ends from the street. Andrés remarks: 'Mirá esa vieja juntando puchos y recitando andá a saber qué antigua maldición de la miseria, una especie de balance del fin del mundo [...] el mejor resumen occidental del setenta es esa mano mugrienta que junta puchos' (*LM*, 278). Yet while Andrés is increasingly affected by the urban (and human) landscape that surrounds them, Francine is indifferent, claiming that 'todo eso lo conozco de sobra, no hay necesidad de venir como un santotomás barato a verificar tanta basura inevitable' (*LM*, 278). Francine's understanding of the surrounding misery as something inevitable and natural encapsulates – or at least this is how Andrés interprets it – the *Weltanschauung* (or 'veltandshaún' as Andrés calls it, *LM* 278) of the bourgeoisie.

Andrés's reaction, once he comes to terms with the fact that he belongs to the same bourgeois world as Francine, where everyone's position in society is seen as 'natural' and inevitable, is one of deep shame and regret: 'si me quedara una nada de decencia debería ir a ponerme ahí para que ese negro en curda me vomitara encima' (*LM*, 280). Andrés suddenly – in an 'epiphanic' moment – understands that he is wrong, that they are both wrong. He realises that poverty should not be seen as natural or inevitable; something can be done to put a halt to that 'perpetuación de la miseria original' (*LM*, 279). It is during this night, when 'las epifanías ocurren [...] entre moscas y sbornias y puchos mal apagados' (*LM*, 281), that Andrés faces up to his own contradicciones and decides to opt for one side of his 'techo a dos aguas', indeed, his 'bifurcación'. This is the night, therefore, when readers expect either 'la muerte de un pequeñoburgués' or 'su confirmación' (*LM*, 292). Andrés decides to join 'la Joda', thereby opting for a life of political action. Somewhat didactically, he is undoubtedly presented by Cortázar as a role model to be followed.

Andrés's political transformation comes hand-in-hand with a cinematic dream, which becomes a *leitmotif* in the novel and which, as the Surrealists would have it, helps him carry out his vital 'leap'.[51] In the dream, Andrés is at the cinema watching a Fritz Lang mystery film which, from the descriptions given, could be identified as *M*. Andrés's oneiric cinema has two perpendicular screens, and although he tries to watch the film from different locations, there is always something between him and the image. While changing seats in the attempt to get a better view, Andrés is repeatedly called by a man – significantly, a Cuban – who wants to talk to him in a different room. As soon as Andrés leaves the cinema to see this man, 'la escena se corta' (*LM*, 103). At this point in the dream, Andrés claims always to be divided ('Soy doble, alguien que fue al cine y alguien que está metido en un lío típicamente cinematográfico': *LM*, 103), yet also

---

[51] André Breton assures us that dreams not only illuminate our inner self, but they also trigger in us vital questions concerning the world in which we live, inciting us to act upon that world and have an effect on its transformation: *Communicating Vessels*, trans. Mary Ann Caws and Geoffrey T. Harris (Lincoln, NE.: University of Nebraska Press, 1990), pp. 59–61.

transformed. He is aware that whatever the Cuban says in the dream is life-transforming, bestowing upon him a sense of responsibility: 'no hay duda que *sé* lo que me dijo el cubano puesto que tengo una tarea que cumplir' (*LM*, 103). But he can never recall the message. It is through his dream and its revelation of his internal schism that Andrés begins to contemplate and search for a possible synthesis. Even before he can decipher his own dream, Andrés knows that he has to act. By means of this obsessive metaphor Cortázar figuratively presents his own aesthetic and political evolution. In other words, Andrés's dream represents that which Cortázar refers to in the prologue as his own 'confuso y atormentado itinerario' (*LM*, 7), which he alludes to in reference to the difficulties that he has faced in his attempt to reconcile literature and politics.

Towards the end of the novel Andrés is finally able to recall his recurrent dream in full, and his duality is unified into a very clear image: 'no puede ser que todo esté tan claro, tan nítido [...] veo mi sueño como soñándolo por fin de veras [...] tan claro, tan evidente' (*LM*, 355–6). Andrés moves on to describe the end of the dream, and thus the most straightforward message of the text is disclosed: 'el sueño consistía nada más que en eso, en el cubano que me miraba y me decía solamente una palabra: *Despertate*' (*LM*, 356).[52] That is: wake up to reality, do something to change it, get involved. Andrés demonstrates his new-found commitment not only by joining 'la Joda'; in taking over el que te dije's role as 'archivist', collecting articles for Manuel's book (*LM*, 369), Andrés also demonstrates his conscious decision to perpetuate the group's political commitment to the future of the *hombre nuevo*. In addition, and as Kathleen Vernon argues, this triumph over detachment and passivity fuses the roles of actor and observer, writer and revolutionary.[53] As Parkinson Zamora suggests, the dedication of Andrés Fava – and to an extent, of all of *Libro de Manuel*'s characters – to historical testimony through the construction of the book for Manuel, implies that their belief in revolutionary change does not rest upon forgetting and obliterating the past, but rather upon recovering it ('¿Olvida? ¿Quién olvida?', *LM*, 9).[54] In this way, the historical fragments presented and preserved for Manuel, and also for us the readers, do not aim to reminisce about the past, but rather point from the past towards the future.

Manuel, the symbol of hope

Also paramount in the political dimension of *Libro de Manuel* is the symbolism of Manuel. Apart from the broader political justifications and possibilities,

---

[52] In very Cortazarian manner, in Andrés's Argentinian mind, the Cuban appears to speak in *rioplatense* Spanish.

[53] Kathleen Vernon, 'Cortázar's 3 R's: Reading, Rhetoric and Revolution in *Libro de Manuel*', *Modern Language Studies*, 16/3 (1986), 264–70 at p. 267.

[54] Parkinson Zamora, 'Movement and Stasis', p. 63.

Manuel seems to be the main reason why 'la Joda' has got together. As Andrés tells us: 'tipos como Marcos y Oscar [...] estaban en la Joda por Manuel, quiero decir que lo hacían por él, por tanto Manuel en tanto rincón del mundo, queriendo ayudarlo a que algún día entrara en un ciclo diferente y a la vez salvándole algunos restos del naufragio total' (*LM*, 183). Through the 'education' that they are providing, the characters envisage in baby Manuel the possibility of a different future, free from oppression and poverty. It could be argued that Manuel is, in many respects, also the embodiment of the reader: the reader of 1973 but also the future reader, being 'instructed' on the politics and history of an era, which, as Cortázar warns in the prologue, might be manipulated by the 'masaje a escala mundial de los *mass media*' (*LM*, 9).

The characters aim to transcend their present through Manuel's memory and, indirectly, through the immortality implied in compiling the book. This awareness is exemplified in the text when, for example, Patricio says, 'Manuel [...] usted me va a justificar ante la historia' (*LM*, 30). The characters' attempt to imprint their reality and history onto Manuel is parallel to Cortázar's longing to convey the historical relevance of his own actions and ideology to his reader, through *Libro de Manuel*. Andrés has confidence in Manuel's (and indirectly, in the reader's) ability to understand their present, their reality, and therefore, through the refusal to forget, contribute to their existence, to the perpetual survival of the novel's political essence: '[Patricio to Andrés] Con tus mezclas refinadas al final nadie comprenderá un belín si le cae el álbum en las manos. Manuel comprenderá – le dije –, Manuel comprenderá algún día' (*LM*, 385).

This explicit will to communicate an understanding to the reader reminds us of the image of the bridge, introduced in *Rayuela* to refer to literature, connecting 'hombre a hombre' (*R*, 400). The bridge metaphor is reiterated in *Libro de Manuel*. In the words of el que te dije:

> La praxis intelectual de los socialismos estancados exige puente total; yo escribo y el lector lee, es decir que se da por supuesto que yo escribo y tiendo un puente a un nivel legible. ¿Y si no soy legible, viejo, si no hay lector y ergo no hay puente? Porque un puente [...] no es verdaderamente puente mientras los hombres no lo crucen. Un puente es un hombre cruzando un puente, che. (*LM*, 27)

The crucial difference therefore is that while in *Rayuela* it was enough for the bridge to exist as the connecting medium, in *Libro de Manuel* it is the action of crossing that makes the bridge exist. In other words, and to draw the analogy with the respective protagonists, while in *Rayuela* Oliveira sees the bridge (or the 'tablón', as in the famous chapter 41), and is content to reflect upon it without feeling an urge to cross it, in *Libro de Manuel* Andrés needs to take action and become involved in order to feel that he has accomplished the mission with which he is entrusted in his dream. That is to say, Andrés needs to cross the bridge and is not satisfied by the mere act of contemplation.

If Manuel is understood to be the reader, then the didactic process inferred for the infant can turn the novel effectively into a political pamphlet. Cortázar is aware of this, tackling the idea with irony as in the words of el que te dije who claims:

> cuando todo eso [la alienación, el tercer mundo, la lucha armada, etc.] 1) es desconocido por el lector [...] el lector es un pánfilo y se merece esta clase de novelas para que aprenda, qué tanto, o 2) es perfectamente conocido y sobre todo encuadrado en una visión histórica cotidiana [...] las novelas pueden darlo por sobreentendido y avanzar hacia tierras más propias, es decir, menos didácticas. (*LM*, 252)

It is thus apparent that the novel assumes its readers to be ignorant of precisely the concerns that the newspaper articles bring to the fore. In that sense too the reader is – for Cortázar – like Manuel: immature and with everything still to be learned. Although the text contains many elements that escape a kind of dogmatic revolutionary literature, its didacticism betrays it and lets it down. It seems that the very awareness of wanting to merge politics and literature, when he had been doing it all along, led Cortázar not to look for an accomplice in his readers (like Morelli does in *Rayuela*), but actually to patronise them in ways that he had proclaimed that he had rejected.

Towards the end of the novel, in a dialogue with Lonstein, Andrés refers to the need to make their present last through Manuel, presenting him once again as 'la Joda's' *raison d'être*:

> —¿Y qué carajo tiene que hacer Manuel a estas alturas?
> —Todo, viejo. Parecería que estamos perdiendo el tiempo con tanto papelito, pero algo me dice que hay que guardárselos a Manuel. [...] No tenemos ningún informe que dejarle a Manuel sobre Roland, digamos, o sobre Gómez. Al fin y al cabo ni se acordará de ellos cuando crezca, y en cambio hay todo esto que viene a ser lo mismo de otra manera y es esto lo que tenemos que poner en el libro de Manuel. (*LM*, 369)

'Todo novelista espera que su lector lo comprenda, participando de su propia experiencia, o que recoja un determinado mensaje y lo encarne' (*R*, 401), asserts Morelli, voicing what is probably the ideal aim of any author. Cortázar can only achieve this with those readers who comprehend, and apprehend, the search for the 'Manuel' within them and who opt to assume Manuel's position in the world. For this is a world laid out *for* Manuel, which in actual fact, from the very start, *belongs* to him (libro *de* rather than *para* Manuel).

Although *Libro de Manuel* appears at points to be somewhat didactic in its contents, it is not strictly propagandistic in that it does not effectively provide any concrete answers. As Miriam di Gerónimo asserts the novel instead offers the means to look for answers.[55] This is clearly articulated in the text; the book *for* Manuel is not an instruction manual as the title of the English translation (*A Manual for Manuel*) might imply: 'Vos ponele las noticias como vengan, rezonga Heredia, a la final [*sic*] el pibe aprenderá a sumar dos más dos, tampoco es cosa de darle las escaleras servidas, qué joder' (*LM*, 307). This is followed by the contrast between two articles side by side: one dealing with a 722 million-dollar loan that the 'Misión Brignone' obtained in the US, and the other, with a letter to God that a 'guerrillero' in Bolivia wrote before dying of starvation (*LM*, 308–9). The book pretends perhaps to be a bridge into the realities presented in the clippings; yet Cortázar offers no firm views, he only suggests a 'bridge' towards them. What these views or answers are or should be, remains conveniently undefined. This is precisely what many committed writers would criticise.

The politics of reception

Cortázar travelled to Argentina to promote *Libro de Manuel* in a journey that would last four months.[56] His arrival coincided with the Peronist triumph in the elections of March 1973, which, ironic as it might sound, Cortázar supported. On the day of the presidential elections, Cortázar wrote to Saúl Sosnowski: 'Esta noche sigo el escrutinio de las elecciones argentinas [...] siento ya que los peronistas han ganado [...] mi libro sale en estos días y habrá una bella pelea alrededor de él. Ves que no hay mucho tiempo para hablar de este maravilloso viaje.'[57] Cortázar's impressions stand in striking contrast to earlier manifestations of his fervent anti-Peronism. As a key example, it is worth comparing the sentiments of this quotation with those from a letter of 1962, when after the ban on Peronism as a political party was lifted, Cortázar, then also back in Buenos Aires, described Argentina as a 'fecundo mar de mierda'. He also claimed to feel, 'acosado, encerrado y [con] mufa'. The return of Peronism onto the political scene had led Cortázar to admit in 1962: 'Te aseguro que no veo la hora de salir de aquí.'[58] Yet in 1973 Peronism meant – or had to mean, so as to be coherent with Cortázar's altered political ideology – a positive rather than a negative factor for Argentinian politics.

Once back in Paris, Cortázar would publish his thoughts on the Peronist victory in *Le Monde*, showing his clear political support and his personal satisfaction at the election results:

---

[55] Miriam di Gerónimo, 'El lector cómplice', in her *Narrar por knock-out* (Buenos Aires: Simurg, 2004), 275–92 at p. 282.
[56] See Goloboff, *Julio Cortázar: la biografía*, p. 222.
[57] Cortázar to Saúl Sosnowski, 11 March 1973, *Cartas/3 1969–1983*, p. 1517.
[58] Cortázar to Eduardo A. Jonquières, 20 March 1962, *Cartas/1 1937–1963*, p. 470.

> La mayor parte de los 'liberales' simulan creer que el peligro del peronismo reside en el riesgo de un fascismo; en realidad, sólo tienen temor a [...] eso que llaman con horror 'el comunismo'. En mi opinión, el peronismo, tal como se muestra hoy día, está muy lejos de ambos 'totalitarismos' [...] y yo llegaría hasta afirmar [...] que este peronismo se encamina en un primer momento hacia lo que allí [en Argentina] se denomina un 'socialismo nacional'. [...] Ni el general Perón ni el presidente Cámpora subscribirán esta profecía, pero yo creo que ahí se encuentra el motor de guía del pensamiento y los actos de miles de hombres y mujeres que apoyan al nuevo gobierno.[59]

Cortázar's optimism would not last long. On 13 July 1973, the elected Cámpora resigned so as to allow Perón to stand for president. Witnessing this kind of political manoeuvring, Cortázar wrote: 'Como para arreglarlo todo, ahí están los acontecimientos en Argentina [...] soy pesimista sobre el golpe de Perón que me parece un giro a la derecha.'[60] Such were the times in Argentina when *Libro de Manuel* came out.

Although Cortázar had proposed *Libro de Manuel* as a text of convergence between literature and politics, when the novel was published criticism from left-wing intellectuals proclaimed that his attempt had simply failed. Critics like Ángel Rama and Jorge Rivera suggested that instead of being a text which integrated political commitment and denunciation with Cortázar's 'old' concept of literature as an artistic medium, *Libro de Manuel* still showed a split between aesthetics and ideology. According to these writers, the Dadaist postulations of the book, interweaving political action with games and humour, could not be taken seriously, let alone as a political novel intending to be 'de utilidad' in the political struggle against the oppression of military governments in the Southern Cone. Critics on the right, on the other hand, also criticised Cortázar for having abandoned precisely that bifurcation which had kept, in their view, politics 'out' of his fictional writings.

When *Libro de Manuel* was published, the Puerto Rican Rosario Ferré wrote: 'Hay una distancia considerable en esta novela entre lo que Cortázar hace y lo que intenta hacer.'[61] This distinction, in turn, was what made some critics value the novel, putting the writer's declared political intention over and above the novel's aesthetic achievements and its actual political 'usefulness'. This is clear in Liliana Heker's review, for example, in which she commended the book for positioning itself on the 'correct' side of politics. The aesthetic dimension of the novel did not seem to matter in her evaluation; what was to be praised about

---

[59] 'La Dynamique du 11 Mars', in *Le Monde*, 23 June 1973, p. 6, translated in Goloboff, *Julio Cortázar. La biografía*, p. 229.

[60] Ibid., p. 225.

[61] Rosario Ferré, '*Libro de Manuel*', *Zona: carga y descarga*, 1/6 (September 1973), 10–12 at p. 12.

Libro de Manuel was 'el planteo de una alternativa, tan clara que deslumbra [...] Cortázar se pone de este lado, del lado de los que van a cambiar la historia [...] Yo no sé cómo se leerá este libro dentro de 15 años: sé que hoy cumple una función'.[62] Yet Heker's criticism is somewhat influenced by the enthusiasm of her own political militancy. With regard to what Heker understood as a very clear political proposition, Ferré, perhaps with more objectivity, claimed:

> A pesar de que estos acontecimientos [los incluidos en el texto] parafrasean una historia verdadera que se repite día a día en la lucha del tercer mundo, es evidente que Cortázar desconoce la experiencia vivencial de los mismos [...] Y no es solamente la falta de experiencia lo que le resta verosimilitud a la obra, sino su ubicación dentro de una visión esperanzadora y optimista de la vida.[63]

A year after its publication, when the news made it to Argentina during November 1974 that *Libro de Manuel* had been awarded the Médicis Prize in Paris, the debate surrounding the text was reignited, so much so that the Cultural Supplement of *La opinión* of 8 December 1974 was entirely dedicated to it, under the title 'Julio Cortázar: la responsabilidad del intelectual latinoamericano: discusiones argentinas sobre *Libro de Manuel* y el premio que acaba de ganar en París'. Amongst the critical writings in English, only Peter Standish seems to be aware of this second round of debates, and even so he only deals with it somewhat superficially. Yet, it is important to consider in more detail the nature of the further debate, especially in the light of Ferro's words, and the overall 'impact' that the novel had, not necessarily on the revolutionary struggle but on Cortázar as a writer.

The discussion included in *La opinión* was presented through the voices of six prominent Argentinian intellectuals of the time, namely Haroldo Conti, Aníbal Ford, Ernesto Goldar, María Rosa Oliver, Ricardo Piglia and Jorge Abelardo Ramos. In general, these figures saw in *Libro de Manuel* a failed attempt to reconcile explicit political content with 'good' fictional narrative, with Oliver claiming for example that: 'Un buen escritor siempre ha logrado unir política y literatura. Siempre que no supedite el escritor al ideólogo. En el *Libro de Manuel* esto no sucede.'[64] Conti, however, put Cortázar's good political intentions over the aesthetic value of the novel and praised it for being 'políticamente útil', and as Heker would have it, for serving a (political) purpose.[65] The other articles simply express disapproval of the aims behind the writing of the novel, and also

---

62 Liliana Heker, '¿Qué opina del *Libro de Manuel* de Julio Cortázar?', *Crisis*, 1 (May 1973), pp. 10–14 at p. 13.
63 Ferré, '*Libro de Manuel*', p. 12.
64 María Rosa Oliver, 'Según su conciencia', *La opinión cultural*, 8 December 1974, 2–3 at p. 3.
65 Haroldo Conti, 'Cuando enmudezcan todas las voces', ibid. 10–11 at p. 10.

of Cortázar himself as a committed writer. Goldar, for instance, belittles *Libro de Manuel* as a mere 'beau geste' which could only 'despabilar la consciencia de algunos'.[66] Accusing Cortázar of promoting a 'guerrillerismo a la francesa', Ford understands *Libro de Manuel* not as a 'propuesta política [sino como] un libro que intenta explicar la literatura de Cortázar, sus búsquedas estéticas'.[67]

Perhaps the most incisive attack in this collection comes from Ricardo Piglia, who read *Libro de Manuel* as the embodiment of Cortázar's long-held 'habit' of 'apropiarse de la realidad a través del mercado'.[68] For Piglia, therefore, the fact that the characters in the novel carry out their *microagitaciones* in 'el espacio de consumo (restaurantes de lujo, teatros, aeropuertos)' is a way of changing or revolutionizing the system in a way that for Piglia can only be equated with consumerism and not with a serious political message.[69] Although he comes to acknowledge that the most prominent political element of the novel lies in its journalism, he nevertheless reads it as a game: 'el juego de leer noticias y pegar los recortes'. For the revolution, or indeed politics, cannot be related to mere hedonistic pleasures; that is part of a bourgeois discourse, he argues, straight out of the experiences of the protests in Paris during May 1968. Piglia asserts that turning politics into a game, and into something that can be consumed, causes the political content of the novel to dissolve and to become another trope within the fictions. He says that 'Esa estetización de la política se corresponde con la práctica estética que los agitadores de [*Libro de Manuel*] confunden con la actividad revolucionaria.'[70] Therefore, Piglia concludes that Cortázar uses politics in a way that is conveniently ambivalent, 'la pone a su servicio, la consume', he argues, so that by privately appropriating a social discourse, Cortázar can remain coherent in the aesthetic ideology of his creative texts.

It was with these debates that Cortázar's days began to be 'numbered' recalling the anecdote by Guillermo Martínez. Piglia was then emerging as a new figure within Argentinian literature and his criticism was decisive. Then came the years of dictatorship in Argentina, and through polemics such as that between Cortázar and Heker (based on Cortázar calling himself a writer in exile), his writings and his politics were progressively sidelined.

In 2001 Saúl Yurkievich wrote that *Libro de Manuel*, 'es un libro que no busca la vigencia intemporal [...] se niega a albergarse en la eternidad ahistórica del humanismo idealista', complementing Saúl Sosnowski's views of 1974 when he asserted that '*Libro de Manuel* queda como testimonio de un momento histórico determinado. Su "vigencia" es momentánea y pronto será

---

[66] Ernesto Goldar, 'La colonización ideológica', ibid, 9–10 at p. 10.
[67] Aníbal Ford, 'Humanismo para europeos, ibid. 7–8 at p. 8.
[68] Ricardo Piglia, 'El socialismo de los consumidores', ibid. 4–6 at p. 4.
[69] Ibid., p. 5.
[70] Ibid., p. 6.

integrada a la historia de la literatura'.[71] In general, Yurkievich's standpoint is echoed by more recent Argentinian academics, with Goloboff himself declaring informally that '*Libro de Manuel* es una obra pésima [...] ni loco [lo] enseño en la universidad.'[72]

As far as can be ascertained, *Libro de Manuel* tends to be ignored within Cortázar's fictional corpus. The novel's political narrative may be effective – as Sosnowski and Ferré argued – but only within a given historical moment. Yet I believe that, as Goldar implied in 1974, *Libro de Manuel* is a book that depicts Cortázar's own 'búsquedas'. In other words, it is not simply the 'product' (as Piglia would argue) of a politicised Cortázar, but rather another step in the aesthetic evolution of a writer who, in his will to allow man to know himself (recalling 'Teoría del túnel'), wanted to explore the potential 'usefulness' of his literature, as well as to put forward other concerns, for him equally important.

An obsolete manual?

The year that *Libro de Manuel* was published was marked by the return of Perón to Argentina, symbolizing the hope of social change for the country. Moreover, the radicalisation of left-wing groups in the entire Southern Cone created great expectations among its intelligentsia. The consolidation of these was not, however, very clear. The concrete threat of a conservative reaction implied that political commitment on the part of intellectuals could play a decisive role in the victory of the Left and, therefore, of the popular sectors of society. As Aldo Marchesi explains, these facts generated a kind of historical and political urgency, whereby the paths that Latin American countries took depended upon all the different agents taking part, including the intellectuals.[73] This urgency demanded a political commitment that was direct and effective on the part of the writer. This is the socio-political pressure that we can assume, from his letters, essays and lectures, that Cortázar, as a then committed Latin American intellectual, was feeling at the time of producing *Libro de Manuel*. This is made very clear again in 'Corrección de pruebas' where Cortázar succinctly states:

> si no lo terminaba [a *Libro de Manuel*] se iba a agriar, sólo serviría para lectores literarios, gentes que todavía creyeran en valores perennes con exclusión de la violenta circunstancia cotidiana. Por todo eso tuve que

---

[71] Yurkievich, *Julio Cortázar: mundos y modos*, p. 239; Saúl Sosnowski, 'Julio Cortázar: *Libro de Manuel*', *Hispamérica*, 2/6 (April 1974), 109–15 at p. 110.

[72] Goloboff, personal interview, 27 November 2007, Buenos Aires.

[73] Aldo Marchesi, 'Imaginación política del antiimperialismo: intelectuales y política en el Cono Sur a fines de los 60', *Estudios interdisciplinarios de América Latina y el Caribe*, 17/1 (2006), 20–34 at p. 29.

autoescupirme del libro sin esperar más y bien que se nota, pero las cosas tienen su precio y mejor Manuel feo y vivo que Manuel hermoso y muerto.[74]

In turn, the pressures that led to the writing of this novel combined and merged with the aesthetic evolution that Cortázar had been undergoing. This was a process which had begun with the more formally conventional novels *El examen*, *Divertimento* and *Los premios*, moved on to break many aesthetic norms with *Rayuela*, concerned itself with metaphysical experimentation in *62*, and with playful combinations of formats in the fragmentary *La vuelta* and *Último Round*, to arrive at *Libro de Manuel*, where many of the elements explored in all the previous writings are combined, with the additional historical urgency and a desire for politically 'useful' effects. It could be argued that, given the negative reception, and even rejection, of *Libro de Manuel* at the time, Cortázar finally decided to separate his longer fiction from his active political life. Politics would remain at the core of some of his most celebrated short stories written after *Libro de Manuel*, such as 'Apocalipsis de Solentiname', 'Segunda vez' or 'Recortes de prensa', yet it would be explicitly absent in other books, such as *Territorios* or *Autonautas de la cosmopista*. Cortázar would, however, also carry on exploring other aesthetic media in order to communicate best the political message in which he believed. Yet, he would never return to the genre of the novel to do so. Good examples of his subsequent exploration are *Fantomas contra los vampiros multinacionales* (which combines comic strips with narrative, Warhol-like photographs, drawings and some facsimile reproductions) and *La raíz del ombú*.[75] Following the perspective of *La vuelta* and *Último Round*, in an attempt – as Marcy Schwartz would argue – to offer alternative systems that require new ways in which to read reality, Cortázar further looked into the combination of image and text in books such as *Alto el Perú* and *Prosa del observatorio*.[76] *Adiós, Robinson*, a radio script written in 1977 for German radio, also reflects Cortázar's political ideology, being a text in which, as Steven Boldy points out, Cortázar's concept of literature corresponds to definitions beyond the exclusively aesthetic.[77] In addition, towards the end of his life Cortázar would also produce *Nicaragua, tan violentamente dulce*, where he put together a collection of essays and articles, written between 1976 and 1983, about his experi-

---

[74] Cortázar, 'Corrección de pruebas', p. 31.

[75] *La raíz del ombú* is one of Cortázar's least known creations. It was written in collaboration with Alberto Cedrón, who created the drawings for which Cortázar supplied the text. It was finished in 1978, shortly after Cedrón's brother, Jorge Cedrón, killed himself in exile after having been persecuted – along with many other Argentinian filmmakers, such as Raymundo Gleyzer, Enrique Juárez and Pablo Szir – by the 'Triple A'. Although written then, *La raíz del ombú* was not published by Cedrón until 2004 (Buenos Aires: Fundación Internacional Argentina, 2004).

[76] "La fotografía, en colaboración con la palabra, ofrece sistemas alternativos que requieren nuevas estrategias para leer la realidad": Schwartz, 'Del lado de acá/del lado de allá', p. 38.

[77] Boldy, 'Prólogo: Cortázar antes y después', p. 10.

ences in Nicaragua, a book which he openly dedicated to the Frente Sandinista de Liberación Nacional, and which can be considered to be 'seriously' and unambiguously political.

Having exposed the self-contradicting and self-mythologizing aspects of Cortázar in relation to the political contents of his writing, it is crucial to point out that even with regard to his most overtly political fictional work, he still could not admit to the fact that *Libro de Manuel* was a political text, possibly in a vain attempt to defend the balance between aesthetic invention and politics that he was searching for. In 1974 Cortázar claimed:

> Yo no sé si llamarlo [a *Libro de Manuel*] un libro político. Ésa es una palabra que me da un poco de miedo, porque política es una cosa muy profesional y muy precisa. Yo creo que es un libro que [...] continúa una especie de *apertura ideológica* en la línea socialista que yo veo para América Latina, y además una especie de pre-crítica a todas las equivocaciones que suelen cometerse cuando se intentan y realizan revoluciones.[78]

The testimonial material inserted in the narrative visually disrupts the narrative. In addition, because these fragments are testimonies of a given 'real' reality, it makes it less comfortable for the reader to completely reject the sense of responsibility implied in the identification with Manuel, and in the fact that this novel is providing the reader with a political history as well as with a fictional story. The novel seems to ask for one fundamental political decision, namely: 'La gran decisión, izquierda o derecha' (*LM*, 351). *Libro de Manuel* is therefore what Umberto Eco refers to as an 'open work', in the sense that its meaning is generated in cooperation with its readers (as opposed to a 'closed work' where the book itself pre-establishes its own interpretation and only necessitates a passive reception).[79] In the novel, the characters themselves seem to allude to this as they criticise the ideology of the bourgeoisie, and thus condemn 'las estructuras y los órdenes cerrados [...] todo tiene que ser cerrado para ellos aunque después aplaudan muchísimo a Umberto Eco porque es lo que se usa' (*LM*, 77). It seems clear that with *Libro de Manuel* Cortázar aims to deliver an open work, facing the readers with their dose of responsibility in literature, but also, as Theo D'Haen argues, responsibility regarding the politics of present behaviour and, I would add, of the reader's relationship with history.[80] Cortázar sketches this out in his Berkeley lectures notes:

---

[78] Prego Gadea, *La fascinación de las palabras*, pp. 220–1. My emphasis.

[79] Umberto Eco, *Open Work*, trans. Anna Cancogni (Cambridge, MA: Harvard University Press, 1989), p. 45.

[80] D'Haen, *Text to Reader*, p. 88.

La	→	*apertura*	Por eso	{panfleto		{esperanza
literatura		cambios de perspectiva	*Manuel* no	{crítica	SIN	{prédica
puede		mostrar al	es un	{contenidismo		{opciones.[81]
		"hombre nuevo"				

It is significant that Cortázar should have written this down as information to be taught about his own literature. In other words, and returning to what he states in the prologue to *Libro de Manuel*, it is somewhat contradictory that Cortázar should have had to clarify that the book is not a political pamphlet and is not a criticism (of the revolutionary cause, we presume), while at the same time claiming that literature is about 'apertura'.

The fact that Cortázar could not bring himself to acknowledge the political dimension of *Libro de Manuel* is reminiscent of the rhetoric that he employed in his letters with regard to 'his own way' of writing revolutionary literature. It therefore seems clear that even at his most openly committed, politically and aesthetically speaking, Cortázar would refuse to succumb to the restrictions of what he understood to be inflexible categories. This in turn meant that he could never actually hope properly to engage with politics as a 'cosa precisa', while at the same time keeping everything open-ended and free. The 'ma façon' behind which Cortázar took refuge when it came to explaining his refusal to conform to revolutionary ways of writing socialist literature, is implied in his assertion that *Libro de Manuel* is the reflection of his own understanding of the direction that socialism should take in Latin America: 'la línea socialista que *yo veo*'.

From allegory to testimonial collage, the political was always present, with varying degrees of emphasis, in the fiction of Julio Cortázar. In this sense, it should not be claimed, as many have done, that *Libro de Manuel* is Cortázar's first and only 'political novel', born from his epiphanic conversion to socialism. It is rather the result of a process by a writer who was constantly searching for innovative ways to represent the reality in which he lived in. The historical present and political urgency that surrounded the writing of *Libro de Manuel* pushed Cortázar to deliver a 'rushed' book, which is perhaps marred, as Boldy would have it, by the repetition of certain Cortazarian formulas.[82] However, it still demonstrates a prevailing will for aesthetic innovation. Although Cortázar fought against dogmatism and the 'quitinosidad', as he called it, implied in revolutionary writing, *Libro de Manuel* is probably, and despite its lack of clear answers, his most didactic work. Outside the socio-political context in which the novel was embedded, *Libro de Manuel* stands nevertheless, and as the

---

[81] Julio Cortázar Papers, Series 1C, Box 2, Folder 43. My emphasis.

[82] Steven Boldy for instance claimed that in *Libro de Manuel*, 'the repetition of structure and character types from earlier works is mechanical; the language is often stereotyped Cortázarese bordering dangerously on rhetoric'; nevertheless, he still calls it 'a brave and honest book': *The Novels of Julio Cortázar*, p. 161.

Latin-Americanist Raymond Leslie Williams asserts, as a 'post-modern novel consist[ing] of a multiplicity of texts', which encourages the reader to think beyond the most immediate political questions so as to consider broader issues, such as humour, language, eroticism and modes of interpretation.[83] It is therefore not simply the product of a 'politicised' Cortázar, but rather the conclusion of an aesthetic, as well as political, evolution.

---

[83] Raymond Leslie Williams, *The Twentieth-Century Spanish American Novel* (Austin: University of Texas Press, 2003), p. 167.

Conclusion

Guillermo Martínez's anecdote, which prefaces this book, epitomises the current critical reception of Julio Cortázar, at least insofar as Argentina is concerned. As Roberto Ferro put it, it seems that the days of Cortázar as a 'gran escritor' ended with the publication of *Libro de Manuel*, and with the labelling of Cortázar as a 'political writer'. The contradictions manifested within Cortázar's construction of his image are to an extent perpetuated in an episode at a book fair in Buenos Aires in 2009. There, the very same writers who were paying tribute to Cortázar in the round-table discussion were simultaneously declaring that his days as a 'good' or respected writer were not only numbered, but were actually over. Meanwhile, *Papeles inesperados*, a volume containing Cortázar's previously unknown manuscripts, was one of the best-sellers at the fair.[1]

In the hope of modifying some of the prevailing preconceptions about Cortázar, this study has attempted to show that he did not 'become' a political writer as a result of his first trip to Cuba, and that the critical claim that divides Cortázar's fictional writings into the apolitical and the political is altogether misleading. Through tracing the evolution of the representation of political elements in his writings, from *El examen* to *Libro de Manuel*, it has been shown that politics had always been a point of reference in Cortázar's fiction. This conclusion has taken into account Jameson's idea that all books have an inherent political unconscious, but it has also demonstrated that for Cortázar, beyond any unconscious manifestation, there was also a quite deliberate exposure of a very concrete – although not always coherently-defined – political ideology. The fact that being an anti-Peronist and expressing this political standpoint in his early literature was problematic *vis-à-vis* Cortázar's subsequent conversion to socialism, is what led the writer to claim and maintain that his writings had been altogether outside historical and political concerns up to his first encounter with Cuba. Thus, the self-constructed image of the politicised Cortázar and the political *vis-à-vis* apolitical binary, made ideological sense at the time of Cor-

---

[1] Susana Reinoso: 'Pero si alguien brilló este año entre todos, ése fue Julio Cortázar. A 25 años de su muerte, vendió muchísimos ejemplares de su reciente legado: *Papeles inesperados*', in 'Autoayuda, ensayo y el plus de la firma en vivo: Julio Cortázar fue un inesperado best seller', *La Nación*, 10 May 2009 <http://www.lanacion.com.ar/nota.asp?nota_id=1126415> [accessed 10 September 2009].

tázar's public adherence to the Cuban Revolution and to socialism. Yet, this contradicts and problematises what his writings in fact contain insofar as their political manifestations go. Therefore I have exemplified what Cortázar's biographer, Mario Goloboff, has referred to as an 'essential unity' in Cortázar's fiction, that is that, contrary to the widespread understanding of Cortázar's fictional works, there is no clear-cut division between the apolitical and political writings, but rather, from the very first fictional writings, politics can be detected in different aesthetic manifestations. Given the more overt commitment required from the intellectual by socialist ideology, the Cuban Revolution and the common beliefs of many Latin American writers of the time, some – and not all – of Cortázar's writings show a more explicit political meaning from the early 1960s onwards, yet this is not an element that emerges anew.

I have shown the extent to which this widespread interpretation is mythologised, in that, ironically, the precise date of Cortázar's pivotal first trip to Cuba cannot be ascertained, yet for almost half a century this imprecision has remained. Whilst it is undeniable that the trip is crucial for the overall appreciation of Cortázar's works and, above all, for an understanding of the role of the political in his fiction, it has been argued that Cuba is central for Cortázar not because it 'transformed' him into a political writer, but rather because it moved him to change the emphasis of an already-existing political dimension in his fictional work. Furthermore, Cortázar's 'autofiguración', which has proven, and still proves, so persuasive and influential on the overall reception of and preconceptions about him, is at points quite at odds with his own work. Indeed, this book has underlined the discrepancies between Cortázar's own elucidations and his fictional work throughout his *oeuvre*.

In chapter 1 it was argued that the interpretative trend that deems Cortázar's writings to be apolitical, largely up until *Libro de Manuel*, is clearly contradicted by the contents of his early novels, namely those which were published posthumously (*Diario de Andrés Fava*, *Divertimento* and *El examen*) as well as his first published novel, *Los premios*. These texts show that Cortázar's preoccupations were, at this point, closely linked to the socio-political reality of Argentina, and that they actually reflect his active rejection of the Peronist regime. This is seen even in *Los premios*, which although written seven years after Cortázar had left Argentina to settle in Paris, is still centred round what Cortázar understood to be the detrimental effects of Peronism on Argentinian society. Mainly through allegorical representation, these early novels moreover prove that, contrary to his own claims, Cortázar was not writing from 'outside history' but was very much immersed in a concrete historical and political context. Furthermore, Cortázar's letters of the time reveal that he understood his anti-Peronism as a political ideology worth fighting for.

The analysis of *Rayuela* in chapter 2 highlighted elements considered to represent its political dimension. Although Cortázar's best-known text is not by any means first and foremost a political work, nor is it completely apolitical. In other words, *Rayuela* is not, as Cortázar hyperbolically claimed, a novel that 'no dice ni una sola palabra de política'.² In examining Oliveira's action versus inaction dilemma, it can be seen that the political element of this novel is primarily located in the protagonist's quandaries, representing an attitude of 'no te metás', which is political in its very abstention from involvement. Cortázar, not yet converted to socialism, seems to condemn this attitude of detachment and 'descompromiso' – recalling Ander-Egg's term – through the unsympathetic portrayal of his character. Attention was also drawn to a sequence of chapters which seemingly has not yet been studied in any detail within critical readings of *Rayuela*, nor within the analysis of politics in Cortázar's fiction in general. By inserting fragments of 'real' history into the narrative, through allusions to explicit images of torture as well as through the interpolation of typographical emulations of newspaper articles dealing with capital punishment, the novel provokes the reader into introspective ethical, social and political questioning. Thus Oliveira's refusal to engage with any sense of responsibility in society, or even in his own circle of personal relationships, may instil in the reader a will to reflect upon his/her own ideological, ethical and political positions, through identification with, or distancing from, the novel's protagonist.

As far as can be ascertained, it was after the publication of *Rayuela* that Cortázar travelled to Cuba and had his 'epiphanic' encounter with the revolution. He became a socialist, though he admitted to never having read Marx, and embraced the role and responsibilities of a Latin American intellectual. Up until his death in 1984, he would remain involved in the revolutionary struggles of Latin America (in Nicaragua, El Salvador and Chile) and would of course condemn the military dictatorships of the region. However, with regard to the representation of the political within his fictional writings, his revolutionary commitment precipitated Cortázar's conflicting notions regarding how to write literature in and for the revolution.

In chapter 3 two extensive quotations, taken from Cortázar's collection of letters, were analysed in an attempt to elucidate how he envisaged his own fiction within the socialist revolution. In his correspondence, as well as in later essays, it is clear that at this point Cortázar was reluctant to confine his literary creation to the dogmatic restrictions that, in his view, came with political commitment. His fervent belief in artistic freedom, and his parallel ambition to be an active participant in the political struggles taking place in Latin America, resulted in the vague concept of an 'opération analogue', whereby somehow (for it remained undefined) Cortázar aimed to be a revolutionary, a 'Che Guevara of language', yet without changing his conception of literature. During this period, when Cortázar had to deal with what for him were conflicting interests, a rhetoric of guilt and duty became increasingly apparent, as did his reliance on a self-constructed image.

---

2 Prego Gadea, *La fascinación de las palabras*, p. 188.

CONCLUSION

This was a stage in his evolution when his ways of writing literature had to split into two different strands, which temporarily ran in parallel.

One of these two strands is epitomised in *62/modelo para armar* as tending towards the completely abstract. Containing no apparent political dimension, this novel encapsulates Cortázar's persistent though undeclared belief in art for art's sake. As the other strand, the collage books include politics in a more explicit manner (for example, through politically provocative images), without giving in to an inflexible aesthetic dictated by a political agenda. Although Cortázar only spoke of the 'failure' of *62* specifically, it can be argued that his whole concept of the 'opération analogue' was altogether unsuccessful.

According to Cortázar, the main purpose of *Libro de Manuel* was that in some way it could be of 'use' to the revolution, asssuming for the first time a more practical end to his literature. Apart from the actual donation of the royalties of the book, and the Médicis prize money, Cortázar did not elucidate clearly how exactly he had planned to carry out his 'opération analogue' without in fact making any aesthetic concessions. The novel was Cortázar's final attempt at performing the 'opération analogue', but given its reception, especially in Argentina, his efforts went unappreciated precisely where they were supposed to be of 'use'. The political dimension manifests itself in various ways in this text. The most explicit is the novel's form, a collage of newspaper clippings reporting the horrors of torture, violence and repression, intertwined with the narrative plot. The form corresponds to the aesthetic exploration already evident in *La vuelta* and *Último Round,* yet whereas in the collage books the insertions varied from the pataphysical to the war in Vietnam, in *Libro de Manuel* they are given an exclusively political dimension. Although this was clearly Cortázar's most blatant effort to come closer to the kind of 'revolutionary' literature that was 'expected' of him and which he had declared he would reject, this final novel still proposed, via its humoristic and erotic dimensions, a kind of revolution which went beyond the political as mere social struggle. For Cortázar, the social and political revolution had to emerge from an internal, personal and individual transformation. The *hombre nuevo* could not just be concerned with political ideologies, but also with those elements in life that would take man beyond that 'underdevelopment' that Cortázar saw in the inflexibility of revolutionary realities. In this sense, this is a book where, in an effort to mirror the political interests and urgencies of its time, the political element is certainly more emphatic than in his previous texts. However, this is not enough to substantiate the claim that *Libro de Manuel* is Cortázar's 'political novel'; rather, it is the product of an aesthetic and ideological evolution, which was permanently looking to experiment with different forms and which, crucially, had politics as a constant source of reference.

A critical approach to outlining the political element in the selected corpus of Cortázar's writings has been achieved by taking into account biographical material and Cortázar's non-literary writings, as well as through textual analysis of the selected texts. Because of the progressive complexity of the role that politics played in Cortázar's life, this was a particularly insightful approach for the reading of the political in his fiction. This is not to say that the political cannot be apprehended solely through studying his fictional texts. Yet, by understanding the evolution of Cortázar's political ideology through the biographical and non-literary writings, it was possible to compare and contrast what his fictional texts show in relation to Cortázar's own views on politics, and what they actually achieved when placed against his aesthetic ambitions. The disjunction between Cortázar's elucidations, paratexts and the actual manifestations of the political in his fictional writings bring to the fore some important contradictions. As expected, the representation of the political in Cortázar's work does not achieve particular coherence, at least not in the longer, fictional writings. However, this could be said to be a faithful representation of the inconsistencies that the meaning of politics had for Cortázar throughout his life.

Moving away from the established critical interpretations that divide Cortázar and his writings into the apolitical *vis-à-vis* the political, I have understood and analysed the corpus here selected as manifestations of a single process, one in which the political is a palpable concern throughout, albeit to different degrees and expressing diverse political ideologies. The ways in which the political element is represented are not consistent, and the stated aims are sometimes in conflict with what the fictional texts actually depict, yet Cortázar did maintain an 'essential unity', with politics as a constant source of reference. It is hoped that this study will lead to further research on the political representation and implications of works by Cortázar which are not analysed here, such as those prior to *Los premios,* which certainly deserve more critical attention, and the short stories for which Cortázar is most widely known and admired.

Martín Kohan, who was also present at that 'homage' to Cortázar at the 2009 Buenos Aires book fair, was similarly vexed by the unquestioned intellectual aloofness with which Cortázar seems to be repeatedly dismissed within Argentinian literary and academic circles. To this effect, he wrote that 'No estoy pensando en algunas críticas muy agudas que pudo merecer Cortázar: [...] sino en otra cosa: en la costumbre displicente de tener en menos a Cortázar [...] como si hubiese medianía en sus novelas, o como si fuese Cortázar el responsable (el responsable, y no la víctima) de las *taras del cortazarismo.*'[3] It is hoped that through the ideas advanced and conclusion reached, this book contributes to the much-needed questioning and gradual untangling of those ingrained 'taras del cortazarismo'.

---

[3] Martín Kohan, '*Papeles inesperados* de Cortázar: sorpresas del cronopio', *Perfil*, 31 May 2009 <http://www.diarioperfil.com.ar/edimp/0369/articulo.php?art=14760&ed=0369> [accessed 01 September 2009]. My emphasis.

Bibliography

Julio Cortázar
Fiction and Critical Work
Cortázar, Julio, *Argentina, años de alambradas culturales*, ed. Saúl Yurkievich (Barcelona: Muchnik, 1984).
—— *Bestiario* (Buenos Aires: Sudamericana, 1951).
—— *Buenos Aires, Buenos Aires* (Buenos Aires: Sudamericana, 1968).
—— *Cartas/1 1937–1963*, ed. Aurora Bernárdez (Buenos Aires: Alfaguara, 2000).
—— *Cartas/2 1964–1968*, ed. Aurora Bernárdez (Buenos Aires: Alfaguara, 2000).
—— *Cartas/3 1969–1983*, ed. Aurora Bernárdez (Buenos Aires: Alfaguara, 2000).
—— 'Corrección de pruebas en Alta Provenza', in *Convergencias/divergencias/incidencias*, ed. Julio Ortega (Barcelona: Tusquets, 1973), pp. 13–36.
—— *Cuentos completos/1* (Buenos Aires: Alfaguara, 1994).
—— *Cuentos completos/2* (Buenos Aires: Alfaguara, 1994).
—— *Diario de Andrés Fava* (Buenos Aires: Alfaguara, 1995).
—— *Divertimento* (Buenos Aires: Sudamericana, 1986).
—— *El examen* (Buenos Aires: Sudamericana, 1986).
—— *Fantomas contra los vampiros multinacionales* (Buenos Aires: Destino, 1975).
—— *Final Exam*, trans. Alfred Mac Adam (New York: New Directions, 2000).
—— *Hopscotch*, trans. Gregory Rabassa (New York: Pantheon, 1966).
—— *La vuelta al día en ochenta mundos* (Mexico City: Siglo XXI, 1967).
—— *Libro de Manuel* (Buenos Aires: Sudamericana, 1973).
—— *Los premios* (Madrid: Santillana, 1960).
—— *Los reyes* (Buenos Aires: Gulab y Aldabahor, 1949).
—— *Manual for Manuel*, trans. Gregory Rabassa (New York: Pantheon, 1978).
—— *Nicaragua, tan violentamente dulce* (Managua: Nueva Nicaragua, 1983).
—— *Obra crítica/1*, ed. Saúl Yurkievich (Buenos Aires: Alfaguara, 1994).
—— *Obra crítica/2*, ed. Jaime Alazraki (Buenos Aires: Alfaguara, 1994).
—— *Obra crítica/3*, ed. Saúl Sosnowski (Buenos Aires: Alfaguara, 1994).
—— *Papeles inesperados* (Buenos Aires: Alfaguara, 2009).
—— *Policrítica en la hora de los chacales* (Buenos Aires: Portocaliu, 1987).
—— *Prosa del observatorio* (Barcelona: Lumen, 1972).
—— *Rayuela* (Buenos Aires: Sudamericana, 1963).
—— *Rayuela*, ed. Julio Ortega and Saúl Yurkievich (Madrid: Ediciones Unesco, 1991)

―――― *62/modelo para armar* (Buenos Aires: Sudamericana, 1968).
―――― *Territorios* (Mexico City: Siglo XXI, 1978).
―――― *Último Round* (Mexico City: Siglo XXI, 1969).
―――― *Viaje alrededor de una mesa* (Buenos Aires: Cuadernos de Rayuela, 1970).
―――― and Ana María Barrenechea, *Cuaderno de bitácora de Rayuela* (Buenos Aires: Sudamericana 1983).
―――― and Alberto Cedrón, *La raíz del ombú* (Buenos Aires: Fundación Interna-cional Argentina, 2004).
―――― and Manja Offerhaus, *Alto el Perú* (Mexico City: Siglo XXI, 1984).
―――― and Julio Silva, *Silvalandia* (Buenos Aires: Argonauta, 1984).

Interviews
Carbono, Alberto, 'Mi ametralladora es la literatura', *Crisis*, 3 (June 1973), 10–15.
González Bermejo, Ernesto, *Revelaciones de un cronopio: conversaciones con Cortázar* (Barcelona: Edhasa, 1978).
Harss, Luis, *Los nuestros* (Buenos Aires: Sudamericana, 1977).
Osorio, Manuel, 'Julio Cortázar: el misterio de escribir y de morir', *Plural*, 157 (October 1984), 2–13.
Picon Garfield, Evelyn, *Cortázar por Cortázar* (Xalapa: Universidad Veracruzana, 1978).
―――― *Julio Cortázar* (New York: Frederick Ungar Publishing Co., 1975).
Prego Gadea, Omar, *La fascinación de las palabras* (Buenos Aires: Aguilar, 1984).
Soler Serrano, Joaquín, 'Grandes personajes a fondo: Julio Cortázar' (Madrid: TVE, 1977)<http://video.google.com/videoplay?doc id=8741130362458662732> [accessed 20 February 2009].

Manuscript Sources
Julio Cortázar Papers, Princeton University Library, Manuscripts Division, Series 1C, Box 2, Folders 42, 43.

Secondary Sources
Abbate, Florencia, 'Al borde del vértigo', *Página/12*, 12 February 2009 <http://www.pagina12.com.ar/diario/suplementos/espectaculos/subnotas/12837□3851-2009-0212.html> [accessed 13 February 2009].
Aínsa, Fernando, 'Las dos orillas de Julio Cortázar', in *Julio Cortázar*, ed. Pedro Lastra (Madrid: Taurus, 1981), pp. 34–63.
Alazraki, Jaime, 'Cortázar antes de Cortázar: *Rayuela* desde su primer ensayo publicado: "Rimbaud"' (1941)', in Cortázar, *Rayuela*, ed. Ortega and Yurkievich, pp. 571–80.
―――― *Hacia Cortázar: aproximaciones a su obra* (Barcelona: Anthropos, 1994).
―――― 'Imaginación e historia en Julio Cortázar', in *Los ochenta mundos de Cortázar: ensayos*, ed. Fernando Burgos (Madrid: EDI-6, 1987), pp. 1–20.
―――― 'Reading "The Night Face Up": Julio Whispers a Key Beneath the Text', *Point of Contact*, 4/1 (1994), 33–9.

—— 'Tema y sistema de *Prosa del observatorio* de Julio Cortázar', *La Torre*, 1/1 (1987), 92–110.

—— and Ivar Ivask (eds), *The Final Island: The Fiction of Julio Cortázar* (Norman: University of Oklahoma Press, 1978),

—— Ivar Ivask, and Joaquín Marco (eds), Montserrat Conill (trans.), *La isla final*, (Barcelona: Ultramar, 1988)

Ander-Egg, Ezequiel, 'Apoliticidad o neutralidad política', in *Formación para el trabajo social* (Buenos Aires: Humanitas, 1987), pp. 29-67.

Anderson, Blanca, *Julio Cortázar: la imposibilidad de narrar* (Madrid: Pliegos, 1990).

Andrés, Alfredo, *Palabras con Leopoldo Marechal* (Buenos Aires: Carlos Pérez, 1968).

Anguita, Eduardo, and Marín Caparrós, *La voluntad: una historia de la militancia revolucionaria en la Argentina*, I: *1966–1973* (Buenos Aires: Norma, 1997).

Arent Safir, Margery, 'Erótica y liberación', in Julio Cortázar, *Rayuela*, ed. Ortega and Yurkievich, pp. 827–38.

Argentina, Comisión Nacional de Evaluación y Acreditación Universitaria (CONEAU) <http://www.coneau.gov.ar/archivos/543.pdf> [accessed 19 March 2008].

—— Honorable Cámara de Diputados de la Provincia de Buenos Aires, 'Leyes y decretos' <http://www.hcdiputados-ba.gov.ar> [accessed 20 March 2008].

—— Legislatura de la Nación <http://www.gov.ar/LEYES/leyesv/1474.htm> [accessed 30 March 2008].

—— Ministerio de Educación de la Nación, *Labor desarrollada durante la primera presidencia del General Juan Perón* (Buenos Aires: Ministerio de Educación, 1952).

Arguindeguy, Diego L., Ricardo De Titto, and Mónica Deleis, *El libro de los presidentes argentinos del siglo XX: la historia de los que dirigieron el país* (Buenos Aires: Aguilar, 2000).

Aristotle, *Politics*, trans. Benjamin Jowett (New York: Dover Publications, 2000).

Arrone-Amestoy, Lida, 'Identidad y diferencia: discursos de la imagen en *Prosa del observatorio*', in *Los ochenta mundos de Cortázar: ensayos*, ed. Fernando Burgos (Madrid: Edi–6, 1987), pp. 55–66.

Barrenechea, Ana María, 'La estructura de *Rayuela* de Julio Cortázar', in *Historia y crítica de la literatura hispanoamericana: época contemporánea*, ed. Cedomil Goic (Barcelona: Crítica, 1998), pp. 410–14.

—— '*Rayuela*, una búsqueda a partir de cero', *Sur*, 288 (May–June 1964), 69–73.

Barthes, Roland, '¿Adónde/o va la literatura?, in *Variaciones sobre la literatura*, trans. Eduardo F. González (Buenos Aires: Paidós, 2002), pp. 175–94.

—— 'Authors and Writers', in *Selected Writings*, ed. Susan Sontag (Oxford: Fontana, 1983), pp. 185–93.

—— *Camera lucida: Reflections on Photography*, trans. Richard Howard (London: Vintage, 1981).

—— *Image, Music, Text*, trans. Stephen Heath (London: Fontana, 1977).

—— *The Pleasure of the Text*, trans. Richard Miller (New York: Hill and Wang, 1975).

—— 'Shock Photos', in *The Eiffel Tower and Other Mythologies*, trans. Richard Howard (Berkeley: University of California Press, 1997), pp. 71–74.
Bataille, Georges, *The Tears of Eros*, trans. Peter Conor (Hong Kong: City Lights, 1989).
Battista, Vicente, 'La corteza de Cortázar', *El escarabajo de oro*, 40 (October 1969), 14–15.
Belgrano Rawson, Eduardo, 'Sacarse de encima la Historia', in L. Lamborghini., *La historia y la política,* 67–72
Benedetti, Mario, *Letras del continente mestizo* (Montevideo: Arca, 1972).
Benjamin, Walter, 'Little History of Photography', in *Selected Writings,* II, ed. Michael Jennings (London: Belknap, 1996), pp. 507–31.
—— 'The Author as Producer', in *Reflections*, trans. Edmund Jephcott (New York: Schocken Books, 1978), pp. 220–38.
—— 'The Storyteller: Reflections on the Works of Nikolai Leskov', in *Illuminations*, trans. Harry Zohn (Glasgow: Harper Collins, 1968), pp. 83–107.
Bernárdez, Aurora, 'Los últimos papeles de Cortázar', *El País*, 5 February 2009, Sección cultura <http://www.elpais.com/solotexto/articulo.html?xref=20090205 elpepicul_1&type=Tes&anchor=elpepicul> [accessed 5 February 2009].
Boldy, Steven, 'Mise en perspective de *Imagen de John Keats'*, in *Cortázar: de tous les côtés*, ed. J. Manzi (Poitiers: UFR Langues Littératures Poitiers, Maison des Sciences de l'Homme et de la Société, 2002), pp. 13–26.
—— *The Novels of Julio Cortázar* (Cambridge: Cambridge University Press, 1980).
—— 'Prólogo Cortázar antes y después', in *Julio Cortázar: obras completas,* II: *Teatro*; *Novelas,* I, ed. Saúl Yurkievich (Barcelona: Galaxia Gutenberg/Círculo de Lectores, 2004). pp. 9–39.
Borello, Rodolfo A., 'Los liberales: de Borges a Murena', in *El peronismo (1943–1955) en la narrativa argentina* (Ottawa: Dovehouse Editions, 1991), pp. 147–82.
Borges, Jorge Luis, *Biblioteca personal* (Buenos Aires: Alianza, 1988).
—— *Obras completas 1923–1949* (Buenos Aires: Emecé, 1989).
—— *Otras inquisiciones* (Madrid: Alianza, 1997).
—— and Adolfo Bioy Casares, 'La fiesta del monstruo', in *Obras en colaboración* (Buenos Aires: Emecé, 1979), pp. 392–402.
Borroni, Otelo, and Roberto Vacca, *La vida de Eva Perón: testimonios para su historia,* I (Buenos Aires: Galerna, 1970).
Bosca, Roberto, *La iglesia nacional peronista: factor religioso y poder político* (Buenos Aires: Sudamericana, 1997).
Brecht, Bertolt, *Brecht on Theatre: The Development of an Aesthetic*, trans. John Willett (London: Methuen, 1964).
Brennan, James P. (ed.), *Peronism and Argentina* (Wilmington: Scholarly Resources Inc., 1998).
Breton, André, *Communicating Vessels*, trans. Mary Ann Caws and Geoffrey T. Harris (Lincoln, NE: University of Nebraska Press, 1990).
—— *Nadja*, trans. Richard Howard (London: Penguin Books, 1999).
—— *Position politique du surréalisme* (Paris: Editions du Sagittaire, 1935).

Bruto, César, *Brutas biografías de bolsillo* (Buenos Aires: Ediciones Airene, 1972).
Buchrucker, Cristián, 'Interpretations of Peronism: Old Frameworks and New Perspectives', in Brennan, *Peronism and Argentina*, pp. 3–28.
Calvino, Italo, *Il Castello dei destini incrociati* (Turin: Einaudi, 1973).
—— 'Right and Wrong Uses of Literature', in *The Literature Machine*, trans. Patrick Creagh (London: Vintage, 1997), pp. 80–100.
Carpentier, Alejo, *El siglo de las luces* (Barcelona: Seix Barral, 1962).
Carreras, Julio, *La política armada: movimientos armados en Argentina* (Buenos Aires: Vergara Grupo Zeta, 2003).
Castro Klarén, Sara, 'Cortázar, Surrealism and Pataphysics', *Comparative Literature*, 27/3 (1975), 218–36.
—— 'Fabulación ontológica: hacia una teoría de la literatura de Cortázar', in Alazraki, Ivask and Marco, *La isla final*, pp. 349–72.
Cavafys, Constantine P., *The Complete Poems*, trans. Rae Dalven (London: Hogarth Press, 1948).
Cavarozzi, Marcelo, *Autoritarismo y democracias (1955–1966)* (Buenos Aires: Eudeba, 2002).
Chávez, Marisol L., 'Entrevista con Julio Silva: papeles, trazos y testimonios', *Revista de la Universidad Nacional de México*, 51 (May 2008), 49–56.
Ciria, Alberto, *Política y cultura popular: la Argentina peronista 1946–1955* (Buenos Aires: Ediciones de la Flor, 1983).
Colás, Santiago, *Postmodernity in Latin America: The Argentine Paradigm* (Durham: Duke University Press, 1994).
—— 'Writing Life and Love: Julio Cortázar and Gilles Deleuze', *Angelaki*, 2/1 (1996), 199–207.
Collazos, Oscar, Julio Cortázar and Mario Vargas Llosa, *Literatura en la revolución y revolución en la literatura: polémica* (Mexico City: Siglo XXI, 1970).
Colominas, Norberto, and Osvaldo Soriano, 'Julio Cortázar: lo fantástico incluye y necesita la realidad', *El País*, 25 March 1979, 3–7.
Conti, Haroldo, 'Cuando enmudezcan todas las voces', *La opinión cultural*, 8 December 1974, 10–11.
Copeland, John G., 'Las imágenes de *Rayuela*', in *Homenaje a Julio Cortázar*, ed. Helmy F. Giacoman (Madrid: Anaya, 1972), pp. 131–50.
Correas, Jaime, *Cortázar, profesor universitario* (Buenos Aires: Aguilar, 2004).
Cosgrove, Ciaran, 'Discursive Anarchy or Creative Pluralism? The Cases of Cortázar and Puig', *Modern Language Review*, 90/1 (1995), 71–82.
Curran, Angela, 'Brecht's Criticism of Aristotle's Aesthetics of Tragedy', *Journal of Aesthetics and Art Criticism*, 59/2 (2001), 167–84.
Darrow, Clarence, 'Closing Argument: The State of Illinois v. Nathan Leopold & Richard Loeb. Chicago, Illinois, August 22, 1924' <http://www.law.umkc.edu/faculty/projects/ftrials/leoploeb/LEO_SUMD.htm> [accessed 20 June 2008].
David-Peyre, Yvonne, 'La Technique des collages et des montages dans *Rayuela* de Julio Cortázar', *Caravelle: Cahiers du Monde Hispanique et Luso Brésilien*, 21 (1973), 65–87.

Dávila, María de Lourdes,'*Buenos Aires Buenos Aires*: ¿ciudad invisible?', in *El mundo Cortázar,* ed. Dulce Maria Zúñiga (Guadalajara: Cátedra Latinoamericana Julio Cortázar, 2006), pp. 129–43.

—— *Desembarcos de papel: la imagen en la literatura de Julio Cortázar* (Rosario: Beatriz Viterbo, 2001).

Dayan, Peter, and Carolina Orloff, 'Finding rhythm in Cortázar's *Los premios*', *Paragraph,* 33/2 (2010), 215–29.

De Campos, Haroldo, 'Superación de los lenguajes exclusivos', in *América Latina en su literatura*, ed. César Fernández Moreno (Mexico City: Siglo XXI, 1972), pp. 279–300.

De Diego, José Luis, 'La transición democrática: intelectuales y escritores', in *La Argentina democrática: los años y los libros*, ed. Antonio Camou, María Cristina Tortti and Aníbal Viguera, (Buenos Aires: Prometeo, 2009), pp. 49–82.

De Diego, Juan, 'De los setenta a los ochenta: la curva descendente en la valoración crítica de Cortázar', in *Actas del II Congreso Internacional CELEHIS de Literatura* (2004) <http://www.freewebs.com/celehis/actas2004/>[accessed 19 November 2008].

De Gerónimo, Miriam, *Narrar por knock-out* (Buenos Aires: Simurg, 2004).

De Ípola, Emilio, *Ideología y discurso populista* (Mexico City: Folios Ediciones, 1982).

De La Guerra Castellanos, Francisco E., *Julio Cortázar: literatura y revolución* (Mexico City: UNAM, 2000).

De La Torre, Carlos, 'The Ambiguous Meanings of Latin American Populisms', *Social Research*, 59/2 (1992), 385–414.

Deleis, Mónica, Ricardo De Titto, and Diego L. Arguindeguy, *El libro de los presidentes argentinos del siglo XX: la historia de los que dirigieron el país* (Buenos Aires: Aguilar, 2000).

Dellepiane, Ángela, 'Otra experiencia para lectores "salteados": *Libro de Manuel*', *Nueva narrativa hispanoamericana*, 5 (1975), 17–34.

Derrida, Jacques, 'Passages – from Traumatism to Promise', in *Points... Interviews 1974–1994*, ed. Elisabeth Weber, trans. Peggy Kamuf (Stanford, CA: Stanford University Press, 1995), pp. 31–52.

De Riz, Liliana, *La política en suspenso 1966–1976* (Buenos Aires: Paidós, 2000).

D'Haen, Theo, *Text to Reader: A Communicative Approach to Fowles, Barth, Cortázar and Boon* (Amsterdam: John Benjamins, 1983).

Dobry, Edgardo, 'Entrevista con Beatriz Sarlo', *Cuadernos hispanoamericanos*, 618 (December 2001), 111–20.

Domínguez, Mignón, *Cartas desconocidas de Julio Cortázar, 1939–1945* (Buenos Aires: Sudamericana, 1992).

Drucaroff, Elsa, 'Fantástico desencantado: los nietos de Julio Cortázar', *Revista Axxón* 155 (October 2005) <http://axxon.com.ar/rev/155/c-155ensayo.htm> [accessed 10 November 2008].

Durán, Juan Luzio, '*Los Premios*, buscadores de hoy día', in *Julio Cortázar*, ed. Pedro Lastra (Madrid: Taurus, 1981), pp. 179–90.

Eagleton, Terry, *Criticism and Ideology* (London: Verso, 1978).
—— *Ideology* (London: Verso, 1991).
—— *Literary Theory: An Introduction* (Oxford: Blackwell, 1983).
Eco, Umberto, 'Lector in Fabula: Pragmatic Strategy in a Metanarrative Text', in *The Role of the Reader: Exploration in the Semiotics of Texts* (London: Hutchinson, 1979), pp. 200–60.
—— *Open Work*, trans. Anna Cancogni (Cambridge, MA: Harvard University Press, 1989).
Esti Rein, Mónica, *Politics and Education in Argentina, 1946–1962*, trans. Martha Grenzeback, Latin American Realities Series (London: M. E. Sharpe, 1998).
Fass, Paula S., 'Making and Remaking an Event: The Leopold and Loeb Case in American Culture', *Journal of American History*, 80/3 (1993), 919–51.
Feinmann, José Pablo, *La sangre derramada: violencia política* (Buenos Aires: Ariel, 1999).
Fernández Cubillos, Héctor, 'La crítica de Nietzsche contra Occidente en *Rayuela* de Julio Cortázar', *Veritas*, 3/18 (2008), 97–126.
Ferré, Rosario, '*Libro de Manuel*, Zona: carga y descarga,' 1/6 (September 1973), 10–12.
Ferrée Chabrier, Christina, 'Aesthetic Perversion: Octave Mirbeau's *Le Jardin des supplices*', *Nineteenth-Century French Studies*, 34 (2006), 355–70.
Ferro, Roberto, 'Cortázar, la trasgresión permanente', *Las palabras y las cosas*, 10 March 1991, 10–15.
—— 'Escritura y vida en Julio Cortázar: cruces y desvíos', *III Congreso Internacional CELEHIS de Literatura* (Mar del Plata: 8 April 2008).
Fiorucci, Flavia, 'Between Institutional Survival and Intellectual Commitment: The Case of the Argentine Society of Writers During Perón's Rule (1945–1955)', *The Americas*, 62/4 (2006), 591–622.
Flaubert, Gustave, 'Lettre à Louise Colet', in *Correspondance,* II, ed. Jean Bruneau (Paris: Gallimard, 1980), pp. 30–3.
Flores García, Víctor, *El lugar que da verdad: la filosofía de la realidad histórica de Ignacio Ellacuría* (Mexico City: Universidad Iberoamericana, 1997).
Ford, Aníbal, 'Humanismo para europeos', *La opinión cultural*, 8 December 1974, 7–8.
Foucault, Michel, *The Archaeology of Knowledge*, trans. A. M. Sheridan Smith (London: Routledge, 1994).
—— *La hermenéutica del sujeto*, trans. Ulises Guinazú (Buenos Aires: Fondo de Cultura Económica, 2001),
—— *Microfísica del poder*, ed. and trans. Julia Varela and Fernando Álvarez-Uría (Madrid: La Piqueta, 1992).
—— 'Power and Strategies', in *Power/Knowledge*, ed. Colin Gordon, trans. Colin Gordon (New York: Pantheon, 1980), pp. 134–45.
Fowler, Rowena, 'Ernest Dowson and the Classics', *Yearbook of English Studies*, 3 (1973), 243–52.
Franco, Jean, *An Introduction to Spanish-American Literature* (Cambridge: Cambridge University Press, 1994).

—— *Decadencia y caída de la ciudad letrada*, trans. Héctor Silva Míguez (Barcelona: Debate, 2003).
—— 'Julio Cortázar: Utopia and Everyday Life', *Inti*, 10–11 (1979–80), 108–18.
—— 'South of Your Border', in *The 60s Without Apology,* ed. Sohnya Sayres *et al.* (Minneapolis: University of Minnesota Press, 1984), pp. 324–6.
Frow, John, *Marxism and Literary History* (Oxford: Basil Blackwell, 1986).
Fuentes, Carlos, 'Cortázar: la caja de Pandora', in *La nueva novela hispanoamericana* (Mexico City: Joaquín Mortíz, 1969), pp. 67–77.
—— 'Julio Cortázar, 1914–1984', in *Julio Cortázar a través de la prensa sudamericana*, ed. Perla Rosenstein (Buenos Aires: Instituto de Estudios de Literatura Latinoamericana, 1984) pp. 35–43.
—— *París: la revolución de mayo* (Mexico City: ERA, 1968).
Gamerro, Carlos, 'Julio Cortázar, inventor del peronismo', in *El peronismo clásico (1945–1955): descamisados, gorilas y contreras* ed. Guillermo Korn (Buenos Aires: Paradiso, 2007), pp. 44–57.
García Canclini, Néstor, *Cortázar: una antropología poética* (Buenos Aires: Nova, 1968).
García Sarria, Alex, and Giraldo Oneida, 'El compromiso ético de la libertad', *Archivo Chile*, 9 October 1997 <http://www.archivochile.com/America_latina/Doc_paises_al/Cuba/Escritos_sobre_che/escritossobreche0188.pdf>[accessed 20 May 2007].
Garrido, Joaquín, 'Operadores epistémicos y conectores contextuales', in *Aproximaciones pragmalingüísticas al español*, ed. Henk Haverkate *et al.* (Amsterdam: Rodopi, 1993), pp. 5–49.
Genette, Gérard, *Palimpsests: Literature in the Second Degree*, trans. Claude Dowinski and Chana Newman (Lincoln: University of Nebraska Press, 1997).
Genover, Kathleen, *Claves de una novelística existencial en* Rayuela *de Cortázar* (Madrid: Plaza Mayor, 1975).
Gilman, Claudia, 'Dame más', *Página/12*, 13 March 2000 <http://www.pagina12.com.ar/2000/suple/libros/00-08/00-08-13/nota1.htm> [accessed 5 January 2009].
—— *Entre la pluma y el fusil: debates y dilemas del escritor revolucionario en América Latina* (Buenos Aires: Siglo XXI, 2003).
Giordano, Alberto, 'Cortázar en los 60: ensayo y autofiguración', in *Modos del ensayo: de Borges a Piglia* (Buenos Aires: Beatriz Viterbo, 2005), pp. 169–76.
Girondo, Oliverio, *Veinte poemas para leerse en el tranvía* (1922), in *Obra completa*, ed. Raúl Antelo (Barcelona: Galaxia Gutenberg, 1999), pp. 3–28.
Goldar, Ernesto, 'La colonización ideológica', *La opinión cultural*, 8 December 1974, 9–10.
Goloboff, Mario, 'En Cortázar no hay dos épocas', *Clarín: Revista de Cultura*, 10 November 2007, 5–6.
—— 'El "Hablar con figuras" de Cortázar', in *Lo lúdico y lo fantástico en la obra de Julio Cortázar II,* coord. Dulce María Zúñiga (Madrid: Fundamentos, 1986), pp. 241–57.
—— *Julio Cortázar: la biografía* (Buenos Aires: Seix Barral, 1998).

—— 'Sumó la realidad a lo fantástico', *Página 12*, 12 February 2004 <http://www.pagina12.com.ar/diario/elpais/1-31438-2004-02-12.html> [accessed 8 February 2008].

González, Aníbal, '"Press Clippings" and Cortázar's Ethics of Writing', in *Julio Cortázar*, ed. Harold Bloom (Washington: Chelsea House Publishing, 2005), pp. 245–63.

—— 'Revolución y alegoría en "Reunión" de Julio Cortázar', in *Los ochenta mundos de Cortázar*, ed. Fernando Burgos (Madrid: Edi–6, 1987), pp. 93–110.

Goux, Jean-Joseph, *The Coiners of Language*, trans. Jennifer Curtiss (Norman, Ok.: University of Oklahoma Press, 1996).

Graham Greene, Patrick, *The Anti-Peronist Ideology of Rhetoric in Jorge Luis Borges and Julio Cortázar* (Ann Arbor: Proquest, 2005).

Guevara, Ernesto, *El socialismo y el hombre en Cuba* (Havana: Cuadernos Erre, 1965).

Guinsberg, Enrique, '*El libro de Manuel*, Cortázar, literatura, política y quitinosidad', *El sigma*, 16 March 2006 <http://www.elsigma.com/site/detalle.aspIdContenido=9524> [accessed 24 March 2009].

Gutiérrez Mouat, Ricardo, 'The Modern Novel, the Media and Mass Culture in Latin America', in *Latin American Literature and the Mass Media*, ed. Debra Ann Castillo and Edmundo Paz-Soldán (London: Routledge, 2000), pp. 71–102.

Gyurko, Lanin A., 'Artist and Critic as Self and Double in Cortázar's "Los Pasos en las huellas"', *Hispania*, 65/3 (1982), 352–64.

Halperín Donghi, Tulio, *Historia de la Universidad de Buenos Aires* (Buenos Aires: Eudeba, 1982).

—— *La larga agonía de la Argentina peronista* (Buenos Aires: Ariel, 1994).

—— 'Nueva narrativa y ciencias sociales hispanoamericanas en la década del sesenta', *Hispamérica*, 27 (December 1980), 3–18.

Hanne, Michael, *The Power of the Story: Fiction and Political Change* (Oxford: Berghahn, 1994).

Heidegger, Martin, *Interpretaciones sobre la poesía de Hölderin* trans. José Maria Valverde (Barcelona: Ariel, 1983).

Heker, Liliana, 'La cultura argentina: de la dictadura a la democracia', *Cuadernos hispanoamericanos*, 517 (July–September 1993), 590–603.

—— '¿Qué opina del *Libro de Manuel* de Julio Cortázar?', *Crisis*, 1 (May 1973), 10–14.

Hernández, Ana María, 'Cortázar: el libro de Andrés+Lonstein=Manuel', *Nueva narrativa hispanoamericana*, 5 (1975), 35–55

Hicks, Emily D., *Border Writing: The Multidimensional Text* (Minneapolis: University of Minnesota Press, 1991).

Huelsenbeck, Richard (ed.), *The Dada Almanac*, trans. Barbara Wright and James Kirkup (London: Atlas Press, 1993).

Hutcheon, Linda, *Irony's Edge: The Theory and Politics of Irony* (London: Routledge, 1995).

—— *The Politics of Postmodernism* (London: Routledge, 1989).

Hutchinson, Sharla, 'Convulsive Beauty: Images of Hysteria and Transgressive Sexuality Claude Cahun and Djuna Barnes', S*ymploke*, 11/1–2 (2003), 212–26.

Jameson, Fredric, *The Political Unconscious: Narrative as a Socially Symbolic Act* (London: Metheun, 1981).
Jarry, Alfred, 'Gestes et opinions du docteur Faustroll', in *Œuvres complètes* (Paris: Laussane, 1950), pp. 187–254.
Jáuretche, Arturo, *El medio pelo en la sociedad argentina* (Buenos Aires: Peña Lillo, 1984).
Jitrik, Noé, 'Notas sobre la "Zona sagrada" y el mundo de los "otros" en *Bestiario* de Julio Cortázar', in *La vuelta a Cortázar en nueve ensayos,* ed. Noé Jitrik et al. (Buenos Aires: Carlos Pérez, 1968), pp. 47–62.
Juan-Navarro, Santiago, 'History and Self-Reflexivity in the Writings of Julio Cortázar', in *Archival Reflections: Postmodern Fiction of the Americas (Self-Reflexivity, Historical Revisionism, Utopia* (London: Associated University Presses, 2000), pp. 196–223.
Justo, Luis, 'Cortázar: ¿misticismo o arte-pop?, *Sur*, 325 (1970), 77–82.
Kelman, David, 'The Afterlife of Storytelling: Julio Cortázar's Reading of Walter Benjamin and Edgar Allan Poe', *Comparative Literature*, 60/3 (2008), 244–60.
Kerr, Lucille, 'Between Reading and Repetition', in *Julio Cortázar: New Readings*, ed. Carlos Alonso (Cambridge: Cambridge University Press, 1998), pp. 91–109.
—— 'Critics and Cortázar', *Latin American Research Review*, 18/2 (1983), 266–75.
King, John, 'Towards a Reading of the Argentine Literary Magazine *Sur*', *Latin American Research Review*, 16/2 (1981), 57–78.
Kohan, Martín, '*Papeles inesperados* de Cortázar: sorpresas del cronopio', *Perfil*, 31 May 2009 <http://www.diarioperfil.com.ar/edimp/0369/articulo.php?art=14760&ed=0369> [accessed 1 September 2009].
Kulynych, Jessica, 'Performing politics: Foucault, Habermas and Postmodern participation', *Polity*, 30/2 (1997), 315–46.
Lamborghini, Leónidas C. et al., *La historia y la política en la ficción argentina* (Buenos Aires: Centro de Publicaciones Universidad Nacional del Litoral, 1995).
Lanusse, Lucas, *Montoneros: el mito de los doce* (Buenos Aires: Ediciones D, 2005).
Lastra, Pedro, *Julio Cortázar* (Madrid: Taurus, 1981).
Leftwich, Adrian, *What is Politics?* (Cambridge: Polity, 2004).
Leonardi, Yanina Andrea, 'Espectáculos y figuras populares en el circuito teatral oficial durante los años peronistas' <http://www.unsam.edu.ar/home/material/Leonardi.pdf> [accessed 31 January 2008].
Luna, Félix, *El 45: crónica de un año decisivo* (Buenos Aires: Jorge Álvarez, 1969).
—— *La comunidad organizada* (Buenos Aires: Sudamericana, 1985).
Mac Adam, Alfred, '*Los premios*: una tentativa de clasificación formal', in *Homenaje a Julio Cortázar*, ed. Helmy F. Giacoman (Madrid: Las Américas, 1972), pp. 289–96.
Mandelli, Huberto, *Las escuelas donadas por Belgrano y su reglamento* (Buenos Aires: Instituto Nacional Belgraniano, 1999).
Manjarrez, Héctor, 'La revolución y el escritor según Cortázar', in *El camino de los sentimientos* (Mexico City: Era, 1990), pp. 129–48.

Marchesi, Aldo, 'Imaginación política del antiimperialismo: intelectuales y política en el Cono Sur a fines de los 60', *Estudios interdisciplinarios de América Latina y el Caribe*, 17/1 (2006), 20–34.
Márquez, Ángel, *Educación y Peronismo (1946–1955)* (Buenos Aires: Centro Editor de América Latina, 1984).
Martínez, Guillermo, 'Los días contados', *Crítica*, 11 February 2009 <http://criticadigital.com/index.php?secc=nota&nid=18661> [accessed 5 September 2009].
Marx, Karl, 'The Metaphysics of Political Economy', in *The Poverty of Philosophy*, trans. Harry Quelch (New York: International Publishers, 1963).
Masiello, Francine, 'Argentine Literary Journalism: The Production of a Critical Discourse', *Latin American Research Review*, 20/1 (1985), 27–60.
Maturo, Graciela, *Julio Cortázar y el hombre nuevo* (Buenos Aires: Sudamericana, 1968; 2nd extended edn 2004).
Mirbeau, Octave, *Le Jardin des supplices*, ed. Michel Delon (Paris: Gallimard, 1988).
Mitchell, William J.T., *Iconology* (Chicago: University of Chicago Press, 1986).
Monsiváis, Carlos, 'Bienvenidos al universo Cortázar', in *Julio Cortázar*, ed. Pedro Lastra (Madrid: Taurus, 1981), pp. 15–33.
—— '"¿Encontraría a la Maga en la manifestación?" Julio Cortázar y la política', *Revista de la Universidad Nacional de México* (2004), 16–19.
Montaldo, Graciela, 'Contextos de producción', in Cortázar, *Rayuela,* ed. Ortega and Yurkievich , pp. 583–96.
—— 'Destinos y recepción', in Cortázar, *Rayuela*, ed. Ortega and Yurkievich, pp. 597–612.
Montanaro, Pablo, *Cortázar, de la experiencia histórica a la revolución* (Buenos Aires: Homo Sapiens, 2001).
Montes Bradley, Eduardo, *Cortázar sin barba* (Buenos Aires: Sudamericana, 2004).
Moran, Dominic, *Questions of the Liminal in the Fiction of Julio Cortázar* (Oxford: Legenda, 2000).
Moreiras, Alberto, *Tercer espacio, literatura y duelo en América Latina* (Santiago de Chile: LOM Ediciones, 1999).
Morin, Edgar, 'Intellectuels: critique du mythe et mythe de la critique', *Arguments*, 20/4, 4–13.
Neves, Alfredo N. (ed.), *Diccionario de americanismos* (Buenos Aires: Sopena, 1973)
Nora, Pierre, *Les Lieux de mémoire*, I: *La République* (Paris: Gallimard, 1984).
O'Connor, Patrick, '"Melancholia Porteña" and Survivor's Guilt: A Benjaminian Reading of Cortázar's *El examen*', *Latin American Literary Review*, 23/46 (1995), 5–32.
Oliver, María Rosa, 'Según su conciencia', *La opinión cultural*, 8 December 1974, 2–3.
Ostria González, Mauricio, 'Sistemas literarios latinoamericanos: la polémica Arguedas/Cortázar treinta años después', in *Crisis, apocalipsis y utopías*, ed. Rodrigo Cánovas and Roberto Hozven (Santiago de Chile: Prensa de la Universidad Católica de Chile, 2004), pp. 423–8.

Otero, Sergio, 'Julio Cortázar: 25 años de su muerte', *El Correo Gallego*, 15 February 2009 <http://www.elcorreogallego.es/popImprimir.php?idWeb=1&idNoticia=395492> [accessed 16 February 2009].
Padilla, Herberto, 'Imagen de Cortázar', *La Nación*, 28 April 1985, 20–1.
Pagani, Horacio, 'El campeón sin corona', *Clarín*, 8 May 2005 <http://www.clarin.com/diario/2005/05/08/deportes/d-08901.htm> [accessed 20 June 2008].
Palapa Quijas, Fabiola, 'Elogian la vitalidad de la obra de Cortázar a 25 años de su muerte', *La Jornada*, 2 March 2009 <http://www.jornada.unam.mx/2009/03/02/index.php?section=cultura&article=a11n1cul> [accessed 2 March 2009]
Parkinson Zamora, Lois, 'Movement and Stasis, Film and Photo: Temporal Structures in the Recent Fiction of Julio Cortázar', *Review of Contemporary Fiction*, 3/3 (1983), 51–65.
—— 'Synchronic Structures', in *The Usable Past: The Imagination of History in Recent Fiction of the Americas* (Cambridge: Cambridge University Press, 1997), pp. 133–55.
Pasco, Allan, 'A Study of Allusion: Barbey's Stendhal in *Le Rideau cramoisi*', *PMLA*, 88/3 (1973), 461–71.
Perón, Juan Domingo, *Doctrina peronista* (Buenos Aires: Volver, 1982).
—— *Perón en doctrina: ayer, hoy y siempre* (Buenos Aires: Megalibros, 1997).
Picon Garfield, Evelyn, *¿Es Julio Cortázar un surrealista?* (Madrid: Gredos, 1975).
—— 'Julio Cortázar's Redheaded Night: Or Notes on Ordering the Universe in *Prosa del observatorio*', *Review of Contemporary Fiction*, 3/3 (1983), 71–7.
Piglia, Ricardo, *Crítica y ficción* (Barcelona: Anagrama, 2001).
—— 'El socialismo de los consumidores', *La opinión cultural*, 8 December 1974, 4–6.
—— 'Ficción y política en la literatura argentina', in *Literatura argentina hoy*, ed. Karl Kohut and Andrea Pagni (Frankfurt: Vervuert, 1989), pp. 97–104.
Pizarnik, Alejandra, 'La condesa sangrienta', in *Textos selectos*, ed. Cristina Piña (Buenos Aires: Corregidor, 1999), pp. 113–37.
Plato, *The Republic*, trans. Alan Bloom (New York: Basic Books, 1967).
Plotkin, Mariano, 'The Changing Perceptions of Peronism', in Brennan, *Peronism and Argentina*, 29–54.
—— *Mañana es San Perón: A Cultural History of Perón's Argentina*, trans. Keith Zahniser (Washington: SR Books, 2003).
Poderti, Alicia, 'Peronismo/antiperonismo y el diccionario de los argentinos (1945–76)', *Rábida*, 25 (2005), 109–18.
Pollmann, Leo, *La nueva novela en Francia y en Latinoamérica*, trans. Julio Linares (Madrid: Gredos, 1971).
Pons, María Cristina, 'Compromiso político y ficción en "Segunda vez" y "Apocalipsis de Solentiname" de Julio Cortázar,' *Revista Mexicana de Sociología*, 54/4 (October – December 1992), 183–203.
Poulet, Georges, 'Criticism and the experience of interiority', in *Reader-Response Criticism*, ed. Jane Tompkins (Baltimore: The Johns Hopkins University Press, 1980), pp. 41–9.
Prieto, René, *Miguel Ángel Asturias's Archeology of Return* (Cambridge: Cambridge University Press, 1993).

Quesada, Luis M., '"Fuera del juego": A Poet's Appraisal of the Cuban Revolution', *Latin American Literary Review*, 3/6 (1975), 89–98.
Ramírez, Sergio, 'El Evangelio según Cortázar', *Revista de la Universidad Nacional de México* (2004), 25–9.
Ramos, Jorge, *Perón: historia de su triunfo y su derrota* (Buenos Aires: Ediciones Amerindia, 1959).
Rancière, Jacques, *Política de la literatura*, trans. Marcelo Burello, Lucía Vogelfang and J. L. Caputo (Buenos Aires: Libros del Zorzal, 2011).
—— *The Politics of Aesthetics,* trans. Gabriel Dockhill (New York: Continuum, 2004).
Reddy, Peter, *Torture: What you Need to Know* (Charnwood: Ginninderra Press, 2005).
Rein, Mercedes, *Julio Cortázar: el escritor y sus máscaras* (Montevideo: Diaco, 1957).
Reinoso, Susana, 'Autoayuda, ensayo y el plus de la firma en vivo: Julio Cortázar fue un inesperado best seller', *La Nación*, 10 May 2009 <http://www.lanacion.com.ar/nota.asp?nota_id=1126415> [accessed 10 September 2009].
Riobó, María Victoria, 'El libro objeto en la obra de Julio Cortázar: *La vuelta al día en ochenta mundos* y *Último Round*', in *Borges/Cortázar: penúltimas lecturas,* ed. Maria Amelia Arancet Ruda (Buenos Aires: Circeto, 2007), pp. 135–60.
Rodríguez Coronel, Rogelio, 'Una revisión ideológica de *Rayuela*', *Inti: Revista de Literatura Hispánica*, 22–3 (1985–6), 91–9.
Roffé, Reina, 'Escritura de la memoria y del exilio', *Jornadas*, University of Poitiers, 22 October 2006 <http://uptv.univpoitiers.fr/web/canal/61/theme/28/manif/134/video/1214/index.html> [accessed 20 October 2006].
Romero, José Luis, *Breve historia de la Argentina* (Buenos Aires: Fondo de Cultura Económica, 2003).
—— *Las ideas políticas en Argentina* (Buenos Aires: Fondo de Cultura Económica, 1956).
Romero, Luis Alberto, *Historia argentina* (Buenos Aires: Fondo de Cultura Económica, 2001).
Ronzitti, Miguel, 'Segundo Plan Quinquenal y Teatro', *Talía*, 1/1 (1953), 20–35.
Rosa, Nicolás, 'Cortázar: los modos de la ficción', in *Ficciones Argentinas: antología de lecturas críticas*, ed. Ana María Barrenechea et al. (Buenos Aires: Grupo Norma, 2004), pp. 201–22.
Rosado Álvarez, Javier, *Historia de la prensa,* coord. Alejando Pizarroso Quintero (Madrid: Centro de Estudios Ramón Aceres, 1994).
Roy, Joaquín, *Julio Cortázar ante su sociedad*, (Barcelona: Península, 1974).
Russek, Dan, 'Verbal/Visual Braids: The Photographic Medium in the Work of Julio Cortázar', *Mosaic: Journal for the Interdisciplinary Study of Literature*, 37/4 (2004), 71–87.
Sábato, Ernesto, *El otro rostro del peronismo: carta abierta a Mario Amadeo* (Buenos Aires: Imprenta López, 1956).
Saccomanno, Guillermo, 'Viñas de ira', *Página/12*, 9 July 2006 <http://www.pagina12.com.ar/diario/suplementos/radar/9-3106-2006-07-09.html> [accessed 10 September 2008].

Saer, Juan José, *El concepto de ficción* (Buenos Aires: Seix Barral, 2004).
Sánchez Martínez, Eduardo, *La legislación sobre educación superior en Argentina* (Buenos Aires: IESALC, 2002).
Sanguinetti, Horacio, 'Breve historia política del Teatro Colón', *Todo es Historia*, 5/1 (1967), 66–77.
Santos Martínez, Pedro, *La nueva Argentina, 1946–1955*, I (Buenos Aires: La Bastilla, 1980).
Sarlo, Beatriz, *Escritos sobre literatura argentina*, ed. Sylvia Saítta (Buenos Aires: Siglo XXI, 2007).
—— 'La novela esperada', in *Escritos sobre literatura argentina*, pp. 239–45.
—— 'Releer *Rayuela* desde *El cuaderno de bitácora*', in *Escritos sobre literatura argentina*, pp. 246–59.
—— 'Una literatura de pasajes', in *Escritos sobre literatura argentina*, pp. 262–6.
Sarmiento, Domingo Faustino, *Facundo: civilización y barbarie* (Buenos Aires: Sopena, 1945).
Sartora, Josefina, 'Jugarse la vida', *La Maga*, 5 (November 1994), 8–9.
Sartre, Jean Paul, *What is literature?*, trans. Bernard Frechtman (London: Methuen, 1950).
Schmucler, Héctor, '*Rayuela*: juicio a la literatura', *Pasado y Presente* (April–September 1965), 29–45.
Schwartz, Kessel, '*Libro de Manuel* by Julio Cortázar', *Hispania*, 58/1 (1975), 238–9.
—— 'Themes, Trends, and Textures: The 1960's and the Spanish American Novel', *Hispania*, 55/4 (December 1972), 817–31.
Schwartz, Marcy E., 'Cortázar Under Exposure: Photography and Fiction in the City', in *Beyond the Lettered City: Latin American Literature and Mass Media*, ed. Debra Castillo and José Edmundo Paz-Soldán (New York: Garland, 2000), pp. 117–38.
—— 'Del lado de acá/del lado de allá: la mirada fotográfica de Julio Cortázar, entre continentes', *Matérika* 9 (2005), 28–39.
—— 'Writing against the City: Julio Cortázar's Photographic Take on India', *Photography and Writing in Latin America: Double Exposures*, ed. Marcy E. Schwartz and Mary Beth Tierney-Tello (Albuquerque: University of New Mexico Press, 2006), pp. 117–39.
Sebreli, Juan José, 'Clase media', in *Buenos Aires, vida cotidiana y alienación* (Buenos Aires: Siglo XX, 1966), pp. 78–107.
Siebers, Tobin, *Politics of Scepticism* (New York: Oxford University Press, 1993).
Sigal, Silvia, 'Intelectuales y peronismo', in *Nueva historia argentina*, VIII, (Buenos Aires, Sudamericana, 2002) pp. 501–46.
Sinnigen, Jack, *Narrativa e ideología* (Madrid: Nuestra Cultura, 1982).
Solares, Ignacio, *Imagen de Julio Cortázar* (Buenos Aires: Fondo de Cultura Económica, 2008).
Solís, Ricardo, 'A 25 años de la partida física del erudito, elocuente y memorioso Julio Cortázar', *La Jornada Jalisco*, 14 February 2009 <http://www.lajornadajalisco.com.mx/2009/02/14/> [accessed 15 February 2009].

Sommer, Doris, 'From Allegory and Dialectics: A Match Made in Romance', *Boundary 2*, 18/1 (1991), 60–82.
Sondereguer, María (ed.), *Revista Crisis: antología 1973–1976* (Buenos Aires: Universidad Nacional de Quilmes, 2008).
Sontag, Susan, *On Photography* (Harmondsworth: Penguin, 1979).
—— *Regarding the Pain of Others* (London: Penguin, 2003).
Sorensen, Diana, 'From Diaspora to Agora: Cortázar's Reconfiguration of Exile', *Modern Language Notes*, 114/2 (1999), 357–88.
Sosnowski, Saúl, 'Julio Cortázar ante la literatura y la historia', in Cortázar, *Obra crítica/3*, pp. 9–31.
—— 'Julio Cortázar: *Libro de Manuel*', *Hispamérica*, 2/6 (April 1974), 109–15.
—— 'Perseguidores', in Alazraki, Ivask and Marco (eds), *La isla final*, pp. 391–410.
Stabb, Martin S., 'Argentine Letters and the Peronato: An Overview', *Journal of Interamerican Studies and World Affairs*, 13 (1971), 434–55.
Standish, Peter, 'Los compromisos de Julio Cortázar', *Hispania*, 80/3 (September 1997), 465–71.
—— *Understanding Julio Cortázar* (Columbia: University of South Carolina Press, 2001).
Stavans, Ilan, *Julio Cortázar: A Study of the Short Fiction* (New York: Twayne Publishers, 1996).
Tansey, Stephen, *Politics: The Basics* (London: Routledge, 2004).
Teitelboim, Vlodia, in Cortázar, *Policrítica,* pp. 29–55.
Terán, Oscar, *Historia de las ideas en Argentina* (Buenos Aires: Siglo XXI, 2008).
Torre, Juan Carlos (dir.), 'Democratización del bienestar', in *Nueva historia argentina*, VIII: *Años peronistas 1943–1955* (Buenos Aires: Sudamericana, 2002) pp. 257–302.
Touchard, Jean, *Historia de las ideas políticas*, trans. Julián Pradera (Madrid: Tecnos, 2000).
Trillo, Carlos, 'Interview to Manuel Barrero', *Tebeosfera*, 10 July 2002 <http://www.tebeosfera.com/1/Documento/Entrevista/Trillo/1.htm) [accessed 3 September 2008].
Trotsky, Leon, 'Revolutionary and Socialist Art', in *Literature and Revolution*, trans. Rose Strunsky (Ann Arbor: University of Michigan Press, 1971), pp. 228–54.
Urondo, Francisco, *La patria fusilada* (Buenos Aires: Tierra del Sur, 2007).
Urstein, Maurice, *Leopold and Loeb: A Psychiatric-Psychological Study* (New York: Lecouver Press Co.: 1924).
Valdés, Mario J., 'Documents and Fiction in Cortázar's *Rayuela*', *Reflexión*, 2/2–4 (1973), 83–6.
Vargas Llosa, Mario, 'La trompeta de Deyá', in Cortázar, *Cuentos completos/1*, pp. 2–8.
Vatican City, 'El himno pontífico' <http://www.vatican.va/news_services/press/documentazione/documents/sp_ss_scv/inno/inno_scv_testo_it.html#Breve%20presentazione%20in%20spagnolo> [accessed 1 April 2008].

Vernon, Kathleen, 'Cortázar's 3 R's: Reading, Rhetoric and Revolution in *Libro de Manuel*', *Modern Language Studies,* 16/3 (1986), 264–70.
Viñas, David, *De Sarmiento a Cortázar* (Buenos Aires: Siglo Veinte, 1971).
—— 'Después de Cortázar: historia y privatización', *Cuadernos hispanoamericanos*, 234 (June 1969), 734–9.
—— et al., *Más allá del boom: literatura y mercado* (Mexico City: Marcha Editores, 1981).
Viñas, Ismael, 'La traición de los hombres honestos', *Contorno*, 1 (November 1953), 7–12.
Weiss, Jason, 'Interstitial spaces (Julio Cortázar)', in *The Lights of Home: A Century of Latin American Writers in Paris* (London: Routledge, 2003), pp. 81–93.
West, Regina, 'La representación fotográfica en la literatura: el caso de *Cien años de soledad* y *Rayuela*', *Lucero*, 2 (1991), 59–72.
Williams, Raymond, *Marxism and Literature* (Oxford: Oxford University Press, 1977).
Williams, Raymond Leslie, *The Twentieth-Century Spanish American Novel* (Austin: University of Texas Press, 2003).
Yovanovich, Gordana, *Julio Cortázar's Character Mosaic* (Toronto: University of Toronto Press, 1991).
Yurkievich, Saúl, *Julio Cortázar, al calor de tu sombra* (Buenos Aires: Legasa, 1987).
—— *Julio Cortázar: mundos y modos* (Buenos Aires: Edhasa, 2004).

Unpublished Dissertations

Ponza, Pablo, 'Los intelectuales críticos y la transformación social en Argentina (1955–1973)' (University of Barcelona, 2007).
Sarmiento Lizárraga, Sylvia, '*Los premios*, *Rayuela*, *Libro de Manuel*: evolución del pensamiento político en la ficción de Julio Cortázar' (University of California, 1979).

Personal Interviews

Fernández Retamar, Roberto, University of Manchester, Manchester, 26 May 2009, [35:10].
Goloboff, Mario, Café El Cisne, Buenos Aires, 27 November 2007 [1:35:10], 19 December 2008 [1:22:15].
Heker, Liliana, Buenos Aires, 1 December 2008 [1:02:45].
Valenzuela, Luisa, Buenos Aires, 19 December 2008 [1:50:08].
Viñas, David, Café de La Paz, Buenos Aires, 18 December 2008 [1:05:00].

Index

Abbate, Florencia 111
Ander-Egg, Ezequiel 72, 79, 90, 91, 93, 198
Alazraki, Jaime 6–7, 51, 56, 66, 108, 116 n. 19, 130
Algeria (political situation in) 77, 85, 99, 112, 113
allegory 194
   in *El examen* 15, 16, 17, 20, 24, 29, 44
   in *Los premios* 48, 50, 53, 54, 55, 109, 165
Alto el Perú 192
Anales de Buenos Aires 48
Andrés, Alfredo 44 n. 90
Andreu, Jean L. 123
Anguita, Eduardo 136
'Apocalipsis de Solentiname' 140, 151, 165, 192
Arent Safir, Margery 84 n. 25
Arguedas, José María 49 n. 106
Arguindeguy, Diego L. 42 n. 84
Aristotle 8, 9, 10, 79, 100
Arlt, Roberto 74
Artaud, Antonin 94, 102 n. 54, 142
Asturias, Miguel Ángel 63–64

'babas del diablo, Las' 95–96
'banda, La' 29, 29 n. 47, 132
Barbey d'Aurevilly, Jules 16, 18, 24, 30
Barrenechea, Ana María 115

Barthes, Roland 98
Bataille, Georges 94, 96, 102, 150
Baudelaire, Charles 94
Belgrano, General Manuel 19 n. 23
Belgrano Rawson, Edgardo 10
Benedetti, Mario 114, 158 n. 8
Benjamin, Walter 91, 165
Bernabé, Jean 77, 112, 123
Bestiario 6, 13, 41 n. 81, 49 n. 101, 77 n. 17
Bioy Casares, Adolfo 15, 48, 138
Blackburn, Paul and Sara 112
Boldy, Steven 7, 23 n. 32, 66, 128, 177, 192, 194
Borello, Rodolfo A. 29
Borges, Jorge Luis 15, 20, 29, 35 n. 69, 46 n. 95, 48, 59, 73, 79, 125, 134
   'El Aleph' 125–26
Borges, Norah 48
Borroni, Otelo 45 n. 92
Bosca, Roberto 46 n. 94
Brecht, Bertolt 100, 139, 165
Breton, André 164, 177 n. 43, 183 n. 51
Bruto, César 74, 76, 87
Buchrucker, Cristián 34 n. 64
Buenos Aires, Buenos Aires 131, 132, 152
Bustos Domecq 29
   'La fiesta del monstruo' 15
cabecitas negras 15, 41, 47 n. 98

Calvino, Italo 133 n. 58
Carpeaux, Louis 96
Carpentier, Alejo 145 n. 88
Carreras, Julio 176 n. 41
'Carta a una señorita en París' 22
Casa de las Américas 115, 149, 154 n. 98, 157
Casa Rosada 14, 41, 43, 44
'Casa Tomada' 6, 20, 29, 48, 50, 54, 55
Cascabel (journal) 74
Castro, Fidel 111, 112, 113, 114, 157, 158, 162
Castro Klarén, Sara 135 n. 67, 139
Cavafys, Constantine P. 37 n. 72
censorship 18, 36, 48, 58
Ciria, Alberto 34 n. 66
Colás, Santiago 134
collage
　books 4, 5, 11, 134, 135, 141, 199
　technique 100, 102
　politics of 133
Collazos, Oscar 122, 124 n. 34, 156,
collective memory 18, 42
Colón Theatre 15, 34, 36, 37, 38, 39, 46, 66, 70
Conti, Haroldo 189
Contorno (journal) 25
Conventillo de la paloma, El 34, 35
Correas, Jaime 18 n. 22
'Corrección de Pruebas en Alta Provenza' 2, 116 n. 20, 139, 162, 191, 192
Cortázar, Julio
　anti-Peronist feelings 41, 49, 63, 67, 68
　apolitical vs. political 1, 3, 13, 71, 83, 90, 153, 196
　artistic freedom 5, 55, 56, 113, 115, 118, 120, 121, 122, 124, 127, 128, 129, 130, 141, 144, 153, 154, 157, 161, 198
　being 'outside history' (*see* 'History – Being outside of')
　committed writer 3, 56, 66, 69, 130, 134, 154, 158, 159, 187, 188, 190
　conversion to socialism (*see under* Socialism – Being a socialist writer)
　evolution (aesthetic, political) 3, 4, 5, 7, 11, 12, 54, 55, 56, 57, 67, 68, 71, 81, 82,102, 110, 113, 140, 143, 153, 161, 180, 184, 191–192, 195, 196, 199, 200
　definition of the modern novel 51–52
　discovery of 'el prójimo' 5, 53, 55, 57, 63, 64, 69, 71, 81, 82, 89, 94, 99, 180
　fantastic element in fiction 54, 55 68, 116, 130, 140, 150, 152, 158
　first visit to Cuba (*see under* 'Cuba')
　use of humour (*see under* 'humour')
　lectures at Berkeley 53, 54 n. 121, 110, 116, 170, 193
　moving to Paris (*see* 'Paris, Cortázar's first arrival')
　political ideology (*see also* ideology) 10, 55, 66, 67, 69, 73, 78, 11
　political writer 3, 10, 71, 110, 116, 124, 146, 196, 197
　rhetoric of guilt (*see under* 'guilt')
　Latin American intellectual 49, 63, 109, 112, 114, 118, 119, 138, 149, 157, 189, 191, 197, 198
　Latin American reality (*see also* Latin America) 3, 82, 83, 120, 137, 154

Crisis (journal) 49 n. 106, 73, 142, 189 n. 62
Cuba
   Julio Cortázar's first visit to 1, 66, 71, 111, 112, 114, 115, 118
   Cuban Revolution 3, 56, 60, 63, 67, 70, 108, 11, 112, 124, 115, 116, 120, 122, 123, 141, 149, 153, 157, 158, 180, 184, 197
   Latin American reality (*see* Latin America)
   Caso Padilla (*see* Padilla, Herberto)

Darrow, Clarence 103
Dayan, Peter 51 n. 110
De Diego, José Luis 49 n. 106
De Diego, Juan 122 n. 28
De Ípola, Emilio 44 n. 91
De la Guerra Castellanos, Francisco E. 6, 128
De la Torre, Carlos 34 n. 63
Deleis, Mónica 42
Dellepiane, Ángela 179 n. 49
democratisation of culture (under Perón) 15, 19, 20, 28
Derrida, Jacques 54 n. 120
descamisados 34, 37, 48 n. 101
D'Haen, Theo 164, 193
Di Gerónimo, Miriam 187
Diario de Andrés Fava 4, 21, 22, 24, 29, 31, 32, 40 51 n. 109, 67, 126, 179, 197
dictadura (*see* military dictatorship)
Divertimento 4, 13, 18, 22, 23, 24, 29, 31, 35, 37, 43, 46, 59, 60, 66, 74, 173, 192, 197
Dobry, Edgardo 17 n. 16
Domínguez, Mignón 17 n. 17
doppelgänger 74
Dostoyevsky, Fyodor 65
Dumas, Georges 96
Duprat, Lucienne de 14, 18, 32, 68

Eagleton, Terry 10, 161
Eco, Umberto 193
eroticism 5, 94, 150, 157, 168, 169, 170, 171, 173, 174, 179, 195
essentialism 51, 145
Esti Rein, Mónica 13, 28
Europe 47, 118, 149, 157
   Cortázar's identification with 117
   Europeanised protagonists 15, 39
   post–war 77
Evita Perón (*see* Perón, Eva Duarte de)
Examen, El 2, 4, 5, 13, 15, 16, 17, 18, 20, 22, 24, 25, 29, 31, 32, 33, 35–40, 43 n. 87, 48, 50, 51, 54, 55, 57, 59–63, 65–70, 73, 74, 77, 80, 87, 92, 97, 109, 132, 150, 165, 167, 169, 173, 179, 182, 196, 197
exile 24 n. 35, 29, 49, 50, 60, 77, 89 n. 28, 132 n. 56, 137, 141, 162, 190, 192 n. 75
Fantomas contra los vampiros multinacionales 7, 192
Farrell, Gral. Edelmiro Juan 13–14, 23, 24, 33, 141
Fass, Paula S. 103 n. 56
Feinmann, José Pablo 2
Fernández Cubillos, Héctor 89, 99
Ferández Retamar, Roberto 50, 66, 117, 118, 120, 121, 123 n. 31, 128, 129, 144, 149, 157
Ferré, Rosario 188
Ferré E Chabrier, Christina 93 n. 39
Ferro, Roberto 159, 189, 196
figuras 35, 68, 126, 128
Final de juego 29, 132
Final Exam 16 n. 13
Flaubert, Gustave 126 n. 37
Flores García, Víctor 90
folklore 15, 38, 39, 40, 47
Ford, Aníbal 189, 190
Foucault, Michel 60–61, 62, 64, 65
   La hermenéutica del sujeto 64–65

Fowler, Rowena 36 n. 70
Franco, Jean 108, 125
Frondizi, Arturo 53, 75, 76, 236
Fuentes, Carlos 71, 113, 114

Gamerro, Carlos 48 n. 101
García Canclini, Néstor 6, 71
García Márquez, Gabriel 114
Genette, Gérard 91 n. 33
Genover, Kathleen 77 n. 17
Gide, André 21
Gilman, Claudia 70, 114 n. 11, 138
Giordano, Alberto 133–134, 138, 153, 154
Girondo, Oliverio 36 n. 71, 40 n. 79
Goldar, Ernesto 189, 190, 191
Goloboff, Mario 2, 3, 48, 53, 67, 115, 129, 160, 187, 188, 191, 197
González Bermejo, Ernesto 10, 54, 67, 82, 89, 90, 128, 158, 161
guerrilla 11 n. 28, 120, 160, 161, 175, 177, 178
Guevara, Ernesto 60, 63, 64, 65, 117, 119, 120, 121, 123, 124, 128, 143, 146, 156, 161, 165, 198
guilt
    Cortázar's rhetoric of 49, 52, 60, 79, 113, 115, 118–19, 121–22, 143, 146, 154, 159, 169, 198
Guinsberg, Enrique 1, 3
Guthman, Fredi 18, 30
Gutiérrez Mouat, Ricardo 38

Halperín Donghi, Tulio 15, 33, 40
Hanne, Michael 10
Harss, Luis 33, 55, 68, 126
Heidegger, Martin 50
Heker, Liliana 49 n. 106, 137, 150, 160, 188, 189, 190
Hernández, Ana María 179
Hernández, José 34, 142
Hicks, Emily D. 161
Historias de cronopios y de famas 134, 135, 177
History
    as reference for Cortázar's fiction 57, 104, 116, 199
    being outside of 2, 51, 68, 82, 104, 120, 197
    manipulation under Peronism (*see* Peronism)
hombre nuevo 7, 13, 51, 53, 60, 61, 63–66, 68, 71, 123, 130, 156, 170, 174, 177, 184, 188, 194, 199
Hopscotch 88 n. 27
Huelsenbeck, Richard 134 n. 61,
Humour 5
    and politics 11, 124, 138, 141
    and César Bruto 74
    in Latin American literature 137, 145, 157, 195
    in *Libro de Manuel* 168–170, 178, 179, 188
    in the 'collage books' 138, 139, 144, 146, 148, 149
Hutcheon, Linda 97

ideology (*see also political ideology*) 5, 9, 10, 11, 21, 33, 39, 45, 56, 57, 66, 69–74, 78, 90, 108, 110, 113, 114, 116, 139, 155, 175, 180, 187, 188, 190, 192–93, 196–97, 200
ideological hegemony 17
Illia, Arturo 136
Imagen de John Keats 134, 144

Jarry, Alfred 135 n. 62, 138
Jameson, Fredric 9, 196
Jáuretche, Arturo 42
Jitrik, Noé 77 n. 17
Jonquières, Eduardo A. 112, 187
Juan-Navarro, Santiago 160
Justo, Luis 148
Kant, Immanuel 99–100
Kelman, David 70, 72, 91
King, John 17 n. 16

Kohan, Martín 200
Kulynych, Jessica 60 n. 127, 62 n. 130

Lamborghini, Leónidas 10 n. 22
Lang, Fritz 183
Lanusse, Lucas 137 n. 68
Lastra, Pedro 55 n. 122, 138
Latin America
    Latin American (political) reality 2, 65, 120, 137
    Revolution in 5, 49, 50, 70, 115, 122, 154, 176, 194
    being a Latin American writer 63, 66, 112, 123, 124, 143, 146, 169
La vuelta al día en ochenta mundos 5, 73, 102, 107, 113, 133, 134, 136, 138, 139, 140, 141,142, 144, 145, 146, 148
Leftwich, Adrian 8, 10–11
Lenin, Vladimir 142, 148, 177
Leonardi, Yanina Andrea 35 n. 68
'Ley 1474' 27
'Ley Universitaria' 19 n. 23, 24, 33
Libro de Manuel 1, 2, 3, 5, 6, 23, 37, 49, 51, 55, 60, 62, 65, 68, 70, 71, 75, 82, 86, 97, 99, 102,104, 110, 111, 113, 116, 122, 125, 128, 130, 131, 134, 136, 139, 140, 147, 152, 154,156, 157–63, 165–94, 196, 197, 199
Luna, Félix 41 n. 83, 44 n. 88

Mac Adam, Alfred 13, 16 n. 13, 17, 61, 62 n. 129
Malle, Louis 151
Mandelli, Huberto 19 n. 23
Manjarrez, Héctor 178 n. 47
Manual for Manuel 187
Marchesi, Aldo 191
Marechal, Leopoldo 44 n. 90
Márquez, Ángel 19

Martínez, Guillermo 8, 196
Martínez Estrada, Ezequiel 21, 153
Marx, Karl 9, 63, 142, 175, 177, 198
    marxist theorists 170
Maturo, Graciela 7, 13, 33, 51, 53, 126, 131
melancholia 17, 18, 31
'Ménades, Las' 132
microagitaciones 68, 125, 128, 174, 175, 177, 178, 179, 181, 190
military dictatorship 15, 67, 69, 116, 121 n. 25, 163 n. 24, 190,198
Mirbeau, Octave 93, 95, 97, 100, 105, 106
    Les Jardin des supplices 93
Mitchell, William J.T. 140
Monsiváis, Carlos 55 n. 122, 82
Montaldo, Graciela 48, 50, 83, 89 n. 28, 109
Montanaro, Pablo 6
Montes Bradley, Eduardo 39 n. 77
montoneros 43, 137 n. 68, 163, 175
Moran, Dominic 62
Mugica, Padre Carlos 158

Neruda, Pablo 26 n. 39
Nicaragua 149, 147, 172, 193, 198
Nicaragua, tan violentamente dulce 192
Nora, Pierre 42
'Notas sobre la novela contemporánea' 51
'no te metás' 5, 39, 59, 65, 69, 72, 73, 77, 83, 85, 90, 93, 99, 100, 107, 108, 163, 176, 180, 198
'nuevo orden' 15, 19 n. 23, 26, 41 n. 82, 45

Ocampo, Silvina 48
Ocampo, Victoria 16–17,
O'Connor, Patrick 31, 46
Oliver, María Rosa 189
Onganía, Juan Carlos 136–37

Ortega, Julio 2 n. 4, 83 n. 23, 84 n. 25
Otero, Sergio 111 n. 1
'Otro Cielo, El' 78 n. 18
Ostria González, Mauricio 49 n. 106

Padilla, Herberto 67, 157, 158, 169
   'el caso Padilla' 180, 182
   Fuera del juego 157
Pagani, Horacio 75 n. 15
Palapa Quijas, Fabiola 111 n. 1
Pampa, la 46, 51 n. 109, 59
Papeles inesperados 8, 71, 82 n. 20, 107 n. 58, 108 n. 62, 156, 196, 200 n. 3
Paris
   Being a committed Latin American writer living in 83
   Cortázar's first arrival (1951) 5, 49, 50, 141, 159 n. 10, 197
   May 1968 146, 147, 176, 190
Parkinson Zamora, Lois 164, 166, 184
Pasco, Allan 16
pataphysics 102, 135, 138, 152, 177, 199
Paz, Octavio 102 n. 54
Perón, Juan Domingo 13–14, 21, 23, 27, 75, 76
   elections 1946 48
   first mandate 19
   relation to the *pueblo* 47
   political manipulation 29, 57
Perón, Eva Duarte de 17, 27, 29, 30, 36 n. 70, 37, 41 n. 82, 45, 46 n. 94
Peronism
   Anti-Peronism 2, 3, 10, 11, 15, 18, 20, 41, 47, 49, 50, 63, 66, 68, 77, 79, 187, 196
   Anti-peronist intellectuals 35, 48, 49, 56, 59
   appropriation of spaces and national symbols 21, 34, 38, 42, 57, 59

Día de la Lealtad 14, 43, 44
and ideological hegemony 17, 21, 27, 55 n. 123, 69
manipulation of history 58, 59
Peronist masses 14, 15, 37, 38, 39, 40, 41, 42, 44, 45, 46, 47, 48, 57, 65, 66, 74, 97 113, 131, 132
Peronist doctrine 14, 21, 33, 38, 45
as political hegemony 34, 39, 57, 58, 69, 72, 79, 181
as political religion 16, 41, 45, 46, 85
University reforms 20, 32, 33
petit-bourgeois 3, 10, 53, 179, 180, 182
Picon Garfield, Evelyn 10 n. 24, 94 n. 41, 112, 129, 138
Piglia, Ricardo 189, 190, 191
Pizarnik, Alejandra 94 n. 42, 101 n. 51
Plato 8, 9, 10
Plaza de Mayo 16, 20, 41, 42, 43, 44, 46, 47, 66, 77 n. 17
Plotkin, Mariano 14 n. 7, 18 n. 21, 33 n. 59, 34, 43 n. 87, 44 n. 89, 45, 46 n. 94, 48 n. 99
Poderti, Alicia 24 n. 34
Policrítica en la hora de los chacales 157, 169 n. 35
politics
   definition 3, 4, 7, 11, 69, 72, 90, 99
   in Argentinian fiction 10
political novel 10, 70, 72, 100, 109
political hopelessness 31, 43, 62, 76
Pons, María Cristina 125 n. 35
Ponza, Pablo 137 n. 67
Porrúa, Fransico 36 n. 70, 37 n. 73, 83 n. 24, 112, 138 n. 70, 146
Prego Gadea, Omar 11 n. 28, 55 n. 123, 109, 111, 139 n. 74, 144, 172, 193 n. 76, 198 n. 2

Premios, Los 2, 4, 7, 24, 26, 46, 48, 50–65, 66, 68, 69–71, 73, 77, 81, 97, 109, 126, 135, 145,159 n. 10, 165, 172, 174, 176, 192, 197, 200.
Prosa del observatorio 129, 130, 135, 192
'Puertas del cielo, Las' 41

Quesada, Luis M. 157 n. 4
Quiroga, Facundo 29 n. 47

Rabassa, Gregory 88 n. 27
Ramos, Jorge Abelardo 43, 189
Ramírez, Sergio 101, 109
Rancière, Jacques 9
Raíz del ombú, La 192
Rayuela 2, 5, 6, 22 n. 31, 23, 46, 59, 60, 68, 69, 70, 71, 72, 73, 75, 77, 81, 82, 83, 88 n. 27, 89, 93, 96, 99, 101, 102, 103, 104, 107–113, 116, 117, 118, 122, 125, 126, 128, 134, 135, 151, 153, 154, 159, 174, 176, 185, 186, 192, 197, 198
'Recortes de prensa' 192
Reddy, Peter 92, 93
Rein, Mercedes 13
Reinoso, Susana 196 n. 1
religious imagery 115, 121, 123
'Reunión' 6, 123, 143
Revolución del '43 13, 32 n. 54
Revolución Libertadora 53, 76
Reyes, Los 23, 142
Rideau Cramoisi, Le 16, 17
Rimbaud, Arthur 7, 16 n. 15, 68, 142,
Romero, José Luis 14 n. 8, 15, 41
Romero, Luis Alberto 13 n. 4
Rosado Álvarez, Javier 58
Russek, Dan 140

Sábato, Ernesto 25 n. 37, 59, 138
Saccomanno, Guillermo 73
sadism 28, 84, 93, 94, 95, 98, 106, 170

Sánchez Martínez, Eduardo 33 n. 58
Sanguinetti, Horacio 34 n. 66
San Martín, José de 27, 28, 29, 30
Santos Martínez, Pedro 15 n. 12, 19 n. 23, 20 n. 26, 24 n. 33, 28 n. 41, 33 n. 61, 35 n. 68, 38 n. 75
Sarlo, Beatriz 17 n. 16,
Sarmiento, Domingo Faustino 15, 29 n. 44, 76
Sarmiento Lizárraga, Sylvia 6, 75, 76
Sartora, Josefina 178–79
Sartre, Jean Paul 24, 30, 62, 115, 137
  Huis clos 24, 26, 62
Schmucler, Héctor 109
Schwartz, Marcy E. 130, 192
Sebreli, Juan José 48 n. 101
'Segunda vez' 125 n. 35
62/modelo para armar 4, 5, 23, 113, 115, 116, 117, 122–132, 133 n. 58, 134, 135, 141, 144, 146, 147, 152, 154, 172, 192, 199
Siebers, Tobin 11, 69, 72, 78, 83, 179
Sigal, Silvia 32 n. 53
Silva, Julio 133, 136, 152
'Simulacro, El' 29
Sinnigen, Jack 9
'Situación de la novela' 51–52
Socialism
  Being a socialist writer 3, 11, 13, 49, 66, 82, 111, 113, 114, 116, 117, 118, 124, 127, 131, 153, 198
Socialist ideology 150, 168, 170, 180, 185, 188, 193, 194, 197
Socialist revolution 10, 117, 118, 119, 120, 123, 147, 152, 154, 156, 169
sodomy 170, 182
Solares, Ignacio 114, 115, 147
Soler Serrano, Joaquín 2 n. 6, 55 n. 123, 135, 160 n. 12
Solís, Ricardo 111 n. 1
Sondereguer, María 142 n. 83
Sontag, Susan 98, 99 n. 48, 131

Sorensen, Diana 177–78
Sosnowski, Saúl 49 n. 104, 66 n. 138, 187, 190, 191
Stabb, Martin S. 24
Standish, Peter 7, 11, 18 n. 19, 74, 94 n. 41, 144, 189
surrealism 5, 22, 119, 134 n. 61, 148, 150, 173, 178, 183
Sur 17 n. 16, 48, 49

Tansey, Stephen 8
Teitelboim, Vlodia 169 n. 36
Terán, Oscar 142
Territorios 192
Thiercelin, Jean 114, 119, 130, 157
Todos los fuegos el fuego 78 n. 18, 113, 115, 116, 123
'Torito' 132
torture 46, 72, 79, 86, 91, 92, 93, 94, 95, 96, 97, 98, 99, 100, 104, 105, 106, 108, 198, 199
Touchard, Jean 9
Trillo, Carlos 74 n. 13
Trotsky, Leon 121 n. 15

Último Round 4, 5, 94, 102, 107, 113, 115, 116, 123, 126, 133, 134, 135, 136, 138, 140, 141, 146–154, 161, 167, 171, 176, 192, 199

Universidad de Cuyo 14, 16 n. 15, 18 n. 22, 20, 23, 32, 48
Urondo, Francisco 163 n. 24
Urstein, Maurice 103

Vaccarezza, Alberto 34, 35
Valenzuela, Luisa 124 n. 32
Vargas Llosa, Mario Vargas 11 n. 30, 114, 122 n. 28, 124 n. 34, 147, 148 n. 93, 156, 168 n. 34
Vatican City 30 n. 48
Vernon, Kathleen 184
Viaje alrededor de una mesa 161 n. 21
Vietnam War 70, 119, 137, 140, 144, 151, 160 n. 14, 199
Viñas, David 49 n. 104, 73, 112, 113 n. 8, 114 n. 12, 122, 137, 168
Viñas, Ismael 25, 59

Warnes, Carlos 74
Weiss, Jason 124
West, Regina 98 n. 46
Williams, Raymond 34
Williams, Raymond Leslie 195

Yurkievich, Saúl 7, 23 n. 32, 48 n. 100, 83 n. 23, 84 n. 25, 190